ELEANOR
ROOSEVELT'S

PHAROS BOOKS
A SCRIPPS HOWARD COMPANY

ELEANOR ROOSEVELT'S

My Day

VOLUME III: FIRST LADY OF THE WORLD

Her
Acclaimed
Columns
1953–1962

EDITED BY DAVID ELMBLIDGE

INTRODUCTION BY FRANK FREIDEL

Frontispiece: Mrs. Roosevelt speaking at the
Democratic National Convention, July 1960.

Copyright © 1991 by Pharos Books

Introduction copyright © 1991 by Frank Freidel

Library of Congress Cataloging-in-Publication Data
(Revised for vol. 3)
Roosevelt, Eleanor, 1884–1962.
Eleanor Roosevelt's My day.
Includes indexes.
Contents: v. 1. Her acclaimed columns, 1936–1945—
v. 2. The post-war years, her acclaimed columns, 1945–
1952 / edited by David Emblidge; introduction by
Pamela C. Harriman–v. 3. The first lady of the world,
her acclaimed columns, 1953–1962 / edited by David
Emblidge; introduction by Freidel.
1. Roosevelt, Eleanor, 1884–1962—Political and
social views.   2. Roosevelt, Eleanor, 1884–1962—
Friends, and associates.   3. United States–Politics
and government—1933–1945.   4. United States—Politics
and government—1945-   .   I. Chadakoff, Rochelle.
II. Emblidge, David.   III. Title.
E807.1.R48A3   1989   973.917'092   88-28821
ISBN 0-88687-407-6 (v. 1)

Book design by Fritz Metsch

Printed in the United States of America

Pharos Books
A Scripps Howard Company
200 Park Avenue
New York, N.Y. 10166

10 9 8 7 6 5 4 3 2 1

Contents

Preface

Eleanor Roosevelt, it was said, more than any other woman, "typified . . . the realization of the dreams of the female Crusaders of the 19th century who threw off the restrictions of the Victorian age."

So begins the United Feature Syndicate November 1962 obituary for Mrs. Roosevelt, and who would have known better how to summarize her life than her editors there, with whom she had worked for twenty-six years? This volume selects and comments upon nine years of Eleanor Roosevelt's writing for the syndicated newspaper column she called "My Day"—1953 through 1962. That column had begun in 1936, and she kept at it, six days per week, slowing down only slightly near the very end of her life. She was still dictating fresh and feisty columns on a broad range of topics after the illness that in the end overcame her had set in, there was still so much to say.

Sampling from this nine-year period, even an intellectually nimble reader will be challenged to keep pace with the globetrotting Mrs. Roosevelt, who moves from subject to subject in her column as easily as she hops from continent to continent on her annual whirlwind tours for the American Association for the United Nations, for lecturing, for charitable activities, or for seeing the world she never grew tired of witnessing anew. She lived to be seventy-eight but had time to acknowledge her advanced age only in her last few weeks. Otherwise it was up in the morning and off to work, or play, with an intensity that left many younger relatives, co-workers, and friends breathless. Eleanor Roosevelt had more than one regular column, carrying forward into this period commitments for a magazine column as well. But as a writer she was not simply a journalist. She also wrote or co-authored numerous books, countless speeches, and hundreds of letters. One of her children, remarking on the frustration their mother must have felt when palsy eventually made it impossible for her to hold a pen, said she had been "the writingest woman alive."

The years covered here begin when Eisenhower enters the White House and end with JFK firmly in place. In between was a long dark night for the Democrats. But for Eleanor Roosevelt the 1950s meant business as usual. Her agenda did not change. Having resigned her post as delegate to the UN to permit Eisenhower to appoint his own team there, she promptly became the prime moving force in the American Association for the United Nations. Only through building up the UN, she believed, did the world have a fighting chance of avoiding a terminal nuclear war. She took a small office in Manhattan and spent dozens of weeks every year attending community meetings in far-flung cities and towns, rallying support for the UN.

A longtime advocate of civil rights, Mrs. Roosevelt already had some dramatic gestures to her credit. She had resigned from the Daughters of the American Revolution because the group refused to let the black contralto Marian Anderson sing in Washington's Constitution Hall. She had resigned from New York's fashionable Colony Club because it refused to consider a Jewish friend for membership. It was no surprise therefore that she would use her "My Day" column repeatedly to promote the desegregation cause as it gained important momentum in these years through Supreme Court decisions, the work of Dr. Martin Luther King, Jr., and congressional equal rights legislation.

There are many columns here also about America's role in the world, particularly with reference to the cold war. The threat of Communist attack from abroad was something Eleanor Roosevelt, like most Americans, took seriously. She tried to build bridges of friendship with the Soviets, visiting the Kremlin, interviewing Khrushchev, and even having him to tea in her New York apartment—where, it was reported by a secretary, "she gave him a piece of her mind." The alleged threat of Communist subversion from within the country—the leftover paranoia of McCarthyism—was something Mrs. Roosevelt took less seriously except insofar as the fight against the so-called subversion might lead toward any abridgement of established liberties for all Americans. There were still the occasional attacks on her character and ideas by right-wing groups who claimed she was a "pinko" herself, and there was even a threat on her life. She shrugged it all off and kept moving.

These years for Mrs. Roosevelt were, as always, active family years. It was hard for her to keep track of all the grandchildren and great-grandchildren by now, plus cousins and their children, plus nieces and nephews—but she did an admirable job. The good fortunes and failures of her own offspring were kept largely out of "My Day," but there is a sweet dose of reminiscing here about jolly days with the children when they and their parents were younger and had time to vacation and play together.

Also conspicuously missing from "My Day" is any discussion by Mrs. Roosevelt of her intense and years-long affair of the heart with Dr. David Gurewitsch. Who was this man who, in a quiet way in the background of a public figure's life, was able to serve her so well as both personal physician and intimate friend? He was in some respects what FDR, as a husband, had not been. There was an emotional warmth between Eleanor and David that surpassed what the last years of the Eleanor and Franklin relationship had brought her. Yet there was a similarity, too, between the two men in her life: each man possessed the qualities of great intelligence, articulate speech and dedication to selfless service in a chosen profession: she respected each of them deeply.

David Gurewitsch was born in 1902 of Russian parents. His father was a Jewish philosopher with mystical inclinations who took his own life when David was still in his mother's womb. His mother trained as a doctor and at the time of the revolution took her family to Berlin. David emerged as a handsome young man with a restless spirit. He dabbled in the film industry, ceramics and farming, and then found his true path when, like his mother, he chose medicine. Fleeing Hitler (David was a Zionist), he went to Jerusalem and, in 1934, came to New York to study at Mt. Sinai Hospital. En route he met Nemone Balfour, of an upper-class Scots family, and they fell in love. After a confused romance, in which she believed a promise of marriage had been made and he apparently did not, he married her, despite reservations on Nemone's family's side about his Jewishness.

In 1940 a daughter was born, but by 1947 the marriage was effectively over, and ended several years later, around 1955, in divorce. Mrs. Roosevelt had met Dr. Gurewitsch some years before in his capacity as physician to her friend, Trude Lash, and as director of a children's medical clinic in the Hudson Valley. He was fifteen years younger than Eleanor Roosevelt, but the two eventually bonded as loving friends. They corresponded frequently; Mrs. Roosevelt's letters sparkled with affection and concern for him. They traveled together. Eventually, they would buy a house together in New York. Adjusting to the presence in David's life of a new wife, Edna, who ultimately became Mrs. Roosevelt's friend, was not easy.

These nine years take us around the world several times and across North America on dozens of occasions with Mrs. Roosevelt, who rarely stayed in any house, apartment, city, or town for more than ten days in a row.

For someone who never held elective office, Eleanor Roosevelt wielded a great deal of political power. In 1956, as in 1952, she actively supported Adlai Stevenson for president. Behind the scenes, and quietly, she helped reform and rebuild a tattered New York State Democratic Party. She gave Stevenson another push in 1960, hoping the White House could finally be his, and then, after some soul-searching and after being charmed during a visit to Hyde Park by John F. Kennedy, she gave her support to the Kennedy campaign and presidency.

Mrs. Roosevelt remained productive and busy, even with new projects, right up until the end. She was always fiercely independent. Treated like royalty wherever she went abroad, Eleanor Roosevelt neither asked for nor expected any consideration at home for having been the wife of a president. When Congress pondered granting presidential widows a pension, Mrs. Roosevelt said she would decline. She would rather proceed on her own resources. Of those resources it was estimated she gave away more than a million dollars to a wide range of charities and needy individuals. Just as she had resisted her children's pleas that she sit for a portrait (though in due time she gave in), Eleanor refused to allow a statue of herself to be placed in a hall dedicated to famous living people. "I can't see why history should be one bit interested in me," she explained. As her United Feature editors wrote, "History apparently thought otherwise."

For their help in preparing this third volume, I want to thank again my editor at Pharos Books, Eileen Schlesinger, and our copy editor, H. L. Kirk; the archivists in the Presidential Library in Hyde Park, New York, and the reference librarian at the Berkshire Athenaeum in Pittsfield, Massachusetts; and the many people young and old—Roosevelt-lovers and Roosevelt-haters—whose unsolicited stories about this great lady confirmed for me the fact that Eleanor Roosevelt had indeed experienced a marvelous transformation from a plain young girl with a shrill voice and no particular self-confidence to a stature unattributed to any other woman in this century: "First Lady of the World."

DAVID EMBLIDGE
Great Barrington, Massachusetts

Introduction

For more than a quarter-century Eleanor Roosevelt shared her life and thoughts with newspaper readers through her column "My Day." Each day was different, varying from quick reports on her doings to an occasional reminiscence and—most frequently—to observations growing out of her innumerable interests and concerns.

Mrs. Roosevelt was already almost as renowned a public figure as her husband, President Franklin D. Roosevelt, when the column began on December 30, 1935, but "My Day" seemed likely to be a short-lived novelty, notable for glimpses of life in the White House. "The house was full of young people, my husband had a cold and was in bed with milk toast for his supper," she wrote on December 30, 1935, chronicling that she went to her own room with a tray of food and a report on educational work in the Civilian Conservation Corps. She went to sleep at 10:30 instead of at her recent customary 1:00 A.M. The next day, after a lunch for sixteen, a young houseguest remarked to her, "Every meal is different in this house. Yesterday we talked about philosophies of government. Today we talked about movies and punging."

"My Day" was much like the White House luncheon conversation, with its familiar, intimate flavor and casual style. It was a marked contrast to the Olympian pronouncements of the public philosopher Walter Lippmann, but it appealed to a broader readership. Mrs. Roosevelt produced her columns at top speed six times a week, turning out five hundred words in less than an hour. When I arrived for lunch at her Val-Kill cottage on May 1, 1948, I could hear her within dictating "My Day." I rang the bell, the dictating stopped, and she herself answered the door. After seating me, she excused herself and resumed dictating as though there had been no interruption. An editor once complained that early chapters of a book she submitted sounded as if they had been written on a bicycle; some of her columns were indeed turned out on bumpy airline flights. (In the last two years of her life she shifted to producing a longer column three times a week. These were more polished and often were commentaries on issues of the day. During her terminal illness she wrote a poignant, semihumorous gem of an essay on what it was like to be in a hospital bed through the night being intermittently queried, medicated, and prodded.)

Eleanor Roosevelt was not a distinguished prose stylist, but her conversational way of expressing herself carried conviction to her following. There were detractors, to be sure, who were delighted when her cousin and Republican rival Alice Roosevelt Longworth, daughter of Theodore Roosevelt, launched a maliciously witty rival column in 1936. It soon disappeared.

Gradually Mrs. Roosevelt devoted more "My Day" space to her concerns and those of the President. Sometimes she floated trial balloons for him. He was keenly interested in what she wrote, and once when she needed a few days' respite offered to fill in for her. She declined. At times she stayed away from topics he did not yet want broached. In July 1944, while she ardently favored the renomination of Vice President Henry A. Wallace and her husband was maneuvering covertly in favor of Senator Harry Truman, at the President's request she withheld a column in favor of Wallace until after Truman had won the nomination.

Eleanor Roosevelt was of vital importance to Franklin D. Roosevelt and was a prime advocate of their intertwining aims. On national issues, in fact, she was often more advanced than he. Altogether they were the greatest husband-and-wife political team the nation has ever seen.

In their youths the Roosevelts were enthusiasts for progressivism under the banner first of Theodore Roosevelt, then of Woodrow Wilson. During the New Deal and World War II, Mrs. Roosevelt was in private a candid adviser and in public a persuasive advocate. After Franklin Roosevelt's death, for more than seventeen years she invoked his name in the cause of a better America, a stronger United Nations, and a world without war and poverty. On all these concerns "My Day" was, to use Theodore Roosevelt's term for the White House, "a bully pulpit."

"My Day" also from time to time gave glimpses of Eleanor Roosevelt's past and clues to the forces that had molded her. Her roots were in the Knickerbocker aristocracy of New York. She reminisced about her grandfather, the senior Theodore Roosevelt, and his houses in which she had spent part of her childhood. And there was a remote cousin, Mrs. Weekes, living on Washington Square who loved to tell "how in her youth she had danced with General Lafayette at a ball" in New York.

There were painful memories of her childhood. Her mother died when she was eight; her father, whom she adored (an alcoholic who had to live elsewhere) died two years later. On January 1, 1945, after she was questioned about her New Year's resolutions, she remarked in her column: "It is many a long day since my grandmother used to suggest that I should make up my mind to be a better little girl—not to steal candy out of the pantry, to take my cold bath in the morning instead of trying to get away with a warm one."

In October 1958, on the hundredth anniversary of Theodore Roosevelt's birth, Eleanor Roosevelt wrote: "Uncle Teddy was always kind to my brother and me because we were the children of his only brother who had died. . . . He was always a fascinating, colorful personality, but I am afraid when I was young I was occasionally more worried by his energy and physical activities he expected of us all than I was impressed by his mental achievements." She had had reason to be apprehensive; as she once explained to me, his method of teaching her to swim was to throw her off the dock at Oyster Bay into deep water. She became a strong swimmer.

But she also expressed her appreciation: "Few young people came in contact with him without being given the feeling that they must do something for the community in which they lived." No one could have become a fuller exemplar of his ideals than his niece, who possessed the same ceaseless energy and became another formidable crusader for progressive causes.

Eleanor Roosevelt was of a generation of young women who gradually assumed leadership in the struggle for social justice among the poor. The beginning of her education as a reformer came at fourteen at Allenswood School outside London, where she became a leader among the students. After three years, although she would have liked to continue, her guardian decreed she must become a debutante. So she did and soon was engaged to her distant cousin Franklin D. Roosevelt, but she also spent much time in settlement-house work among slum dwellers. At the end of her life she was still proud that she had shown her fiancé conditions he had not known existed.

After her marriage, childrearing years ensued. Household responsibilities and summers at Campobello Island—the "beloved island" she calls it in "My Day"—filled her time. In addition, from the time her husband was elected to the New York state senate in 1910, she began to absorb knowledge of issues and political skills.

Mrs. Roosevelt's metamorphosis into a reform and political leader in her own right was rapid. It began with work at a Washington serviceman's canteen during World War I. In 1918 came estrangement from her husband when Eleanor Roosevelt discovered he was in love with her social secretary, but they did not separate. Then, ironically, when Roosevelt became permanently crippled with polio in 1921, she cemented with him their enduring political partnership. For months she was his surrogate at Democratic meetings and herself rose rapidly in the hierarchy of Democratic women.

Even when Franklin Roosevelt, learning through use of braces and crutches to give a semblance of being lame, not a paraplegic, made his reappearance at political functions, she continued to serve as his ears and eyes. During his two terms as governor of New York she managed, in addition to teaching at Todhunter School in New York City, to perform numerous political errands for him. He taught her how to see more than officials intended when she inspected state institutions. (She was proud of this skill and demonstrated to readers how sharp her eyes still were when she set forth in her March 12, 1960, column a detailed account of conditions in a New York City vocational school.)

Several times when I saw Mrs. Roosevelt she demonstrated disarming warmth, candor and modesty, and yet at the same time exhibited the firm self-discipline she had nurtured through years of public appearances. That first noon in 1948 we dined at a simple table in an alcove off her kitchen. As we ate, with the President's dog Fala begging for scraps at our feet, she remarked that in September 1944 Winston Churchill had lunched with her at that same table. She did not add— as I discovered years later—that she had engaged in lengthy and energetic debate with Churchill over how to maintain the peace, a feat that she hoped to accomplish through the United Nations.

During my few interviews with her she always spoke with admiration of her husband's ideals and achievements; there was a personal side to her relationship that she kept hidden. One summer morning, I witnessed her standing beneath an ancient oak (long gone) in front of the Roosevelt Library, answering the questions of a visiting group of southern women. I was startled when one of them asked Mrs. Roosevelt if she and her husband had been planning a divorce when he was Governor of New York. Unruffled, she answered firmly with a simple "no." Once, when talking to me about her children's various divorces, she commented that when she was young it was assumed that when one made one's bed, one had to lie in it. On the last time I saw her, when she was soon to die, she revealed that her husband had often baffled her by the way he concealed his feelings. How, she asked, had he been able to talk so enthusiastically to Harry Hopkins about horse racing, when, as she knew full well, the subject bored him?

Many years earlier, in 1932, on the night Franklin Roosevelt was first elected president, Mrs. Roosevelt was subdued. She seemed to fear she would have to be a conventional first lady and give up the dynamic role she had been playing in Albany. Far from it. She shifted her activities from the state to the nation. She was patroness of a model community, Arthurdale, in the Appalachians. She concerned herself with the welfare of the dispossessed; she pressured the administration to place women in responsible positions; she fought for the civil rights of blacks, on issues like antilynching legislation, pushing well ahead of her politically cautious husband. Yet he welcomed her radio broadcasts, public speeches, and voluminous writings, all of which helped budge public opinion. One of the most important of these outlets was "My Day."

In the late 1930s Mrs. Roosevelt increasingly worried about the threat to peace from Germany and Japan. She helped the President by promoting in "My Day" the cause of collective security. When the young British king and queen came to visit in June 1939, an occasion that generated public sympathy for the British, Mrs. Roosevelt wrote in warm detail of their reception in the White House and at Hyde Park.

During World War II, Mrs. Roosevelt's and the President's concerns focused on the battle lines, the home front, and the winning of the peace. She served as a particularly effective representative of the President, crisscrossing the nation, visiting London, and raising the morale of American forces from the Caribbean and Brazil to Australia and the South Pacific. All these journeys she chronicled in her column. She saw less and less of him, and in 1944 worried about his failing health. He encouraged her to write about the postwar future as he spun dreams of projects to keep the peace and raise the living standards of peoples throughout the world.

On April 12, 1945, when Mrs. Roosevelt suddenly received word of her husband's death, she responded with dignified stoicism. She did, however, misgauge the effect upon her. She remarked to a reporter concerning her future that "the story is over," but quite the reverse was true.

Years of growing renown lay ahead as Eleanor Roosevelt became first lady of the world. Through "My Day" in 1945 she continued to voice her views on many issues—on July 10 in favor of Senator Claude Pepper's bill to require "equal pay for equal work for women," and on September 7 Senator Robert Wagner's bill to create a national health insurance program. The explosion of the atomic bomb, bringing an end to the war with Japan, brought her immediate comment on August 8: "We have only two alternative choices: destruction and death—or construction and life!"

During the intensifying cold war Mrs. Roosevelt never wavered in her conviction. She sincerely hoped that the United Nations could act as peacekeeper, but her years of service during the Truman administration as one of the delegates to it convinced her of the need for the Truman Doctrine and the NATO alliance. Her crowning achievement was her several years of leadership in shaping the United Nations declaration of human rights.

During the Eisenhower administration, with which this third volume of "My Day" columns opens, Mrs. Roosevelt worked informally for the cause of the United Nations through the American Association for the United Nations. She was also active in Democratic politics through Americans for Democratic Action, ardently supporting Adlai Stevenson, Democratic candidate in 1952 and 1956.

As the Democratic convention of 1960 approached Mrs. Roosevelt, finally persuaded that support of Stevenson was a lost cause, gracefully admitted that John F. Kennedy would make a better candidate. She hailed his first State of the Union address, writing on February 1, 1961, that she sensed in it "a will which has not existed before . . . to face the realities before us at home and abroad." The President appointed her to chair the Commission on the Status of Women.

Most of the issues Mrs. Roosevelt was espousing in "My Day" through the 1950s are still on the American agenda—among them equal rights for women, blacks, and Native Americans; improvement of public education; and prohibition of school prayer. She was appalled by children's ignorance of geography and believed federal support would raise educational standards. Despite her own private education and that of her children, she wrote in March 1961 that "the public schools would probably be better off if all of us felt an obligation to send our children there."

International affairs continued to be in the forefront of Mrs. Roosevelt's interests. On December 20, 1961, she began "My Day" with a challenging question: "What can one woman do to prevent war?" She was receiving many letters containing this query. Her answer was that each woman (and man) should take an active interest in government, work for worthy political candidates, help build the United Nations, work against the proliferation of nuclear armament, and hope in the end "such lethal weapons can be destroyed." She was outlining a course of activity she herself had long followed. She kept herself well-informed, reading in addition to many American publications the *Manchester Guardian* and, to keep up her French, *L'Express*.

Through the last decade of her life, Eleanor Roosevelt continued to travel broadly, bringing to her readers her impressions of other peoples and world leaders. She was queasy about German reunification even before she interviewed the Soviet leader Nikita Khrushchev, who "spoke to me of the loss of his son and 12,000,000 men in the war." Her column of October 3, 1957, carried a transcript of the interview.

Mrs. Roosevelt enjoyed her visits to Israel and the Middle East. On one trip she gave in to the pleas of her granddaughter Nina and impulsively bought her a camel, which, when she learned of the stringent

American import regulations, wound up in the Jerusalem zoo. She sought a way to ease pressures upon Israel, coming at that time from the Saudis, and on April 16, 1957, expressed her wish that the United States and the Soviet Union could come to an agreement not to supply arms to any Middle Eastern countries.

As Mrs. Roosevelt turned seventy-seven, she was not feeling well and was forced to slow down. She knew how serious her illness was but went on one final tour of Europe and Israel. From Paris she confessed that while the youngest members of her party went out for more entertainment, she opted for "a good night's sleep." Yet on April 30, 1962, she reported that, after her plane had landed late that morning (from the West Coast), she had gone to a hearing on equal pay for equal work, to a Brandeis University committee meeting in the morning and board meeting in the afternoon. She had dined with Indira Gandhi and then taken her to a performance of Tennessee Williams' *Night of the Iguana* (which left both of them "a little baffled").

Despite Mrs. Roosevelt's illness (a rare, incurable form of tuberculosis of the bone) in August she visited Campobello Island and wrote in warm reminiscence about her own and her husband's energetic summers there before he was stricken with polio. Three days later she was writing about her own overnight ordeal in a hospital. The illness intensified, but she still wrote her column. In September she was pointing out that "we might profit by the study of other cultures of the world."

On November 7, 1962, Eleanor Roosevelt died at the age of seventy-eight. In her June 4, 1962, column undoubtedly thinking of herself and her husband and his "great ends," she had written:

"A human life is like a candle. . . . sometimes the inner light is strong and bright from the beginning and grows with the years. . . .

"The great people of the world spread the major light. . . . But they . . . perhaps could never have accomplished their great ends without the little lights which reached out and inspired them."

FRANK FREIDEL
Cambridge, Massachusetts

1 9 5 3

The transfer of power from one administration to another in the White House is always a complex procedure, sometimes a real sea change of ideology. In 1953 it was all that and a housecleaning too. After decades of Democratic hegemony, at last the Republicans were moving back into 1600 Pennsylvania Avenue. Though Eleanor Roosevelt had had dreams of being asked to stay on as a U.S. delegate to the United Nations under the new Eisenhower administration, she quickly saw that such was not to be. The year began with her resignation from the post that had established her professional diplomatic credentials around the world. Almost immediately she began to work for the American Association for the United Nations, becoming busier than ever during the year that in October saw her sixty-ninth birthday.

As he left office President Harry Truman warned, in his final State of the Union address, of the increasing dangers of atomic war, setting the tone for a year characterized by a steady buildup of worry in many quarters of American life about Communist attack or influence. The day after Dwight Eisenhower was inaugurated in late January, a federal jury in New York convicted thirteen Communists on charges of conspiracy to overthrow the U.S. government. The political atmosphere in the country was set for McCarthyism to flourish.

In February, Joseph McCarthy, the Republican senator from Wisconsin, alleged that the Eisenhower foreign policy was being sabotaged by the Voice of America radio network. Throughout the year McCarthy made numerous outlandish, usually unsubstantiated claims, often about specific individuals, generally insinuating that Communist subversion was rampant. In November, responding to the pervasive Red Scare, the President decried McCarthy's tactics and defended Americans' right to confront their accusers face-to-face—something McCarthy never seemed willing to do. The very next day the Senator

1

declared that the entire Truman administration had been "crawling with Communists."

McCarthy's influence and that of the House Un-American Activities Committee were spreading, despite the apparent illogic of so many of their allegations. In a still-famous trial and subsequent June execution by electrocution, Julius and Ethel Rosenberg were put to death for espionage related to Communism, the first American civilians to be executed for treason. The General Electric Company and other major businesses declared that as a matter of policy all Communist employees would be fired. Mrs. Roosevelt joined President Eisenhower and many other more sensible Americans in continuing to question McCarthy's and HUAC's good sense and intentions.

The Republicans did not favor wage and price controls as had the Democrats and thus, beginning in February, the structure of bureaucracy and executive orders that had controlled everything from the price of eggs to automobile tires, as well as the workingman's wages, since the early days of World War II, was dismantled. The laissez-faire philosophy of Republicanism was taking hold in Washington again after an absence of many years. Eleanor Roosevelt, long a supporter of moderate price and wage controls, was skeptical about the changes but saw no chance of stemming the Republican tide or the pent-up demand for a freer market among workers and consumers.

The country suffered three astonishing tornado disasters in 1953 (during May and June, in Texas, Ohio, and Massachusetts), causing the death of 349 people. And there was other violence that was hard to make sense of in 1953. In March the United States protested the Soviet firing on an American bomber in international airspace. At the end of July a U.S. B-50 bomber was shot down off Vladivostok, Siberia, by Soviet forces. These political and military confrontations added fuel to the anti-Communist fires.

While Mrs. Roosevelt was away from the country on a prolonged Far Eastern trip (from late May to early August), a Korean armistice was finally signed at Panmunjon. That war was not resolved, but it was over. Even so, 1953 held other military events for the United States. In the fall, over much protest from the liberal establishment, including Eleanor Roosevelt, the administration struck a deal with Spanish dictator Francisco Franco, promising to provide military and economic aid in exchange for the right to build air and naval bases there—all part of a strategy to augment U.S. influence in the Mediterranean and North Africa.

One of Mrs. Roosevelt's great heroes in public service, former Secretary of State George C. Marshall, architect of the Marshall Plan for postwar European recovery, was awarded the 1953 Nobel Peace Prize.

For a brief period after Eisenhower was elected but before Truman left office, Mrs. Roosevelt held to the belief that she could continue to work in her role as a UN delegate, even under a very different White House. But she listened to her Democratic political friends who told her bluntly that her time was up. Nor could she ignore the fact that no invitation to stay on had come from Eisenhower. There were rumors that FBI Director J. Edgar Hoover wanted her out. The die was cast, but the change in her life by no means meant that she would slow down. She took various feminine steps to enliven her appearance (including new hair styles and brighter clothes). She launched into new work for the United Nations and renewed her friendship and discreet romance with Dr. David Gurewitsch. January 1953 was not an ending for Eleanor Roosevelt: she seized the moment to make a new beginning.

HYDE PARK, JANUARY 5—On New Year's Day many of my close neighbors came to call on me at home in the afternoon, and I was asked quite frequently whether I would now be staying here more of the time. Suddenly I realized that I would probably be here less.

As my readers doubtless know, all Democrats who have been presidential appointees either to the U.S. delegations to the UN General Assembly or to any of the UN councils or commissions are expected, with the change of administration, to send in their resignations. It is, of course, only fair that a new president should have an opportunity to appoint people of his own choice to represent him in these positions. For this reason I have sent to the State Department, for presentation at the proper time, my resignation as a delegate to the present General Assembly, which has only adjourned and will reconvene in February.

Having resigned both from the General Assembly delegation and the Human Rights Commission, and not having lost any of my interest in the United Nations, I tried to think of the most useful thing I could do. It seems to me that the most essential thing is to strengthen the American Association for the United Nations in this country. This, of course, can only be done by finding ways to enlarge our existing chapters, to increase the number of chapters throughout the nation, and to make all of them centers from which information flows to every other organization in the community. In that way, knowledge of all UN activities will not only be available, but practically thrust upon the attention of every American citizen. Therefore I am going to start work on Monday morning as a volunteer under Mr. Clark Eichelberger, and I hope that I can be of use to him and to the United Nations.

. . . .

Eleanor Roosevelt had a fine sense of humor about the family lineage. Keeping track of all the Roosevelts, whose American forebears went back

. . . .

as far as the early Dutch settlement of the Hudson Valley, required, as she said, skill in higher mathematics. The Roosevelt grandchildren referred to here are both children of her fifth son, John. Haven Clark Roosevelt was born in June 1940; Anne Sturgis Roosevelt (Nina) was born in December 1942.

NEW YORK, JANUARY 13—Because of the miserable weather over the week-end we all decided not to go to the country, so I took my two grandchildren, Haven and Nina, to Roosevelt Memorial House at 28 East 20th Street. Mrs. Joseph Lash brought her son Jonathan to meet us and we went through the house, beginning with the nursery on the second floor.

I had had the great privilege many years ago of going through that house, which was the birthplace of my uncle, Theodore Roosevelt. At that time I was with my aunt, Mrs. Douglas Robinson. So, on last Saturday I tried to remember all the stories she used to tell us.

There is the story of his saying his prayers, as a little boy, to his mother's half-sister. This half-sister later became Mrs. James K. Gracie, a great-aunt whom we all adored as children. She must have really suffered in those early days when she and her mother were sheltered in their Northern son-in-law's house when all of their interests were wrapped up in the South. The story of the prayer was that little Theodore prayed for the success of the Northern army and his aunt was beside herself in tears. His mother heard him from the corridor and came in to reprove him for being so thoughtless and unkind. His answer silenced her, for he said: "But, mother, I thought I could tell the truth to God."

Down on the second floor the middle room has the old horsehair furniture of that day and I could remember Auntie Corinne telling us how much as children the horsehair scratched their legs and how they squirmed and were reproved by their father. She even remembered the Bible verses she had first read aloud as a child in that room.

We went through the museum side of the house also, and the children were interested to see some things similar to what I have and which they had seen at home. For instance, there are some samples of the pink-and-white china that belonged to my grandmother Roosevelt, who was their great-great-grandmother.

It is a little confusing to them, however, to follow the family lineage that leads back to Theodore Roosevelt, Sr. on my father's side and on my husband's side to Isaac Roosevelt. There is one less generation on his side and that is also confusing, and to work out that their grandfather, Franklin D. Roosevelt, and I were fifth cousins once removed is a real problem in higher mathematics.

Having visited India and seen firsthand what had been accomplished under the guidance and inspiration of Mohandas Gandhi, before and after his assassination in 1948, Mrs. Roosevelt was deeply moved. Her own spirituality was grounded in the Episcopal denomination of the Christian faith, but her attitude was ecumenical. When she saw wisdom in another tradition, she tried to bring it home into her own. This column displays a close parallel to the spirit and ethical stance of Gandhi. Perhaps it was Mrs. Roosevelt's own deep conviction that even the most intractable of political problems begins to be solvable when the individuals involved open their hearts to loving one another that most attracted her to Gandhi's similar philosophy.

WASHINGTON, JANUARY 27—"I prophesy that if we disobey the law of the final supremacy of spirit over matter, of liberty and love over brute force, in a few years' time we shall have Bolshevism in this land which was once so holy."

What Gandhi said about India is something for every one of us to ponder. Most of us are constantly concerned about material things and yet the people whom we like best to have with us and who make the best impression on those with whom they come in contact are the people who rarely give much thought to material things. Their minds dwell on the deeper questions of life.

Mahatma Gandhi often urged that we "turn the searchlight inward." By this, of course, he meant that we must understand our own weaknesses, our own faults, before we can conquer them. All these teachings of Gandhi are applicable to our modern way of life just as they were in the kind of life he was urging on his people. His inspirational leadership finally won freedom for his people—and it was achieved without war.

I do not know that Gandhi's plans for living could be applied to modern life, but there is no doubt in my mind that the more we simplify our material needs the more we are free to think of other things. Perhaps what we all need to do is to sit down and think through how this could be accomplished without the loss of gracious living.

I used to think that, of necessity, comfort and beauty cost a great deal of money. I have learned that that is not true. But I still think we encumber our lives with too much, and that perhaps that is the part of Gandhi's teaching that should remain with us today.

No one who has been in India and seen some of the things that he established and felt the impact that his presence has left on material things—such as the feeling one gets when one enters the very simple room he occupied so frequently at the boys' school for Untouchables—

can doubt the power of the spirit. Gandhi used to sell his autographs in order to keep this school going.

Some of the things the boys are trained to do, such as spinning and weaving, seemed to me less necessary now that India is free and they do not have to prove that they can live independently of any goods brought from outside. But the spirit is as valid as it ever was.

I think that here in our country it would be well for us to give more time to studying how we must preserve our freedoms and our liberties and, above all, how we must preserve our belief in one another.

....

In the early 1950s telephone calls passing through a switchboard were still routinely handled one at a time by an operator plugging in and unplugging one phone-line jack after another, often in a tangled nest of wires. It took specialized skill; more than that, it took fortitude if the switchboard was in the basement of the White House. Here Mrs. Roosevelt gives the same kind of enthusiastic praise to a retiring White House worker as she did, in other "My Day" columns, to retiring cabinet members and Supreme Court justices who also served the public well.

NEW YORK, FEBRUARY 12—I have just read that Miss Louise Hackmeister will no longer be at the switchboard in the Executive Offices in Washington. I think anyone who has ever watched her at work or had anything to do with her would want, as I do, to pay her a tribute for work well done over a long period of years.

I have never known anyone more resourceful in tracking down people nor more even-tempered and calm when good temper and calmness were essential. There must be many people, both Republicans and Democrats, who will want to say a word of thanks to a public servant who has carried on in her job over a long period of years in a completely nonpartisan manner.

....

Inside the circle of power was a place Eleanor Roosevelt loved to be. Even though the Democratic Party had lost the White House in the 1952 election, it had held on to its majorities in both houses of Congress. It was not a party in disarray, but it did feel the need to lick its wounds and regroup with an eye toward the future. It also wanted to honor Adlai Stevenson, who had carried the Democratic presidential banner in 1952 and lost the race to Eisenhower.

This "My Day" column reads like a who's who of the Democratic establishment of the time and includes Senator Herbert Lehman, governor of New York from 1932 to 1942, director of the Office of Foreign

Relief and Rehabilitation (whose activities Mrs. Roosevelt actively sup-
ported), and senator from 1949 to 1957; Margaret Truman, the former
president's daughter; Representative Sam Rayburn, Speaker of the
House, who served in that body during the remarkably long period 1913–
1961 and engineered the passage of much of FDR's New Deal legisla-
tion; and William Averell Harriman, who had served as ambassador to
the USSR from 1943 to 1946, secretary of commerce 1946–1948, and
would later be governor of New York, undersecretary of state, and am-
bassador-at-large.

NEW YORK, FEBRUARY 16—I was very much a Democrat on Saturday. In the morning I spent a little while listening to reports at a meeting called by Stephen Mitchell, chairman of the Democratic National Committee. These reports were made by men and women representing their organizations, and were certainly encouraging. They voiced determination to make advances by 1954 which would show tangibly that the people had returned to their Democratic allegiance.

Saturday night at the dinner given to Adlai Stevenson, where he made his first major speech since the election, I was very proud of the leadership he was giving the Democrats. Mr. Stevenson painted the ideal role for a party out of power to follow, but was realistic enough to say that we would doubtless fall to the temptations of partnership now and then. In everything which concerns the welfare of our country, however, we must try to back the administration when we are convinced that the policies advocated are for the national good.

In responding to Mr. Stevenson's speech, Senator Lehman made a very moving appeal in which he said if we did not remain the party of progress, of progress for all the people, we would not deserve a return to power. I think one of the most effective speeches of the evening was made by Miss Margaret Truman in a few short words. She looked charming and, when she said she thought the time had come when every Democrat should stand up and be counted, I think she gave just the right touch to the gathering.

It was an enormous gathering that did not bear the signs of a party in defeat. I have rarely seen tables in both tiers, as well as covering the entire floor, of the ballroom at the Waldorf. They told me with satisfaction that 1,780 people were present, and since most of them had paid their $100 it must have been a help to the party's treasury!

President Truman sent a signed $100 bill even though he could not be present.

I sat by Mr. Sam Rayburn, who has been so long the Speaker of the House that it seems almost impossible not to consider him "Mr. Speaker." Averell Harriman, presiding, did a really wonderful piece of work in getting everything exactly on time. He made an amusing crack at one point while we were waiting for TV to pick up Mr. Stevenson. Looking at the gathering with satisfaction, Mr. Harriman said: "You see, the Union Pacific always runs its trains on time." This was good preparation for some of Mr. Stevenson's witticisms, which kept the crowd both laughing and applauding.

The two Congressional speakers seemed well content, from the Democratic point of view, with some of the recent Washington happenings. Mr. Rayburn remarked that he was "glad to come to New York City," where occasionally he heard "people talk sense."

. . . .

One of the quirks in Eleanor Roosevelt's otherwise peace-oriented thinking about the U.S.–Soviet cold war was that while she urged both sides to get on with disarmament talks, she also urged Congress to bring about universal military training—not just for young men but also for women. This column explains her thinking on the subject without using the key term that by this time had begun to appear in every State Department speech and report to Congress on the perceived worldwide Communist threat: deterrence. It was this so-called deterrence theory that lay behind even Mrs. Roosevelt's thinking: If America and the West were to keep their military forces strong and up nearly to maximum size, the likelihood that the Russians would ever attack would go down.

Mrs. Roosevelt does not seem to have remembered that often, elsewhere in her "My Day" columns and in her other writing, she criticized both U.S. and Soviet foreign policies because they led to frequent arms sales to smaller countries so they could in turn deter either a Communist or a Western attack. She argued that building up armies and armaments leads inevitably to war. Evidently, she did not think the same would be true in America.

NEW YORK, FEBRUARY 28—Yesterday I visited New York University's uptown campus in the Bronx for a lecture. The audience was wonderfully attentive, and I enjoyed my trip to and from the school along the East Side highway. The weather was so wonderful one almost felt that spring was on the march.

I never face a group of young men, as I did at NYU on Thursday, without the great sense of responsibility that no member of the older generation can escape when he realizes the kind of world these young people are going to live and work in.

This reminded me of a dinner party the other night when I sat beside one of my husband's old friends, who brought up one of his pet theories. This theory is that if we had established universal military service years ago, the Russians would never have dared to become the menace they are today.

. . . .

I always listen with interest because I realize that our haste in disarming has cost us a great deal. It probably has been far more costly than it would have been to remain more constantly in complete readiness to defend ourselves, if necessary. We ended the war at the top of our military power and it has taken us up to now to rebuild even a part of that power and we probably are not at the top even now.

We have discovered from our experience in two major world wars that in our desire to keep them away from our own shores we are necessarily dragged into them. The next world war, which I hope will never come, may well be in our country from the beginning because we will be vulnerable to attack from the start.

This is why I look at our young men and young women with a deep sense of the realization of the kind of world they live in and the decisions they have to make in order to keep their future secure. Perhaps all of them will have to submit to universal military training simply because we may feel that a trained and hardened youth is essential to the safety of our nation.

Even if the Soviets give us assurances that they are not going to try to communize the world in the next 50 years and agree to the kind of inspection that we think is necessary to safeguard the nations of the world if atomic energy is controlled by the United Nations, we may feel we need to be constantly prepared for defense. If this is so, I hope that this training can be made as valuable as possible to the physical and mental development of our younger generation.

Many families dread the thought of universal military training. First, it delays the time for a young man to begin to earn his own living and establish his own place in society. And, second, many fear the temptations that confront the youngsters in training camp areas far from their home towns. I have never been concerned about the latter, even granting the fact that the boys are away from home influences. But we must acknowledge that it troubles many families, so we must be sure that the opportunity of training given to these boys is many-sided and as healthy for the body, mind and spirit as it is possible to make it.

. . . .

Only in the late 1950s, after Adlai Stevenson had twice lost a presidential race to the Republicans (demonstrating en route that, brilliant though he was as a policy analyst, he lacked the charisma and the human warmth necessary to inspire the voters), did Mrs. Roosevelt begin to recognize the irreversibility of his limitations. In his first presidential campaign in 1952, she had sensed his stiffness and unapproachability but was so impressed by his intellectual command of a vast array of complex subjects that she could not see why Stevenson would not in

. . . .

9

the end make a good president, and in 1953 her references to him were still warmly laudatory. In this column she quotes from a recent Stevenson speech various lines that neatly sum up several of her own most deeply held philosophical and political principles.

(Adlai Stevenson was governor of Illinois from 1949 to 1953.)

WASHINGTON, MARCH 3—"We live in a time for greatness and greatness cannot be measured alone by the yardsticks of resources, knowhow and production. There are moral dimensions, too. It is the urgent duty of a political leader to lead, to touch, if he can, the potential of reason, decency and humanism in man and not only the strivings that are easier to mobilize.

"The challenge of our faith and time is the insensate worship of matter organized in a vast international conspiracy. But the goal of life is more than material advance. It is now and to all eternity the triumph of spirit over matter, of love and liberty over force and violence."

In those last words Governor Stevenson has set down for us the great differences between ourselves and the Soviet Union.

I will acknowledge there are cruelties that we find in our system because there are failings in human nature.

I will acknowledge that we do not always find the way of love and liberty, but that is our goal. We strive, and the striving is probably what is really worthwhile in human life. You rarely attain finality. If you did life would be over, but as you strive new visions open before you, new possibilities for the satisfaction of living.

. . . .

Stephen Vincent Benét's long narrative poem about the Civil War, John Brown's Body, *had captured a Pulitzer Prize in 1929. Throughout his career Benét was known for vivid literary treatments of American folklore and history—art well suited to please the mind and tastes of Eleanor Roosevelt, who enjoyed plays and poems with political and historical themes.*

DETROIT, MICH., MARCH 9—On Thursday evening in New York I went to see a performance of "John Brown's Body." It happens to be one of my favorite poems, and I was dubious about whether I would enjoy it on the stage. But Charles Laughton has done a wonderful job of directing it, and Raymond Massey and Tyrone Power both give their parts vital meaning. I am frank to confess that I had not expected Mr. Power to give a performance which would satisfy me as this did. I enjoyed the whole evening, which certainly leaves with you an unforgettable impression.

. . . .

This was a benefit performance for the Citizens Committee for Children, and I was glad that it turned out to be such a full house. I saw many of my friends, so that it was a pleasant social evening as well as one of great artistic satisfaction.

....

The next two columns concern observations Mrs. Roosevelt made about the working and living conditions for blacks in Florida. In the first we sense that, like anyone else, occasionally she failed to see a broader point, having become caught up in the details of a story. It did not seem to have occurred to Mrs. Roosevelt that the shortage of black domestic servants in Florida cities might have some other remedy than bringing in more black people to fill such jobs. Or she could have been poking fun at the white residents who felt dependent on blacks for such help.

The second column shows that Mrs. Roosevelt believed the civil rights struggle would not be won all at once in a set of rapid, sweeping changes. Indeed, she seems to have recognized that the road to victory, when equality of opportunity would be a fact of life and not just a dream, would be a road paved with a thousand compromises, some of them quite humbling. Mary McCleod Bethune was the black founder and president of Florida's Bethune-Cookman College and former adviser on minority affairs to FDR. (The "young trustee" she refers to is a member of the board of the college.) The seventeenth child of former slaves, Bethune was a heroine in Mrs. Roosevelt's eyes; Bethune's opinion counted.

SARASOTA, FLA., MARCH 18—There is one amusing situation here: people are in great need of domestic servants. Colored people have always filled these positions, but the white population has increased so much more rapidly than the colored population that there simply are not enough colored people to meet the needs, regardless of what wages or what living conditions are offered. They would like to attract more colored people to the area. Already 60 modern houses have been constructed for their use, and another 100 are being planned. This hardly seems adequate to me, however; I would say the population of the city had increased by the thousands, not by the hundreds.

NEW YORK, MARCH 20—Daytona is considering the sale to Negroes of a certain area that can become one of the finest beach resorts anywhere in the South, which would be named Bethune Beach. Again, this is segregation, but Mrs. Bethune feels that it is a first step—the bridge between having no recreation for the colored people and the time when all public beaches would be open to all citizens.

....

I do not like segregation any more than Mrs. Bethune does, but I can see that in the South these steps are almost essential. How must young colored people feel about segregation of the ocean? They see young white people enjoying the natural sport of their age, but for them these areas are forbidden.

In Sarasota I was told that the local government had been considering for a long time a beach for the colored people but could not arrive at a final decision. It is felt that such a recreation area would be a safeguard and should be provided.

I hope that in more and more of these Florida cities the present pattern will be changed, not by Northerners, who would be intruding, but by the Southerners themselves.

....

Nobody likes to see a house they have helped to build torn down or abandoned. Eleanor Roosevelt had to swallow a bitter pill at this point in her life when she realized that the Republican administration, having been heavily influenced (some said intimidated) by the likes of Senators Joseph McCarthy of Wisconsin and John Bricker (Ohio Republican), would not subscribe to the UN's Declaration of Human Rights or the covenants supporting it. The administration argued that U.S. foreign policy might be hampered by restrictions about dealing with countries not in agreement with the legally binding promises on human rights.

Mrs. Roosevelt, of course, considered the Declaration of Human Rights by the United Nations one of its (and one of her own) most important accomplishments. She had given almost seven years of her life to the project as chairman of the Human Rights Committee at the UN. Even if she had not been the U.S. delegate, it is likely that her moral principles and her sense of how foreign policy ought to be conducted would have led her to the same somewhat embittered critique of the Eisenhower–Dulles–Republican Party position.

NEW YORK, APRIL 9—I was not really surprised when I read in the newspapers yesterday about Secretary of State Dulles' testimony on the subject of executive agreements and treaties. I had heard rumors that this abandonment of the human rights covenants was to be the position of the State Department and the administration, but it was hard to believe that it would be done in quite the way it has been done.

It is quite evident, as the Secretary of State said, that executive agreements are necessary for the safeguarding of the country in certain situations and to prevent them or insist that they be accomplished only in cooperation with the Senate would be endangering the working of our foreign relations.

To say, however, that it is improper to have a treaty that is going

....

to change the social customs of a country and its legal practices as regards the protection of its individual citizens and their civil liberties seems to me an utterly strange position to take. I wonder if all of the Republicans will agree with this stand on the human rights covenants.

I am very happy to say that the present administration did not carry on the bipartisan policy followed by the Democratic administrations in the immediate past by which many Republicans were given opportunities for service, and gained experience. Had the present administration carried on this bipartisan policy, I might have been asked to finish out my last year on the Human Rights Commission. Had I been asked I probably would have felt obligated to accept and now I would be in the unpleasant position of having to resign in the face of the administration's attitude toward these covenants.

Mrs. Oswald Lord, now representing the United States on the Human Rights Commission, must find herself in a curious position. She has joined representatives of 17 other nations in Geneva, where they are scheduled to draft two covenants that her government has announced it will not present to the Senate.

It would seem more logical to withdraw from the Human Rights Commission if this is to be the U.S. attitude. Even the Soviet Union, though many of us are fairly sure it will not ratify, have not announced through their government that they will not ratify. The Russian representatives are not in quite as awkward a position as those from the United States.

True, this attitude will not take away from us in this country our social, political or civil rights, but there are many areas in the world where our leadership, even if it had been confined to civil and political rights, might have helped vast numbers of people to gain these rights.

In spite of all that has been said, we would have been in no danger of losing any of our rights, and there were many ways—either through reservations, through working for a federal–state clause, or in improving the wording of the present articles—in which we could have made it possible to ratify the covenant on civil and political rights. But now we are not even going to try.

We have sold out to the Brickers and McCarthys. It is a sorry day for the honor and good faith of the present administration in relation to our interest in the human rights and freedoms of people throughout the world.

NEW YORK, APRIL 10—I read with great interest this morning President Eisenhower's letter to the United Nations Commission on Human Rights, meeting in Switzerland, which he sent through the United States representative, Mrs. Oswald B. Lord.

The President states that freedom is indispensable for the achievement of a stable peace, that people everywhere are seeking peace and freedom, and that we must press ahead to broaden the areas of freedom. He regrets the fact that in totalitarian governments there is no respect for freedom or for the dignity of the human person and considers this a basic cause of instability and discontent in the world today. These are wonderful sentiments and entirely true statements, but they give no indication of how those people, or we ourselves with them, are going to work together to attain the ends desired.

Secretary of State Dulles' letter to Mrs. Lord is a clearer statement. In brief, he says that no legal instrument capable of wide ratification in the world today would have any value, since it could not be as good as the actual practice in the advanced democracies and would have no advantage in the countries where the people have few, or none, of the traditional human rights, nor could it be applied in totalitarian states.

We can assume, I think, that the Secretary looks upon the Universal Declaration of Human Rights as being in somewhat the same category as the Emancipation Proclamation of Abraham Lincoln.

It was of value to declare the slaves free. By the same token, it was of value to set down in the Declaration of Human Rights—even though it had no legal binding value—certain standards for human rights and freedoms throughout the world and to accept the resolution saying we would try to attain these standards and also that we would acquaint the people throughout the world with these desirable human rights and freedoms.

No one will deny that writing these covenants was difficult. Great Britain recognized this a long while ago, and I imagine the British are relieved that the burden of having to make a decision as to what their attitude will be has now been taken over by the United States. They can simply say now that they follow our position.

The Soviets will excoriate us unless the dove of peace is very strongly flying toward the United States at this time and they feel they must appease us. In the old days they would have said we had no interest in the well-being of people throughout the world. It will be interesting to see what their delegates actually say at the present meeting.

The representatives of many other nations will feel lost and perhaps a little contemptuous of our fears.

We are not willing to sign anything that binds us legally in the field of human rights and freedoms. Yet, we in the United States find legal decisions helpful in gaining rights for our own people.

Other nations may bind themselves if they wish, but we feel that it is impossible "to codify standards of human rights as binding legal obligations," and the Eisenhower administration does not want to fight a section of the American Bar Association, or the isolationists or those who might vote for the Bricker amendment.

In other words, we use high-sounding phrases but we are afraid— afraid to tackle a difficult thing and try to improve it and accept it ourselves as far as we are able.

....

Envy is always a troublesome motivator. Mrs. Roosevelt had good reasons for her chilly feelings about Clare Booth Luce. The lady had deserted FDR to support Wendell Wilkie in the former vice-president's renegade run for the presidential nomination in 1940. Mrs. Luce, for her part, did not always have kind words for Eleanor Roosevelt. Nonetheless, Mrs. Roosevelt cited Mrs. Luce as an admirable model in certain respects. Clare Boothe Luce had distinguished herself as a playwright (her best known work is a witty satirical 1936 piece called The Women) *and as congresswoman from Connecticut (1943–1947). She was the wife of a giant in American publishing, Henry Luce (founder of* Time, Fortune, *and* Life). *Mrs. Roosevelt at sixty-eight also had something else on her mind: how to stay trim after fifty, certainly a bipartisan question.*

NEW YORK, APRIL 13—On Thursday afternoon of last week I went to a tea given by the N.Y. Newspaper Women's Club in honor of Mrs. Clare Booth Luce, our new Ambassador to Italy. It was her 50th birthday and, she told us, someone had said to her: "Well, the worst part of the century is behind you."

Mrs. Luce does not look 50. She is a very lovely-looking woman who has kept her slim, slight figure, and she has much charm. They say the Italians were uncertain about accepting a woman as ambassador, for it was a somewhat new departure in their area of the world. But in Mrs. Luce they will find not only a beautiful woman, but an able ambassador, with brains which any man might be proud of. I feel Mrs. Luce will represent us well. Her powers of observation and analysis, sharpened by her training both as a writer and as a member of Congress, should make her very valuable.

....

On April 12, the eighth anniversary of FDR's death, Mrs. Roosevelt lost a co-worker and companion who had been with her for decades: Her secretary, Malvina "Tommy" Thompson, died. What did it mean to be secretary to Eleanor Roosevelt? For one thing, there had been for years now a team of secretaries to help carry out her work. Some of them handled correspondence only. Others were researchers, tracking down facts and figures to give Mrs. Roosevelt's arguments in her "My Day"

....

columns, magazine articles, and hundreds of speeches reliable author-ity. But Malvina Thompson was her closest personal secretary, some-thing of a cross between confidante and administrative director. They worked together virtually every day, and on most domestic and inter-national trips of more than a day or two, Miss Thompson went along.

Eleanor Roosevelt had gone up to Hyde Park from New York at 4:45 A.M. to be there in time for the ceremonies at FDR's grave. As soon as that event was over, she went directly to the hospital, and Tommy died just as she arrived. Miss Thompson had indeed been a Roosevelt family member. Anna wrote to her mother after the death: "I know there is no use dwelling on how much you (& we . . .) will miss her but still, not having her around is going to be hellishly hard to take."

NEW YORK, APRIL 14—Miss Malvina Thompson, who had been my secretary for 29 years and who is known to most of my friends and to all my family as "Tommy," died on Sunday afternoon in New York Hospital after 12 days of very serious illness. We all hope that she suffered very little pain.

I am quite sure that no one ever lived a more selfless life. She gave of herself willingly and lovingly. She had a tremendous sense of re-sponsibility about her work and a great sense of dignity. But because to her what she did was so important, whether the task was little or big or whether it was menial or intellectual made no difference what-soever. She did every job to the best of her ability, and her greatest satisfaction lay in helping me to do whatever work I was doing as well as she thought it should be done. Her standards were high for me, as well as for herself, and she could be a real critic.

She had met a great many of the great in her life, but she always valued them as people and not because of their names or their position. A young friend of hers and mine said to me after her death that one would always have memories of good times with her, for she had humor, was a shrewd judge of people and could be caustic, though never really unkind.

One does not weep for those who die, particularly when they have lived a full life. And I doubt in any case whether the gauge of love and sorrow is in the tears that are shed in the first days of mourning.

People who remain with you in your daily life, even though they are no longer physically present, who are frequently in your mind, often mentioned, part of your laughter, part of your joy—they are the people you really miss. They are the people from whom you are never quite separated. You do not need to walk heavily all your life to really miss people.

The children who have so constantly come into Tommy's living room, who have used her typewriter—and sometimes abused it—who have been scolded, who have been cared for, who have been loved, they will talk of her as naturally and as often as they do the things in which she played so big a part. Their elders might make their memories into sadness. Children will keep them bright with laughter.

I am sure that no day will pass when in her own family, among her brothers and sister, her nieces and nephews, someone will not remember kindly her loving deeds of remembrance. I know that in my large family, with its many ramifications, there will never be a day when Tommy will not live.

. . . .

One thing that helped in putting the sadness of Malvina Thompson's death behind was simply getting on with the kind of high-spirited extended family gatherings that were typical at Hyde Park. By this time in her life, Mrs. Roosevelt could count on the unscheduled appearances, at Val-Kill or in her New York apartment, of Roosevelts from any of four generations: her own, her children's, her grandchildren's, and her great-grandchildren's—not to mention assorted nieces and nephews.

NEW YORK, MAY 12—Sunday was our first real summer day at Hyde Park and all our young people were out on the tennis court for the first time.

We had a buffet luncheon for Mr. and Mrs. Henry Morgenthau, who came over to join Mr. Leo Mates, Yugoslavia's permanent delegate to the United Nations, and Mrs. Mates, who were spending the week-end with me.

A number of young people "dropped in," including William Donner Roosevelt and a friend, a student from Spain. Elliott Roosevelt Jr. came from Andover to spend a long week-end—or what is called a long week-end in Andover! Chandler Roosevelt came up from Newport, where he finished a two-week refresher course for the Marine Corps. John and his wife and family were up in their house for the week-end and Trude and Joe Lash were in their house. So we all came together for luncheon, and when that happens only a buffet lunch is possible. We had much good talk and laughter.

On Saturday we took the young people, including my grandchildren, Jonathan Lash, Nicky Pratt, Grania Gurewitsch and her friend, Ann Carlton, to West Point. There was no parade because the grounds were too soggy from the recent rains. So we went to the beautiful chapel, and Mr. Myers, the organist, who has been there 40 years, played some selections for us. The most impressive and unforgettable selection is the "Alma Mater" preceded by music that depicts a storm almost matching the sound of battle.

We all had a picnic lunch with Colonel and Mrs. Frisbee in their

. . . .

little garden and together with Mrs. Frisbee's preparations and ours we really had a feast.

The boys chose to go to the baseball game afterward but the rest of us visited the mess hall and the kitchen.

In that mess hall 2,500 boys are fed within a half-hour sitting and, in addition, they frequently feed as many as 200 members of visiting athletic teams on week-ends. I never saw such a clean kitchen, and the efficiency with which everything is prepared and put into the hot-plate servers to keep warm just took my breath away. All the 2,500 boys at the dining tables are served with a hot dinner three minutes after the first boy is seated.

Mrs. Lash asked the cook what happened with the leftovers. He seemed bewildered for a minute and then responded, "There are no leftovers."

. . . .

Mrs. Roosevelt was busy making last-minute arrangements before taking one of the longest trips of her life. The nearly continuous stream of "My Day" columns that had begun in 1936 and was interrupted only for a few days after FDR died would now be shut off for approximately two months. The trip would take her all the way around the globe, heading westward to the Far East—Japan. She was accompanied by Maureen Corr, her chief secretary, and by Minnewa, her son Elliott's wife. The trip was underwritten by the U.S. Committee on Intellectual Exchange. Following her work in Japan, she would meet David Gurewitsch in Athens; together they would visit Yugoslavia.

Out of courtesy to the White House, Mrs. Roosevelt had asked Secretary of State John Foster Dulles if he might have preferred sending a Republican woman to Japan. His lofty response, explains biographer Joseph Lash, indicated his indifference, based on the fact that Mrs. Roosevelt would not be representing the United States anyway. Dulles ignored her offer to come to Washington to be briefed before the trip.

The social invitations Mrs. Roosevelt had to decline because of her travel plans show clearly how highly she was held in the esteem of world leaders; this column refers to Ambassador Abba Eban of Israel; Queen Elizabeth II of England; and to the Norwegian royal family.

NEW YORK, MAY 13—I have found much to my regret in the past day or two that I have to have time to do a few personal things before leaving next week for Japan and Europe.

As a result, I had to forgo the pleasure of attending on Monday night the dinner given by the United Jewish Appeal for Ambassador Eban. It was a real disappointment to me personally, but I was somewhat relieved because I felt it would cause less consternation than if I had

. . . .

had to give up something where I was the only speaker and the whole meeting depended on my being there.

As always happens when one is going away, unexpected things come up and one has to try to finish odds and ends hurriedly as the date for departure draws closer.

I am prepared to work very hard in Japan but on leaving there I hope to travel in more leisurely fashion, not spending much time anywhere except in Yugoslavia, where I will be for about two weeks. And I hope there will be no speeches or official engagements, so that I can really enjoy sights and sounds of new places and get a little impression of the places and peoples.

I was very much touched the other day to be invited to the coronation by Queen Elizabeth, and I was very sorry that, because of my commitments in Japan, it wasn't possible for me to accept.

In the same way I would have liked very much to be at the wedding of Princess Ragnhilds. I felt it was very kind of Prince Olaf and Princess Martha to invite me and because of old associations I would have liked to have been there. I am glad, however, to hear the young people will be coming to New York, as the young husband's family has business connections here, and I look forward to someday soon when I shall see them.

. . . .

"East, west, home is best" goes the children's rhyme, and as much as Eleanor Roosevelt loved globetrotting, few pleasures in her life could compete with family gatherings and community activities at Hyde Park. The Roosevelts were not passive observers; they were competitive and playful participants. Entering animals in contests at the county fair, marching in the town parade: There isn't much in America that is more middle-class.

Mrs. Roosevelt used these occasions for wry observations about human behavior—about how often vanity precedes a fall, or how we all tend to hear just what we want to hear while disregarding the rest. The inspirations for these bits of common wisdom were the personalities and antics of her children and grandchildren.

HYDE PARK, SEPTEMBER 3—We went this morning to the opening of the Dutchess County Fair. My first interest was of course to visit Franklin Jr.'s Hereford cattle and his sheep. They had changed the hour for judging the cattle so they will not be judged until tonight and I do not know at what hour the sheep will be judged. Going so early we missed some of the exhibits.

I always enjoy the flower shop, particularly the flower arrangements, and I was looking forward to seeing them today and comparing what

. . . .

I saw with what I had learned about flower arrangements while I was in Japan. I brought home two books on the subject and watched many classes, even those in factories where girls were being taught to arrange flowers. In our hotel a lady who was taking courses arranged the flowers in the lobby each day and I watched with keen interest to see how she created such a variety of beautiful designs and used comparatively few flowers. Since the flower show was being judged and we could not go in, neither could we see the arts and crafts show nor the grange exhibits, as the judges were busy.

I did get into the 4-H Club building, however, and looked with interest on what the boys and girls were doing in dressmaking, in food preparation, in craft work of different kinds and even in flower arrangements. I saw some of their animal exhibits, too, and spent a little while watching some of the horse show entries. While we were there they were showing medium-sized ponies and large-size ponies. Miss Deborah Dows with her beautiful white stallion won first prize with her really beautiful little horse.

Our children went through all the booths of different kinds for entertainment and tried their hands at many things. Only two of the small boys were lost when it was time to go home. We had their names called over the loudspeaker, but when they finally appeared they blandly said they hadn't heard a thing, which shows how easy it is not to hear when you do not want to.

We all went to lunch at the Vanderbilt Inn on the way home and I felt that when we walked in we must have looked like an invading army: 11 children and eight grownups. That really is quite a crowd!

Sad to say, I will not be able to go again since I go to New York early tomorrow morning and my niece with her four children and a friend, Mrs. Wagner, will be leaving here for Michigan. I shall be anxious to hear what happens to Franklin Jr.'s pet bull because he thinks he should win over anything in his class. But every owner has that feeling about his particular pet animal and I learned long ago not to count my chickens before they were hatched. This is a very valuable lesson which I hope Franklin Jr. has also learned.

HYDE PARK, SEPTEMBER 22—Saturday, September 19, was Community Day in the village of Hyde Park. As a family we were out bright and early because my granddaughter Nina, Johnny and Ann's oldest daughter, was marching in the parade with the schoolchildren. It was a wonderful parade, a high school band and the band from the village of Tivoli some 25 miles away kept them all moving, automobiles with prominent citizens, all the fire department, every business in town with a vehicle of some kind and the Park Service, not to be outdone, with a very attractive float covered with green and with a bust of my husband, all swept by us as we stood watching on the main road. At one o'clock we were back again in front of the town hall, this time to watch the children in a bicycle parade.

There were any number of children on tricycles, so there had to be two types of prizes, three for the older children who rode bicycles and three for the younger children who rode tricycles. All the bicycles were to be decorated, which really meant much work on the part of the older members of the community, and the winning of the prize depended largely on the ingenuity of the parents who could think up some way of presenting their child and bicycle in a unique manner.

One of the tricycles had two large paper bunnies cut out from painted brown paper fastened on either side of the wheels and handlebars and each bunny had a nice little piece of white cotton for a tail. The little rider rose out of the center of the bunny's back and he was so young that he was entirely oblivious to what he was supposed to do or in fact what anybody else was supposed to do. He kept riding around in his own little circle and I saw innumerable people rescue him and try to put him in the line where he would follow some one of the others.

I don't know who finally won in the tricycle races but a little boy whose bicycle had been transformed into an exhibition stand for fruits and vegetables and who was himself like Carmen Miranda with a little hat on his head set on one side in which fruits were held at rather a precarious angle won first prize for the bicycles. The boy had been made up with rouge and blacking around his eyes and he really looked like a good imitation of a sophisticated chorus girl.

I thought our own Sally looked very sweet with her bicycle all decked out with red, white and blue crepe paper and little whirl-around pinwheels on either handle. She was wearing a little Austrian peasant girl's dress with an apron which I brought her from Vienna and little wreaths of flowers in her hair.

Finally at four o'clock, I, myself, went to speak at the town hall, so we felt that as a family we had been very active in Community Day!

. . . .

The Red Scare of the 1950s pushed some people well beyond the outside edge of reason when it came to thinking through what did and did not constitute a Communist threat to America. Occasionally a truly absurd and comic instance of such unreasonableness would surface, and Mrs. Roosevelt could laugh at it heartily. But she also saw in such off-balance thinking a serious point, for she feared such people might themselves become arbiters of power. This column both makes fun of a worried right-winger and reminds "My Day" readers to beware—an illustration of a key element in Eleanor Roosevelt's thinking: how the dualistic

. . . .

attitudes that lead to simple black-and-white judgments about human behavior are almost never very close to the truth—the truth that lives in no specific place in the gray area in between.

NEW YORK, NOVEMBER 21—I saw something in the newspaper the other day which seemed to me to show the change in the climate of our thinking rather dramatically. The article read that a lady who frequently consulted with Senator Jenner and who was a member of the textbook committee of the State of Indiana had just suggested that Robin Hood might well be removed from all libraries because it would contaminate our young. The reason: Robin Hood took from the rich to give to the poor and that is a Communist theory!

Strange to say, when I was young a great many years ago we read Robin Hood and nobody thought of its being communistic. At least my grandmother never mentioned it. All I learned from it was that you could be a bad man and yet not wholly bad; that even in evil sometimes good could be found. I felt the charm of the characters who were part of the Robin Hood surroundings and I enjoyed the story and I must say that I never felt too sorry for the people whom he robbed because they always seemed to be able to get along without the worldly goods which he removed.

What a shame it is that the young people of today cannot have the pleasure that we had without being threatened by this new fear of communism. I seem to remember in a book that many of us revere that there is a story about the young man who asked the Master how he could be saved and that the answer was "Give all your worldly goods to the poor." Is that story looked upon as Communist today?

Much more serious, however, is this same lady's recommendation that the mention of the Quakers should be expunged from our young people's knowledge. They must not learn about the Quaker religion nor about famous Quakers in this and other countries because the Quakers do not believe in war, and if we had fewer soldiers that would encourage the Communists.

To what absurdities are we really coming? Is the State of Indiana going to accept such foolish recommendations? Do they keep someone on their textbook committee who has as little breadth and understanding as this lady seems to have? Does Senator Jenner really consult with this lady? Or does she consult him before she presents such opinions? If he agrees with them then I am not surprised that these investigation committees suggest that the Protestant clergy are riddled with Communists. Most of our clergy would like to see people think more of peace than of war and they certainly advocate that the rich should give to the poor. Not always voluntarily, either, but on the urging of those who see how some of their money can be better spent.

To be sure, Robin Hood was a fabulous robber, but perhaps all of us who ask for money for good causes from those we know have it to give might be considered as robbers because sometimes I am quite convinced that the giving is not completely voluntary. Either the force of public opinion suggests that, or their next-door neighbor may think less well of them if they are not gracious givers.

What is the use of dwelling on such absurdities, except to give you a laugh and perhaps to make you examine a little into what some people call communism? If Robin Hood and the Quakers are to be classed as Communist influences, we are living in a topsy-turvy world!

1 9 5 4

The threat of communism at home and abroad fanned a smoldering debate all year long in 1954. Everyone seemed to have a theory about the scope and seriousness of the threat and proposals about how to handle it. At the federal level there was plenty of action, some of it productive, some of it self-contradictory. Many of Mrs. Roosevelt's "My Day" columns wrestled with the details of particular cases of alleged Communist influence in foreign or domestic affairs. While her positions were usually consistent, she joined in the country's frustration over the excessive expenditure of energy on a single but amorphous issue—especially because she saw so much else that the society should be doing to improve itself and to help the less fortunate elsewhere.

In Eisenhower's State of the Union message in early January the Congress heard a call for cuts in military spending. Five days later Secretary of State Dulles announced a U.S. commitment to a policy of "massive retaliation" against any nuclear attack and promptly suffered a barrage of domestic and foreign criticism. On January 21 the United States launched its first nuclear submarine, the *Nautilus*. Within the next six weeks Eisenhower reported twice to the nation that the military had successfully tested the new hydrogen bomb on two atolls in the Pacific. While America was building its nuclear arsenal it also participated in unsuccessful Big Four talks on the reunification of Germany. Mrs. Roosevelt was as eager as anyone for Europe to be stabilized, for oppressed people to be free, for the spreading influence of Soviet-bloc communism to be checked. But she maintained her skepticism about a reempowered Germany.

Foreign policy and military activity in 1954 seemed to draw the United States repeatedly to Asia. In mid-March the French reported that U.S. military aid was in fact carrying the burden of the cost of the French-Indochina war in which France, a former colonial power in Southeast Asia, was trying desperately to stave off Communist control in Vietnam. The United States opposed a negotiated settlement, fearing that communism would spread even faster in its wake. Dulles urged air support for the French battle at Dien Bien Phu, but Congress was leary without some cooperation from at least one other Western power, Britain. On April 7 Ike gave a speech, using the phrase "falling row of dominoes" to describe what he feared the Southeast Asian countries would become if the United States did not take a military stand there against communism. The "domino theory" prevailed in U.S. foreign policy thinking as a corollary to the containment theory, for years to come. Eleanor Roosevelt had little argument with this, though she believed humanitarian aid might work better in the long run than arms.

In early May, Dien Bien Phu fell to the Communists. The French began to back out, American commitments to the French unraveled, and the Communists took over North Vietnam. By August a situation with similar potential confronted the State Department. Having lifted its protective blockade of Taiwan earlier in the year, the U.S. found itself and its ally, the Taiwanese non-Communist government-in-exile of China, threatened by invasion from Communist mainland China. Eisenhower did some saber-rattling, reminding Chou En-lai, the Communist foreign minister, that the U.S. Seventh Fleet could easily interpose itself, but by mid September the United States had decided not to get involved in a direct military way. Nonetheless, the seeds had been sown for U.S. commitments in Southeast Asia (defense treaties were signed in 1954 too), and prognosticators like Eleanor Roosevelt could see that there would be trouble for years to come as long as America continued in its role as chief defender of democratic rights worldwide.

Among the more successful battles being won on the home front, however, were two that Mrs. Roosevelt was particularly pleased about. The Salk polio vaccine was out of the lab and into the doctor's office, at least in Dr. Jonas Salk's own office in Pittsburgh, where real testing on children began and appeared to be working. And in a landmark case, *Brown* v. *Board of Education*, the Supreme Court pushed the country a giant step forward in achieving justice in civil rights. *Brown* concerned the issue of segregation in elementary schools. The ruling proclaimed segregated schools that are "separate but equal" to be "inherently unequal." It demanded desegregation "with all deliberate speed." Liberals cheered; outraged Southern conservatives showed their resistance to change by refusing to implement the Court's orders. Mrs. Roosevelt praised the Court and pressed for reasonable discussion and obedience to the law, yet she knew the struggle would take years.

Another grand drama and debate also absorbed the nation—primarily on television—throughout much of 1954. Republican Senator Joseph McCarthy of Wisconsin opened hearings in April into his allegations that the Army was in some quarters infiltrated by Communists. His tactics in the hearing room and in press conferences were so outlandish (characterized by gross and irresponsible insinuations which threatened to ruin many careers) that his Senate colleagues realized at last something must be done to put him in check. By June McCarthy had expanded his charges, claiming that the CIA too was infiltrated by Reds. In August a Senate committee began to investigate charges of misconduct by McCarthy himself.

McCarthy and his allies were still having some success, however. They had engineered legislation called the Communist Control Act, which Eisenhower signed in late August. By mid-October—just after Eleanor Roosevelt's seventieth birthday—the Civil Service Commission, using this new law, had dismissed more than 2,600 employees suspected of having Communist sympathies. Nonetheless, by the end of September, the evidence against McCarthy had become overwhelming. The Senate committee unanimously recommended censure; on December 2 he was condemned by the full Senate, and within weeks his power was gone.

There were engineering feats in 1954 as well. The St. Lawrence Seaway Project got under way with massive commitments of capital from both Canada and the United States. Groundbreaking took place for the first atomic power plant, at Pittsburgh. Two Americans of note were awarded Nobel Prizes in 1954: Dr. Linus Pauling, for his work in biochemistry (largely on the role of vitamins in health), and the coveted prize capped Ernest Hemingway's career as a writer. The name of America's most popular fiction writer at midcentury barely receives even a brief mention, if that, in the whole run of "My Day" columns. Hemingway's male chauvinism, belligerent personality, heavy drinking, and conviction that politics never really solves any problems were all anathema to Eleanor Roosevelt.

. . . .

Some foreign policy analysts specialize in counting dollars, guns, tons of grain, and other quantifiable things when assessing the likely success or failure of a potential move. Others say that the real issues cannot be quantified; that they are more a matter of attitudes, beliefs, even feelings. Mrs. Roosevelt was by no means oblivious to the value of the first approach. As an adviser to FDR and as a delegate to the United Nations, Eleanor Roosevelt was renowned for being well-informed about the objective facts of any situation under discussion. Yet her basic style in evaluating a complex issue involving a contest of wills (between

. . . .

two countries) was to look at the overriding feelings being expressed by the governments and the people in general.

Such was the case in her review of a thorny problem faced by the State Department concerning India and Pakistan. Mrs. Roosevelt tries here to consider all sides objectively. Her underlying concern is that U.S. foreign policy work consistently to contain communism within the borders of the Soviet Union, China, and the Warsaw Pact nations in Eastern Europe. Although she differed on so many points with the Eisenhower program, in this respect, Eleanor was right in step with mainstream U.S. thinking at the time. She does express again, however, her one reservation about this policy: that humanitarian aid may do more to win friends in the battle against communism than will all the arms America could ever supply.

NEW YORK, JANUARY 7—Day by day we see the question of military aid to Pakistan or a military agreement with Pakistan discussed in our newspapers and each time it seems to me it is being made more clear to us that, whether reasonably or not, still the Indians are completely opposed to this arrangement. They feel that Pakistan is safe from the Soviet Union, having both Afghanistan and India on its borders, and that in accepting military aid from the United States, Pakistan will bring the cold war to the Indian world.

We seem to be jeopardizing the friendship of 370 million people in order to establish a military agreement with 70 million people It is certainly not fear of Pakistan that makes India appear to object to this, for even with the United States military aid Pakistan would not be a threat to India because of India's predominance in her area of the world as to resources and population.

It is perhaps natural that Pakistan should seek to strengthen her position. From the United States point of view there is undoubtedly no feeling that we want to control either India or Pakistan and because the idea of political control is very far from our thoughts we are sometimes surprised that the rest of the world does not take it for granted that our intentions are good—that all we are trying to do is to make the world safer for democracy.

In the old sense of military bases and military alliance this arrangement with Pakistan seems to be entirely different. We are simply willing to strengthen Pakistan against the Communist world. It is true that India has tried all along to remain completely neutral in the cold war and this strengthening of Pakistan by a Western democracy might well seem from the point of view of the Indians a dangerous step. There is no question that we want to be friendly with both India and Pakistan and there is no question that we trust both countries as far as their desire for freedom and democracy goes.

It may well be that we would strengthen Pakistan more by economic aid than by military aid and perhaps give India less cause for suspicion. This whole question it seems to me requires careful study and thought. It is important for the people of the United States to demonstrate in every possible way their friendship for both countries and their feelings that it is important not to do anything that endangers that friendship. It may well be that a change in the type of aid that we propose may be the solution to this problem. All of us may feel that India is unreasonable but there are times when all nations are unreasonable. Some people have even felt that that could be said sometimes of the United States.

. . . .

Eleanor Roosevelt was the guest of honor at an almost countless number of testimonial dinners. Her work with all sorts of Jewish refugee relief agencies and fund drives, as well as with the Bonds for Israel program (to raise investment capital for the new nation), brought her many such invitations from Jewish groups. Her ruminations here about one event of this type reveal her sincere interest in American history and in how the Roosevelt family line traces back to its beginnings. Given the history of anti-Semitism in America, and perhaps given Eleanor Roosevelt's own youthful attitude toward Jews (which biographer Joseph Lash indicates was less than sympathetic), Mrs. Roosevelt goes to some length in several "My Day" columns to show clearly that the old Roosevelts and the early Jews in America were friends.

NEW YORK, JANUARY 8—Monday evening at a dinner which Mrs. Dick Sporborg gave for me, I was presented by Dr. de Sola Pool with a most interesting volume called "Portraits Etched in Stone—Early Jewish Settlers, 1682 to 1831." This volume covers much of the early history of New York City.

The Jewish people have been among the earliest settlers in our country. On October 12, 1492, Luis de Torres was the first Jew to land from Columbus' caravel "Santa Maria" and he gave thanks to God for having safely crossed the uncharted seas. There were other Jews in the crew and from that time on their people were a part of all the settlements of this continent.

The history of New York City includes the story of many Jews and intertwined with their story is that of many other New York families, among them my own Roosevelt ancestors.

Dr. de Sola Pool tells the story of the old Chatham Square Cemetery and in the book there is a picture of it in the early 20th century. In presenting the book to me he told the story, too, of the friendliness that existed between some of the early Roosevelts, among them Isaac,

. . . .

who helped to ratify the Constitution of the State of New York and who was my husband's direct ancestor.

The Roosevelts owned farms and land in this area and were connected in this way with the acquisition of this first Jewish cemetery in Chatham Square. The tablet over the cemetery reads:

This Tablet Marks What Remains of
The First Jewish Cemetery
In the United States
Consecrated in the year
1656
When It Was Described as "Outside the City"

During the War of the Revolution
It was Fortified by the Patriots
As One of the Defenses of the City

Erected in 1903 under the Auspices of
The American Scenic and Historic Preservation Society
and of
The American Jewish Historic Society

. . . .

Among the numerous malignant effects of McCarthyism was that it caused liberal-minded career service people in government to leave their jobs lest they end up being unfairly accused (by McCarthy, his Senate cronies, or by HUAC) of having Communist sympathies. The net result was a serious brain drain from several departments in the federal government. And the Red Scare drove people away from even applying for government jobs for fear that their reputation might someday be ruined by unfounded insinuations. Eleanor Roosevelt lamented these developments and saw that they did not bode well for the political health of the country. The Mr. Ford she refers to is Henry Ford, II, grandson of the great automobile industrialist, who became president of the Ford Motor Company in 1945. Ford had given a speech on world peace when accepting the Poor Richard Club Medal on January 16, 1954.

NEW YORK, JANUARY 23—I think Mr. Ford's statement the other day that he found many of the foreign representatives in the United Nations mystified about our attitude on communism in this country and feeling that we were a great big frightened giant looking for a mouse with a club, was most interesting. It never does give confidence to people to find that someone they feel they should rely on for calm and clear judgment is frightened.

. . . .

This mad rush on the part of Senator McCarthy to accuse people in government of communism has forced us into searching for Communists under every bed when as a matter of fact the Senator discovered comparatively few in positions of importance. I think the performance has been harmful to the trust that citizens as a whole have in the conduct of their government and in their government servants.

Mr. Dulles may well believe that in the Foreign Service the witch hunt in the Department of State has had no effect. On the whole our people are so loyal and courageous that as long as they stay in the service they will try to send in reports which do represent their thinking. However, I know of a number of young people in the service who were just beginning to be of value who had resigned because they did not feel it was worth staying in under present conditions. That is a loss to the Foreign Service in the future and the mere fact that in the recent past fewer young people have been applying to enter is an indication of how they feel.

. . . .

One of Mrs. Roosevelt's most far-sighted and well-argued "My Day" columns on Mideast foreign policy explains a number of her ideas about where the situation there would carry us if left unchecked. Her sympathies clearly lay with the young Israeli government. Her opposition to indiscriminate arms sales to every country in the region, especially to Arab nations, was by this time well known. What stands out here is the effective interweaving of several different kinds of factors, in several countries, all working on one another at once. Mrs. Roosevelt was an expert at succinct expression. The guiding principles in her thinking here are consistent with other writing of hers elsewhere: Belligerence does not breed reconciliation; weapons acquired for defense eventually become weapons used for aggression; the United States cannot buy peace by selling the instruments of war.

MONTREAL, JANUARY 28—I was very much interested the other day in a statement made by the new King of Saudi Arabia to the effect that 10 million Arabs should be sacrificed to get rid of the Israelis. In one way I imagine the people of Israel should be proud of the fact that the Arabs estimate they will need 10 million to be sacrificed in war to subdue a couple of million people.

In another way it seemed to me, as a citizen of the United States believing in the United Nations and in the hope of a peaceful world, that this was a shocking statement. The United Nations resolution dividing Palestine did not please many of the people immediately interested, but the Israelis have accepted it and gone ahead and built

. . . .

on that tremendous influx of immigration from the Arab states and Europe which include many people who have become a burden on the country. Still, democracy has been preserved and economic and political stabilization are moving forward.

The problems are great in Israel but they are being met and conquered, and since in that area of the world this is one of the strongholds of democratic government it would seem that it was a paramount interest to the countries of the West to support and help it grow.

This in no way means antagonism or unwillingness to help the Arab states to grow, but two of the Arab states, Egypt and Syria, are under a dictatorship. Even though that dictatorship may have been necessary and may be the most benevolent government that can be developed at present, it still means that these states are not democratically governed and may still have political and military upheavals. This group of Arab states has expressed its loss of confidence in the United States and in the West by remaining strictly neutral in the differences between the Soviet Union and the United States. As far as the Korean War is concerned, they have shown in every possible vote their mistrust of the UN cause in Korea.

Many people deplore the loss of friendship for the United States in the Arab states and feel it is due to the fact that the United States was willing to back the United Nations proposal for the division of Palestine. Whatever the cause, the results are deplorable and the policies now pursued are far more disturbing than the creation of the government of Israel.

It seems to me a most shocking thing for the head of a government in these days of tension to announce what is tantamount to a verbal declaration of war. For the United States, therefore, to contemplate giving arms to the Arab countries seems to me a highly questionable policy. I am sure we have the most laudable intentions, first of showing that we are willing to help both Israel and the Arab states on an equal basis, next we are undoubtedly hoping that these arms will make the Arab states feel that they can put up some fight if the Soviet Union should decide to attack them.

I can see no reason whatsoever which will prevent the Arabs from using these arms against Israel, if they are so inclined, and once that happens a bitter war will ensue in that area of the world and we will be forced to take a stand which would certainly complicate matters considerably and face us with an increasingly difficult problem.

. . . .

Like the "My Day" column of January 23, this one makes an almost mournful plea: Americans must stand up and take stock of themselves,

. . . .

for they have been cowed by the likes of Senator McCarthy into a weak-
ened condition of self-doubt and lack of trust in one another.

NEW YORK, MARCH 10—In The New York Times Magazine on Sunday there was an article by John B. Oakes entitled "This Is the Real, the Lasting Damage." It talks for the first time very openly about the fear that is prevalent in the land today where everyone is fearful of saying anything which may cause him to be called a Communist by many who do not even know what it is to be a Communist. The fear has fallen on our public men, on our teachers, even on our ministers and certainly it has fallen on our young people.

Those of us who understand communism know that it is because it creates fear in people that we dislike it. Communism enslaves both the bodies and the minds of men. Because of the fear that we are creating at home, the same situation is developing in what is supposed to be the land of the free and the home of the brave. We might almost as well be living under a totalitarian government for the effect upon us all is much the same as it would be if we did not have our freedoms guaranteed by law.

The laws are all there and they are all good but they no longer protect us. I do not belittle the harm that undetected Communists might cre-ate in this country but something has happened to us when people who are not Communists are still afraid of being called Communists, so some of the things said in this article we should take to heart.

Here is a quote to remember: "The only antidote, therefore, to the influence these people exert (those who would frighten us) is a deter-mination not to be frightened by them. There is no trick to recovering the full expression of freedom. But it requires constant exercise of that privilege, for nothing atrophies from disuse so quickly. Americans in their hearts know this, and despite momentary aberrations they have always come back to it."

. . . .

Here is an uncharacteristic pat on the back for the Roosevelt family and
its style of debate—for its members, a form of entertainment.

CHICAGO, APRIL 6—I have had young people tell me they found family gatherings somewhat boring, a situation which I think never exists among our young people. They may violently differ with each other and I have had strangers present when Roosevelt arguments were going on who thought that we were about to kill each other. But as a matter of fact this intensity only stimulates thinking and interest and I think has a good deal of value. Somebody said about the United States that

. . . .

we have unity through variety, and that is what I always feel exists in my own family. Plenty of variety but basically a great deal of unity.

. . . .

Mrs. Roosevelt quotes from a letter from an association of Japanese women who protest the radioactive contamination of Japanese fishing grounds as a result of recent American hydrogen-bomb tests in the Pacific. Her ambivalence about the value of the tests is clear in the following two columns. Mrs. Roosevelt wants the United States to retain its military superiority but fears that the very weapon designed to accomplish that end is too dangerous for anyone to manage. Her numerous "My Day" columns, many speeches, and other writing on the topic in magazines amounted to a substantial contribution (though in the minority report) to the policy-formation process. In the end the American government came to believe that the best defense against a Soviet nuclear attack was to arm America to the teeth with nuclear weapons sufficient to deter any such hostile initiatives by the enemy.

New York, April 13—"Under these circumstances it is difficult to convince the Japanese that these tests are made in order to protect all of us, as some Americans seem to insist. We now know that these tests, if given in Bikini, will threaten our survival. We cannot be convinced that further tests are necessary. Is it not enough to know how horrifyingly powerful and unpredictable they can be? We understand that the next test is already planned for April 22nd. Will you not take a stand in an effort to stop further tests in this area—for our sake, for yours and for the sake of all the people in the world?"

We women are far away from the problems of the Pacific in this country. But we have heard a great deal about the force of the bomb and to most of us the real value of this bomb is that it may awaken people to the fact that we can now destroy our civilization completely. Therefore, perhaps it will give all of us everywhere in the world, including the Soviet Union, the determination to prevent war, if we possibly can. If it has that effect, the explosion accomplished a desirable result, but whether we should continue the experiments is something I think our government should seriously consider.

New York, April 16—Increasingly people are talking to me about the new H-bomb and its dangers. Even on "Meet the Press" I was asked if the knowledge that one could carry a devastating bomb in a suitcase didn't frighten me, and so I have decided to tell you what I feel about this whole situation.

It seems to me that the discovery of this latest bomb has actually outlawed the use of atomic bombs. The power of destruction is so

. . . .

great that unless we face the fact that no one in the world can possibly use it and therefore it must be outlawed as a weapon, we risk putting an end to all civilization. However, this realization makes it necessary to think of other things much more critically.

The day that we agree the world over that no one can use an atom bomb, we must either agree immediately on total disarmament, except for a united force in the United Nations, or we must make sure that we have better weapons than anyone else. We must have the best of the less destructive weapons, such as tanks, guns, etc. We are not equal as to population with the Communist world.

Therefore, the free world must stand together to defend itself. It will not do to rely on a weapon that we cannot use for protection. It is entirely obvious that were we, because we had no other strength, to use the H-bomb, let us say against an enemy that seemed to threaten us or that seemed to threaten the security of an area of the world that we felt should not fall to Soviet domination, instead of having the sympathy of the world we would, by that one action, have created fear and hatred of us.

No one can use this new destructive weapon without destroying innumerable innocent people. It would not be only our enemies that would condemn us, it would be our own conscience.

The conscience of America is a very real thing and if, because of any temptation whatsoever, we use this terrific weapon first, there are few of us in this country who could live with our own conscience.

Before we drift into war in one way or another, I feel that every possible agency, primarily the United Nations and its negotiation machinery, should be called into play. Sometimes I think we rely too much on negotiation only among the great powers. True, there is no force set up in the United Nations and you cannot rely on the enforcement of peace through an already set-up compulsory force provided by every member nation in the United Nations.

Just because of this, however, the mobilization of world opinion and methods of negotiation should be developed and used by every nation in order to strengthen the United Nations. Then if we are forced into war, it will be because there has been no way to prevent it through negotiation and the mobilization of world opinion. In which case we should have the voluntary support of many nations, which is far better than the decision of one nation alone, or even of a few nations.

I dislike fear and I confess to being on the whole rather free from it. But not to look at the dangers of the present and make up our minds that we do not want to drift, but that we want to use all the machinery there is to prevent war, seems to me foolhardy.

I think the women of this country, if they face the fact of the present situation, will agree with me that this is a time for action—not for war, but for mobilization of every bit of peace machinery. It is also a time for facing the fact that you cannot use a weapon, even though it is the weapon that gives you greater strength than other nations, if it is so destructive that it practically wipes out large areas of land and great numbers of innocent people.

. . . .

For one who was by nature fundamentally an optimist, Eleanor Roosevelt had an impressive capacity for staring in the face unpleasant truths about the failings of human society. There may have been some degree of compensation going on in her mind in these early postwar years, compensation in the form of legitimately deep sympathy for the sufferings of Jews and others oppressed by the Nazis—because at the time of the Nazi terror, few Americans had any clear idea about the scope of the horror. Whatever the roots of Mrs. Roosevelt's compassion, her outrage at what the Nazis did to people in the mostly Jewish Warsaw ghetto is clear, as is her high admiration for the strength of character shown by all those who rose up in their helplessness to make a last stand against such humiliation.

EAU CLAIRE, WIS., APRIL 22—In my home city of New York, April 20th was declared Warsaw Ghetto Day by Mayor Robert F. Wagner to commemorate the eleventh anniversary of the Jews of Warsaw against their Nazi oppressors. This day has a meaning for all people everywhere because it proves that in the face of almost impossible difficulties men and women preferred certain death and fought together for the reputation and dignity of the individual human being. Warsaw was the center of Jewish spiritual and cultural life. We are apt to forget history and it is well for us to remember such incidents as this one that occurred in Poland.

After conquering Poland, the Germans created the world's largest ghetto and set about exterminating all life within that ghetto. Every method was tried to instigate division among the Jews. Setting one group against the other, they made it more and more difficult for anyone in that area to get enough food, and starvation seemed to be spreading everywhere. They treated all Jews with utter contempt and the spiritual degradation that was forced upon them was more humiliating, and in some ways more terrifying than the outright murder which they often found awaiting them in unexpected places.

These Jews of the ghetto were allowed no weapons and very few could be concealed. So it was an incredibly grave decision when finally in 1943 the Jews of the ghetto decided to strike back at the Germans. All they had to fight with were their minds and their bodies and they

. . . .

knew that every modern mechanical instrument of war would be opposed to them, as well as a trained army personnel.

You might call it the courage that comes from desperation, but it is a page in the history of the Jews of which as a people they must be very proud. For it was a great triumph of the mind and spirit to fight in the face of certain death, for only a minute number of people escaped alive from that uprising of the ghetto of Warsaw in 1943.

The book "Martyrs and Fighters" by Philip Friedman contains accounts gathered from the few surviving eyewitnesses of the events which occurred during the uprising. They saved a few documents, battle reports, and last testaments. So this book published by the Anti-Defamation League of B'nai B'rith and the Club of Polish Jews is to honor the many heroes who died.

To paraphrase, "when the bell tolls, ask not for whom it tolls for it tolls for everyone of us." In commemorating this great heroic action we commemorate not only the high spirit and the courage of these Jewish people, we commemorate and call to mind also the many instances in history when men and women in other areas of the world belonging to other nations, members of other races and of other religions, have also chosen death rather than humiliation and slow extermination.

Human beings rise to great heights at certain times and it is well to commemorate those heights and not to forget them, for they spur others to live with high standards and to dare greatly and to face even death with great fortitude.

. . . .

The next column is as much a piece of loving praise for the work of Mrs. Roosevelt's intimate friend Dr. David Gurewitsch as it is a commentary on some advanced practices in pediatrics being used at his clinic not far from Hyde Park. To say that Eleanor Roosevelt was filled with admiration for David Gurewitsch is an understatement. The doctor could deliver both physical and psychological help to a patient in ways that were direct and often tangible—at least when compared to the more abstract efforts a writer, diplomat, and intellectual like Mrs. Roosevelt could make to improve someone's or society's lot. Undoubtedly, among other things, it was the immediacy of David Gurewitsch's impact on his young patients that made him so admirable and attractive in her eyes. He was her personal physician as well. Her correspondence with Gurewitsch reflects again and again this respect and enthusiasm.

Accompanying Mrs. Roosevelt on this trip was Bernard Baruch, the financier who served as adviser to presidents Woodrow Wilson and Franklin Roosevelt and who shared with Eleanor Roosevelt the experience of working as a United Nations delegate.

. . . .

ATHENS, OHIO, APRIL 28—Just in a week, spring is with us. Last Saturday I drove to Westchester County and all of the blossoms were out. Dr. Gurewitsch and I went with Mr. Baruch on a visit to Blythedale Hospital. Dr. Gurewitsch is the medical director there and he was anxious to show Mr. Baruch the experimental work being done for handicapped children.

There are children in plaster casts lying on their stomachs. There are others lying on their backs and many who look perfectly normal but who have some disease which requires bed rest and treatment. There are others with deformities of one kind or another, but for all of them treatment is being administered. The experimental part is the effort to find out how to treat the whole child so that one handicap will not mean that the child acquires several handicaps during the years required for a cure or for amelioration of the condition that he may suffer from.

I saw, in walking around, great improvements in the training of the staff since I had been there a few years ago, and much had been done to develop the specific things needed by certain children. They were dedicating last Saturday a dental clinic with a movable chair so that a child who was in a bed could be wheeled in and treated without leaving his bed. They had also enlarged and improved the examining room so that one felt the doctors had a much better opportunity to make really satisfactory examinations of their patients. Altogether, I thought the board of directors and the administration director were doing a fine piece of work in cooperation with the medical director.

Dr. Gurewitsch has with all his patients, but especially with children, a very remarkable intuitive way of knowing what they need. They are taking advantage now of psychiatry for the children but I think every doctor practices psychiatry, even though a specialist is essential to help fully meet the needs of the patients.

. . . .

From this column about the Supreme Court decision in Brown v. Board of Education *it is clear where Mrs. Roosevelt's sympathies lay on the school segregation issue. It also sounds as if she may have assumed at least temporarily that the Court's decision had in fact solved the problem. Her columns over the next several years would show that after some reflection Mrs. Roosevelt saw the ruling as critically important but not by itself adequate to bring about the social change she hoped to see. There would be a major test of wills between the federal government and school administrators, state and local government officials, and even between ordinary citizens and the National Guard before black children could safely attend classes in previously all-white schools.*

. . . .

NEW YORK, MAY 20—While I was on the "Tex and Jinx [television] Show" I was given the news of the unanimous Supreme Court decision that wiped out segregation in the schools. I am delighted this was a unanimous decision because I think it will be difficult for the states with segregated school systems to hold out against such a ruling.

If it were not for the fact that segregation in itself means inequality, the old rule of giving equal facilities might have gone on satisfying our sense of justice for a long time. It is very difficult, however, to ensure real equality under a segregated system, and the mere fact that you cannot move freely anywhere in your country and be as acceptable everywhere as your neighbor creates an inequality.

Southerners always bring up the question of marriage between the races, and I realize that that is the question of real concern to people. But it seems to me a very personal question which must be settled by family environment and by the development of the cultural and social patterns within a country. One can no longer lay down rules as to what individuals will do in any area of their lives in a world that is changing as fast as ours is changing today.

....

Nostalgia and sentimentality were not often strong in Eleanor Roosevelt. She loved history, whether family lore or national events, but she looked forward to a better tomorrow more often than backward to a lost paradise in yesterday. Every once in a while, though, Mrs. Roosevelt slipped into the pleasure of a truly nostalgic gathering of old friends. In this case most of the friends were FDR's classmates, for here we see her attending the fiftieth reunion of his Harvard class in Cambridge. She and other Roosevelt family members, some of whom were Harvard men, were guests of honor.

NEW YORK, JUNE 19—Then we all lunched together and proceeded to the Harvard–Yale baseball game, in which Harvard, unfortunately, came out the loser. I hadn't seen a baseball game in so long that I was really interested in watching such a close one, as well as watching the crowd. To me the most interesting thing was the parade of the classes and the attention they gave to the class of 1904.

I wished so much my husband could have been there, because he had the quality that some men have of remaining, in some ways, always young. That is what comes out in most men at a reunion. You look at them and you realize that they have behind them years of struggle in a difficult world, and yet, for the few hours of the reunion, they relive their college days and are young again. I think this is a very good thing.

....

Mrs. Roosevelt's reading habits were eclectic, to say the least. Here she comments on a bank report—not usually the stuff of light literary entertainment. Indeed, Mrs. Roosevelt draws a serious inference from this weighty material, an inference about a sociological trend in American society: the expansion and rise of the middle class. Eleanor Roosevelt, and perhaps others writing as social historians, called this process a "bloodless revolution" because in effect it had redistributed wealth more extensively than had many bloody revolutions in Europe and Latin America. Though the revolution was something America should be proud of, Eleanor Roosevelt believed, it did mean that there were proportionately far fewer families like the Roosevelts at the top of the financial pyramid.

HYDE PARK, JULY 15—A reader has sent me an extract from an analysis in the New England Letter written by an economist connected with the First National Bank of Boston. Here is a quotation which may interest you.

"Our marketing system has been in a state of flux because of the impact of many factors. There has been a revolutionary redistribution of income in this country in the past quarter of a century.

"In 1929, for instance, the net income after taxes of those in the income group under $5,000 a year constituted a third of total disposable income, while in 1953 it amounted to around two-thirds. The top tenth of the nation's families in 1929 were getting 46 percent of all personal income before taxes, but by 1950 the share had dropped to 29 percent.

"What has happened is that a large proportion of the people who used to be in the bottom brackets have graduated into the middle class. The narrowing of the gap between the lower and the upper income groups has been brought about by a combination of factors, including progressive taxes, high level of employment, marked increase in the number of women workers, sharp increase in wage rates, and extension of welfare programs.

"The leveling down process has also been at work on a regional basis. Industrialization and improvement in agriculture have brought the Southeast, Northwest and Southwest into a stronger economic position, while the rest of the country has lost ground relatively. In the Northeast, for instance, the share of total income payments has declined from 36.4 percent in 1939 to 29.7 percent in 1952. On the other hand, the South gained from 20.6 percent to 23.8 percent, and the Pacific Coast rose from 9.4 percent to 11.9 percent."

If these figures are correct, there has been a very great change since 1929, the year of the stock-market crash—which was the first financial result of the bad conditions in our farming areas which had spread at last even to our industrial centers. When you realize that one-tenth of the nation's families were getting 46 percent of all personal income before taxes in 1929 and that the distribution gradually accomplished by 1950 meant that the families in this same category were getting only 29 percent, you see the magnitude of the change.

In this little quotation, so dryly stated, is really hidden the bloodless revolution which has occurred and which I believe has enormously strengthened our country. We have fewer people at the top with very great wealth, but we also have fewer people at the bottom who are barely existing and we have a tremendous broadening of the middle group.

It is this middle group which distinguishes us from Communist countries and from the type of capitalist countries that exist in certain areas of the world. In a rather different way we are approaching the situation that prevails in the Scandinavian countries, which have long been areas where a majority of the people lived comfortably. It is interesting to note that the marked increase of women workers has brought about some of this change, but other factors play a more important part.

I think this little report is something to be very proud of and I am sure the situation it recognizes contributes to our security as a nation.

. . . .

Visiting son Elliott and daughter-in-law Minnewa at their ranch in Meeker, Colorado, Mrs. Roosevelt was presented a challenge, the new word game sweeping the country: Scrabble. Evidently being one of the most articulate women in America did the former First Lady little good in the competition with her grandchildren. It was back to the famous Eleanor Roosevelt knitting needles for her.

NEW YORK, JULY 24—On my return to the ranch I was introduced to Scrabble, which practically has become an obsession with some of us. Those who play it know how competitive one can become in finding combinations of words. In spite of the fact that I found it extremely irritating because I was so slow at making these combinations, I think I shall get a game and start the children at home on it. I am so bad at games, though, that I always find I can start and teach the children and then they rapidly become so much more proficient that I am again relegated to my knitting.

. . . .

A theme running through a great deal of Mrs. Roosevelt's writing about foreign policy and the seemingly eternal to and fro of domestic political

. . . .

*competition is that difficulties between and among powerful institu-
tions like governments or political parties will continue unabated until
the individuals involved achieve some degree of peace within themselves. Few of our diplomats and tough-minded political infighters have
had the wisdom and the self-confidence, as Mrs. Roosevelt did, to be
able to talk in public about the role of love and forgiveness in the wider
world of adult behavior. But over the years Eleanor Roosevelt had positioned herself uniquely to do such philosophizing without apology
and without fear of being labeled a sentimentalist.*

HYDE PARK, AUGUST 25—The sermon in our church on last Sunday
dealt with the admonition to love one another, and the misunderstandings which might arise over the question of forgiveness and how
often that forgiveness should be granted.

In thinking it over afterwards, it seemed to me that in the world
today it is sometimes rather difficult to follow the spirit and the teachings of Christ.

I long ago ceased to have the slightest feeling about anything which
is said about myself or done by people who want to hurt me. But
sometimes it is hard to keep down resentment when things which you
know are untrue are said about the dead. And it is even harder to keep
down that resentment when things are said to harm and when truth
is distorted about the living.

I do not think I really hate anyone in the world, but I must say that
sometimes I find it puzzling to separate the sin which is being committed from the sinner. I am sure of one thing, however. If in any way
we can keep from war during the next few years, that achievement
certainly will be one of the things that church people will feel has
helped them to achieve the ideals of their religions. For war certainly
intensifies all the hatreds between people.

Some people I know feel that the strain today—the possibility of
atomic war—is unbearable. But that, I think, is really a challenge to
those of us who believe that God will not destroy willingly. Only if we,
through our blindness, fail to carry out His will as we have in the past,
and perhaps will again, will we (not God) achieve destruction.

That knowledge should make us work harder than we have ever
worked to build a better world. We have to follow our own lights, of
course, and others may feel that what we do is not the kind of thing
they consider good. Here again we have to rely upon the majority of
people coming together on what is the best method of developing the
good in the world in which we live.

It seems to me that our best instrument, internationally, for bringing
people together is found in the United Nations, and I hope and pray
that we may strengthen that organization and allow it to do the best

possible work for keeping peace. Without a forum of this kind and a meeting place for the representatives of the people it is difficult to imagine how greater understanding among people can be developed and a world kept at peace.

I am convinced, however, that one of the essential steps that must be taken throughout the world is for individuals to try to set their own houses in order, to get rid of feelings of hate and to try to develop charity and understanding in the circles that they individually touch.

. . . .

The summer of 1954 found Eleanor Roosevelt writing a number of "My Day" columns about domestic matters and family issues. Sometimes humorous and at others quite serious, Mrs. Roosevelt was very much at home with subjects like how to be a good grandparent and what to do when the kids have grown up and flown the coop. She knew there were no easy answers and her call for heavy doses of common sense may strike a later generation as a bit too easy to say and too hard to implement. But throughout her tenure as one of America's leading newspaper columnists, Eleanor Roosevelt was considered a model parent, a model working woman, a model senior citizen. What she recommended was taken to heart by her readers.

NEW YORK, SEPTEMBER 3—I have just been sent an amusing and quite charming little booklet entitled "How to Be a Grandmother." The traps that await any prospective grandmother, or even one who has been a grandmother many times, are well described. We are told that we must welcome our grandchildren; that we must not, however, swallow them up, but leave them to their own parents.

I think one might sum it up by saying that a grandmother should have a great deal of common sense, not be given to interfering, know when to give and when not to give financial help. A special contribution to the life of children is to have time to be leisurely with them. The closing paragraph sums up the booklet: "Being a modern first-class grandmother is a challenge. Take it, live up to it—and you will have three generations rising up to call you blessed."

NEW YORK, SEPTEMBER 4—I had a letter in the mail recently which reminds me of so many things I have heard middle-aged women say in the past. "I am 54 years old. My family is grown up and as I review the years and look into the future I feel so terribly useless. I have heard all the nice things about raising a nice family, etc. But somehow they seem so commonplace and a little false. Besides, there were other things I wanted to do too!"

Only initials are signed to this letter, so I cannot answer it personally,

. . . .

but I would like to say something about the problem. It is a problem that faces almost all married women once their children are grown.

I don't know whether my correspondent is a widow or still has a husband to look after. But I would like to say that it never seems to me false to be proud of having brought up one's children, if one has done the best one could for them. All of us, as we look back, can see many mistakes that we made, and we may wish that we could change the way we did things when we were in our twenties. But that is out of the question.

If we loved our children, and did the best we knew at the time, all we can hope for is that, if we are blessed with grandchildren, we may be able to help a little out of the wisdom which the years have brought us. It may be possible, when the children who took up so much of our time and thought have gone, to create new associations with one's husband and perhaps learn together to enjoy new things. It is also possible to develop new activities out of interests that have been very slight in the past. And if one is alone, this is essential.

I have seen women become a great influence in their neighborhood, both in city and rural areas, just because they had free time to undertake a number of little civic, church or philanthropic chores—things that none of the younger women felt they had the time to accomplish. I will give you an example.

I know of a retired schoolteacher who is active as treasurer for a fund in her village from which money is loaned to students who could not quite cover their expenses. It fell to this woman's lot to look into each case. She became interested in the young people, kept in touch with them, watched them, not only through their college days but through their first jobs.

She saw them repay the money they had borrowed and go ahead with their careers, perhaps into married life. For that teacher the little job she undertook, without pay, has brought her endless interest.

She also has found jobs in the neighborhood that could bring her in small sums of money now and then. I think one can multiply the number of middle-aged people who are doing such things. So I would urge all those who find themselves facing the same kind of frustration and despair, because their main object in life seems to have come to an end, to realize that new interest can be created and life can be kept exciting and useful.

. . . .

Earlier "My Day" columns had advocated that parents read aloud with their children, and although those columns may have been derived from press releases sent out by the literacy and library organizations Mrs. Roosevelt supported, they were written with conviction. This column

. . . .

....

describes a pleasant literary event at Bard College in Annandale-on-Hudson, near Hyde Park, in which Mrs. Roosevelt herself leads an evening of reading aloud for a student literature club. We learn something new about her literary tastes as well. We already knew that in drama Eleanor Roosevelt preferred scripts with clearly recognizable social and political themes. But in poetry and fiction, we discover that her enthusiasms include playful children's stories, the mysterious challenges of modernist poet T. S. Eliot, and the charming romantic fantasies of the Irish novelist James Stephens—quite a literary smorgasbord.

In the second column here we find Mrs. Roosevelt once more thoroughly enjoying the written word—both the whimsical rhymes of Phyllis McGinley and the provocative intellectual challenges of Eliot's longer poems.

NEW YORK, OCTOBER 21—After the luncheon, I spent a little longer at the office than I intended, so we did not leave New York for Hyde Park until after four o'clock. The sky looked most threatening and the wind, which must have been the edge of the hurricane, was blowing hard but we made fairly good time. We stopped for just a few minutes to leave the dogs and bags, etc., at my cottage, and then went on to the home of President Case of Bard College, where I dined.

After dinner I read to the students. The room was filled again, but I hope very much we can use a smaller room next time as it is difficult to get as much discussion about what you read if the group is so large and not close around you. I feel that a smaller room will give us all a greater opportunity for interchange of views on what we read. The young people tell me each time what they would like read the next time. They had asked for "Winnie the Pooh" last Friday and I was delighted to see that even grown-ups can rock with laughter over that altogether delightful children's story.

They also had asked for T. S. Eliot's "The Love Song of J. Alfred Prufrock." Sometimes I find Mr. Eliot difficult to read because, for me, he is difficult to understand. But this happens to be one of my favorites so I was delighted to have the chance to read it.

By request, I also read "Animula," which is another of the poems that I really delight in. I had promised to bring some of Edward Lear's "Nonsense Rhymes" but forgot, so I read instead two chapters from "The Crock of Gold," by James Stephens. One can only hope that in reading aloud one stimulates the desire to read on the part of young listeners. I certainly enjoy these evenings and hope that the audience does also.

NEW YORK, OCTOBER 25—I was given a new book of poems by Phyllis McGinley the other day, and have very much enjoyed reading it. The

....

book has humor and is written in the lighter vein, although some of
the poems I found very moving. The author has a real gift and much
skill in her writing.

I particularly relished one poem called "Meditations During a Per-
manent Wave." I join with her fervently when she says:
"Of the small gifts of heaven
It seems to me a more than equal share
At birth was given
To girls with curly hair."
Those of us who are unblessed know only too well how true that is!

Miss McGinley's reflections on the poems and plays of T. S. Eliot
also struck a responsive chord, as when she writes: "T. Eliot, the An-
glican, who feared God Removing his bowler, furling his umbrella,
Set down, in riddles, dogma for the crowd."

I subscribe to that heartily, for a great deal of what T. S. Eliot has
written is a riddle to me. Nevertheless, his poetry has a fascination,
and I find I have to read it!

....

*Throughout 1954 Eleanor Roosevelt's schedule of speeches and meetings
with the various state and local chapters of the American Association
for the United Nations made the pace of her life hectic indeed. At this
point we find her on the West Coast, making some observations about
living conditions in the City of Angels—conditions that even then were
beginning to trouble anyone with high standards about the quality of
urban life. Smog was not yet a common word, but the seriousness of
the problem was becoming all too clear to civic leaders and to visitors
like Eleanor Roosevelt—though her basic optimism made her suspect
a solution would soon be found. Almost all her life, in New York or
any other city with a good system of subways or buses, she had no qualms
about riding as a straphanger. The absence of effective public transport
in Los Angeles seemed to her very conspicuous indeed.*

LOS ANGELES, NOVEMBER 6—On arrival in Los Angeles I went directly
to Long Beach, where a very charming hostess allowed me to bathe
and change and have a little rest before their buffet dinner. This was
an informal and delightful party in a house situated on a hill, with a
beautiful view of the many lights far below. In the daytime it must be
really gorgeous. These California houses seem almost to take in the
outdoors—you feel that you live outside and the world of nature is
very close. Flowers are everywhere. Trees and vines apparently grow
with great rapidity.

Smog, however, is what seems to be on everybody's mind. They told
me all sorts of things that would have to be done. I had not realized

....

quite how bad smog can be. People say their throats are raw, their eyes are runny and it is really a great discomfort.

Governor Knight recently called some specialists together who said it was not really dangerous to health. But others believe it may have lasting bad effects, so no one is very happy about the situation. In spite of the beauty of nature and the fact that today the sun is shining and everything looks lovely to me, my hosts last night were troubled by the whole smog situation.

Los Angeles is a city with rather poor public transportation, so there are an enormous number of cars. And while there are machines that can be placed in oil-refining plants which might do away with smog, nothing small enough has yet been invented to use in motor cars. I suppose, with the need, inventors will go to work and the problem will be solved. But at present it is a very unpleasant situation, I gather, for those who live in this whole area.

....

The foundation for the next column—it concerns Norman Thomas, America's most famous socialist—had been laid, stone by stone, over the many years Eleanor Roosevelt had spent trying to explain satisfactorily to her readers how to distinguish among capitalism, socialism, and communism. There were plenty of social critics on the right in America who believed that any ideas originating in the socialist camp were in fact communist ideas in disguise: and therefore, beware. But Mrs. Roosevelt looked at socialism through a different lens. Had she been a European intellectual, it is fairly likely that she would have been a socialist herself. In any case, in modified form, many of the American socialists' better ideas had in fact worked their way into the New Deal and into subsequent legislation sponsored by the liberals in the Democratic party.

It was therefore natural for Mrs. Roosevelt to toast Thomas, who joined the Socialist party in 1918 and helped found the American Civil Liberties Union in 1920. A perennial socialist candidate for president (1928–1948), the record of his ideas later enacted into law is impressive: unemployment insurance, minimum wage laws, five-day workweek, abolition of child labor. A prolific author, Norman Thomas spent many of his last years campaigning for nuclear disarmament. He died in 1968.

NEW YORK, NOVEMBER 23—On Saturday last Norman Thomas was 70 years old. He has led American socialism in this country for a half century. He still seems full of vigor and enthusiasm. He is no more afraid of new ideas today than he was 50 years ago.

It seems to me that men who have had a purpose, and have really worked for it, come to their older years still with a vitality and an

....

interest in life which is lacking in those who have been less dedicated. Though he has not been elected to public office, Mr. Thomas has seen many of the ideas that he tried to persuade people to accept finally become acceptable in the most conservative circles. So I think he must have the satisfaction of feeling that he has done something to make the world a better place for the majority of people to live in.

....

One of the virtues of Eleanor Roosevelt's style of thinking about weighty issues of government is that she never saw the issues in the limited way of someone who places the natural prejudices of gender before the objective demands of truth. But Mrs. Roosevelt was a leading woman too, and from start to finish in her career as a newspaper columnist, the majority of her readers were women. Hence her freedom and expertise in passing judgment on women's fashions of decades gone by. Always the opinionated adviser-at-large, she even goes so far here as to lay down a few laws about how to establish a personal style in dress. All this from a woman whose own wardrobe as First Lady met with howls of complaint from fashion critics who found her dresses too dull and her hats too bizarre.

NEW YORK, DECEMBER 3—On Tuesday night I went to see "The Boy Friend," an entertaining musical comedy that satirizes the '20s. The dresses of the period were very ugly, from my point of view. The ladies had no waists, only a line that came around the lower part of their hips, and skirts that came to their knees, which was not too bad if they had pretty legs but terrible for the fat ones.

In the play, of course, all the girls had beautiful legs and one wonders if they are chosen for legs rather than faces, though there were pretty faces, too!

If you want to see a procession of ladies' styles, the next time you are in Washington go to the Smithsonian Institution, where there is on display the inaugural gowns that were worn by each of the Presidents' wives. Thus, the fashion picture is recorded at least for every fourth year. I think you will come away with a feeling that the woman who dresses to suit her particular type, with only a moderate bowing acquaintance with fashion, comes out better than the woman who is a slave to the designer of the moment.

When one is very young, very slim, and very pretty, one can afford to go from one extreme to the other—and even can wear rather ridiculous clothes, at times. But later on, it seems to me, though one must keep a nodding acquaintance with the fashions so as not to be too conspicuous, it is not such a bad idea to find a style that suits and stick to it.

....

The mainstream is filled by many tributaries. President Dwight Eisenhower or Secretary of State John Foster Dulles, if asked why the United States should not unilaterally move toward complete nuclear disarmament, would have offered a set of reasons quite different from those delivered here by Eleanor Roosevelt on the same question. Nonetheless, both conservatives and liberals in the mid-1950s found themselves in a surprisingly impromptu harmony about the need to carry on with the development of "the bomb" (as the only effective deterrent against the potential onslaught of communism and its nuclear arsenal)—while at the same time swearing off the bomb's use (because its damaging consequences were unconscionable).

In the 1950s no one wanted the disarmament talks to move forward more than Eleanor Roosevelt, yet here and in several other "My Day" columns she defends the deterrence theory about the bomb, a theory that effectively ensured the cold war's long continuance. Mrs. Roosevelt gives a twist to the conventional deterrence viewpoint, however, in the way she suggests that America may even need the bomb as a substitute for democratic will-power sufficient to resist the Communist ideological challenge.

NEW YORK, DECEMBER 29—I have a wire asking me what I think of a letter written by C. Rajagopalachari of Madras, India, and which appeared on the editorial page of The New York Times last Sunday.

This gentleman's letter is a plea that we in the United States have the courage, as a people, to do away with the use of all atomic weapons. Because we used the bomb to end the war with Japan he feels that it would be a privilege for us to renounce the use of all such weapons now. He says that germ warfare has been practically ruled out because no nation feels that it could possibly use that kind of warfare—and yet the accusations were made in the Korean War that we had used germs. We insisted that we had not, but the accusations were nevertheless made.

Mr. Rajagopalachari insists that as long as we negotiate about how to control atomic weapons we will be on the verge of using them.

It is true that these negotiations keep us constantly wondering what may happen, but at the same time and on the same page of The New York Times there was an article by James Reston which reminded us all that in Washington (and I think in the whole United States) peace is everybody's most-important business.

I am wondering, however, if it is possible for a nation to give up a weapon which it has grown accustomed to thinking is not a weapon to use for killing, but a weapon which, unused, may be the one real assurance of peace on earth.

Unless a country has an idea in which it believes so fully that that belief is stronger than any weapon, it would be impossible to throw the weapon away.

In our early days when we were fighting against great odds, we believed strongly that the democratic idea, which we were establishing in this country, in itself was strong enough to sweep the world. We felt we had evolved a new way of life, a way of life in which people who had always known slavery suddenly were going to be made free.

Many of the men who held to this idea were aristocrats and yet they had a vision that not just they, themselves, but all men were going to be free. All men were going to have an opportunity to take part in their own governments, and they hoped for peace just as we do.

Now, I think if this idea were as strong with us today as it was in 1776, perhaps we could do as our Indian friend suggests. But unless we are convinced that this idea has such vitality that in itself it will win the world to its banners, I do not think there is any hope that doing away with the bomb will accomplish the ends desired.

The belief in the idea must come first, and then perhaps the other gestures will come as a matter of course.

1 9 5 5

If the airline companies Mrs. Roosevelt used in this one year alone had offered frequent-flyer mileage credits, her 1955 travels would have put a considerable dent in their revenues. She circled the globe and crisscrossed the nation in a flurry of activity, driven by her abiding political and moral passions but at times, like the United States itself, somewhat uncertain of her focus or of the impact her work might have.

In January, Eisenhower's Foreign Operations Administration made the fateful decision to begin sending military aid to Southeast Asia (Cambodia, Laos, South Vietnam). Few people, Eleanor Roosevelt included, foresaw the protracted struggle there in which America would eventually become embroiled. Sam Rayburn was re-elected Speaker of the House of Representatives when the 84th Congress convened; he would wield the gavel for another six years. Among the Senate's early 1955 actions was an 84–0 vote to continue its investigation of Communist activities by government employees: The spirit of McCarthyism lived on. If such behavior was old hat for the Senate, President Eisenhower tried something new by giving the first televised presidential news conference.

Typical of Mrs. Roosevelt's hectic schedule was a winter trip to the Southwest for AAUN lectures and meetings. In a span of a few days she covered Little Rock, Memphis, New Orleans, Houston, Dallas, Corpus Christi, Denver, and Odessa, Texas. When she hit the ground again in New York, she was still running. She was a young seventy. Another ten-day trip (to the Midwest) followed in February. By March she was en route to France and visits in Italy and Israel.

Although now ten years past, the geopolitical aftermath of World War II was still current business. In April 1955 the Senate agreed to negotiations on the future of West Germany, and the Big Four powers consented to the establishment of sovereignty for the Federal Republic of Germany. Eleanor Roosevelt kept a close watch on Germany's political behavior. Austria's status, too, was clarified in 1955 by a Big Four treaty: its borders returned to their pre-1938 positions; economic union with Germany was prohibited; occupying forces were withdrawn.

There were relatively few giant steps forward in 1955 for the social causes liberals such as Mrs. Roosevelt supported, but among those, two are worth noting. In May the ruling elders of the Presbyterian church decided to admit women to the ministry through ordination. Late in the year, the Interstate Commerce Commission banned segregation on trains and buses that crossed state lines.

Reflecting the continuing tensions between the United States and the Soviet and Chinese Communists, Congress extended Selective Service for another two years. In June the Soviets shot down an American military plane over the Bering Strait, which did little to calm American nerves upset about the prospect of nuclear war. Not long after a July summit meeting in Geneva that did little to advance the cause of peace, President Eisenhower suffered a heart attack.

Late summer saw Eleanor Roosevelt heading west to Asia for an extended trip, including visits in Tokyo, Hong Kong, Manila, Djarkarta, the island of Bali, and Bangkok. Much of the trip was devoted to work for the international federation of United Nations associations.

Toward year's end Mrs. Roosevelt celebrated one traditional occasion and a new development. About Thanksgiving at Hyde Park she wrote: "We were only seventeen for Thanksgiving dinner Thursday evening here. . . . But we had six children, which always makes a celebration at home more worthwhile." And the labor movement gave her something new to applaud: Under the leadership of George Meany and Walter Reuther, their two nationwide organizations (American Federation of Labor and Congress of Industrial Organizations, respectively) joined forces to create the AFL–CIO, which meant more strength from greater numbers, a positive fact for working men and women.

. . . .

Eleanor Roosevelt respected a certain category of artists above all others: those who not only found ways in their art to tell the truth about human experience in terms everyone can understand but who also found ways beyond their art to contribute productively to society. The hugely successful photography exhibit called The Family of Man *at the Museum of Modern Art in New York was the brainchild of one such artist, photographer Edward Steichen. Born in Luxembourg in 1879, Steichen was brought to the United States in 1882 and was in the vanguard of photographers in America throughout a period that produced such other luminaries as Alfred Stieglitz. Together, around the turn of the century,*

. . . .

they organized shows and galleries that included works revolutionizing the public's concept of photography as art.

Steichen served his adopted country in both big wars: in World War I he led the photo division of the air service and pioneered aerial photography; in World War II he headed the naval combat photo unit. Garbo and Chaplin were among his famous portrait subjects between the wars.

The Family of Man exhibition showed the human race to itself in all its splendor and shame, its joy and agony. The photographs, from every corner of the globe, represented many races, creeds, political systems, and cultures. The exhibit attracted other artists with similarly broad sensibilities, among them the American poet and biographer Carl Sandburg, Steichen's brother-in-law who wrote a fine prologue for the exhibition catalogue.

SARASOTA, FLA. JANUARY 27—On Monday evening I attended a preview of the photographic exhibit called "The Family of Man" at the Museum of Modern Art in New York. This collection of 500 photographs by 280 photographers from 68 countries was conceived and prepared by Mr. Edward Steichen, director of the museum's department of photography.

Mr. and Mrs. Carl Sandburg were there to commemorate the occasion and it was a joy to see them. In fact, there were many people I was glad to see, such as Mr. and Mrs. Eugene Meyer, who had come on from Washington, and Dorothy Norman, and Nelson Rockefeller, who paid tribute to Mr. Steichen in a stirring short speech.

Thousands and thousands of photographs were examined before Mr. Steichen made his choices, which makes "The Family of Man" a memorable exhibit.

Some of the young people who worked under Mr. Steichen, like my young friend, Doris O'Donnell, told me that his favorites are the collection showing birth and motherhood. There is one among these particular pictures of a baby's arms that I thought simply entrancing.

The captions were not as yet on all the pictures when we viewed the exhibit, and that was because at the last minute they did not entirely please Mr. Steichen.

I could not, however, have enjoyed anything more than I did the first impact of the collection. Joy is depicted by such a beautiful collection of photographs—fun, enjoyment, and, finally, the pleasures of food, drink, of daily living, of the dawn of love. Eventually, one comes to the sorrow of death, the horror of fear and despair and the cruelty of man to man.

How strange it is that there can be such perfect love and such cruelty side by side!

I liked the photograph of the United Nations General Assembly with the words of the Charter, which are used as a caption for the entire exhibition. In a way they symbolize the hope of man. If enough of us can cling to those aims, some of the cruelty will disappear and more of the maturity of love and understanding may emerge.

It seemed to me that perhaps one area was somewhat neglected, and that was the area of the work of man. That is a most-important part in the lives of men and women, in some lives the most important part, particularly when the work is creative work. It is often such a large part of man's existence that it would seem to be essential to mark it more clearly in a collection such as the museum's.

Perhaps I am wrong, however. There was such a crowd at the preview that even with Mr. Rene d'Harnoncourt's kind guidance I had difficulty in not starting at the wrong end of the exhibition and going backward. I may well have missed some of the photographs.

There is one special photograph of Mr. Steichen's own mother, showing her bringing out food from the house, which one should not miss. I know I shall return to be sure I have not missed any part of this remarkable exhibition.

. . . .

Undue fear of Communist subversion in the United States and the spread of Communist influence abroad were major headaches of the fifties; Mrs. Roosevelt's prescription for a cure was more education. Whenever and wherever she could, she praised those who were making an effort to clarify for the public, for elected officials, or just for themselves the origins and meaning of the Communist phenomenon. And, of course, with her "My Day" column available as a lecture platform, Mrs. Roosevelt frequently stepped up to the podium and delivered what by this time had become an almost set speech on the differences between Communist ideology and Communist practice, in America and abroad.

The next three columns all concern the debate about communism. Robert Hutchins was perhaps the most distinguished administrator in higher education in America, having been dean of Yale Law School; then president and chancellor of the University of Chicago; and then a top-level administrator for the Ford Foundation, the Fund for the Republic, and, eventually, the Center for the Study of Democratic Institutions. To study the essence of communism and report to the American public, this near-perfect liberal was teamed with Clinton Rossiter, an American history professor from Cornell whose best books, such as Conservatism in America, gave an even-handed treatment to the ideology from "the other side of the aisle." Mrs. Roosevelt believed that such joint efforts could not help but shed light.

Mrs. Roosevelt herself struggled with the implications of the containment theory of foreign policy. She stood firmly with those who would resist the spread of communism into lands where the people were given no choice about their political systems; yet she also campaigned for years for what a later generation would call détente, or disengagement by the major powers so as to enhance the chances of avoiding war. Should the United States or the United Nations get involved in defending islands like Formosa (off the coast of China) against attacks from the Communist mainlanders? Her analysis pushed and pulled her in both directions.

For Eleanor Roosevelt the subject of communism versus democracy was so fascinating that it could serve equally well as dinner-table conversation and grist for the after-dinner debating mill. Her column dated February 12 gives an excellent outline of Marxist doctrine considered ideally and a comparison to Marxism in its not-so-ideal practice. Why some respectable intellectuals were attracted to communism was a question Mrs. Roosevelt was not afraid to ask.

In that column Eleanor Roosevelt refers to Mr. and Mrs. Julius Rosenberg, but she does not mean the recently convicted spies. This Mrs. Rosenberg is Anna Rosenberg, a figure who appears frequently in Mrs. Roosevelt's private correspondence of this period. Anna was a close adviser and friend of Mary Lasker, the wealthy art connoisseur and supporter of medical research and public health, causes that had Mrs. Roosevelt's support as well. Anna was also a staunch supporter of Adlai Stevenson and was active in the National Democratic Party.

NEW YORK, FEBRUARY 2—The president of the Fund for the Republic, Robert M. Hutchins, announced a short time ago that there has been an allocation of $250,000 by the fund for a factual study of the influence of communism, past and present, on all aspects of American life. A group of scholars under the direction of Clinton Rossiter, who is professor of government at Cornell University and who wrote the prizewinning history "Seedtime of the Republic," will make this study.

This study will contribute greatly to our knowledge and should be of help in basing future action on facts rather than on fears.

NEW YORK, FEBRUARY 8—It is true that the island of Formosa was acknowledged as a part of China, but that was before the mainland was overrun by the Communist forces in China. Once that had happened, naturally the area to which non-Communist forces had retreated became an area which must be defended by the non-Communist world against aggression.

Both the Soviet Union and Communist China should recognize the fact that no one intends to interfere with them within the borders that they now control. On the other hand, the rest of the non-Communist world does not intend to have Russia and Red China swallow up little by little other areas of the world, nor do they intend to have them, through infiltration, gradually induce more areas of the world to develop discontent at home and eventual revolution.

We are making a very concerted attempt to try to bring about a peaceful world within which people may live together in spite of differences of economy and political beliefs, but we cannot sit by quietly and see new areas swallowed up by constant Communist aggression.

To take Formosa would be the beginning of the use of force by the Communist Chinese. It is true that Communist China has not as yet taken over satellites in the manner of the Soviet Union, but it might easily become a practice of the Chinese Communist government, as it has become a habit on the part of the government of the Soviet Union.

There is certainly no desire on the part of the U.S. to bring about active war, but if we are to have a world with some kind of security there must be some understanding of the fact that communism cannot spread beyond its present boundaries and territorial ambitions.

NEW YORK, FEBRUARY 12—Last Wednesday evening I went to a most interesting dinner party at the home of Mr. and Mrs. Julius Rosenberg. There I had the pleasure of talking with Senator William Benton at the dinner as well as with my hostess and many other delightful people.

After dinner the group gathered together for general conversation, an enlightening procedure that is rather rare at a dinner party nowadays. At an appropriate time I asked a question which had been asked of me during the day:

"How do you explain why communism has any appeal at all to intellectuals or to the intelligent people of countries that are not suffering from great economic distress?"

The consensus, as I judged it, was that many people did not think of communism in the terms of what actually exists today in the Soviet Union. They thought of it primarily as a Marxist doctrine, more or less of an economic Utopia with ideals that are similar to those phrased for me some time ago by Marshal Tito.

I had asked Marshal Tito to give me his definition of communism. His answer was that no country had real communism as yet—least of all Russia, where there existed state capitalism and an imperialistic form of government. He disclaimed true communism in his own country, saying that they were trying in Yugoslavia to establish a socialist state, which was only the first step toward true communism.

True communism had not yet been achieved anywhere, he said, since it required that all people should cease to be greedy and be willing to see each individual receive according to his need from communal production.

I pointed out to Marshal Tito that this existed in an Israeli kibbutz, and he insisted this could not exist anywhere since people were not unselfish enough as yet to live together in this way!

I think the feeling in our group at the dinner party was that it was this idealistic concept which appealed to intellectuals, the idea of reaching a state where no one suffered and where there was a standard of achievement that was not financial, so that everyone could share in a decent and happy existence.

But, since this ideal does not resemble what actually happens in those countries where there is so-called Communist rule today, it did not entirely explain the acceptance by certain types of people in different parts of the world.

It was finally suggested that to these people the faults that exist today probably seem the necessary steps, in themselves wrong and perhaps reprehensible, but steps that must be gone through before the desired goal could be reached.

One of the members of the group pointed out that we were not taking into consideration the differences in the characters of people throughout the world, and the fact that communism might never have an appeal to people in certain countries because bread might mean more to them than ideas. In other countries, however, the appeal of martyrdom for an ideal might be much more compelling than any financial success.

. . . .

What does it mean to be rich? Some who have never had much money might understandably find it hard not to answer such a question by rattling off a list of things they'd love to possess. But to those who, like Eleanor Roosevelt, had had financial comfort all their lives, a different perspective is possible.

NEW YORK, MARCH 9—Among a group of people the other night of which I was a part there was a discussion as to what riches really are. One of those present said that when she was young she had lived in a small town in which her father was a banker and the richest man in town, so by comparison with others in that town they were rich. But when she moved away from the town she found she was not rich at all.

It seemed to me that definition of riches, which is one purely of comparisons (you are rich if you have more than the people with whom your lot in life happens to be cast), is most unsatisfactory.

As I think of the people I know, I consider that those are rich who are doing something they feel worthwhile and which they enjoy doing. They seem to be so content with their possessions as not to be con-

. . . .

stantly striving to accumulate more of the kind of things that only money can buy and which they may see in greater abundance in homes around them.

One of the real gifts that brings you riches, I think, is the power of appreciation. If you can enjoy the blue sky, the beauty of the fresh snow, or the first green of spring, if you can hear music and have it leave a song in your heart, if you can see a picture and take away something that is real and vital to dream about for days, then you have the ability to get joy out of your surroundings. That kind of appreciation is perhaps more valuable than some more tangible kinds of riches.

The first foreign trip of the year begins for Mrs. Roosevelt with visits to several sites in France, among them Cambous, where she inspected a refugee camp for Jewish orphans being prepared for removal to Israel. Since the end of the war ten years earlier Eleanor Roosevelt had sustained a serious and active interest in the fate of displaced persons, particularly Jews whose deepest hope was to resettle in Israel—where, presumably, security could be found at last. Trude Lash, one of her traveling companions, was an old friend from New York and the wife of Mrs. Roosevelt's eventual biographer, Joseph Lash.

ROME, MARCH 17   The land in the Montpellier region is not rich soil. For that reason Cambous was chosen for the Jewish refugee children's camp. The soil and climate conditions are much similar to those in parts of Israel.

The children have to carry their own water in the camp. This is looked upon as a good thing because if they go to live in the Negev water may be scarce and they may have to carry it there. Twice a week in winter the youngsters have to take hot showers and the showers are in the same building as the kitchen where, of course, there is running water. In summer they have cold showers every day because the heat there is similar to what they will experience in Israel.

To make anything grow the children must take infinite trouble, and that is good preparation, too, for Israel. The mountains are forbidding. Outcroppings of rock are everywhere and stones look almost more plentiful than dirt except in the little valleys.

To illustrate some of the fears and superstitions these children come with, let me tell you the story of one little boy who arrived a week ago with his brother. He told us there were nine children in the family but six had died, and his mother said that she would lose all the children if they stayed with her, so he and his brother had been sent away. He had a watch on his wrist that his father had given him as a parting gift and he said he would keep it carefully. One little brother, aged seven, was left behind, and quite simply this little boy said: "He stayed with my mother to die."

One little girl there, we were told, is 18 years old, but physically and mentally her development is that of a child of 12. She has been sent to Switzerland in the hope that she will grow. She is getting special care and special food, but so far she is still at the age of 12 and very envious of her sister, who is normally developed. She feels so inferior that she has asked not to be sent to Israel at the same time.

After we left Cambous we stopped for a little time in Nîmes and Avignon, two of the old French cities which I had not seen for many, many years.

We drove in late to Marseilles and I met the deputy mayor and his wife, who were very kind and hospitable, and also our American consul general and his wife, Mrs. Wharton, were equally warm in their hospitality.

Mrs. Lash and I, however, had both wanted to eat bouillabaisse and walk along the docks for a little way even though it was late at night. Our young days were very far apart but we seem to have done somewhat the same things, though she is some 25 years younger. I was a little shocked when I remembered that the last time I had eaten bouillabaisse in a restaurant in Marseilles I had been 16 years old. It does not seem so long ago!

. . . .

Of all the Israeli leaders Mrs. Roosevelt met, none impressed and delighted her more than the young country's elder statesman David Ben-Gurion, whom she visited this time at his charming home in Tel Aviv. Repeatedly on her visits to Israel, Eleanor Roosevelt welcomed opportunities to see kibbutzim in action, possibly because in her own country the idea of government-sponsored living and working cooperatives was seldom heard of. She admired the high spirits of the young workers, married and single, who chose to help build the still-new state of Israel by forsaking certain personal needs to devote themselves to working for the benefit of the group.

New York, April 1—In Tel Aviv last week we arrived just in time to keep an appointment with Mr. Ben-Gurion. We were met at the door by his wife, who greeted us warmly, and it was a great pleasure to see the Minister of Defense himself in such good physical health and such happy spirits.

Mr. Ben-Gurion typifies, as does Mr. Baratz of Degania, the pioneer in Israel, a man who felt he must live on the soil and make things grow and be as self-sufficient as possible. It was characteristic when he said

. . . .

to me, "The happiest years of my life were the first years I spent in Israel in a kibbutz and the last ones I've spent in the Negev."

He lives in a new settlement not far from the Egyptian border and he says, "God made the rocks but forgot to put soil on them. Therefore, it is up to us to do it."

In his mind's eye he sees the picture of his home surrounded with flowers and fruit trees and a garden and green grass everywhere. As I left he said, "One must see the picture and then one can make it come true."

....

"Strong and fearless public servants." Mrs. Roosevelt's experience in the White House and on all the levels of government she observed at close hand during her husband's climb to the top taught her a simple but important lesson: Good government, whether liberal or conservative, depends on the trust placed in leaders and their assistants by both the electorate and by colleagues in government. Where suspicion runs rampant, wild accusations will ensue. And when they do, otherwise admirable careers are damaged irreparably. Here again is a "My Day" column about the ghost of McCarthyism, still haunting Washington.

HYDE PARK, APRIL 12—I wonder how much longer the Administration is going to think it wise, the minute there is an attack by some member of Congress, to get rid of the person involved no matter how valuable a public servant that person may have been in the past or how valuable he might well prove to be in the future. The attack is usually made because of an independent opinion expressed or because of an independent action taken.

I have in mind, of course, the abrupt dismissal of Mr. Edward J. Corsi as special assistant to Secretary of State John Foster Dulles on refugee and immigration problems.

I am a Democrat and would certainly evaluate with a good deal of objectivity the way a job is handled by a Republican liberal. I have watched Mr. Corsi's work on refugees and immigration for a long time and I can only say that even though Rep. Francis E. Walter of Pennsylvania is a Democrat I think Mr. Corsi knows more about the subject, which the McCarran–Walter Immigration Act so badly mishandled, than does Mr. Walter, one of the co-authors of the legislation.

As for Mr. Scott McLeod, administrator of the immigration act, I can't think of anyone whose background has provided him with less understanding of the whole situation. Mr. Walter and Mr. McLeod evidently felt that they wished to get rid of a public servant who happened to disagree with them. So they began to find things in Mr. Corsi's past which tied him to Communist organizations.

....

I haven't the remotest idea whether he may have mistakenly contributed to an organization that turned out to be Communistic. That has happened to a great many people. He may even have worked for a time with a group that later proved to be subversive.

I say I don't know and I hope it didn't happen to him, but even if it had it would not warrant the treatment that has been meted out to him in this present State Department situation. His record of fine public service in the Republican Party over a long period of years stands for all to read.

If Mr. Walter and Mr. McLeod have been successful in getting him out of this particular State Department appointment where they felt he has interfered with them, then again it has been shown that it is possible for people with special interests of their own to hurt the general interest of our country.

It is a curious thing these days how difficult it seems to be for the heads of departments to stand up for their appointees if a breath of suspicion is cast upon them by any member of Congress. Mr. Dulles has stated, and so has the President, that there is no question of Mr. Corsi's loyalty. That is kind and truthful, but we hardly needed to be reassured.

The fear of McCarthy is still with us, though we may try to think of his power as being at an end. I was hopeful that it might at least be reduced to the point where we would have no more dismissals of this type, but I am very much afraid that I hoped for the impossible. This type of treatment of appointees does not build strong and fearless public servants.

. . . .

The success of the Salk polio vaccine was one of the great triumphs of science and public health administration for Mrs. Roosevelt's generation of Americans, and especially for their children. But it must have been a bittersweet triumph for her and her family as they remembered the painful effect of the disease on FDR throughout almost his entire adult life.

NEW YORK, APRIL 15—I was much touched some days beforehand to receive a letter from Dr. Jonas Salk telling me that all through his work he had had in mind my husband's illness and the interest and satisfaction that he would have taken in the final results.

I know that would have meant a great deal to my husband. Though be accepted the blow of the crippling attack of polio and went forward with never a complaint, still anyone remembering him as a young athletic and strong man could not fail to realize what a terrific battle must have gone on within before this acceptance was possible.

. . . .

60

Though we can look back today and realize that the character developed at that time—the enforced thinking and feeling—probably prepared him for much of the work that he was to do in the future, still we cannot minimize the agony of soul that must have been endured. His interest in helping others came from the understanding of his own battle, which must have been a motivating force.

Therefore I realize what it would have meant to him to know that the two most dangerous forms of polio can now be handled with such a tremendous percentage of success.

The work that it has meant for Dr. Salk and all his associates is tremendous, but I also think their satisfaction must be very great.

Naturally, much work remains to be done. A long time will elapse before all children in this country and those in other parts of the world will have been immunized and also for a long time progress in treatments will have to go forward for the many persons who have suffered during the last few years.

. . . .

Seldom did a play review take up nearly an entire "My Day" column, and even more rarely did Mrs. Roosevelt find herself positively moved by drama that exposed the seamy or neurotic sides of life. Yet two of Tennessee Williams' plays that do so come in for high praise in her comments about his Cat on a Hot Tin Roof. *Though her sense of propriety kept her from discussing explicitly some of the characters' unsavory problems with sex and drink, the fact that these plays were moving even if unpleasant comes across clearly. (The cast Mrs. Roosevelt saw included Burl Ives as Big Daddy, Barbara Bel Geddes as Maggie, Ben Gazzara as Brick, and Mildred Dunnock as Big Mama.)*

HYDE PARK, MAY 2—On Friday night I went to see the new Tennessee Williams play, "Cat on a Hot Tin Roof." This is real theater, I must acknowledge. It deals with a problem almost as prevalent as alcoholism, and with other problems which are equally well known, though we look at them frequently as a result of neurotic disturbances, either mental or emotional. Any psychiatrist or psychoanalyst who attends the play must feel that he is spending a few extra hours in his consulting office. Nevertheless it is a play dealing with real problems, beautifully acted and well written.

One wonders what it is that is making this play such a success. It cannot be that people like to contemplate human suffering. It must be something that goes deeper and is a problem for many people today. I think perhaps it is because here, as in his earlier play, "The Glass Menagerie," Tennessee Williams is showing us the difficulty of communication between people who spend their lives saying and doing

. . . .

things they do not mean and do not feel. That must hit home to many individuals, and the play leads one to think beyond just people in their daily contacts. This inability to communicate is what makes it difficult for groups of people to understand each other, for nations—above and beyond the difficulties of language and the meaning of words—to get at the realities that lie in the minds and hearts of the peoples of other nations. This is the real tragedy beautifully shown in "Glass Menagerie" and again expressed in this play. I think it is this underlying theme which gives Tennessee Williams' work a real appeal.

To come back to the individuals in the play: how difficult it was for them to be honest with each other, probably because it is so difficult to be honest with oneself. Shame or pride keep many people from expressing even to themselves things that might better be brought out into the open for the ultimate peace of the individual.

It isn't a pleasant play. Many will be shocked by it. Some will feel they prefer not to think about such things. But those who feel the need of greater communication with their fellow human beings will go away thoughtfully and recognize that something fundamental is dealt with here.

. . . .

In a column that sounds as much like something from the 1990s as from the 1950s with its concern for the relationship between physical and mental health and the question of what fosters longevity, Mrs. Roosevelt waxes anthropological. She may have chuckled to see in the newspapers a report that women were living longer than men and were holding onto more power in society (at seventy, she was herself a prime example of the gerontomatriarchy she describes here); but basically she was compassionate toward men whose stressful lives took their toll and toward the women they left behind. Eleanor Roosevelt had been a widow for ten years.

NEW YORK, MAY 13—Few people may have noticed a little item in the newspapers the other day under a dateline from Washington. The Population Reference Bureau says that since 1900 the proportion of persons over 65 has doubled from four to eight percent. There also has been a steady increase in the proportion of women, particularly in the age groups above 20.

In terms of voting power, ownership of land and corporate equities the United States could be seen on the road toward a gerontomatriarchy—"control by aging females," the bureau said.

This will make us smile, particularly in a country where for so many years women were scarce and the young man held the important position in our population.

. . . .

This fact, however, should give us a little food for thought. Why do women live longer than men? They are the "weaker" sex, they bear the children and, therefore, should wear out more quickly since we no longer live in a time when men must run the daily risks of hunting for their food and having to defend by physical prowess their homes on a day-by-day basis.

Is the answer perhaps that women, through the ages, have had to learn how to conserve their strength and to build resistance?

More and more in the modern world men have been obliged to set their goal for success in a competitive atmosphere. One may be under as great a strain when sitting quietly at a desk as in the days when one went out hunting to sustain himself. So, since men must work every minute in order to excel and must work at high tension in constant competition with all those around him, men often die earlier than do women.

The modern killers are heart disease and cancer and brain hemorrhage—all of which represent the pace at which modern man lives. Transportation and communication have so greatly increased in speed that man can cover more ground and do more than he could in years gone by, yet he stood up better apparently under hard physical labor than seems to be the case under the modern type of strain.

I wonder if there is not something in teaching children how to acquire an inner calm. It seems to me that in some of the books written in days gone by there was more emphasis on serenity. It may be that we must learn how to have inner serenity in spite of outward speed and activity.

Certainly, we should find ways of keeping a better balance in our population, for whether in youth or in age I think too great a predominance of one or the other sex is a distinct drawback. Our doctors had better start finding out why men wear out faster than women and they had better keep them alive for the happiness and contentment of all.

. . . .

There were few women in America Eleanor Roosevelt admired more than Mary McLeod Bethune, whose death she laments here. If Bethune had been white and had accomplished the same things—rising from poverty to obtain a fine education; founding and running a college for decades (Bethune-Cookman College, Daytona, Florida, and its normal-school predecessors); serving the country as director of the Division of Negro Affairs during the New Deal—she would certainly have deserved praise. But, in fact, Dr. Bethune demonstrated to both the white and black worlds that with supportive parents and a commitment to endless hard work, even a poor black girl could achieve great things. She was an inspiration.

. . . .

NEW YORK, MAY 20—I was distressed to read in the newspapers Thursday morning of the death of a really great American woman, Mary McLeod Bethune.

Dr. Bethune started life under conditions which must have made her education seem almost impossible, but both she and her parents had a great desire for her to gain knowledge and they seized on every opportunity. And the opportunities came, as they so often do, when people are ready to use them.

The newspapers were full of stories of how she led her remarkable life. Beginning with a dollar and a half she built a Negro college in Florida. She fought for the rights of her people but never with resentment or bitterness, and she taught both her own people and her white fellow Americans many a valuable lesson.

I always liked the story of how once a patronizing Pullman car conductor, asking her for her ticket, said: "Auntie, give me your ticket." She let him repeat it twice. Then, looking up sweetly, she said: "Which of my sister's sons are you?" This was a way of turning the tables on a gentleman, which was far more effective than any amount of anger would have been.

She had a deep religious faith and religion was not academic with her. It was both a weapon and a shield. She has told me very simply how time after time she has prayed for things, never for herself, but she always believed that if they were good things the Lord would hear her prayer. And there must have been many, many times when people were moved to answer her needs just because of this faith. She helped herself and the Lord helped her.

I knew Dr. Bethune best, of course, in the years when she worked for the National Youth Administration and she did good and courageous work for the young people of her race in a difficult period. But I have kept in touch with her all through the years and I will miss her very much, for I valued her wisdom and her goodness.

I would like to be at her funeral but I doubt if that will be possible. I have many commitments that would mean disappointment to various causes, which I think Dr. Bethune would be the first to feel should come before one's personal desires. Nevertheless, I will cherish the spirit she lived by and try to promote the causes that she believed in, in loving memory of a very wonderful life.

....

Perhaps in anticipation of her upcoming trip to the Far East Mrs. Roosevelt wrote several "My Day" columns in the summer of 1955 on Oriental topics and issues. The two included here contrast in tone but show the breadth of her interests. In the first she argues for careful preservation of Oriental customs and against a wholesale adoption of Western

ways—which, from her viewpoint, were no better, no worse, just won-
derfully different. In the second she turns to a dark subject: the dev-
astation caused in Japan by the atom bomb. In reviewing Hiroshima
Diary, *by a Japanese physician who survived the blast, Eleanor Roos-*
evelt remarks on the unusual absence of bitterness among the Japanese
and seizes the occasion to reiterate that these bombs must never again
be used against people.

HYDE PARK, JUNE 4—I saw an article in one of our metropolitan papers
on Thursday saying that the children in the schools of Thailand are
being taught to shake hands, in preference to the traditional "wai"
greeting.

I have always thought that this customary method of greeting, which
varies a little in different Oriental countries but is somewhat the same
in India and other countries, has back of it not only charm but good
common sense for medical reasons.

In Thailand the old custom is to press the palms of the hands together in front of the body. For greeting a superior the hands are held
on a level with the forehead, for an inferior they are held on the chest.

Some of the native tribes in New Zealand greet you by touching the
foreheads together, which actually means that mind speaks to mind.

These ways of greeting have meaning and are graceful, and I am
not sure that they are not far better than our habit of shaking hands
or the European habit of a gentleman kissing a lady's hand. The latter
may be a charming and pleasing custom to the ladies but may not be
so sanitary.

In any case, before the Orient adopts Western customs I hope they
will think twice, for some customs might well be adopted by the West
from the East.

NEW YORK, JUNE 18—I have just read a new book called "Hiroshima
Diary," the journal of a Japanese physician from August 5, 1945, to
September 30, 1945.

Dr. Michihiko Hachiya, who kept this diary, was the director of an
important hospital in Hiroshima. He was himself wounded in the blast
and his hospital was partly demolished by the fire that followed. To
every American reader this book will bring some of the horror of what
dropping the first atomic bomb meant.

It was an unknown weapon then and those who suffered from it,
like Dr. Hachiya, not only coped with many day-to-day physical needs
but were overwhelmed by the scientific mystery of a weapon they knew
nothing about and whose effects they had never heard of and could
not gauge.

It is a book written with an extraordinary lack of bitterness, and one must marvel at the doctor's reflection of the human spirit, its nobility and strength under such terrific pressures.

To me it has been a painful book to read, but that is because I still have the feeling that I had the day I spent in Hiroshima when I felt that all about me death was still a companion. But there is in this book not only horror but tenderness, gentleness and compassion and power to forget to blame in the overpowering need to help.

. . . .

In a brief section of a column devoted to other subjects, Mrs. Roosevelt returned to a favorite political and philanthropic theme: the plight of political refugees. But she also referred to a political figure not all that well-known at the time, a name that would eventually come to dom-inate the American landscape: Senator John F. Kennedy. Theirs was an unsteady friendship until well into the presidential race of 1960.

HYDE PARK, JUNE 28—Senator John F. Kennedy has written a letter to Senator William Langer, chairman of the Senate subcommittee on refugees and escapees, that should be read by all of us. Senator Ken-nedy suggests amendments to the Refugee Relief Act of 1953 in order to allow more help to be given to escapees and refugees from behind the Iron Curtain, so that they may be resettled in other countries. Secondly, he wants the expiration date extended and unused quotas made available to other groups, such as Greeks, Italians, Poles, French, etc., and he hopes the limit will be raised far over the present 209,000 people.

I like the quotation at the end of Senator Kennedy's letter in which he says the Refugee Relief Act should not be what John Boyle O'Reilly once termed:

"Organized charity, scrimped and iced

In the name of a cautious, statistical Christ."

Let us hope that we can approach this question in our Congress, in our homes, and in our communities with generosity, for in the end we will benefit.

. . . .

Summer pleasures—in particular relaxation outdoors in any number of different settings—were frequent "My Day" subjects. In a column on the conductor Serge Koussevitsky of the Boston Symphony, Mrs. Roosevelt not only makes a fund-raising pitch for the Koussevitsky scholarship fund at the summer music school founded in his name at Tanglewood (in Lenox, Massachusetts) but also spins out a few thoughts on a broader theme: the importance of the arts to the health of society, both in history and now. She had been the narrator in a

. . . .

performance of Prokofiev's Peter and the Wolf *at Tanglewood, directed by Maestro Koussevitsky, and she had a deep affection for him.*

The Fourth of July was a holiday the Roosevelt family never ignored. They enjoyed the festivities in their village of Hyde Park, and the day offered a welcome excuse for family to gather at Mrs. Roosevelt's Val-Kill cottage. But kids will be kids, and despite urgings from the adults that the day was a good one on which to sit still briefly for a reading of some words written down long ago by the Founding Fathers, other activities were clearly more important to the youngsters. Eleanor Roosevelt had a forgiving heart whenever children were involved.

HYDE PARK, JUNE 30—From many parts of our country people have journeyed year after year to Tanglewood in Berkshire County, Mass., to enjoy the music. And these visitors have been interested in the various teaching activities that go on there during the summer and which the late, great conductor, Mr. Koussevitsky, took such a keen interest in developing.

After his death some of the people in the county formed a committee to raise $15,000 in his memory to provide a yearly scholarship for one student. So far only $7,000 of that sum has been raised. And since the opening at Tanglewood takes place this year on July 4, and Mr. Koussevitsky's birthday comes later in the month, I have been wondering if the many who enjoy year after year the fruits of his labors would not like to make sure that between the date of the opening and the time of his birthday the rest of this fund was contributed. This achievement then could be announced at the memorial concert that is usually given on his birthday.

Mr. Koussevitsky would have liked to feel that one young person could come and have the opportunity to study there every summer. I think he understood very well that everyone was not gifted with genius, but in order to have genius discovered and rewarded there must be a vast number of people musically educated. Perhaps they would never be great artists but they would contribute to the musical appreciation of our audiences, and that is the only possible way that you can support great artists.

The countries that have had the greatest musicians, the greatest actors, the greatest writers are the countries that have appreciation of the arts among the people as a whole. It is a sign that a nation is growing up, is coming to maturity when it is really concerned to support the arts.

In the Middle Ages every artist had to have one individual patron who was willing to support him and let him do his work. That was a sign that civilization was still in a more or less primitive state. But the greatness of France, for instance, has been the fact that appreciation of art was present in the people as a whole. You have but to go into an art gallery in France to see that the public is there—even the people from the farm areas.

I remember seeing a woman with a market basket on her arm sitting before one of the masterpieces in the Louvre. It was her way of giving her soul a chance for a moment of peace and contemplation before the work of the day went on.

One of the things that troubles me about the future of the living drama in our country is the fact that it is so expensive that the vast majority of the people can see a play only on very rare occasions. Many people throughout our nation who live in rural areas have never seen live actors perform on the stage.

For a really healthy development of all the arts you need an educated audience as well as performers.

HYDE PARK, JULY 7—We celebrated the Fourth here in very quiet fashion, staying at home most of the day but having a goodly number of people to play tennis during the morning and for lunch.

I asked my son John to read the Declaration of Independence and the Constitution to all of the young people, for we had 10 youngsters between the ages of two and 16 over the past week-end. The youngsters, however, were much more interested in sparklers after dark and spending all possible time in the pool. The Declaration of Independence and the Constitution and the Bill of Rights remind them of school!

It was a good thing that the long week-end came during such a hot spell, for many people were able to get to the country and find some relief. Our swimming pool has been in almost constant use. I don't think anything gives the children more comfort than being able to plunge into the pool and stay there for an hour at a time. They have a wonderful game they call "Red Rover," and that seems to take all their interest and energy for long periods of time.

. . . .

Blessed with good health and too busy to fret over small ailments, Eleanor Roosevelt was the exact opposite of a hypochondriac. For her a visit to the doctor was an amusing nonevent.

HYDE PARK, JULY 18—I think I can say that Thursday was for me rather a waste of time. I went for a physical check-up to the Rip Van Winkle Clinic in Hudson, where a most comprehensive and thorough job was done in what I think would be considered record time. Yet, is there anything duller than doing things about your health when you feel completely well and, as far as you can see, are completely well! They tell me, however, that when people reach old age they should go and

. . . .

have periodic physical examinations. Since this is the thing to do, I suppose I should feel satisfied that it is over, and perhaps I will never have to do it again.

. . . .

FDR had given Eleanor Roosevelt more than enough to be disappointed about in their marriage. Even at the time of his death, his dalliance with another woman was not entirely over. But whatever lingering pain such disappointments may have left with her, she never washed such emotional laundry in public. In the public arena she was still the President's wife, and he had been the country's leader. She took pleasure in fulfilling sincerely what she must have seen as a civic duty—to give her late husband all the praise he was due for his illustrious career.

Many writers had tried to distill from FDR's long and complex story the essence of his genius for leadership, of his contribution to American history. Few had succeeded as well as political historian and literary critic Isaiah Berlin whose forte, Mrs. Roosevelt thought, lay in seeing patterns in both the facts and in the human feelings behind the actions.

Berlin had emigrated in the 1930s from his native Latvia to England, where he became a lifelong Oxonian as both student and as professor (although he taught at prestigious universities in many other countries as well). Among his better-known works is the study called The Hedgehog and the Fox, *about Tolstoy's view of history (1953).*

NEW YORK, AUGUST 1—In the Atlantic for this month there is an article entitled "Roosevelt Through European Eyes," by Isaiah Berlin. It is most interesting to me that someone who never met or saw my husband, but only heard his voice over the radio, could write this article. He was writing, however, of how Franklin D. Roosevelt appeared to Europeans, and most of them could not see or meet him and probably did not often hear him on the radio.

Mr. Berlin says certain things that to me are very interesting as coming from an outsider, so to speak. He writes, for instance, "It is not too much to say that he altered the fundamental concept of government and its obligations to the governed. In this respect Lloyd George was no more than a forerunner. The welfare state, so much denounced, has obviously come to stay: the direct moral responsibility for minimum standards of living and social services which it took for granted, are today accepted almost without a murmur by the most conservative politicians in the Western democracies. . . . But Mr. Roosevelt's greatest service to mankind (after ensuring victory against the enemies of freedom) consists in the fact that he showed that it is possible to be politically effective and yet benevolent and civilized: that the fierce left and right wing propaganda of the thirties, according to

. . . .

which the conquest and retention of political power is not compatible
with human qualities, but necessarily demands from those who pursue
it seriously the sacrifice of their lives upon the altar of some ruthless
ideology, or the systematic practice of despotism—this propaganda,
which filled the art and talk of the day, was simply untrue."

To have changed permanently a concept of government and made
it more humanitarian, to have won a further victory over the enemies
of freedom and to have proved that you may hold power and still be
a really human being—that isn't a bad summing up as the results of
an active political career. I am grateful to Mr. Berlin for his insight
and understanding.

....

*Eleanor Roosevelt always had good times when she visited her son El-
liott's ranch at Meeker, Colorado. Entertainments under the Rocky
Mountain sky were decidedly different from anything she was likely to
experience back East. A visit to a trout hatchery provoked memories of
deep-sea fishing FDR enjoyed with his political cronies, often on the
waters off Campobello Island, New Brunswick. Though Mrs. Roosevelt
enjoyed energetic horseback riding until late in her life, that was about
the extent of her participation in vigorous sports. Otherwise she was
content to watch, to knit, to think, and to chat.*

MEEKER, COLO., AUGUST 4—Early this morning I walked over to see
the state fish hatchery, which is not far from my son's ranch house.
Walking along the stream it was amusing to see the little trout swimming against the current, and when I got down to the place where
they were loading trout into tanks to take them over to Rifle Creek,
which is about a three-hour drive away, I was surprised to see how big
they were. I am sure anyone would have liked them for a morning
meal.

I am not a fisherman, however, though from watching people fish
for trout I have decided that it must be far more interesting than the
deep-sea fishing which I used to watch my husband enjoy.

I realize, of course, that there is much skill and muscle that goes
into the catching of certain of the big-game fish, which my husband's
parties used to go after. But it always seemed to me so difficult and to
require as much skill as trout-fishing does.

The need to acquire these skills always frightened me, and I suppose
I never tried long enough to have them seem attainable as far as I was
concerned. So I contented myself with knitting and watching those
enviously who could do the things I could not do.

I am hoping that while I am here some of the household will be
trout-fishing. Eating them is something even unskilled people can do.

....

Anyone who stays in public life long enough to have her views become widely known has to expect that crackpots will eventually take shots at her ideas and even at her personality. Mrs. Roosevelt was used to hearing criticism of her political thoughts; it rolled off her back like the proverbial water off a duck's feathers. She publicly ignored most of the frivolous criticism that came at her from ill-informed people. Occasionally, however, the virulent immorality of the thinking in a piece of hate mail Eleanor received was just too much for her restraint. Her "My Day" column would then pillory the hapless fools who had written the piece. In the following column, it is surely the evidence of anti-Semitism and anti-United Nations thinking (about which Mrs. Roosevelt had become particularly sensitive over the years) that provoked her.

MEEKER, COLO., AUGUST 11—I received a copy of a sheet from a newspaper that was sent by some people in Princeton, N.J. This printed material, from my point of view, is a rather shocking document. In the first place, it is openly anti-Semitic, so violently anti-Semitic that it allows itself to say things which are completely untrue. In the second place, it attacks President Eisenhower in an outrageous way. I am not a Republican but I believe that all of us Democrats and Republicans alike owe the office of the President, as well as the man who occupies it, respect and truth in our criticisms. The criticisms in this sheet are far from true. It is headed with a hammer and sickle on both sides of the banner headline: "The Coming Red Dictatorship." As one reads on, one wants to point out the inaccuracies in almost every paragraph but, suffice it to say, that the anti-Semitism is not hidden but stares out from every line.

Here is one statement which, it seems to me, is inexcusable: "Eisenhower is completely subservient to the Jewish plotters and is carrying forward their protocol plots steadily."

What nonsense! How gullible can people be?

One must suppose that the people who get out this sheet are writing what they believe, but if that is so one can only say that they are stupid beyond belief. And if they are writing what they do not believe, then they are doing it for some purpose, perhaps to fool the public. Apparently they hope people will be gullible enough to accept without real analysis their idiotic statements.

One thing about which I personally know the truth they say: "The human rights covenant drawn up by Eleanor Roosevelt, Dean Acheson and two Russians gives the government of any member nation and the U.N. the right, if it thinks itself threatened, to curb the freedom of the press and impose martial law and to take over all industry and all labor."

Just to point out how inaccurate they are, here are the facts: No human rights covenant has been accepted by the General Assembly of the United Nations. The Universal Declaration of Human Rights was not legally binding and could not do any of the things here put down and it was written by the representatives of 18 nations who worked together for over two years. So, picking out the United States and the Soviet Union as responsible for it is rather absurd to say the least.

One might laugh at a publication such as this—which is called "Commonsense" and carries a subtitle, "The Nation's Anti-Communist Paper"—if it were not so tragic that such nonsense can exist in a country like ours.

....

Here begins a travelogue from a trip Mrs. Roosevelt had looked forward to for years. Although Japan had been as much an enemy of the Allies in World War II as had Germany and had even attacked the United States directly at Pearl Harbor, she was somehow able to move much more quickly toward forgiveness and rapprochement with the Japanese than she ever was with the Germans—whom she held responsible for starting not one but two world wars. Thus little sense of animosity, resentment, or fear appeared in Mrs. Roosevelt's string of columns from this trip. She is, instead, mostly enthralled or at least charmed by the very foreignness of Japan and the Far East.

Eleanor Roosevelt the travel writer: Never one of the world's great stylists, she could nonetheless evoke a scene quite well. And she had a knack for seeing below the surface details to meaningful patterns of cultural values underneath. On this trip she was accompanied by her close friend, David Gurewitsch, director of a children's medical clinic at Blythdale Hospital in Dutchess County, near Hyde Park. Mrs. Roosevelt had an admirable capacity to take pleasure in customs and objects that were completely new to her, such as the rigorous discipline of the Japanese tea ceremony and the mysterious calm of the Buddha.

TOKYO, AUGUST 20—Mr. and Mrs. Matsumoto and Dr. Takagi joined us at noon and took us to a delightful Japanese restaurant for lunch. The first dish placed on the table was so lovely in color and so artistically arranged that Dr. Gurewitsch insisted on having it carried out into the sunlight so that he could take a picture of it in color. The charming courtesy of everyone in Japan impressed you wherever you go but especially when you go to the kind of restaurant we went to today. After our very delicious lunch the lady who owns it showed us the tea ceremony. Only the very best Japanese tea is used and they do not ship it to the U.S.A. Dr. Gurewitsch was instructed in the

....

guest's role of the ceremony by Mrs. Matsumoto, who showed him how to turn his bowl and hold it correctly but he liked the tea—which proved that he is more adaptable than I am, for I have never quite been able to get used to the taste.

I remember that when I was here two years ago I was envious of my daughter-in-law, Minnewa, because she had shoes that she did not have to untie every time we went into a shrine or into a house. So this time I brought a pair to wear that I can just slip on and off without bothering to tie them.

NIKKO, JAPAN, AUGUST 26—In the treasure house of one of the shrines at Nara, there is the most beautiful of all the buddhas I have seen so far. You come upon it after you have seen many other lovely buddhas, but this one stands tall and slim with one hand extended palm up as though it is pleading for something, and the expression is one not of suffering but of calmness. Somehow this figure seems to me to have almost a Christian concept.

． ． ． ． ． ． ． ． ． ．

Though far from home, Mrs. Roosevelt kept as close a watch on domestic political events as she could through foreign newspapers and communications from her staff in New York. One particularly ugly story of absurd racial discrimination in Texas reached her halfway around the globe, in the Phillipines. And she sent a message back to her readers in the United States about how embarrassing it is for the country, in the eyes of foreigners, when again this lamentable side of the American character rears its ugly head.

MANILA, SEPTEMBER 2—When one is far away from the United States certain things which happen there and pass almost unnoticed by the average citizen at home take on an entirely different color when seen through the eyes of the people of another country.

A few days ago there appeared in the paper a story of a manager in an airport restaurant in Houston, Texas, who had mistaken the Indian Ambassador and his companion for Negroes and had requested them to move from the regular restaurant to a small room reserved for Negroes.

The Indian people vary in color from light brown to dark brown. Our American Negroes vary in color from very light brown to black. And where segregation is practiced incidents of this kind are apt to happen.

Every person I have met almost since this came out in the papers has spoken to me of it with indignation, surprise and horror. How

． ． ． ． ． ． ． ． ． ． ． ． ． ． ． ． ． ．

could an ambassador be treated in this way? A better question is: How could any human being be treated in this way?

The restaurant manager in Texas was probably carrying out a rule made to cover citizens of the United States who happen not to be white. Have we a right anywhere in the United States to assume that the accident of color changes our rights as citizens?

Many of us have looked charitably on the difficulties of the people in our country who have grown up for generations thinking of colored people as slaves and, therefore, inferior, but it is a long time since President Lincoln declared that we have no slaves in the United States and only citizens of our country. Whether the color is yellow or white or brown, the rights are equal and the mere fact of citizenship gives us these rights.

. . . .

Peasant life on the canals near Bangkok, Thailand, became the subject for one of Eleanor Roosevelt's most vivid travelogues.

BANGKOK, SEPTEMBER 17—We were called at 6:00 A.M. and went out on the river to see the floating market from the river. Canals have been dug to carry the water back onto the land, which is very fertile and grows crops in abundance.

Rice is the basic food here, as in many other countries in this area, but unlike Japan, for instance, which must import much of its rice, the people here have a surplus and export to many countries.

We saw the people this morning who live on the land and in the boats. In some cases without boats these people would be bereft of all means of transportation. The small children go to school by boat, all the produce goes to market by boat, all the necessities of life come to their door by boat. The ice-cream vendor rings a bell, the butcher blows a horn, someone else sounds a bugle, and the housewife knows just what she will find by her float.

Everyone bathes in the canal. All the wash is done in its muddy waters and, strangely enough, comes out looking clean and white. And, of course, the canal is the only outlet for sewage disposal.

Our guide remarked that a child becomes accustomed to germs from birth, and I'm sure that is so or the infant mortality rate would be even higher than it is.

The life on the river is the life of the people of Thailand and a picturesque life it is and full of color. The boats are laden with fruits and vegetables and usually are towed in long strings. The women often do the rowing and, as you look at some of the older women who cut their hair short like the men, it is sometimes hard to decide whether you are looking at a man or a woman.

. . . .

The children are very friendly and wave at the sightseers' boats as they pass.

Late in the morning we went to see the royal barges, which are only used on state occasions—one barge for the coronation, one for the yearly state visit to the temple and the smaller ones for members of the royal household. The barges are beautifully decorated but on state occasions they are also gaily decked with flowers and other decorations and rowed by men in gorgeous costume. Our guide evidently loved all the pageantry, as people do in every part of the world.

Eleanor Roosevelt had been among the first to read the English translation of The Diary of a Young Girl *in the winter of 1951. Over the next five years, as* The Diary of Anne Frank, *the book became a bestseller in many countries, and now a dramatic adaptation appeared in New York. It moved Mrs. Roosevelt deeply; she saw in it a hard lesson about the need for vigilance against losing our freedom to demagogues and totalitarian systems. In her view, one could not be reminded too often of these dangers.*

St. Paul, Minn., October 15—Before I took off on this trip I saw earlier in the week a most remarkable play, "The Diary of Anne Frank." This was adapted from the book of the same name—a book that could be read the world over with pleasure and profit because it describes man's inhumanity to man in the words of a child. The play brings the message home even more keenly because it is so dramatically done.

There is humor in this play; there is tenderness and love; there is hate, and human frailty is not hidden.

Susan Strasberg's acting is superb. I can think of no one who could do the part of Anne better than she does. Anne was an exasperating child, completely normal in many ways, wanting fun and noise and action. Yet, in other ways she was so sensitive, so thoughtful and so conscious of her own personality that she must have been the most trying child to her elders.

From Joseph Schildkraut we have come to expect an outstanding performance in his every appearance and this play is no exception.

The humor, the gentleness, the patience, the courage which lead to that last wonderful line, "We have been living here in fear, now we can live in hope," are all so naturally portrayed that it is hard not to feel the actor is not really Mr. Frank.

Would we all have had courage to approach such moments in the way Mr. Frank did!

Then there is his courage, when the personal trials are over, to accept the death of a dearly loved wife and daughter and pick up the pieces of life and still go on. This seems to me an almost incredible strength of character.

I have marveled at Mr. Frank in real life and the highest tribute I can pay the actor is that I think he has portrayed a remarkable character convincingly and with deep insight.

Every member of the cast is good, and at many points I laughed and enjoyed myself. But as I left the theater my heart was heavy, for I realized that people had actually lived through these scenes—and can we say with absolute assurance that they will never live through them again?

I think we can say that the conscience of human beings was greatly awakened by what happened to people before and during World War II but was it enough to keep us from ever permitting ourselves or our neighbors to indulge in hate of our brother now?

Do we understand, at last, that freedom must be universal and that all men must be assured that there will be respect for the individual human being, regardless of his race, his creed or his color?

Without that assurance we have practically no certainty that for one reason or another Anne Frank's diary might not be written again by some little girl in the future.

I hope this play will be very successful and have a long run, for I am sure it will bring to many people a greater understanding of the things that must never happen again anywhere in the world.

. . . .

"Workers of the world, unite!" In many different ways Eleanor Roosevelt used her "My Day" columns to encourage various groups of workers within the American economy to stand up for their rights and to demand respect. Each of the next three columns is informed by this spirit.

In the first, Mrs. Roosevelt gives a ringing defense of housewife, *a term she believed deserved as much standing in the marketplace as any other job title. Feminists of a later day with a more conventional sense of professionalism may find Mrs. Roosevelt's argument merely quaint at best or reactionary at worst. But the political message here derives from the moral values at its base: that there are no more important roles to play in society than parent, spouse, and homemaker. If we dishonor these roles, Mrs. Roosevelt believed, the fabric of society comes undone, and no governmental leadership can knit it together again.*

Early in December Mrs. Roosevelt and many other liberals were shocked to learn that the Civil Service Administration had been systematically collecting and holding on file the names of some two million people who allegedly had been connected to subversive organizations. In the second column here she maintains that such lists are incendiary. They implicitly convict people of crimes no one has even

. . . .

tried to prove, and they represent an underlying paranoia—the polar opposite of the pride in the vitality of American institutions that Mrs. Roosevelt always considered the country's best defense.

Returning to the women-and-work theme, in the third column she makes a strong call for a shift in policy in the two major national political parties, a call to bring more women into positions of real leadership. Though she makes no claims, as later feminists would do, that female leadership would be inherently better—more intelligent or more effective—than male, she certainly knew it would be different. For one thing, women would focus their attention on different issues, and schooling would be one of them. Mrs. Roosevelt contended that eventually the presence of more women in positions of party leadership would have a positive, liberalizing impact on platforms and policies; that all this would help push the country toward solutions for knotty problems like segregation.

NEW YORK, OCTOBER 17—Recently I received a letter which raised a question of interest to many women. It reads as follows:

"Reading your article in the August Safeway Magazine gives me the inspiration and opportunity I have long been looking for, namely to 'speak' to you regarding the word 'housewife,' used to define the greatest profession we women perform.

"QUESTION. What is your occupation?
ANSWER: Housewife, wife of a house.
QUESTIONING A CHILD: What does your father do?
ANSWER: He is a lawyer on Wall Street, N.Y.C.
QUESTION: What is your mother's occupation?
ANSWER: Oh, she is just a housewife.

"I have heard this on TV. I am sure other women have cringed at the term. The dictionary defines the word as 'the woman in charge of a household.' Wife is defined as 'a woman joined in marriage to a man as husband.'

"Surely there is another name for us. How do you feel about it? Why not write an article which will bring opinions from other married women?"

I must confess that in days gone by I have often entered myself on questionnaires as "housewife" without feeling the slightest embarrassment. Now I put down "writer" or "lecturer," because the major part of my life is taken up in this way rather than in running a home and watching over the daily needs of a household and children plus guests, as it used to be in earlier days. I am not sure, however, that I did not feel more useful when I had to be home the greater part of the time. I had to make very careful plans when I left home so that all would go on in the same way while I was gone. I was limited in my free time. One could never be sure that there would not be sudden illness which would make a change in plans inevitable, or that home tasks would not clash with some demands outside my family—and of course, the demands outside the family were always secondary.

Those were the days when on a questionnaire I would put down "housewife" and feel very proud of it, and I am quite sure that no woman has any reason for feeling humiliated by the title. It is one of the most skilled professions in the world. When one adds to the business of running a house the care and bringing up of children, there is so much needed preparation for this occupation that I think it could be classed today among the most skilled occupations in the world. To be sure, there are good and bad homes; and there are children who are well brought up and children who are badly brought up. This happens in any business or professional activity. But when one adds up what it means to a nation, one must concede that the well-run home and the well-brought-up children are more important even than a well-run business. More people are affected by the occupation of a housewife and mother than are ever touched by any single business, no matter how large it may be.

BALTIMORE, DECEMBER 2—I was shocked to read the other day the revelation by Mr. Philip Young, chairman of the Civil Service Commission in Washington, that the commission maintained a card index file with names of two million persons "allegedly affiliated with some sort of subversive organization or activity."

He went on to explain that they did not even try to substantiate any of the accusations which they took from many different sources, and he said that perhaps three-fourths of the people dismissed from government service never had the least idea they were dismissed because of security questions. The official reason given might have been something like "excessive drinking."

It seems to me that the Civil Service has a very grave responsibility when it lists against a name the word "subversive" without verifying the information that has brought about the accusation.

NEW YORK, DECEMBER 7—I would like to state again what I have said so often in the past. The time has come, I think, for all political parties to give more thought to including women on the policy-making level. It may well be that we have reached the stage when separate divisions for the work of men and women in political machinery may not be necessary.

But there is no doubt in my mind that women work differently from men, and they will put a different emphasis on certain issues. The temptation to use them exclusively on the uninteresting chores that have to be done, and very often are done by volunteers, in any political organization is very great because women have more time in their localities. They can address envelopes and stuff them with literature. They can undertake ringing doorbells, and plenty of them will be content to do it.

But there must be women included in the upper stratas so that all women will know that their voices are being heard.

If women really understand the issues they will probably talk more effectively to their neighbors than any of the men, especially if the issues are such that they affect their daily lives. For instance, I think we are going to hear from the women before long on the school question. More and more women find their children going at different hours because of the overcrowded schools and most of them do not like it.

I am sure, also, that in the South if women find that because of the state policy against integration they cannot send their children to schools that are free, there will be a reaction in a very short time. They may not like desegregation but they are certainly going to dislike having the white children as well as the colored without opportunity for education.

. . . .

Mrs. Roosevelt reports on the experience of her first drive on a super-highway and marvels over engineering that was soon to become commonplace. But the bridge she describes and the view downstream to New York City are powerful images that only the most jaded of travelers in any generation could ignore. The technical details she offers about methods of bridge construction make one ponder: Was there any subject that could not draw Eleanor Roosevelt's serious attention?

NEW YORK, DECEMBER 16—I had the great pleasure of driving across the new Tappan Zee Bridge that crosses the Hudson River from Nyack to Tarrytown and is a link in the Thruway to Buffalo.

I had never been on the Thruway before and we drove a short distance on it. It is certainly a mode of rapid transportation and very cleverly engineered to try to do away with some of the difficulties that straight parkways create. An effort has been made to overcome these with carefully engineered curves and rises.

One can go so steadily at the same speed on many straight highways that some people find it hard to keep awake. Some drivers advise that if you are alone to turn the radio on really loud and not to play soft music. The engineers of the Thruway told me, however, they had

. . . .

thought of this and tried, by creating different levels and widening the middle part of the road in different places, to make enough variety to break the monotony.

They still say, however, it is wise to stop about once an hour and walk around your car or stop to get a cup of coffee.

The bridge itself across the Hudson is quite low for part of the way where the river is shallow, and as it follows the contour of the land it curves. This makes it very attractive. It is high enough where it rises for an ocean-going steamer to pass underneath it.

The construction of this bridge presented some very serious difficulties. To reach the rock in some places the engineers had to go down 300 feet below the level of the river bed, and they used a clever device of floating concrete in other places to carry some of the weight of the steel.

On the whole it is a very remarkable engineering feat, and as it crosses at the Tappan Zee, which is one of the most beautiful places in the Hudson River, a special effort was made to design a railing to permit a view in both directions. I have always found it tantalizing to cross a bridge and not be able to see over the parapet, so I was particularly glad to notice this innovation.

At one point from the bridge you can look down the river and see the New York City skyline, and on a clear day you can see the outline of the George Washington Bridge.

1 9 5 6

The new year began with a burst of energy from Eleanor Roosevelt. In its first month alone she visited at least these cities on two trips for the American Association for the United Nations and to keep other business and social appointments: Bellingham, Seattle, and Longview in Washington state; Los Angeles; San Antonio, Houston, Lubbock, and Dallas in Texas; Philadelphia; Albuquerque, New Mexico; Phoenix, Arizona; and, of course, New York City and Hyde Park.

Tensions were rising in the civil rights debate. Early in February the University of Alabama broke the color line by enrolling its first black student, Autherine Lucy. Liberals hailed the step. Overnight, riots ensued on the campus and within days, to restore order, the school suspended Lucy, a major setback for desegregation. A week later a federal court in New Orleans declared all state laws supporting segregation invalid. By March 1 the National Association for the Advancement of Colored People had sued the University of Alabama to force readmission of Lucy, but, to get clear of the problem, the school countered by expelling her altogether. In May the Methodists joined the Presbyterians who, the preceding year, had voted as a church to call for an end to segregation. Eleanor Roosevelt had been for some time a director of the NAACP, and in midsummer she agonized over whether to vote to obey a court order segregationists had obtained to force the organization to surrender its membership lists.

Springtime brought some charming and some encouraging news of different kinds. Royalty-watchers everywhere were given a rare treat when an uncommon commoner, the Academy Award-winning actress Grace Kelly, married Prince Ranier III of Monaco. Dr. Jonas Salk, a hero in Mrs. Roosevelt's and many other people's minds, announced in June that the polio vaccine he had developed with colleagues stood a good chance of eliminating the disease in America within three years.

81

International tensions in the Middle East boiled over into armed conflict in July. The United States had offered fifty-six million dollars to Egypt to support the Aswan Dam project on the upper Nile, but shortly withdrew the offer on learning of Egypt's close political ties to the Soviets and of Soviet arms sales to Egypt. Even larger World Bank loans were offered for the project and then withdrawn under U.S. pressure. Egyptian President Gamal Abdel Nasser retaliated by nationalizing the Suez Canal (which had been an open waterway, under British control, since 1875) and by withdrawing guarantees of safe passage for Israeli ships. By autumn Israel and Egypt were in military battle over land rights in the Sinai Desert, which Israel had occupied. British and French troops fought on the Israeli side until the United States was successful in arranging a cease fire—to be enforced by United Nations troops. Mrs. Roosevelt saw the entire string of events (particularly the lack of coordination among the Western powers) as a monstrous foreign policy debacle for the Eisenhower administration.

It was an election year. Ike and Vice President Nixon were renominated by the Republicans after the Democrats had renominated Adlai Stevenson for president, this time with Senator Estes Kefauver for vice president. Mrs. Roosevelt squeezed in a month-long European trip just after the conventions, visiting Holland, Denmark, and France. Back home by mid-September to join the campaign, she fought hard for Stevenson and other Democratic candidates. She took the unusual step of closing up part of her Hyde Park house because she simply didn't have time to go there. In mid-October, after noticing that, like Moby Dick, Mrs. Roosevelt seemed to have the knack of being everywhere at once, the *Boston Globe* sent a reporter to follow her: The editors could not believe anyone of seventy-two could keep up the pace of her travels and appointment schedule. The reporter was soon exhausted and went home.

The incumbents held fast in the White House, garnering almost seven times as many electoral votes as the losers. But the liberals held sway and even gained seats in both houses of Congress. Mrs. Roosevelt and other political observers foresaw a difficult four years ahead resulting from this ideological stalemate between the White House and the Capitol.

Election week in America, no matter how it turns out, demonstrates at least one thing: that political choice is relatively free here, at least for those who can muster the necessary funds to run for office. But in the Eastern-bloc countries of Poland and Hungary, early in the same week when Americans were choosing new representatives, the Soviets used massive military force to crush popular uprisings against Communist control by the Kremlin, uprisings which many people at the time, including Eleanor Roosevelt, thought stood a good chance to blow apart the ten-year-old Warsaw Pact alliance of Soviet satellites. They were wrong. It would be another thirty-four years before real political freedom would begin to return to Eastern Europe.

....

Any serious thinker whose social or moral philosophy is as subtle or multifaceted as was Eleanor Roosevelt's resists easy summary. But she found the right phrases to encapsulate her philosophy of interdependence in a statement issued in a Philadelphia ceremony celebrating Benjamin Franklin. The venerable Franklin would no doubt have been an admiring friend of Mrs. Roosevelt.

NEW YORK, JANUARY 21—In Philadelphia's continuing celebration of the 250th anniversary of Benjamin Franklin's birth, a foreign-born chemist whom I met the other night has been awarded the Franklin Institute's highest honor, the Franklin Medal. His name is Professor Arne Tiselius, a delightful, modest scientist who was the Swedish winner of the 1948 Nobel Prize in chemistry.

At Independence Hall on the same day there was also a ceremony that launched an interesting document entitled "A Declaration of Interdependence." This is a small but impressive pamphlet sponsored by the Interdependence Council, Inc., which was formed to develop an increasing sense of "interdependence among all peoples."

Five years of study in many countries of the world have gone into this document, which is signed by 1,371 persons in 51 nations. It reaffirms man's dependence on man without regard to religion, color or geographical boundaries.

In the foreword this declaration states "people have the power to help or harm each other. Which shall it be? Nations can live in peace or die in war. Which shall it be? The fate of humanity depends on the feelings of individuals toward one another."

And then it says what I think is all important for all of us to remember:

"I am only one. But I am one. I cannot do everything. But I can do something. What I can do I ought to do. What I ought to do I will do."

This organization may be only a candle lighted in a world which at present seems very dark, to those who would like to see peace and goodwill established. But even a candle is better than no light at all, as many of us have discovered who live in areas where occasionally electric light is cut off for a time.

....

Mrs. Roosevelt shared with her "My Day" readers a prayer spoken by the American Indian chief Yellow Lark that captures much of the essence

....

*of her own philosophical orientation. In so much of her political anal-
ysis—of great issues and small—we see her explanations of combatants'
anger and hostility coming down not to ideological causes but to unresolved conflicts within the individual personalities themselves. She
acted on the basis of the belief that before one can make peace in the
world, one must first make peace in one's own heart.*

NAHUNTA, GA., FEBRUARY 10—February 17 is the date this year on
which World Day of Prayer will be observed. The sponsor of this day
in the United States is the General Department of United Church
Women of the National Council of the Churches of Christ.

The purpose of the day is to unite all Christians in a bond of prayer,
and this will be the 70th year of the observance in the United States.
Thousands of communities will participate.

I like particularly a prayer that was written by one of our Indian
chiefs, Chief Yellow Lark. It reads:

"O, Great Spirit; Whose voice I hear in the winds, and Whose breath
gives life to all the world, hear me. I come before You, one of Your
many children. I am small and weak. I need Your strength and wisdom.

"Let me walk in beauty and make my eyes ever behold the red and
purple sunset. Make my hands respect the things You have made, my
ears sharp to hear Your voice. Make me wise, so that I may know the
things You have taught my people, the lesson You have hidden in
every leaf and rock.

"I seek strength not to be superior to my brothers, but to be able to
fight my greatest enemy—myself. Make me ever ready to come to You
with clean hands and straight eyes, so when life fades as a fading sunset,
my spirit may come to You without shame."

. . . .

*Only rarely did Eleanor Roosevelt venture into the kitchen to claim
any authority as a cook. It was not her bailiwick. From time to time,
however, in a completely lighthearted way, she used her "My Day" column to convey some observations about food, usually about putting
food by for the winter, an activity she enjoyed every year at Hyde Park.
This time a famous snack or dessert recipe, dear to the hearts and palates
of young Americans coast to coast, was given detailed attention.*

NEW YORK, FEBRUARY 14—I also find material here from another
group, doing much good work on the development of young American
girls—the Girl Scouts of America. Girl Scout Week this year is from
March 11 to March 17. Many of us will buy cookies that week and
enclosed with them will be a recipe for making a favorite Girl Scout

. . . .

dish, called "Some Mores à la Girl Scout." I quote it here because I think many non-Girl Scouts will enjoy it.

All you need is four thin squares of plain chocolate, two Graham crackers and one marshmallow. You toast the marshmallow slowly over coals or in the oven until brown. You put the chocolate square on the Graham cracker, then the marshmallow, then another Graham cracker. And you will want "some more," as the Girl Scouts say. If you get tired of the chocolate, use slices of apple, pineapple or peanut butter instead.

. . . .

Well before the military conflict between Israel and Egypt broke out later in 1956, Mrs. Roosevelt tried to persuade Eisenhower's foreign policy analysts to see the tensions there as involving not just Mideast countries squabbling over land rights but as by-products of the interaction of much larger forces from outside the region: Soviet and American intentions and claims concerning the Suez Canal, access to oil, and general political influence. She recognized the Mideast tensions as a tinderbox, dangerously awaiting a spark to ignite it.

NEW YORK, FEBRUARY 24—I anxiously await our government's realization that this whole Near East problem is not just an Arab–Israeli dispute but a problem of the influence of the West as opposed to that of the Soviets. We want no wars, but we do not want a Sovietized world. We would like to have people develop their own forms of government, make changes in their mode of life without dominance by outside influence and pressure.

We would like to see the people move forward to a better economic status for the betterment of the whole world. We would like to see the Soviet Union develop in its own way in its own areas. We would like to see it allow freedom to the rest of the world, to develop as they wish.

But the Soviets, wherever they can, exert influence. They do this not only by persuasion but frequently through gaining control in many ways. This is a menace to those of us who wish to live in a free world.

Israel is the one place in the Near East where we can be sure that life is being made worth living and where freedom will be fought for. Therefore, it should be of special interest to the United States. For if, in the long run, Israel remains free, the whole Near East may remain free. At the same time, our oil interests will be better protected in free Arab countries that are developing themselves than in Arab countries under Soviet domination.

. . . .

Though Eleanor Roosevelt was not so saintly that she never took potshots at presidents in office or in retirement when she thought their

. . . .

policies needed amending, she was consistently deferential toward all First Ladies, past and present, Democratic or Republican, and First Daughters as well. One of her favorites was Margaret Truman, whose recently published memoirs began to tell the story of her own experience as a private and public person—a theme Mrs. Roosevelt knew all too well.

NEW YORK, MARCH 9—There is a charmingly told story in Good Housekeeping called "Margaret Truman's Own Story." It is simple and straightforward and Margaret comes out as the very nice child she certainly must have been. No wonder her father and mother adore her.

Some of the stories she tells—and they are told with humor—are most entertaining. What she says of her father and mother is said with the warm devotion of one who was a happy child.

She certainly is one of the few children of her generation who was born at home, not in a hospital. All of my children were born at home, too, and I have the same feeling that it really was a distinction not to arrive in this world in the impersonal confines of a hospital. I hope my children agree!

So much that Margaret tells of the routine of her early life sounds like it belongs to a generation older than hers. That habit of driving out to Sunday dinner with grandmother was a regular one when I was young, too.

Margaret Truman's story of Christmas is particularly charming. And the practice of preserving Christmas-tree ornaments is one which I think, too, must belong to a generation ahead of Margaret's.

I added some new decorations from Sweden the year that I went there with my son, Elliott, and his two older children. And two years ago his daughter, Chandler, made me some lovely white-spangled balls to hang on the Christmas tree. But I still preserve the little ceramic figures representing the Holy Family. They always have had their place under the Christmas-tree branches.

One can see from Margaret's story how difficult it must have been for her to get accustomed to Washington after the easy life in Independence, Mo. But Margaret Truman is adaptable today, probably because she had to be adaptable in her early youth.

There is, of course, much of history in these memoirs. And as they go on there may be more, but seen from the viewpoint of the daughter of the man who was making it. I think this will be a real addition to her father's memoirs, for here one gets the feeling of the family life and the background of a Senator and, finally, a President.

The clear sense that the desegregation struggle would be a long and protracted one comes through in this column about the early boycotts of buses with "whites only" sections in Alabama. Easy as it was to articulate the humane logic of a change in racial policies and habits of thought, Mrs. Roosevelt knew that it would be years, if not decades, before the structure of customs and laws that kept segregation in place could be thoroughly revised. As a guideline, she consistently recommended the same course of action that would soon be recognized also as Dr. Martin Luther King, Jr.'s—nonviolent, passive resistance to segregation.

NEW YORK, MARCH 12—I think everyone must be impressed by the dignity and calmness with which the boycott of the bus companies in Montgomery, Alabama, has been carried on by the Negroes. Gandhi's theory of nonviolence seems to have been learned very well.

I would also like to speak in praise of those white people in the South who have long fought for the rights of all their fellow citizens. They are probably being made to suffer more than any of us in the North can imagine at the present time. I am interested to find that there is even a group of University of Alabama students who want to know how they can restore sanity to their fellow students. They do not regard with fear the admission to the undergraduate body of one young woman, and they deplore the methods used to keep her out.

I feel Miss Autherine Lucy has behaved with a great deal of dignity. She has apparently not enjoyed the publicity which the NAACP has thrust upon her; but she has acted with quiet dignity both in Washington and in New York, and her attitude gives one confidence that if she can be given a chance in the university she will act with wisdom and discretion.

Personally, I would like to see not one student but ten admitted. Also, if there are others at the present time that the university is considering, it would be well to bring their consideration to a rapid close and accept these students, as well as to rescind their foolish refusal to permit this rather gentle and mild young woman from returning to the university.

The Supreme Court recognized that there must be local adjustment in certain states in desegregation of the schools. They placed good faith in moving forward in the hands of the courts, and we must wait to see how this progresses. But there is nothing which prevents the Administration in Washington from moving at once in the area of protection for all citizens who desire to vote. In many states, this means paying a poll tax. That in itself may make voting difficult in some cases and really requires two campaigns:—(1) to get people to pay their tax, and (2) actually to get them to the polls.

No matter how many promises the NAACP wishes to extract from candidates at the present time, nothing can be achieved of real value for the coming ten months except by the Republican party and the Republican administration, since they are now in power. The question now being addressed to Democratic candidates might much better be addressed to the President of the United States. He can act, and where he cannot act he can ask Congress to give him the power to do so, or to give it to his Department of Justice. I think it is fair to ask any candidate what his position is. But I think it is a waste of time, if you want something done in the next few months, not to concentrate your continuing efforts on the only people who can actually do anything—the President and his administration.

. . . .

One of the quiet heroes of the 1950s was Edward R. Morrow, the television news journalist. Television broadcast journalism was still young, and there were few truly successful models for anyone to follow when taking on unusually complex or sensitive subjects. But, tempered by his wartime radio news reporting and gifted with an inner confidence and razor-sharp mind, Morrow was eminently well suited for the difficult task of covering foreign affairs broadcasting. Mrs. Roosevelt by this time had appeared on television frequently enough to realize the ways that pressure created by the technical demands of production could interfere with clear thinking by the reporters. She admired anyone (but Morrow especially) who could remain an island of calm in the turbulent seas of excitable interviewees and anxious television directors.

NEW YORK, MARCH 16—I watched with great interest Tuesday night Edward R. Morrow's remarkable television presentation of the Egyptian and Israeli situations. Abdel Gamal Nasser, the Egyptian prime minister, was somewhat more flexible in his thinking than one of two of the Egyptian refugees who were interviewed.

But I found Ben-Gurion, the Israeli premier, a much milder and more appealing gentleman than Mr. Nasser. He seemed to have a mellowness which, perhaps, comes with age.

The disturbing thing, of course, was that the Egyptians repeated points of view which I do not think can be upheld by the facts, though I don't question for a minute that they believe them. The Israelis, of course, took opposing views.

For instance, I think it can be proved that the refugees who left Israel during the war did not leave just because the Israelis were dropping bombs on their homes and had committed atrocities.

. . . .

In war, atrocities are committed on both sides, and I think it can be proved that the Mufti in Jerusalem broadcast the appeal that the Arabs leave temporarily, with the promise that they would be back within a few weeks.

I think it also can be proved that the lorries which took them out were furnished by the British. It also is probable that certain Arab sheiks remained in Israel, together with other Arabs who still live there, for they have eight representatives in the Knesset (parliament) today.

It is true that these Arabs, as a minority, are not entirely happy within the borders of Israel. Life is hard there, and a few complain of being detained in an old walled city north of Haifa and of having their land taken away from them. I did not visit this city, but if injustice is being done, the representatives of these people could bring the complaints before parliament.

I sympathize with those who want to return to their own land and their own homes. But they must know that this land is occupied largely by refugees from other Arab countries and that their homes have been wiped out.

I understand the deep pull that their own land has for the Arabs. But war always brings dislocation and hardship, and it seems to me they must accommodate themselves and stop looking backward. They must start looking forward to the best they can do under the new conditions.

. . . .

She had natural instincts for the ritual rhythms of springtime shopping for something fresh to wear, but she had as well a single-minded passion for leadership in the political and social areas where few women had dared to work. Eleanor Roosevelt was completely comfortable with the blend in her personality of the ordinary and the unique.

NEW YORK, MARCH 20—One almost expects blizzards early in March, but this one was a little late.

And since Friday was a difficult day to get around on the streets of New York, I decided to go out and buy myself a spring hat! I bought two of them, in fact, in Sally Victor's and I hope that by April, when I finally receive them, the weather will not resemble that of last weekend.

Saturday morning I gave a short speech on "The Changing Role of Women in the Modern World." This subject seems to be one that is growing in interest. It perhaps has particular value at the present time, since women are playing a larger and larger part in developing areas in many countries. So this is a good subject for study by women all over the world.

. . . .

89

It wasn't just the fact that President Woodrow Wilson had been a Democrat that made Mrs. Roosevelt sing his praises in later years. She had her doubts, as many Americans did in hindsight, about his handling of America's delayed entrance into World War I, though she blamed the Germans for almost everything in that war. Yet her highest praise for Wilson concerned his postwar efforts to secure passage in Congress of the treaty creating the League of Nations, a task at which he failed and a labor that, finally, exhausted him. Looked at through the lens of Eleanor Roosevelt's now eleven-year-long commitment to the United Nations, an institution she saw as the only hope for peace among all nations and which she no doubt suspected could have done much to prevent World War II had it been in place, Wilson's efforts on behalf of the ill-fated League appeared to her all the more heroic.

NEW YORK, MARCH 21—This year is the 100th anniversary of Woodrow Wilson's birth and various meetings are being held and lectures being given in his memory.

But there is one memorial which I think many people will be particularly anxious to have a part in, and that is the Woodrow Wilson Memorial in the Washington, D.C., Cathedral.

In early March, the last of the cut stone arrived from Indiana to complete the beautiful little chapel, which is more than half built. The intricate carving remains to be done, the marble floor still must be designed and laid and the tomb installed.

It is hoped that the chantry chapel be in readiness for the memorial service on November 11 this year, when it will be dedicated.

An appeal has come to me asking that friends, and particularly those who hold Woodrow Wilson's memory in respect, will send in contributions to swell the funds which so far have been raised. These funds as yet cover only about half the cost and the Cathedral is anxious to see the full amount raised this spring, if possible.

I think President Wilson would have liked to feel that as many of his fellow citizens as possible had a part in this memorial, for he loved the Cathedral and would have taken pride and comfort in the feeling that a chapel there would be built and used as a memorial to him.

Much that has happened for the benefit of our citizens in later years stemmed from Woodrow Wilson's administration. It is fitting, I think, that his 100th anniversary should be remembered in this way.

. . . .

Clear evidence that the child within Eleanor was still very much alive in her seventy-first year appears in a column telling about her reaction to a freak snowstorm that brought New York City to a standstill.

NEW YORK, MARCH 22—On Sunday afternoon I went out to speak in the evening in Englewood, N.J. A car came for me and we simply crawled the whole way. But the car was heavy and the driver was excellent, managing to keep control so that we did not go too fast down the hills.

I arrived on time to find that, in spite of the snowstorm, a full attendance was present for the dinner. The only thing that worried me was how, in returning, I could climb the hills I had come down. Another route was suggested to my driver and he took it successfully, bringing us back safely at about 11:30 P.M.

With my usual passion for fresh air at night—which, I am told, is quite out of fashion now—I could not resist opening a window before retiring and at 6:00 A.M. I awoke to find that the snowstorm was in my bedroom!

I got up and found a dustpan and pail, filling the pail with snow over and over again until my poor maid woke up and put the finishing touches on my efforts to remove the outdoors from my bedroom. Everything within reach of the snow was soaked, and from then on I kept my window closed!

I was supposed to go to Philadelphia for the whole day on Monday, for both lunch and dinner speeches. So I decided that if I could do nothing else, I could walk to 59th Street, get a subway and then shuttle across to Pennsylvania Station.

But the Pennsylvania Railroad would give me no assurance that the trains would be on time going over or coming back. At the same time, it occurred to me that in this weather there would be no audience in Philadelphia, so I called those in charge there and they promptly agreed, asking me to give them a "snow" check for later on.

I had a free day! Such a wonderful thing!

First, I took my little Scotty, who loves the snow, for a walk. Then I did all the dictating that has been accumulating for months, some reading, wrote letters, talked on the telephone with my snowbound son, Franklin Jr., on his farm. I also talked with my son Johnny, who had managed to get out of Hyde Park and catch a train down, but the rest of his family was snowbound in Hyde Park.

I called my office and asked if they really needed me and, if so, I could have walked there, if necessary. But I was allowed to stay home.

Then I was told that a grandson was marooned, unable to fly or catch a train to join his family in Florida, and I was asked if he could stay with me. Of course, I was delighted to have him.

All of this was pleasant, but I wish the snow were gone.

The superintendent of our building has just told me there is no oil for the furnace and we will have no heat except from our two fireplaces!

I mildly protest that the oil should be allowed to get so low, but we are fortunate to have fireplaces and wood!

....

The next day's column went back to serious business and to a theme Mrs. Roosevelt took up many times in the years after the war: resettlement of refugees. Though Israel could easily claim Mrs. Roosevelt as its most loyal and active American supporter outside the Jewish group itself, that loyalty by no means blinded her to the needs of Arab refugees, many of whom were in their sad state as a result of Israeli military and political actions. While expressing concern for these refugees, she also tried once again to suggest political solutions to the apparently endless Arab–Israeli conflict.

NEW YORK, MARCH 23—I have an anonymous letter which asks me what is being done by the United Nations about the plight of the nearly one million Arab refugees of Israeli aggression.

Isn't it astonishing how many mistakes can creep into one sentence!

There are 800,000 refugees who are being cared for by the United Nations and have been cared for since, during the war, their own Moslem mufti in Jerusalem called upon the Arabs in Israel to leave.

Israel was not the aggressor in this war. The Arabs were the aggressors. The partition of Palestine and the creation of the State of Israel was the result of UN action.

The Arabs did not accept the new state. So Israel fought and gained more land, holding it by defeating her Arab attackers.

The Arabs who did not heed the call of the mufti and leave Israel during the war are still living in there. As a minority, they have certain grievances. But, by and large, with eight representatives in the Knesset (the parliament), they have a voice, as citizens of Israel, to demand redress for their wrongs.

No one can blame the poor people who left Israel. They were told that in a few weeks they would be back and would receive not only their own land and belongings but that of the Israelis, who would be driven into the sea.

Unfortunately for the Arabs, this did not come to pass. Israel remained a state and those poor refugees were the saddest and most miserable people I have seen in any refugee camps.

The worst of their plight was that, being in Arab countries where they didn't want to feel they were permanently settled, they were not even allowed to find jobs to keep up their skills, to set up work within the refugee camps for this purpose or to train young people.

Whenever a few people were settled and left the camp, people seeped in from the desert overnight. This was because the food in these camps

....

was better than what they could obtain through their own efforts outside. This sounds incredible, but the head of the authority, who was an American, told me this when I visited these camps.

So the United Nations has done all it could to care for these people, who are victims of the Arab government's decision that they should leave Israel. Every effort should be made now to resettle those who can return to Israel. The rest should be indemnified and settled where they are needed in Arab countries.

In large part, these people's homes in Israel have disappeared and their possessions are no longer there. The face of the land has changed because Israel has taken in thousands of refugees from other Arab countries who now occupy most of the land.

I was never so sorry for any refugees in my life as I was for these poor people. But war always brings hardships and injustices and people always suffer for what governments have done.

The Israelis did not instigate aggression and they did win that war.

The most friendly things that have been said concerning the Arabs appeared in an editorial in Life magazine last week and I suggest the sender of this letter read that editorial. Then he will recognize the fact that both Arabs and Israelis have made many mistakes, both are the friends of the United States as far as we are concerned, but that the basic mistake is that the United Nation's creation of the state of Israel was not accepted by the Arabs from the start. It will have to be accepted in the long run.

In the meantime, much has been lost that might have gone into constructive improvement of the life of the people in Israel and the Arab states. And refugee camps still are not wiped out.

. . . .

On the tail end of the late-March snowstorm Eleanor Roosevelt went home to Hyde Park for the Easter week-end. In an unusually relaxed mood she enjoys commenting on New Yorkers' Easter finery and then indulges herself in a universal week-end pleasure: sitting before an open fire.

HYDE PARK, APRIL 2—I returned to New York right after lunch and arrived in time to make a train up to Poughkeepsie at 6:25. There is still snow on the ground and it is hard to believe that Easter is here. In New York, my taxicab driver insisted that the people would be out in all their finery in the city on Easter Sunday. When I suggested that it might be too cold, the answer came at once: "These New Yorkers will wear their finery anyway."

I am afraid that up here in the country, however, I am not going to be very springlike, for it seems to me much too cold to go out in

. . . .

any new finery. But perhaps I will overcome my backwardness and wear my new straw Easter bonnet.

I found my cousin, Mrs. Forbes Morgan, here with the two children when I arrived. More of our friends will arrive during the day, but I am afraid there is not very much in the country even for children to do just at the present time. There are no winter sports, yet enough snow on the ground to keep you from walking comfortably in the woods; and we can't do any of the things which we will do once spring is really here, such as putting the tennis court in order. Actually, the only reason we come to the country just now is to rest, to sit in front of an open fire and read a book or sleep through a good part of an afternoon. Those are the real reasons for whatever time you spend in the country at this season. Shortly, however, I hope we can see the snow melt away and a few of the early spring flowers come up. Then the busy planting time will be here and we can begin to plan for the summer flowers.

....

A year before his death, Admiral Richard Byrd, polar explorer and author, was feted at a gala dinner in New York. Ever since the expeditions into the Wild West by the likes of Lewis and Clark and before the explorations of outer space by astronauts, opportunities for anyone truly to be an explorer on earth were limited. Byrd found his niche in the pantheon of explorer heroes with exploits concerning both the north and south poles, with flights over both and travel to the poles on the icecaps as well. His career in daring exploration had begun in the mid-1920s, and Mrs. Roosevelt had followed it admiringly. FDR was assistant secretary of the navy from 1913 until 1920 and kept a particularly strong interest in naval affairs throughout the rest of his life. He too thought Admiral Byrd was outstanding. Both Roosevelts recognized the important role inspiring heroes play in the national memory.

NEW YORK, APRIL 5—On Tuesday evening I went to the dinner given by the International Rescue Committee in honor of Admiral Richard Evelyn Byrd, who just returned from his latest Antarctic expedition.

Admiral Byrd is honorary chairman of the IRC, which was founded in 1933 as a voluntary American organization to aid escapees from dictatorship, terror and oppression. It has a very strong board.

There was a large attendance at the dinner, even though it unfortunately was held at the same time the Overseas Press Club was giving its dinner at which former President Harry S. Truman spoke.

The dinner for Admiral Byrd opened with an address by Angier Biddle Duke, with Leo Cherne, chairman of the IRC, presiding. Richard C. Patterson, New York City's commissioner of commerce and

....

public events, represented the mayor in presenting the medal to Admiral Byrd for distinguished service to science and the world.

As Admiral Arleigh Arthur Burke reviewed Admiral Byrd's whole career, I remembered the boy we knew so many years ago when my husband was Assistant Secretary of the Navy and Richard E. Byrd was a graduate of the Navy Academy who, because of an injured knee, was threatened with retirement from the service.

I can remember his joy when his knee soon healed and he was returned to active service, and recall many of the good times we had together.

My husband and I once gave a fancy dress party to which all the guests were invited to come dressed as characters out of books. Young Richard E. Byrd had no way of getting a costume so, prophetic as it may have been, I dressed him up as one of the Gilbert and Sullivan opera "admirals."

None of us knew what fate held for him then, but certainly no one has had a more fruitful and satisfactory life. Even now there is something of the young man about him. But I must say that Mrs. Byrd looks even younger than he does and is much the same person whom I knew as a young woman—gentle, self-effacing, disliking publicity, but pretty and full of charm and tact.

....

About once a year Eleanor Roosevelt took up the broad issues of curriculum reform in the nation's schools in a "My Day" column. Concerning school issues such as equal opportunity for all races, or for girls and women, or fair wages for teachers, she was resolutely on the liberal side of the argument. However, when it came to the question of subjects to be taught, Mrs. Roosevelt usually took what later would be seen as a conservative position—conservative in the sense that traditional subjects should not, in her view, be lightly tossed aside in favor of trendy but less useful material. Foreign languages, ancient and modern, seemed to her essential ingredients in the educated mind. She was a lover of clear expression, logical debate, the well-written paragraph; it is no wonder that she defended the status of Latin and Greek in the schools. Such training had been part of her education and that of her children. She saw no reason in the contemporary world to make a change.

New York, April 10—I have a letter of protest concerning my statement a short time ago that French was being taught badly in our public schools, colleges and universities.

The writer of the letter points out that I remarked that an audience I was in could understand a French play and insists that this was true

....

because "the methods of teaching French and other languages have undergone a remarkable revolution in the course of the last few years."

I am delighted to hear that such is the case but sad when told that fewer and fewer young Americans are taking any foreign language at all at the elementary level.

I think that any young American, understanding how rapidly the world is being drawn closer and closer together, should take at least two languages as well as his own. French should be studied because it is spoken by many people around the world, nearly as many as speak English. And the student should take another language—the native tongue of the country he or she may be interested in and hopes to visit.

Incidentally, I think Latin and Greek provide valuable background for nearly all modern languages, and if I were young today, I would take both of these, as well as the modern languages!

. . . .

Commenting on one of the numerous books that tried to capture the essence of her remarkable life (Eleanor Roosevelt books for both children and adults are still in print in several languages), Mrs. Roosevelt shared with her readers her sense of humor about the past. One suspects that among the qualities in Eleanor's personality that kept her young at the age of seventy-one was her ability to laugh at herself.

HYDE PARK, APRIL 14—I had completely forgotten the photograph of me when I was five years old which the library seems to have preserved. And the thing that amuses me most about it is the absurd clothes that we wore as children.

I have thought some of this year's hats are ridiculous, but as I look at some of the hats I wore in previous years, I realize they were just as ridiculous. And even the way we did our hair then seems absurd at the present time.

Men have an easier time. Styles, in hair or in clothes, don't change so much for them!

. . . .

Was there no cause too humble to deserve Mrs. Roosevelt's support? She traveled the entire globe to meet with national leaders, great artists, and thinkers, always in search of ways to make a contribution to peace. And she also took a little trip to Bayside, Long Island (in the New York City borough of Queens) to lend her support to a Cub Scout program. Eleanor Roosevelt saw such activities for children as character-building for them, as good stepping stones toward responsible citizenship. In her

. . . .

view, parental and neighborly help for the Scouts was just as important as anything she might have done at the United Nations.

The same column gave her readers a glowing report on the biggest hit play of the Broadway season. Mrs. Roosevelt had little enough time for the theater, but My Fair Lady was to become one of the few shows she ever saw twice.

John Golden was a theater producer and friend of the Roosevelts.

NEW YORK, MAY 3—Sunday afternoon I went out to Bayside, Long Island, to see a small group of Cub Scouts given their charter and their flag. This little pack is named after John Golden, who helped to start it because of his great sympathy for retarded children who never before had an opportunity to join in scouting.

It is a pilot project but it seems to be working out very well. It was a touching ceremony and one, I hope, that might be repeated for the many handicapped youngsters in other communities.

In the evening I was taken by a friend to see "My Fair Lady." Shaw's "Pygmalion" has been made into a delightful musical comedy, starring Rex Harrison and Julie Andrews.

Moss Hart staged the production and I wonder how he managed to make it so nostalgic to those of us who think back with joy to Gertrude Lawrence in "The King and I" and to "South Pacific."

Somehow I kept being reminded of both productions and wishing that John Golden could be here to see this perfectly delightful and enchanting musical, which I am sure he would have enjoyed as much as I did.

. . . .

During the years of Eleanor Roosevelt's close involvement in American political life, she listened to and trusted completely only a handful of sagacious commentators and advisers. One was Chester Bowles, whom she knew from New Deal days. After the war he served as director of the Price Stabilization Board; he became chairman of the International Advisory Committee for the United Nations Appeal for Children, then governor of Connecticut, and in 1951 the United States' ambassador to India. Bowles knew life at the top rungs of society and at the bottom, and his thoughts about the American racial problem struck Mrs. Roosevelt as eminently sensible. Her own analysis of the American dilemma, as sociologist Gunnar Myrdal called it, included a not-too-subtle reminder to segregationists that nearly a full century had already passed since emancipation. Patience, she warned, does not last forever.

HYDE PARK, MAY 5—I was rereading on Wednesday evening an article written for The New York Times magazine of February 7, 1954, by

. . . .

Chester Bowles. It was called "The Negro, Progress and Challenge" and in it Bowles brought out one of the basic factors in the solution of the racial problem in the United States.

On January 1, 1963, we will celebrate 100 years of emancipation of the Negro. In other words, we are very near the 100-year mark, and that is a long time—if we really mean to carry out Lincoln's Emancipation Proclamation—to correct the evils of slavery and prove to the world that we really do believe in equality of all human beings.

Of course, equality is conditioned by the gifts that God gave us, and all that human beings can do is to refrain from creating inequalities of opportunity which prevent people from rightfully reaching their full development.

White people do not attain the same conditions of either intellectual or material achievements, but they do not spend their lives battling man-made discrimination. We know that there is the opportunity to develop that which we have within us and that no one will turn against us because of our race, religion or color.

In this article, Bowles brought out that the future of the white peoples of the world well may hang on our ability to solve the racial problem in the United States and that time for this is running out.

One hundred years is a long time to wait. Our Negro citizens have been patient beyond belief. The question that so many of us have been asked over and over again, "Do you believe the Negro as capable of development as the white man?" should be answered once and for all with "I do believe that, given the same opportunity with discrimination removed, the Negro is as capable of achieving any standard of success."

God has not put any more limitations on the Negro than he has on the rest of us. But man-made circumstances perhaps have made it more difficult for him to develop his potentialities. These circumstances men can change.

The other question often asked is: "Would you like your daughter to marry a Negro?"

Intermarriage of races does not of necessity follow the granting of equal opportunity, for marriage is purely a personal matter. But I think we must face the fact that, while people of the same color and race generally prefer to marry each other, there have been mixtures of races just as there have been mixtures of religions, and no one can either prevent them or make them successful or unsuccessful. This is one of those things time alone can resolve, with the individuals themselves making the decisions.

For the people of this country, the question is whether they can continue to exist without giving all citizens full equality before the law and equal dignity as human beings. We must make this decision and upon it depends our whole future and that of white peoples everywhere.

....

The civil rights struggle of the 1950s and 1960s brought forth some great leaders and some embarrassing scoundrels whose names and egos filled news reports across the nation. But much of the real work in winning recognition for equal rights for black people was done by strong-willed, courageous, intelligent folk who otherwise made no claim to fame. One such heroine was Rosa Parks, the black woman who started the successful Montgomery, Alabama, boycott to force the bus company there to allow blacks to sit anywhere whites could sit on the city buses. Quite probably, from Mrs. Roosevelt's viewpoint, it was she who was having an interview with a powerful person, not the other way around.

NEW YORK, MAY 14—A few days ago I met Mrs. Rosa Parks, who started the nonviolent protest in Montgomery, Alabama, against segregation on buses. She is a very quiet, gentle person and it is difficult to imagine how she ever could take such a positive and independent stand.

I suppose we must realize that these things do not happen all of a sudden. They grow out of feelings that have been developing over many years. Human beings reach a point when they say: "This is as far as I can go," and from then on it may be passive resistance, but it will be resistance.

That is what seems to have happened in Montgomery, and perhaps it will happen all over our country wherever we have citizens who do not enjoy complete equality. It may be that this attitude will save us from war and bloodshed and teach those of us who have to learn that there is a point beyond which human beings will not continue to bear injustice.

....

A continuing dilemma in the debate about the Second World War was the question of whether using the atomic bomb against the Japanese had been morally justifiable. No one doubted that it did, indeed, help significantly to bring the war to a rapid conclusion after years of seemingly endless killing. At the same time, the bombs dropped on Hiroshima and Nagasaki did considerably more short- and long-term damage than even the most optimistic physicists and generals had predicted. Had it been a case of illegitimate overkill?

Mrs. Roosevelt received a steady stream of mail from the "kooks," mail she usually ignored publicly. And, from time to time an apparently radical opinion would appear even in the mainstream publications sent to her. Such was the stimulus of the following column, about the atomic bombs and the guilt Americans presumably should feel. Mrs. Roosevelt tried to resolve the dilemma by re-examining the facts, by seeing that President Truman hardly had any other choice, and by putting some emphasis on the obligation Americans had in the postwar years to help rebuild the two targeted Japanese cities.

HYDE PARK, MAY 31—I was surprised to see an article from The Pilot, an official publication of the Catholic Archdiocese of Boston, reprinted in large quantities and sent out by the American Friends Service Committee of Cambridge, Mass., entitled "I Confess."

The article was reprinted with the permission of the editor of The Pilot, America's oldest Catholic weekly newspaper, and, therefore, editorial boards of both the newspaper and the Friends Service committee seem to have approved it.

It was written some time ago marking the anniversary, August 6, of the day ten years before when we dropped the first atomic bomb on the city of Hiroshima, Japan.

The purpose of the article is to say that the American people and their leaders who were responsible for dropping the bomb on Hiroshima, and on Nagasaki the following day, should have confessed their "guilt" long ago.

It goes on to say that the people of Asia feel that much of the aid we have given them since that time came from a feeling of guilt, but that until we confessed this guilt, nothing would be of any avail.

I would like to review the circumstances which led up to this first use of the atomic bomb.

Our military people were almost ready for the last stage of the war, which was the actual attack on Japan. They had counted the costs such an attack would have involved—at least a million lives of American soldiers in addition to complete destruction of as much of Japan as would have been defended. This would have meant cities, towns, villages, men, women and children, for modern war is no longer a war between soldiers; it is a war between peoples.

Because of the plea of one of our American art lovers, we never had bombed two of the historically beautiful cities in Japan, Kyoto and Nara. These, of course, would have had to be destroyed.

All of these facts were presented to the President. In addition, he was told that one bomb would not be sufficient. Two, in quick succession, were our only hope of bringing about complete and rapid surrender. The reason for this was that we had people who had seen the defenses in Japan and they reported that these were so strong it was not believed possible for any army to penetrate to the interior.

So the only possible chance was to deal the Japanese such tremendous blows that they would realize that if they wanted to save themselves from complete destruction, they must surrender at once.

I think everyone in this country should have a horror of the conditions which brought about the need for using the atomic bomb. They should have grief and pity for the people affected and do all in their power to help the innocent who suffer.

But if you had to make this decision, I do not think any decision could have been made other than the one that was made. Leaflets were dropped over Hiroshima before the attack, warning the people to leave the city, and the same thing was done at Nagasaki. But it is human nature to stay where you are and not believe the worst until it happens.

I would not confess guilt for the American people or their leaders, only pity and a deep desire to aid those who suffered through no fault of their own and certainly through no fault of the American people and their leaders.

....

A day's work for Eleanor Roosevelt often ranged fluidly over personal and family matters, local political issues, larger international concerns, and sometimes (usually in her writing or speeches) reached far back or far forward in time as she tried to articulate where we have come from and where we are heading. She had what a later generation would call a global vision. It was not an abstract concept; it grew out of years of personal interaction with people from all walks of life, from all corners of the globe. Here is a "My Day" report on one such day's worth of work and play.

HYDE PARK, JUNE 19—The meeting of the African groups at New York's International House on Friday morning seemed to be very successful and those participating told me they all enjoyed hearing Chester Bowles the day before. Their motto is "Unity in the Family of Man," and I was particularly impressed by the type of questions asked me.

We Americans have much to learn about other peoples of the world, and I think we know less about those on the African continent than anywhere else. It is impressive and encouraging to find so many of their students over here and able to compete on a high intellectual level with our own, in spite of differences in their educational backgrounds, particularly when they come from the areas of South Africa.

The young woman who came for me was from South Africa and had been in this country for two years. No one could have asked for a more charming, gracious and poised person, and her introduction of me as the speaker of the morning was beautifully done.

....

As I left International House, I drove straight to Hyde Park where everything is now lush and green, perhaps even more beautiful for the slowness of spring. We have jumped quickly into summer. I picked rhubarb and asparagus Saturday morning in the garden, and many flowers are beginning to be available for the house.

At teatime, Abdul Sbihi from Morocco came with his daughter, who is studying in this country and will return to her homeland next autumn. Several other persons were with them and all spent a little time with me before going over to the Memorial Library to lay a wreath on my husband's grave.

Dr. Nyozekan Hasegawa, an 80-year-old Japanese professor, in this country on the cultural exchange program sponsored by Columbia University, came with his interpreter for dinner and to spend the night.

The children were fascinated by the Japanese kimono he wore and the way he wore his hair, which made him look somewhat like our own Walt Whitman. He told us he once was called the Japanese version of Tagore, the Indian poet.

We found him an altogether delightful person and only wished he could have stayed longer, but on Monday morning he left for New York after I had taken him over to the Library.

Dr. Yasaka Takagi persuaded Dr. Hasegawa to come for the visit, and the latter has the same gentle philosophy and charming approach to life which endears Dr. Takagi himself to everyone.

The interpreter who came with him from Japan was taken ill Sunday. He is 30 years younger than Dr. Hasegawa, and the professor twinkled when he mentioned this difference in age.

Dr. Hasegawa has a delightful sense of humor and was particularly pleased to see my youngest granddaughter, Joan, at breakfast. But she would not approach him very closely, being, I think, awed by his hair and his clothes!

He told us that when he was young he hated to go to the barber, so he found a way that he could cut his own hair and he never has been to the barber since!

. . . .

Not long before this column appeared, Mrs. Roosevelt had commented on the stabbing of a Brooklyn teacher by a girl student, from a girl gang, to the effect that the teacher had probably provoked the assault. A torrent of criticism rained down upon her for failing to see how morally depraved the girl's attack had been. In this second attempt to deal with the ugly incident, she yields somewhat to the more conventional view that the girl's social background and domestic life must have been largely at fault. But Eleanor Roosevelt does not here succumb to the temptation of assuming that such a crime could only have been committed by

. . . .

someone whose mind and soul were irreversibly depraved. She was too much a liberal optimist to believe that such a criminal could not be helped.

HYDE PARK, JULY 27—It is shocking to hear of girl gangs committing murder, and for two high schools in Brooklyn, N.Y., to have gangs that actually fight each other seems to me an extraordinary situation.

A few weeks ago I wrote of a teacher who was beaten up by a student and I said that I felt that the teacher was partially to blame. I have had a number of letters telling me that it is outrageous to hold the teacher to blame in a situation of this kind, and that if I were a teacher in the public schools today, I would know that the homes are to blame and that there are incorrigible children who cannot be controlled either in school or at home.

My writers say that these pupils are just "bad children."

I did not make it clear that I think one of the things in which every teacher should be trained is careful observation of the children in her classes, from the very early years. Psychiatrists say that many young children need psychiatric help and the future difficulties could be obviated if they received help when they were at that age.

This does not mean that every teacher must be a psychiatrist. It means, however, that neither the teacher nor the mother must be afraid to face the fact that a child found backward or difficult to handle may need care and understanding beyond what they themselves are able to give.

There is real responsibility on parents and teachers to report symptoms of trouble in children as early as possible. With the older children, whom my correspondents seem to consider beyond control, I think the teacher, in her dealings with her pupils, has some responsibility in finding those who are uncontrollable and reporting them immediately.

The head of the school who does not at once have such a child examined is also negligent, because I question how many "bad" children there are.

Without question, there are sick children. These girls forming gangs and committing murders are sick children who should have been reported long ago.

I realize that it takes courage for a mother to say her child seems to be behaving badly. She does not want to suggest that there is anything abnormal, or emotionally or mentally wrong, with her child. But it is a good deal better to face the facts before a crime is committed than to have to acknowledge it afterward.

It is even harder for a teacher to report a child, but at least she has the support of the people above her, and they have a responsibility to the community which they cannot well escape.

I have been told that it is not uncommon for youngsters of 12 and 13 to think they are behaving in grown-up fashion if they can get some liquor and drink it. I don't think at that age anyone really enjoys liquor. But, in any case, the desire to ape one's elders is nothing new, and I believe if more honesty were practiced in the home and in the schools between the young people and their elders, some of these difficulties could be controlled.

It is when you set standards for youngsters and do not live up to them yourself that the youngsters begin to question the validity of the standards. I have been reading the manuscript of a book, which I will mention in a later column, and the author makes the point of this need for honesty between generations.

....

Mrs. Roosevelt agonized about a tough decision concerning the NAACP (National Association for the Advancement of Colored People). As a director of the group she sat on the board, whose membership records had been subpoenaed by a federal court in a suit brought by segregationists. The plaintiffs would have been happy to use those lists to identify NAACP members for public attack, either verbal or physical. Looking at this incident in Eleanor Roosevelt's political life, one can see easily why the Chinese expression "May you live in interesting times" is considered a curse.

NEW YORK, JULY 31—On Saturday I went to Washington for a few hours and then caught the train in the afternoon back to Hyde Park and our usual busy routine there.

As one of the directors of the National Association for the Advancement of Colored People, I was consulted on a very difficult situation created by the injunction against the NAACP in Alabama and the court order demanding that the membership lists for Alabama be produced in court Monday morning of this week. The judge imposed a $10,000 fine for contempt of court if these lists are not produced as specified, and the threat of a $100,000 fine also hangs over the organization.

It is a very difficult question between a legal duty, which in this country requires you to obey a court order, and a moral duty, which I think binds an organization not to put its membership in jeopardy.

In the present temper of "white citizens' councils" in certain Southern states and with the knowledge of what has been done by them, one realizes that those lists produced in court may put many people in a position where their economic situation and even their physical safety may be far from secure.

....

Under these circumstances what should an honorable group of people do? The majority, of course, will decide, but I find it a very difficult decision to make.

. . . .

It was a hot summer in the civil rights struggle. In one of the most dramatic demonstrations in American history of black outrage at white domination, an entire chain gang of black prisoners in Georgia revolted in a way that shocked even seasoned veterans of the political struggle. Eleanor Roosevelt was always concerned about the negative impact such ugly events on the American domestic scene would have on the country's image in the eyes of critical foreigners. This incident was one, she said, for which we could only feel shame.

HYDE PARK, AUGUST 2—That was a most shocking story in the Tuesday papers describing how criminals (36 inmates of Rock Quarry State Prison in Georgia) broke their legs with 10-pound sledgehammers in protest against working conditions. Mr. Forrester, the state director of correction, said the men were working at a rock quarry and he described them as "among the most hardened in Georgia."

Have you ever seen a chain gang in Georgia working along the road? Have you ever watched the men in charge of these road camps, with their whips and their pistols in their belts?

I still remember one man's face which I saw 20 years ago in one of these camps. I was more afraid of him than I was of the prisoners.

It is bad for any man to have complete control over another human being, and this whole system in Georgia is a bad system. Men do not inflict such pain and serious injury on themselves merely to get out of doing hard work. There must have been unbearable conditions. And we call ourselves advanced in our penal institutions!

. . . .

Into the hurly-burly of presidential politics once again: the Democratic National Convention, 1956. Eleanor Roosevelt at seventy-one was tough, observant, fast-moving, inexhaustible; just the kind of player Adlai Stevenson was glad to have on his team.

Shortly before going to Chicago to help engineer the Stevenson nomination, Mrs. Roosevelt and the rest of the country had been surprised by former President Truman, who announced he would support Averell Harriman, not Stevenson. Seasoned political observers reported that Eleanor Roosevelt's presentation at a press conference held immediately after she arrived from New York (a forty-five-minute conference in which she deftly put the Truman move in the background, brought Stevenson's stellar record out front, and shifted everyone's attention to the platform

. . . .

committee's fight over the civil rights plank) was a bravura one. One of Stevenson's top aides, Arthur Schlesinger, Jr. commented, "It was an adroit and ruthless performance."

Faye Emerson was son Elliott's third wife (1944–1950).

CHICAGO, AUGUST 15—The season of hurricanes seems to be upon us. I read in the Monday-morning paper that one they have named "Betsy" was on its way to Miami.

I could not help thinking that a convention, in a way, is somewhat like a hurricane. The lobbies of the hotel and the streets near the hotel are all jammed.

One poor, patient donkey has been outside the Sheraton-Blackstone, where I am staying, all day and probably a good part of the night, so I hope he can sleep, regardless of noise, standing up. The noise is deafening. At 6:00 A.M. yesterday morning a band was playing outside the hotel.

I am grateful for the fact that it is cool, though on Sunday afternoon from four to six o'clock Adlai Stevenson did not think so. He mopped his brow and seemed quite appalled by the crowds attending his reception. I think that, being less accustomed than I am to shaking many hands, he became more weary than I did as the people streamed by us.

Someone told me that there were at least 10,000 people at this reception. Certainly no other candidate can claim anything like the jam that surrounded us during those two hours.

I visited a number of delegations with Stevenson during the day and was happy to meet the people from Colorado and many other states.

We ended up with a big meeting of the Michigan delegation, and there I saw some familiar faces and enjoyed meeting again young Governor G. Mennen Williams. He was in his shirtsleeves, partly because of the heat and partly, I think, because he felt this was a working meeting and sooner or later they must get down to business, which was symbolized by shirtsleeves.

People keep asking me if women get into smoke-filled rooms at a convention. I have yet to find any room really smoke-filled. But I think the women at this convention are getting into all of the political caucuses in very great numbers.

A buffet supper was given Sunday evening by the Chicago host committee. It was a pleasant party and I also enjoyed going to the reception for House Speaker Sam Rayburn of Texas. There I saw my old friend, Senator Tom Connally, whom I had not seen for a long time; Senator Lyndon Johnson; Grace Tully and, as we were leaving, Governor Averell Harriman of New York.

Bright and early on Monday morning I was called for and driven out to Faye Emerson's television show, which took place outside the convention hall. I enjoyed being with her, but it was a rather windy day and I don't know how tidy our hair looked as we discussed politics and conventions in general, with considerable emphasis on this one!

I got back in time to visit the Stevenson headquarters, the National Democratic Committee headquarters and to attend the National Democratic Women's breakfast, at which some clever skits were given. Then I attended briefly the opening session of the convention and had lunch out there.

. . . .

After the convention and before the campaign itself got fully underway, Mrs. Roosevelt spent three weeks in Europe on another of her succession of grueling lecture tours, mixing AAUN and other work with an equally rigorous social schedule. With her were grandsons Johnny (John Roosevelt Boettinger), her daughter Anna's third child, born in 1939; and Haven (Haven Clark Roosevelt), her son John's second child, born in 1940.

ST. LO, FRANCE, SEPTEMBER 1—Our next stop was Omaha Beach, where one can still see some of the boats which were beached on D-Day. All the steel on them is being salvaged, but the hulks will remain until they disintegrate.

We visited the American cemetery there and the war memorial. I liked the memorial very much, but I still think the most impressive one I know is at Chateau-Thierry.

In the Omaha cemetery General Theodore Roosevelt, Jr., who was killed at Utah Beach, is buried, and the body of his youngest brother, Quentin, an aviator who died in 1918, has been brought from its former resting place to lie here beside his brother. The site of this cemetery is very beautiful and the planting of the flowers and the upkeep generally is well done.

The chapel is not yet quite finished but will be simple and beautiful when it is ready for use.

It seemed fitting that our soldiers should lie looking out over the sea they had to cross before they could help liberate this land, which had to be freed from Nazism to keep our own land free from the scourge of totalitarianism.

The directors in charge of the cemetery told me that about six or eight families of the boys buried there came every week during the summer to look at their graves.

But I am surprised that these cemeteries are not visited by many more Americans who aren't looking for particular graves but who want to see what is done to honor those who died to protect us all.

. . . .

I brought my grandsons there because I think all young Americans should not be allowed to forget the sacrifices of a previous generation and all of us should take an interest in seeing that the small organization which cares for the cemeteries and the battle monuments of our country is always supported with interest and affection.

....

In a quintessentially hard-nosed campaign-season column, Eleanor Roosevelt took on the top three players in the Republican administration: President Eisenhower, Vice President Nixon, and Secretary of State Dulles. Together, she argued, they had so badly botched U.S. foreign policy in recent years that even America's best allies, Britain and France, had taken to vetoing U.S. proposals in the UN Security Council. Stevenson would set things right again, if only the citizenry would vote him into office, and America would be proud.

Never one to simplify complex issues just for the sake of making a point, Mrs. Roosevelt nonetheless knew that in a political campaign there is little room for subtle thought. There are bad guys and there are good guys, and she wanted her readers to know which were which.

SAN FRANCISCO, NOVEMBER 2—Like most other persons in the country, I felt that the last few days have been painful, indeed. Every day the news from the Near East has been full of anxiety—anxiety for which we had not been prepared by the administration nor by the President himself, who only a week ago told us that the news from the Near East was good.

Most of us then had some misgivings but hoped that perhaps there might be some truth in what the President was saying. Our common sense told us, however, the situation could not be as rosy as we were led to believe.

The greatest shock came when a resolution presented by the United States in the United Nations Security Council was vetoed by the two most important allies of the United States—Great Britain and France. How could such a thing be?

It could not be possible that our Secretary of State had let our relationships so deteriorate with our closest allies and our most important friends that we were not aware they would veto our resolution!

It could not be possible that we would present such a resolution, knowing that we would find ourselves lined up with the Soviet Union and the dictator of Egypt, against Great Britain and France and the only democratic country in the Near East—Israel! What a false and confusing situation!

If we felt our allies' position was wrong, had we lost all our influence that they would not listen to us? Something must be seriously wrong.

....

Then on Wednesday morning I opened a metropolitan paper to see on the front page that our Secretary of State accused our allies, Great Britain and France, of having entered into an agreement and instigated Israel's latest action in Egypt.

Again my heart sank. Did we not know whether or not our allies had entered into any such an agreement with Israel? What had happened to our relations with these two important countries in the world?

Then I read that Vice President Richard M. Nixon said in a speech that now, of course, the people of this country would decide that they must keep a tried-and-true general as our leader and as our President because it would be unwise to change at this crucial time to untried and poor leadership.

I could not believe my eyes! How could we have had worse leadership than that which brought us to this present situation? Do we want to continue with the kind of leadership that has led to a war in which, if we are not with our old allies, we have to side with the Kremlin and the dictator of Egypt? What a decision to have to make!

Where has our influence, which ought to help shape such decisions in the world, failed so that we find ourselves today in such a position?

I listened to the President on television and noticed that he never mentioned a most important point, namely that the Kremlin has succeeded in dividing the West and we are, indeed, weakened. Does he not realize the seriousness of the situation he and John Foster Dulles have created?

I feel sure that every woman in this country will feel it her obligation to beg her friends and neighbors—men and women, young and old—to change this leadership as quickly as possible.

I think if we elect Adlai Stevenson and Estes Kefauver next Tuesday and give them the support in the Senate and the House which they need, we will not find ourselves unexpectedly in situations of this kind. We will have a leadership which, I hope, will give us a knowledge of what conditions really exist in the world and, therefore, will ensure greater security for us and for the world as a whole.

. . . .

After the crushing defeat Stevenson suffered at the hands of the Eisenhower–Nixon team, the gloom in the Democratic camp was thick. Never a sore loser, Mrs. Roosevelt was also a compassionate comrade who recognized that the defeated candidate needs and deserves friendly support. She admired Adlai Stevenson enormously and suffered his humiliation with him, as this report of a postelection visit to him attests.

A few days later her column contained a poke at the victorious Vice President. Such jibes at Mr. Nixon came along more and more fre-

. . . .

quently as his political stock began to rise and an eventual presidential bid of his own became more likely.

ST. CATHERINES, ONT., NOVEMBER 14—I left New York around noon Saturday for Chicago, where I made a talk in the evening and in the afternoon had the pleasure of visiting for a short time with Adlai Stevenson.

Stevenson has taken defeat as I knew he would—philosophically, with a long look into the past and into the future and with a greater interest in what will happen to the country and its people than in himself.

NEW YORK, NOVEMBER 20—No matter how fine certain people may think Vice President Richard M. Nixon is, I suppose it is permissible to say that I far prefer President Eisenhower.

. . . .

If Eleanor Roosevelt had had more administrative ability (something she herself confessed she lacked), she might have made a colorful, provocative Secretary of State. From her vantage point as journalist, as ex-United Nations delegate, and as former First Lady, she certainly saw the larger foreign policy issues broadly enough to feel secure in formulating a critique of the Eisenhower administration's activity in this realm. As tensions in the Mideast heated up, with British and French troops helping Israel in its struggle in the Sinai against Egypt, Mrs. Roosevelt believed that the Republican leaders were simply too tangled up in their concern over placating Arab interests to protect the flow of oil to America. And she sensed a weakness on President Eisenhower's part that she thought could have dangerous long-term consequences: kow-towing to the Soviets just to keep them quiet. Her long years of international political experience had taught her that appeasement does not work.

HYDE PARK, NOVEMBER 26—In our own country we are faced with a difficult decision in the Egyptian crisis. Egypt is demanding that all troops from Great Britain, France and Israel be removed from Egyptian territory at once, and that the UN police force be in no way considered as a "military presence." But the British, French and Israelis, before they withdraw their military forces, want some assurance that Egypt and the other Arab states will negotiate a permanent peace. They feel that otherwise they are apt to find themselves in the same position which existed when they were goaded to the point of making this attack.

It is reported, however, that President Eisenhower feels the best way

. . . .

to proceed "for the solution of the basic problems of the area" is to get all military personnel out of this area as soon as possible. If one could also move all Arab military power from the area, this might be a satisfactory solution. But, I must say, one does not have a great sense of confidence that the Arab states will be moved by any kind of reasonable attitude. If the UN force was considered a real military force and of sufficient size to constitute a power that would enforce all United Nations decisions, this would seem to me a very wise solution. But if it is merely to be a token police force, with no ability to enforce the will of the majority in the United Nations, then I can see a real dilemma for the United States. We will be asking our best allies to withdraw with the possibility that we are reducing them to a hopeless situation, with arms coming into the Arab states from the Soviet Union and nothing being done to protect the interests of the world in the Suez Canal and to assure the safety of Israel, all of which is essential to the survival of democracy in the Near East.

. . . .

Mrs. Roosevelt's intimate decades-long political involvement in the struggle for black civil rights inevitably provoked those who hated her liberal position into demanding that she admit to having some "Negro blood" in her veins and in her immediate family. She seized upon the chance to explain to her uninformed readers, once again, a few biological facts of life.

NEW YORK, DECEMBER 5—I received a most amusing postcard the other morning. Unfortunately, it was not signed in a readable manner so I cannot answer it privately. But it comes from Mobile, Ala., and says: "Dear Mrs. Roosevelt: You have not answered my question, the amount of Negro blood you have in your veins, if any."

I am afraid none of us know how much nor what kind of blood we have in our veins, since chemically it is all the same. And most of us cannot trace our ancestry more than a few generations.

As far as I know, I have no Negro blood, but, of course, I do have some Southern blood in my veins, for my Grandmother Roosevelt came from Georgia.

. . . .

The year stumbled toward its conclusion with disturbing news from Hungary, where workers' councils were disbanded under Soviet orders. Angry over the Soviet actions that had crushed democratic uprisings in Hungary and Poland only weeks before, Mrs. Roosevelt points out somewhat acidly that communism was supposed to have brought power to

. . . .

the workers, not tanks in the streets to stifle their expressions of political unrest.

NEW YORK, DECEMBER 12—The news from Hungary is ominous. The government has dissolved the workers' councils and little by little the people are being shorn of what meager freedom they have had.

It is hard to understand how a Communist regime can forbid workers' councils when the Communists always act in the name of the workers, just as though the workers decided everything.

It is convenient to make speeches glorifying the rights of the workers. But when these rights are completely ignored after they have been demonstrated to vary in some ways from the Soviet pattern, it seems that the Soviets are proving their utter lack of interest in the rights of human beings.

． ． ． ． ． ． ． ． ． ．

A hint of things to come: the first mention in "My Day" of the civil rights leadership of Dr. Martin Luther King, Jr. Eleanor Roosevelt recognized in the wisdom of his thoughts and the eloquence of his expression that, like Mahatma Gandhi, King's greatest strength and best contribution to the struggle would be in the symbolic power of his own nonviolent resistance to discrimination.

HYDE PARK, DECEMBER 24—Throughout the country our eyes are turned on Montgomery, Alabama, as the Supreme Court's order ending segregation on buses goes into effect. The Negroes celebrated this order at mass meetings on Thursday night and they have already gone back to using the buses on a nonsegregated basis. Their spiritual leader, Rev. Martin Luther King, Jr., cautioned them not to allow any violence. "This is a time when we must observe calm dignity and wise restraint," he said. "Emotions must not run wild."

Only one or two minor incidents occurred the first day of nonsegregation on buses. The Negroes in Montgomery had been given careful schooling in a nonviolent approach to any difficulties that might arise. Special emphasis had been laid on "remaining peaceful even if others strike first." It is to be hoped that everything will continue to move quietly, for this experiment of nonsegregation is already in force in the airlines in the South, and in the North there is no place where one may not sit next to an individual of any nationality or color in public conveyances. Once it is accepted, I am sure it will seem as natural for the people of the South as it does for the people of the North.

． ． ． ． ． ． ． ． ． ． ． ． ． ．

1 9 5 7

President Eisenhower and his foreign policy advisers, including Secretary of State John Foster Dulles, believed in early 1957, when they articulated what became known as the Eisenhower Doctrine—a guarantee of U.S. arms sales to any Mideast country requesting them—that providing arms would help stabilize an area of the world threatened from without by Soviet communism and from within by ages-old ethnic and political conflicts. The White House unwittingly fueled the possibilities for armed conflicts there, conflicts that rarely resolved anything for the better or for long. By early March Congress had approved the Eisenhower Doctrine, and there was no turning back. Mrs. Roosevelt wanted to see Israel kept strong enough to defend its borders, but she was among the first to call for a serious reconsideration of arms sales as an instrument of foreign policy. Her voice went mostly unheard.

In the meantime, Ike was inaugurated for his second term as president, riding a high tide of popularity. Eleanor Roosevelt continued to scurry back and forth across the United States, in fair weather and foul, mostly for AAUN meetings and lectures, occasionally stopping to see friends and family en route. In January she went to Florida and the Midwest; in February to Washington state and to California, Arizona, and Texas; in March to Minnesota and Iowa—for several days of grueling work and travel in each state. Also in March, Mrs. Roosevelt and an entourage of friends (including David Gurewitsch) and secretaries took an excursion to Morocco and other parts of North Africa. Though she had been practically everywhere else in the world, the lure of exotic places like Casablanca was still strong for her.

At the end of April the United States dedicated its first working nuclear reactor for domestic electricity production, at Fort Belvoir, Virginia. The event was hailed as the harbinger of an era of safe, cheap power.

Senator Joseph McCarthy died in early May, just about the time Mrs. Roosevelt was filing the first of her "My Day" columns from London at the start of a two-week trip to the United Kingdom and the Continent (primarily Vienna). Also early that month, the young, ambitious senator from Massachusetts, John F. Kennedy, captured the year's Pulitzer Prize for biography with his book *Profiles in Courage.*

President Eisenhower was concerned about the potential spread of communism in Southeast Asia, too; in May he met with South Vietnam's president, Ngo Dinh Diem, to firm up commitments between the two countries in the struggle against the Soviets and the Chinese— a step similar to that of the French there years before. But a happier historical note was also sounded at midyear: the *Mayflower II*, a replica of the boat that brought the Pilgrims to Plymouth Rock, in Southeast Massachusetts in 1620, arrived at the same spot after a fifty-four-day commemorative voyage across the Atlantic.

Blowing off the Gulf of Mexico uncommonly early in the hurricane season, a terrible storm took 531 lives along the Texas–Louisiana coast at the end of June. By late summer another type of storm was brewing in the South. The Civil Rights Act of 1957 was signed by the President in late August. The act included strong provisions to protect voting rights and induced very strong opposition: South Carolina Senator Strom Thurmond set a filibuster record (twenty-four hours, twenty-seven minutes) in his attempt to thwart the bill's passage. Only days later, in defiance of federal Supreme Court rulings calling for school desegregation, Governor Orville Faubus of Arkansas called out his state's National Guard to prevent black students from entering the all-white high school in Little Rock.

Much of the nation was shocked and outraged, though the action won much praise also from fellow segregationists—who immediately lionized Faubus. Ike and the governor conferred a few days later. A federal injunction ensued to force the governor to withdraw the National Guard. The black students entered the school, and riots that lasted several days broke out. Finally the President had to send in soldiers to make peace and to protect the nine black students who had tried to integrate the school. Federal authorities and the black students prevailed, but enormous damage had been done both to America's image in the eyes of the world and to the segregationists' political position, for the string of events radicalized a great many otherwise patient black people, making them now quite willing to fight for their rights.

While all this turmoil was upsetting America, Eleanor Roosevelt was engaged in a drama of her own. She made her first visit to the Soviet Union (both Moscow and the deep interior), and came back after a month's stay with highly valuable reportage on many aspects of Russian life. Her interviews with Khrushchev were given additional space in her "My Day" columns. Overnight, in addition to being a leading expert on United Nations affairs, Mrs. Roosevelt now became, at seventy-two, a much-sought-after expert on Soviet affairs. Invitations to lecture on the USSR all but swamped her already overly packed schedule.

An unflattering surprise was given to the U.S. space program, and indirectly to the American educational system (especially the sciences), when the Russians launched the first unmanned satellite, Sputnik, on October 4. Though Eleanor Roosevelt never became a fan of the space program, thinking that all those dollars could better be spent solving earthly problems, she quickly joined the critics who said Sputnik's success was a litmus test for the parallel success of the Soviet educational system—and by implication for the sluggishness and failure of its American counterpart.

Another flying object of 1957, initially unidentified for many first-time viewers but eventually to become as common as the hula hoop, was the Frisbee, brought to us by a company named Wham-O, and appropriately situated in sunny, carefree California. There is no record that Eleanor Roosevelt ever tried one.

. . . .

At the beginning of 1957 the Scripps-Howard newspaper chain did not renew its contract for Mrs. Roosevelt's "My Day" column. The New York World-Telegram *had carried the column for several years but had begun omitting it frequently in recent times, presumably because its editors believed their readers were losing interest in what Mrs. Roosevelt had to say. Disappointed at this partial loss of readership, she was shortly pleased that the New York* Post *took it over. The* Post's *publisher, Dorothy Schiff, was instrumental in arranging Mrs. Roosevelt's trip to the Soviet Union later in the year.*

Though Eleanor Roosevelt was not trained as a historian or political scientist she had an uncanny knack for seeing where things were probably heading. Such was the case with events in Hungary. It would be a generation before her hunches about the eventual results of Soviet domination there would play themselves out, but she was right on target. Of course, Mrs. Roosevelt worked from certain assumptions, too, one of them that no people will remain willingly and forever under authoritarian control.

NEW YORK, JANUARY 2—I find the appeal to the West by the present Hungarian government one of the most astonishing that has come from any Soviet-controlled government. The newspaper representing

. . . .

the regime has asked that the West give the present Hungarian government financial assistance and share its technical knowledge.

The lack of technicians is certainly developing in Hungary as a result of the flight of many of their best technical people. Because they had worked closely with Western scientists and kept in touch with Western scientific publications, these men knew what was going on in the world outside and could not be fooled by Soviet propaganda spread in every Soviet-controlled country against the West.

It is extraordinary to find an organ of the present government acknowledging that living standards for people in similar positions outside Hungary, even in Austria, are higher than they can be in Soviet-controlled Hungary. If this fact is generally accepted and known it will fan the flames of discontent in every Soviet satellite.

. . . .

Mrs. Roosevelt could sometimes pull off with a few hundred words, in a tour de force of succinctness and clarity, what other writers might need thousands of words to accomplish. This column covers the rising political tensions in the various Mideast countries. Among the exercises that taught Mrs. Roosevelt how to report so efficiently on complex subjects was probably her job of reporting to FDR when he was president and was unable to travel to see conditions in far-flung places around the country. It was often said that the First Lady had become the President's eyes and ears. The President needed to know quickly and clearly what she had witnessed. Mrs. Roosevelt's own hearing had been deteriorating for almost a decade. Her reference to a new hearing aid reflects her newly found relief from this frustration.

NEW YORK, JANUARY 8—I spent Friday and Saturday in Washington and on Saturday had the good luck to be able to hear and see the President in the Capitol when he addressed the joint session of Congress. My son was able to get me a ticket, and I was particularly anxious to go, as I felt I had not as yet fully understood what the President hoped to accomplish in the Near East.

I listened carefully to the speech, using a new type of hearing aid which is attached to a pair of glasses. It has revolutionized my ability to hear, both at meetings and when people are speaking, so I am sure I heard everything the President said. I read the speech again Sunday morning in the paper on the way up to New York in the plane.

I know that this authority which the President is asking from Congress is intended to prevent any Soviet attacks on countries in the Near East, but I am not sure that the Soviets intend any open military attack in the Near East. It would seem entirely unnecessary for them to

. . . .

undertake a military attack when they are accomplishing their desired ends without one.

Both in Egypt and in Syria the Soviets have offered arms and technicians and, in both cases, they have been received with open arms. Now, it is obvious that there are certain states in the Near East that have been much more closely tied with the West and they may have received arms and technicians from us.

In certain places we have bases, but I do not yet quite see how this plan for military aid is going to meet and solve the two real problems which keep the Near East in turmoil.

It is true that the President said we would use economic aid and work closely with the United Nations, but I came away from his speech with a feeling that I still lack a clear picture of how we are going to try to meet the real challenges in the Near East: The settlement of the Suez Canal dispute and the bringing about of a peaceful acceptance of the state of Israel. There must be a willingness to recognize Israel's existence and to cooperate for mutual benefits that would appeal to both the Arab states and Israel.

I have begun to feel that a little of our firmness should not only be addressed to the Soviet Union, Great Britain, France and Israel but also should be directed at Egypt and Syria. I was told in Washington that the Syrian ambassador had gone to the State Department and expressed his great displeasure with some of the things the United States was saying and doing.

Sometimes I wonder whether President Gamal Abdel Nasser of Egypt is not calling the tune in the Near East rather than any one of the great powers. I have no objection to that, for I believe that every small country should call the tune in its own country and should decide on its own relations with other countries.

But when we cannot induce Syria to rebuild pipelines its army has wrecked or to let us rebuild them, it is harmful to the interests of many countries. It seems to me now that we should turn to the countries that are willing to cooperate with us, and not behave like white rabbits when we deal with those who seem to scorn us.

. . . .

As the civil rights struggle approached the boiling point, Eleanor Roosevelt was often one of those liberal critics who regularly pointed out that Northerners had more than a little housecleaning of their own to do concerning racism, that the accusatory finger could be pointed not only at recalcitrant Southern segregationists. Public housing projects struck Mrs. Roosevelt as one of the most important kinds of places where Northerners could and should show the rest of the country that integration was right and would work.

. . . .

SAN FRANCISCO, JANUARY 26—I have said on several occasions that we in the Northern cities must desegregate housing before we can hope to comply with the Supreme Court decision. Therefore, I was very much interested to read what Dr. Roma Gans, professor of education at Teachers College of Columbia University, told the Board of Education of New York City at one of its hearings.

She said New York City would have to have legislation forbidding discrimination in all multiple housing projects, whether they are aided by public funds or not. In other words, if the Supreme Court ruling is to be obeyed, we will have to set a pattern of life which will run through everything we do.

There is no segregation now in the North in public transportation and, though there is not supposed to be in hotels, restaurants and theaters, I think in subtle ways there have been restrictions for our colored citizens.

All this has to come to an end. Why it should be so difficult for us to accept the fact that all of our citizens must be treated on a completely equal basis I have never been able to understand. This does not mean that if you do not like someone you are obliged to invite him into your home. It only means that you have to be willing to share public facilities on an equal basis with everybody.

Whether the apartment next to you is occupied by a Greek or an Indian or a Negro or a Jew should make very little difference to you. My experience is that in New York City one sees very little of his next-door neighbor, and unless you want to know him, you certainly are not obligated to make friends. But you are obligated to be courteous and to willingly share the facilities which have to be used in common.

In New York City we have not only Harlem but the gradual development of a Puerto Rican section. We would not like to be told that we were behaving toward our citizens the way certain unenlightened governments in Europe, in Africa and in Asia have behaved toward minority groups in general and Jewish groups in particular in their midst.

We do not like to be told that we have ghettos in our big cities, but that is exactly what we have, and we will continue to have them until we get over the idea that we cannot live in the same houses and share all public facilities on an equal basis with all of our citizens.

. . . .

Few serious theatergoers in New York did not make an effort to see Eugene O'Neill's Long Day's Journey into Night; *the 1954 production was too well reviewed and too moving to resist. Eleanor Roosevelt added her applause to the many ovations. But her notice is uncharacteristically terse for a play about which her own family experience had prepared her*

. . . .

to say much more. The word alcohol *is conspicuously missing from this comment on the best American play yet written on the destructiveness of addiction to drugs. Mrs. Roosevelt's early childhood had been sadly marred by the alcoholism of her father—who had been sent away, to protect his own children, when Eleanor was still less than ten years old.*

WASHINGTON, FEBRUARY 5—I went on Friday night to see Eugene O'Neill's "Long Day's Journey into Night." The drama provides an evening of agony but of intense interest. Every member of the cast does his or her part beautifully and from the viewpoint of characterization, I think it is most remarkable writing and very good theater.

I do not recommend it for a pleasant evening, but if you feel strong, you certainly will be rewarded by gloom that holds you tense every minute.

....

If Eleanor Roosevelt had had her way, American politics would have worn a coat of rather different colors. Having watched and participated in so many political contests, Mrs. Roosevelt formulated quite a number of still-radical ideas for changes in the way Americans finance their campaigns. Here we see that her thinking was thoroughly egalitarian insofar as the two major parties were concerned, but she makes no mention of third-party or other political groups who might also want or deserve a slice of the pie.

The column for February 18 shows Mrs. Roosevelt once more an intensely loyal Democrat, a fine reporter of behind-the-scenes political party activity, and a sharp critic of those Southerners who were contemplating another secession—if not from the Union, at least from a too-liberal Democratic Party that would force them to support the movement for civil rights.

SEATTLE, FEBRUARY 13—The cartoon on this newspaper's editorial page dealt with a subject which is of interest to the whole country. It showed a GOP elephant and a Democratic donkey, the latter warming his hands at a little wood fire and looking very ragged, having spent only $10 million on the election campaign. The GOP elephant, having spent $20 million on the campaign, looks resplendent in good clothes and a diamond pin. He says, "Money well spent, I say."

I wonder if others throughout the country feel strongly enough about this situation to do something about campaign expenses. I have long felt that the same amount should be spent by both parties, that both should be given free radio and television time, and that an equal amount of newspaper advertising and railroad travel should be allowed in the different categories and paid for by the public.

....

SAN FRANCISCO, FEBRUARY 18—My first greetings in the hotel here were from delegates from Hawaii who had come for the national meeting of the Democratic Committee and the Advisory Committee, which met at the same time. Saturday night the big fund-raising dinner was addressed by Adlai Stevenson, but panels on many subjects continue to be held. My son James and Senator Lehman [of New York] were on the panel on human resources, where the Senator brought up the question of the attitude of the Democratic Party on civil rights. The papers have long articles on the subject.

Governor Harriman was here only for 24 hours, but like many others he agrees with Senator Lehman that the President and the Republican Administration have not faced up to their responsibility as regards integration in this country. They agree also that the Democratic Party, because of its Southern membership, has not come out strongly and honestly in its stand, and they are determined that there shall be a clear-cut decision as to where the Democratic Party does stand.

They acknowledge the fact that this may bring a political explosion, since this is the question which deeply divides the Democratic Party. The South—solidly Democratic for many years, though it is now beginning to move into a less solid status and show signs of having a two-party system—still has held, because of seniority, many of the most important and influential party positions in the Congress. The Congressional leaders in both the Senate and the House are opposed to anything which will mean a clear-cut stand on civil rights legislation.

There are among the Southerners those who realize that change must come. But they are also faced with the fact that they must be re-elected, and their role is a difficult one. For the liberals in the North to force on the whole party a stand which is impossible for the South to accept is going to be a very serious step, and I hope that wisdom and patience will be used in the discussions which are to go on in the next few days.

. . . .

At first it might seem that the hero of this story is FDR in the heyday of his New Deal presidency. Then one might think that the protagonist, a poor farmer from Columbus, Mississippi, named Sylvester Harris, was the hero. However, one also has the sense that Eleanor Roosevelt used this story in her "My Day" column as a way to remind her readers that sometimes it is the political system and moral fiber of a nation that deserve applause.

NEW YORK, FEBRUARY 23—When I hear it said that people in trouble aren't worth helping because if they had what it takes they wouldn't be in trouble, I like to remember the story of Sylvester Harris.

. . . .

The delightful story of Harris is told in the March Ebony magazine.

Harris, who lives on a farm at Columbus, Mississippi, is supposed to have ridden into town on his mule, Jesse, during the Depression and, according to legend, there put in a call to the President to ask help in saving his farm.

Harris says the truth of the story is that he did not ride his mule but got into an old truck which managed to get him into Columbus. He was told that the call to the President would cost him $4.80, so he stacked the nickels and quarters in front of him in the telephone booth and put in the call.

He got an assistant and a secretary, but he insisted on talking to the President. He was about to lose his mule and his farm and he would talk to no one else. Finally, he did get the President on the phone.

Two days later appraisers came and went over Harris's land, got him a government loan at the Federal Land Bank of New Orleans which satisfied his mortgage, and overnight he and his mule became a symbol of the "forgotten men" of that day.

Harris is 65 now and has a modern farm with a tractor, cultivators and trailers. His old mule, Jesse, is dead but he has two new ones. His home was electricity, a refrigerator, a radio, a washing machine and two TV sets, and he cooks with gas.

A gentleman in Texas asked me the other day if giving economic aid to people in countries which do not seem able to get along by themselves has any value. I told him that without aid these people would go on being helpless, but with it we might see miracles occur. He looked very doubtful.

I wish now I had told him the story of Sylvester Harris.

. . . .

One of the emerging luminaries of the Democratic Party at this time was Senator Hubert Humphrey of Minnesota. Humphrey had helped form the Democratic Farm-Labor Alliance in Minnesota in 1944, then served as mayor of Minneapolis for the next four years. He went to Washington in 1949 as a senator and continued in that post until his death in 1978 (with a four-year interruption for his service as vice president under Lyndon Johnson in the late 1960s). Mrs. Roosevelt saw in Humphrey a man with enthusiasm for projects and problems that were not great vote-getters in the 1950s (the arts, child care, civil rights), and in this respect he was to her one of the quiet but powerful leaders of the day. Neither Senator Humphrey nor Mrs. Roosevelt was an artist, yet both realized the importance the arts play in the health of the national spirit.

. . . .

NEW YORK, FEBRUARY 27—Senator Hubert H. Humphrey of Minnesota has sent me copies of three bills he has introduced into Congress in the interest of the arts.

One of the bills, S 967, provides for the establishment of a federal advisory commission on the arts to encourage cultural and artistic endeavors nationally and internationally. The commission, at the same time, would stimulate a greater appreciation of the arts in the American public.

Another bill, S 966, provides for the transfer of the Civil Service Commission Building in the District of Columbia to the regents of the Smithsonian Institution for use in housing the national collection of fine arts and for a national portrait gallery. The bill also provides for the international interchange of art and craft work.

The third bill, S 965, broadens the composition and activities of the 47-year-old U.S. Commission of Fine Arts, which now functions primarily in the District of Columbia, by providing representation of the living arts—music, drama, poetry, the dance—and the graphic arts—motion pictures, radio, television, literature and the crafts.

For a Senator to interest himself in the arts in our country is encouraging, for this is an area in which we have lagged far behind many other countries. We have been so preoccupied with our industrial growth that we have thought of little else. The culture of a nation is, after all, as important as its economy.

. . . .

The congressional career of Adam Clayton Powell, Jr., of New York City's Harlem, the nation's biggest black ghetto, was tempestuous—to say the least. His principles and behavior posed a serious problem for Mrs. Roosevelt, who often wanted to lend her support to the civil rights cause and to other issues concerning blacks and their needs. But the congressman and the former First Lady mixed about as well as oil and water. More often than not Mrs. Roosevelt viewed Powell's positions and tactics as so radical and aggressive that they were sure to backfire and set the struggle for civil rights back a few hard-won steps. The tactics Powell used to achieve his desegregation goals were not uncommon in Congress; he would often attach civil rights amendments to bills unrelated to those issues when he was sure the bills stood a good chance of passage. Mrs. Roosevelt thought such maneuvering was cheap and too sly to merit respect, yet she usually would have supported Powell's ideas about desegregation had they been put forth in a different way. Her criticism of the congressman's approach went on for years. (He served in the House from 1945 until 1967, when he was barred by his colleagues on accusations of having misused public funds.)

. . . .

EN ROUTE TO MOROCCO, MARCH 21—Congressmen opposed to all federal aid to education defeated the school construction bill in Congress last year by taking advantage of the Powell amendment, sponsored by Representative Adam Clayton Powell, Democrat of New York, who represents a Harlem district.

The Powell amendment would have denied federal aid to school districts that had not complied with the Supreme Court decision to integrate their schools.

Those who opposed federal aid to schools, in principle, supported the amendment and so it went into the bill. But when the bill came up for a final vote, they voted against it together with the Southern Congressmen whom they knew well in advance would not accept a bill containing a mandatory integration provision.

These opponents of federal aid were aware of the fact that many of their fellow legislators from the South were coming up for re-election shortly and that support of the bill by a Southern Congressman would mean his defeat.

Many of those who voted for the amendment did so because they believed in the principle it set forth, and they followed through on their convictions by supporting it in the final vote.

But their strength was not enough to pass it, for they were stymied by the double-cross that was so apparent that everyone in the country interested in the bill must have known what happened.

Respect is due those Congressmen who felt strongly that it was unfair to pay federal school funds to states which were doing their best to defeat the purpose of the Supreme Court's integration decision.

It seems to me that this year the school crisis is so great that the harm, both to white and Negro children all over the country, resulting from a shortage of classrooms is apparent to all. Overcrowding and split sessions in schools have had such a bad effect that even those who believe in the principle of the Powell amendment must realize that our first concern is to get school construction under way.

If this is done, then it would be possible to carry the fight for integration in the schools through the courts of the various states.

I hope that Representative Powell will see the inconsistency of his position and refrain from offering an integration amendment to the bill this year. And I hope the bill can be discussed early enough so there will be plenty of chance for it to pass in this session.

I feel, however, that this important legislation will not pass unless the people of the country express their opinions, not merely by talking at home but by organizing groups to go to Washington to see their representatives and by writing personal letters to these representatives telling them of the feeling in their communities.

No representative will vote contrary to what he feels is his community's real nonpartisan attitude on the bill. If he is a Democrat and hears only from Republicans, he might well say that these people wouldn't vote for him anyway, and vice versa.

But if the letters come from both Republicans and Democrats, and if his visitors represent both parties, he will realize that this question of federal aid to education transcends party lines.

....

As the dateline of the March 21 column indicates, Mrs. Roosevelt was traveling abroad again. After a stopover in Madrid to see masterpieces at the Prado museum there, she and her entourage headed for their primary destination, Morocco. As usual, even though she traveled as a private citizen, she was received as though she were a high government official. Her travel reports in the "My Day" column combine elements of a friendly letter home to loved ones and the careful descriptiveness of a guidebook.

CASABLANCA, MOROCCO, MARCH 27—By special arrangement, three of us went with the U.S. minister and his wife, Mr. and Mrs. Homer Byington, Jr., to the Prado in Madrid, one of the best museums in the world.

We concentrated on three Spanish painters, El Greco, Velasquez, and Goya, and these collections are magnificent. Mrs. Byington had taken two courses at the museum and had attended more than 50 lectures, so she was able to tell us the legends and stories about the painters or paintings.

Goya went through a period before his death in which he was old and bitter, so he decorated his home with horrible paintings. Then, suddenly, at the end he painted his last canvas—a sweet and charming milkmaid in Paris.

Two of the El Grecos will stay long in my mind. One is of the Crucifixion in which you feel an ascending movement I have seen in no other painting. The other is a portrait of a monk.

I had not realized that Velasquez had always lived and painted at court, so he never had to sell his paintings.

The flight from Madrid to Casablanca took about three hours, with an hour lost because of the time change. These time changes are somewhat confusing!

We arrived in the dark to be met by what seemed to be a crowd of people. My son, Elliott, and Dr. Gurewitsch greeted Kenneth Pendar with joy and he will be helpful to them in planning our visit here. The white-robed Governor of Casablanca and a representative of the Sultan also were on hand to greet us.

The Hotel Anfa, where I am staying in Casablanca, was the place where the conferences were held in World War II between my husband and Prime Minister Winston Churchill. Elliott was there with his Air Force unit at the time, so he was assigned to his father. He has been describing for us all the people who came in and out of the hotel during those historic days.

After a late dinner, a few of us went for a short time to the home of our Consul General, Henry H. Ford. The United States government has bought for its consulate the house in which Mr. Churchill stayed while here for the war conferences. Elliott remembered the room where the maps, which Mr. Churchill always insisted accompany him to keep him briefed on troop movements, were hung.

I remember when Mr. Churchill came to Washington during the war, one room had to be set aside for his maps despite the fact that a room my husband had on the lower floor of the White House was fully equipped with maps of the world.

The next morning I awoke early and went for a walk before breakfast. Few people were about, but a young American Army officer, driving by in his car, stopped to say good morning. It was foggy, but later the sun burned away the fog.

The flowers are lovely here now, and soon there will be a riot of color. Palms, cedars and eucalyptus trees grow close to the hotel. The eucalyptus were imported from Australia and do well here.

The peach trees already are in bloom and the fruit will be ripe in May. The orange season is almost over, but the grapefruit is just beginning to ripen and those I have seen are very large.

FEZ, MOROCCO, APRIL 2—Here we are in the old capital of Morocco and I feel sure that we will find it interesting.

The Hotel Palais Jamai is on the outskirts of town, but as the city lies in a valley and the walls and defenses were built all around it, the view of the city from the top of the hill in approaching it is lovely.

As we were driving along this morning, we came through a village in which the whole population seemed to be trekking to a hill covered with trees. We decided to join the procession and discovered they were going to the weekly fair.

We wandered among the vegetables and fruits, dyes and spices. Then we came upon the meats, and here again I was struck by the cleanliness. There were few flies and everything was washed and fresh-looking. One should not eat uncooked food here, but it is hard to follow the rule when everything looks so sanitary.

We looked at the sheep and cattle, and I spoke to a young man bargaining for them with the Moroccan farmers. This young man, a Swiss, was buying cattle for three farms and he told me he bought sheep at about $6.25 a head, fattened them for a few months, and sold them at the time of the great religious feast for a neat profit.

We lunched in the town of Meknes with the Pasha and had an even more sumptuous meal, if that were possible, than the day before. The food here is rich, prepared with much butter—very good, and very fattening!

We saw the Sultan's imperial palace—enormous but largely in ruins—and then drove through the town and saw a beautiful mosaic-covered gate where the letter-writers were plying their trade. Finally, we came here by the most direct road, for we were rather tired of sightseeing.

The Hotel Palais Jamai was built as a private house, but a strange house it must have been, with many stairs and many rooms at different levels. It has a lovely garden and terrace.

My son Elliott is managing his big party of travelers well, and the Sultan has provided us with a delightful traveling companion. The Sultan also notifies his governors along the way to look after us, and they are more than kind.

This country needs more industries and help from various sources. I heard an amusing story about the labor unions. They are struggling to get recognition for collective bargaining, and so far the industrial leaders will not accept them. Consequently, there are strikes.

One strike was called at one of our United States bases where the strikers announced that they understood that in the United States employees are always paid by their employers while on strike. They were surprised and aggrieved when they were told this was not the case.

Perhaps some of our good labor leaders should come over here and help them organize. It would be better than leaving it to the Communists.

....

Just over a month before the next column was written Congress had given its overwhelming approval to the Eisenhower Doctrine. The doctrine seemed to most American politicians a natural extension of other broadly popular measures the country had taken in the postwar years, such as the Marshall Plan. And it fit neatly with the containment theory, which held that although it would be impossible and illegitimate for America to try to eliminate communism in countries where it was already well rooted, it was America's duty to the free world to act as global policeman, surrounding and containing communism so that it could spread no further.

Mrs. Roosevelt was never afraid to take a stand with a small, vocal minority. She had come to the conclusion that while communism did indeed need to be resisted wherever possible, the notion of selling arms to anyone and everyone in a self-evidently unstable political area of the world like the Middle East could only lead to continued and increasing conflict. To her, the Eisenhower Doctrine, no matter how popular, was a recipe for disaster.

NEW YORK, APRIL 16—I was very much disturbed last week to see that in spite of our conciliatory attitude toward Saudi Arabia in accepting a clause forbidding some of our citizens to be employed on American installations in that country, Saudi Arabia is now making more trouble for Israel and insisting that they will bar Israel from use of the Gulf of Aqaba. This only goes to prove, I think, that a weak attitude will increase our difficulties rather than lessen them, and this holds for the United Nations as well as for the United States.

As the days go by, I wish more and more that the United States would make the effort to come to an agreement with the Soviet Union by which neither of these two countries would provide any arms to Near Eastern countries. This would remove all question of attempts on either side to control these nations, and we could leave the inspection to the United Nations forces so that we would be sure no arms were coming in surreptitiously.

These nations could then proceed to receive economic aid from either the Soviet Union or the United States for projects to improve the standard of living of the people of their countries. Whatever they obtained in the way of arms they would buy from other countries not controlled by the USSR and we could be pretty sure that it would be a small amount. It seems a very short-sighted policy to tie our economic aid always to military aid. I hope this incident with Saudi Arabia will teach us that we have no friends in countries like this and can only hope for respect—and respect is not gained through weakness.

. . . .

Having recently returned from North Africa, Mrs. Roosevelt was especially interested in the struggle toward freedom going on in Algeria. This "My Day" column is a masterly, if small, example of her sense of realpolitik: that in every complex situation there are several rights and wrongs, and reality consists of a tricky balancing act among them all. Neither France, as the outgoing colonial power, nor Algeria, as the emerging new independent nation, had all the right on its side. Patient, steady, difficult negotiations, taking into account the needs of all parties, were the only sane way through such a thicket, according to Eleanor Roosevelt.

NEW YORK, APRIL 19—The fact that Tunisia and Morocco have achieved freedom of government and now are attempting to work out

. . . .

satisfactory political and economic ties with France and the Western world has made the question of Algeria's future all the more important.

As you know, France is facing armed resistance in Algeria and has been obliged to put an army of somewhere around 500,000 men and large supplies of military materiel in that area.

While I was in Morocco recently, I was visited twice by groups of people from Algeria. Quite naturally, the French say they have been in Algeria 150 years, that they consider it an integral part of France, and that there are no separate people called Algerians—they are all French.

One Frenchman said to me, "To ask France to give up Algeria is like asking the people of New York to return Manhattan Island to the Indians."

I smiled at this because there do not seem to be any Indians clamoring violently to have Manhattan returned to them.

Large numbers of Algerians, on the other hand, do not feel they actually are Frenchmen, or that they ever have been given equal representation with the French in the control of their government. It is this control which they wish to gain.

The whole situation is complicated by the fact that France's economy would be benefited greatly by an economic arrangement on the development of the new oilfields, which are said to be extensive.

I personally feel that if it were possible to make such an economic arrangement equitable to both Algeria and France and then a reasonable agreement for Algeria's ultimate independence with constantly increasing autonomy, France itself would be better off. At the same time, some form of federation of the three North African states could be planned, with a real tie-up with France and the West.

Then France could work out further economic agreements with Algeria and the other North African states which, in the end, would be advantageous to her and to them.

....

Underlying Mrs. Roosevelt's appreciation of the movie version of Reginald Rose's teleplay Twelve Angry Men *was her well-known opposition to the death penalty. She believed that in most cases it was nearly impossible for a jury to be absolutely sure that no contradictory evidence could ever be found that might influence them to make a different decision. Thus, a well-crafted film drama illustrating this point, and others about the psychology of back-room political decision making, was bound to get a rave review from her.*

NEW YORK, APRIL 20—The other night I saw a private showing of Henry Fonda in "Twelve Angry Men." He is magnificent, but the whole cast is made up of excellent actors.

....

As a character study, this is a fascinating movie, but more than that, it points up the fact, which too many of us have not taken seriously, of what it means to serve on a jury when a man's life is at stake. In addition, it makes vivid what "reasonable doubt" means when a murder trial jury makes up its mind on circumstantial evidence.

....

One of the United Nations' chronic problems has been that the great powers could still act unilaterally to satisfy their own purposes, sometimes completely disregarding whatever the General Assembly or even the Security Council might have ruled.

Mrs. Roosevelt feared for the health and viability of the United Nations when major powers acted in such a way. Though she remained resolutely opposed to world government, she yearned to see the day when all difficult international disputes would be taken voluntarily, as a matter of course, to the floor of the United Nations for open debate. She wrote the next column in London, where she was beginning her second foreign trip of the year. The May 15 column gives us a glimpse of the British royal family's private life.

LONDON, MAY 4—There is a feeling over here, I am told, that a number of European countries are becoming discouraged with the ability of the United Nations to cope with world problems and that we are leaning toward a return to the old power politics.

I do not think the evidence will bear this out.

For instance, one rather conservative U.S. senator from a Middle-western state sent a letter to his constituents, asking whether or not they supported the United Nations. Eighty-four percent of the answers favored greater support of the UN.

I personally think that what the United Nations really needs is more leadership by the great nations and implementation of UN decisions through the support and power which can be brought to bear by the great nations.

Every time we in the United States act on our own instead of through the UN we weaken this great organization. Our country has been saying, for instance, that all nations should act through the UN. Yet we belie our own words by negotiating outside the United Nations and by using a show of military power to further our position.

Jordan had to be strengthened and kept free, but I cannot see why this could not have been done through the United Nations as well as it was done by a show of force on our part alone.

The fact of power is undeniable, but how this power is used and how UN decisions are implemented depends on the way the great

....

nations decide to work and cooperate within the framework of the United Nations Charter.

NEW YORK, MAY 15—I had an appointment to see Queen Elizabeth in London, so George Spencer, who accompanied us from Nottingham on the train, urged the engineer to see to it that we arrived on time, and we did.

It was very kind of the Queen to receive me, since she had not realized that I was leaving Britain so soon and little Prince Charles had had his tonsils and adenoids out the day before.

I arrived at the Palace at 6:30 P.M. to be met by a charming young man who took me into a small sitting room where the Queen's lady-in-waiting came to speak to me. Then we went upstairs to another small sitting room where in a few minutes someone came to say the Queen was ready.

I went into the Queen's study and found her just as calm and composed as if she did not have a very unhappy little boy on her mind. I asked if he had felt well enough yet to demand ice cream and she said he already had had two portions, making me feel that he probably was on the mend.

Forty minutes after I had arrived and after a nice talk, the Queen thoughtfully said she knew she must not keep me longer, as I had a dinner engagement, and we parted.

I have the greatest respect for this young woman who must combine the responsibilities of a Queen with the requirements and emotional stresses of a young mother. I think, too, the British people are fortunate in having the royal family to hold them together. Everywhere you go, you see that the Queen, Prince Philip, the Queen Mother, and Princess Margaret are loved as well as deeply respected.

. . . .

It was one thing for Eleanor Roosevelt to write from the distance of New York about the Southern states' problems with desegregation and something else altogether to find herself on the hot seat in the South, a barrage of testy questions coming at her from prosegregation reporters. However, Mrs. Roosevelt was a pro at handling aggressively critical newspeople; her experience reached back to the early days of the New Deal. What stands out here is the clear consistency of her position: that the law of the land must be obeyed; that the best tack to take in the fight against discrimination is nonviolence. The emerging civil rights leadership of Martin Luther King, Jr. is noted as well.

HOUSTON, TEX., MAY 24—I am in Texas for two lectures on behalf of Bonds for Israel and arrived in Houston when a court hearing was

. . . .

being held on the speed for compliance with the Supreme Court's order on desegregation of schools.

This led the press to ask me a number of questions which, as a guest, I felt it was unfortunate for me to have to answer, particularly since I feel that my attitude and beliefs on this question have been so well known.

I was glad, however, to be able to express my strong feelings against violence in this issue anywhere in our country. And so I regret the decision made in Texas against the National Association for the Advancement of Colored People, for it seems to take away the right to use legal action to enforce the desegregation decision and, in a way, makes it more difficult to prevent violence.

I hope that I am wrong and that we will see a continuation of the staunchness shown by the citizens in Montgomery, Ala., who under the leadership of the Rev. Martin Luther King have adhered to non-violence.

But human beings have a breaking point if denied an outlet for their emotions and convictions. Then violence may seem to be the only answer, and that hurts us, both at home and abroad.

....

Public figure though Mrs. Roosevelt was, she was also still a homemaker, and from the predictable frequency with which she reported in her "My Day" column on domestic activities at Val-Kill, in Hyde Park, it seems that a good portion of her readership was interested in such news.

HYDE PARK, JUNE 1—I have been gradually bringing a little order to my Hyde Park home after having been away so much during the past year. The winter blankets have been put away and the summer ones taken out of storage. I need a number of slipcovers for furniture, but that cannot be done without a delay.

I rather love short intervals of intensive domestic activity, but whether I would like it over a long time, I do not know. But picking rhubarb in the garden and eating fresh asparagus, which is still coming up, certainly is satisfying!

....

The environmental protection movement that began to have an impact on American business and government about twenty years later was just being born in the 1950s. The country was still enthralled with what chemical fertilizers and pesticides could do to increase crop production. Very few observers of the agricultural and medical scenes in the 1950s stepped back from the practice of using pesticides indiscriminately to develop a critique of the way America made its decisions about agri-

....

*cultural chemicals. Though she worked with only a lay person's un-
derstanding of both farming and medicine, Eleanor Roosevelt was
among the first to call for careful study rather than blind acceptance
of powerful but potentially harmful fertilizers and pesticides.*

NEW YORK, JUNE 28—There is great anxiety, particularly in some sections of the East, as to the dangers in the widespread spraying of DDT.
Many organizations are concerned about its immediate effect upon
wild life, including native birds, fish ponds and streams and other forms
of life in the natural control system of nature.

Many people have been worried over spraying of any kind. One of
my sons, Franklin Jr., believes that all artificial sprays are detrimental
to plants and to the creatures who eat them, be they human beings
or cattle.

This is becoming quite an important controversy. A decision, it
seems to me, can be made only by a group of persons appointed by
the Secretary of Agriculture who cannot be influenced by special interests.

Such a group could ascertain whether spraying actually can be
harmful to animals and humans and whether the food value of anything that has been sprayed really has been injured.

....

*It didn't matter to Eleanor Roosevelt whether Democrats or Republicans
had been up to procedural shenanigans in Congress; she never liked
such ways of pushing a bill through to approval. That was the essence
of her criticism of Adam Clayton Powell, Jr. in a March column. In
this one the same sort of criticism is directed at the Republicans. The
issue Congress was debating was essentially the same as in Powell's
case: how to provide additional federal aid to the public schools.*

NEW YORK, JULY 30—I do not believe in crying over spilt milk, but in
the case of last week's House action in defeating the federal school aid
bill, I think it is important that we all understand how the milk was
spilled. The antisegregation amendment was adopted, at the suggestion of the Republicans, and then many of the Republicans voted
against the amended bill—thus making the defeat sure, since they were
of course joined by the Southern Democrats. This coalition has used
the same tactics before.

It is a clever trick, but I hope the colored people of this country are
going to awaken to the fact that—by voting for the antisegregation
amendment and then voting against the bill—the Republicans are
friends neither of Negro nor of white children. They simply make sure

....

that no federal money will be spent on constructing new schools, and both Negro and white children suffer.

I have said repeatedly that, in view of the situation as it now stands, it would be better to refrain from putting this antisegregation clause into the bill. Without it, we could get a clear-cut vote as to who wants new school construction and an improved school situation for the children of our country as a whole.

I think the segregation question will have to be fought in the courts anyway, and Congress should consider the school construction problem on the simple basis of needed school facilities. The legal fight for antisegregation would then proceed, school by school and case by case, wherever it is not accepted. This may take more time, but at least all of our children would not suffer as they now do, in overcrowded buildings with overworked and—in some cases—poorly trained teachers.

For this year, the school bill fight is over—but it will have to begin again in the next session of Congress. I hope everyone will understand clearly what Republican trickery has done.

. . . .

In an odd twist of political sympathies, Mrs. Roosevelt, in a column about the prospects for German reunification, expresses an implicit sympathy for the Soviet Union's position. That sympathy arose much less from any softening of her dislike for communism than from her decades long antipathy to German governments and military forces. In Mrs. Roosevelt's view the only appropriate policy toward the Germans was one of caution and wariness. She had not yet forgiven Germany for its part in initiating the two world wars, without doubt the darkest periods of Eleanor Roosevelt's long life.

NEW YORK, AUGUST 1—One wonders what the West's stand on the question of free elections on the unification of Germany will actually bring about.

The four great powers have a responsibility to restore one Germany by bringing about unification, but quite naturally the Soviets hope that unification will create a new pro-Soviet area, while the West hopes it will widen the area where there is attachment for democracy rather than for communism.

I can hardly imagine the Soviets agreeing to a free vote unless they are quite sure that Germany will not become a military menace. Yet the Western powers feel strongly that the unification should not be tied, in any way, to promises of neutrality.

The basic fact of Germany's right to be unified is, I think, incontestable. But we cannot forget history, and since Germany has started two world wars the anxieties on the part of the Eastern nations are

. . . .

understandable. Perhaps it is not unnatural to expect something a little more reassuring for peace in the future than has been forthcoming so far.

. . . .

Eleanor Roosevelt's approaching trip to the USSR was to be her first behind the Iron Curtain, and through her eyes many Americans would get their first glimpses of everyday life in the mysterious, threatening country that long before Churchill had described as "a riddle wrapped in a mystery inside an enigma." Mrs. Roosevelt is no ordinary tourist or even an ordinary journalist. The breadth of her interests and the ambitiousness of her plans indicate how seriously she took this opportunity.

NEW YORK, AUGUST 30—I am about set to leave for the Soviet Union, where I hope to arrive fresh and ready to do anything that comes my way. That is why I am making two stops on the way, one for 24 hours in Berlin and one for overnight in Copenhagen. This means I should arrive in Moscow next Tuesday afternoon. On the return trip, I will fly straight through.

During my time in the Soviet Union I will write only two columns a week, and if it is possible for me to get them out, these will arrive in this country for publication on Tuesday and Friday.

Through the Russian ambassador in Washington, I have requested interviews with as many Soviet government heads as possible, as well as political leaders. I told him that, of course, I am most interested in health, education and welfare, and if at all possible, would like to see an area for rest and recreation for young people as well as what is being done in housing for old people. I have been told that good work is being accomplished in these fields.

I want, of course, to see factories, collective farms, schools, museums and the cultural facilities available to the people. I have asked permission to travel when my interviews are arranged.

I would love to take a two-day trip on the Volga River, stopping overnight on the way. I want, too, to see what is being done to rebuild Stalingrad. During World War II I was given a description of the way supplies were brought throughout the night for the defense of this city. It certainly was a dramatic story of one of the most valiant defenses in history.

I wish to visit Leningrad, Kiev, Yalta, Baku and, if possible—because the names have intrigued me since I was a child—Samarkand and Tashkent.

I would like the opportunity to visit some churches, synagogues and homes. But I want to do this casually, not as a prepared arrangement.

. . . .

One cannot feel one knows people unless one has seen them in their home environment.

. . . .

The next two columns were wired to America from within the Soviet Union and were subject to censorship. Though Mrs. Roosevelt's report-age is colorful here, her political opinions about the Soviets are muted.

Tashkent, the fourth largest city in the USSR, is located in Central Asia far to the east of Moscow. Both a major oasis and a manufacturing center, it is the capital of the Uzbek Soviet Socialist Republic.

TASHKENT, USSR, SEPTEMBER 20—Before coming here to Central Asia I visited a Baptist church in Moscow and had the opportunity to talk with the head of the church. My interpreter was a young organist who has studied in Britain for six months and was going back for another six months.

I was told there are about half a million Baptists in the Soviet Union and the number is growing at a rate of 15 to 20 thousand a year.

I looked at this church congregation with great interest, for the church was packed. In all Russian Orthodox churches I have visited so far a great majority of worshipers have been middle-aged or older women, but in this Baptist church there were young men and women. They seemed to take a great interest in the service and told me that the church was supported entirely by the congregation.

From the Baptist church we drove to a synagogue, where I talked with the chief rabbi. He gave me some information which I previously had obtained from one of the Soviet ministries and ended by asking me to tell the American people there is a great need for peace.

This emphasis on peace has been made over and over again to me by all kinds of people. The implication seems to be that the Russian people want peace but the American people want war. I don't know whether or not my assurances that we also are anxious for peace have fallen on deaf ears.

I returned to the hotel just in time for a recorded interview I had been requested to give to a Russian correspondent. I approached this interview with considerable trepidation, but I don't think it proved to be as formidable as I had feared.

I was only a few minutes late in greeting my guests, United Press correspondent Henry Shapiro, with his wife and daughter, and NBC correspondent and Mrs. Irving Levine.

We had a pleasant hour together at tea, and then a young Russian who had piloted my granddaughter, Kate Roosevelt, around on her trip here last year came to bring me some long-playing recordings for

. . . .

her because she had told him she was going to learn the Russian language.

He also brought for her a photo of himself and his wife and a box of her favorite candy in her favorite kind of box.

Kate seems to have left remarkably pleasant memories everywhere she went. One of her other admirers remembered that she admired the kind of cap worn by the women of Uzbekistan, and I believe he obtained one for her. So some good feeling was engendered by her visit.

That evening we went to a concert which was more like a vaudeville show. The singing wasn't very remarkable, but there was some good dancing.

The next day we went to see the new buildings of Moscow University on the outskirts of the city. They are almost as far away as the airport, but the transportation to that area by bus and subway is frequent. Six of the faculties are housed there, while six others are in old buildings downtown.

This university is set up quite differently from our universities, and the degrees are given in quite a different way. But I'll tell you about the educational setup here in greater detail later.

There are 120 elevators in the Moscow University buildings, making one wonder why it was necessary to build such high buildings when there was so much ground all around them. But from the top of them the view is magnificent.

Looking down, you see a park in one area with a statue of Lomonosov, the university's founder. There are some fine botanical gardens for use in studies of agriculture and science. Directly in front, as you look down, you see the dove of peace outlined in what looks like white rock.

I am constantly struck by the amount of emphasis that is put on peace here and wonder why that is done.

We lunched at the Indian embassy with Ambassador and Mrs. K. P. S. Mennon, who were delightful hosts. Their embassy and those of Britain and the United States are the only ones in Moscow that have gardens, enabling them in summer to have their parties outdoors.

After lunch the ambassador walked us down to see a little house on the grounds which he had planned to turn over to a member of his staff. The Soviet government, however, was horrified at the idea, explaining that Napoleon had used that house for two nights.

The house, therefore, stands empty. The area below it, which might be turned into a beautiful garden, also is empty because, as the ambassador explained, the summers are so short that it is hardly worthwhile to do much in the way of developing gardens.

After leaving the embassy we drove to Pushkin Museum to see a beautiful collection of modern French paintings which Ambassador Llewellyn E. Thompson had told us about. All of the paintings were bought before 1917 by someone who did a remarkable job, showing every period in the various artists' lives.

MOSCOW, SEPTEMBER 27—We started our morning at Tashkent in Central Asia at a collective farm, and now I can tell you the basic difference between a state farm and a collective farm.

The collective farm is owned by an organization of farmers. Seven percent is taken from the collective income for land and seven percent is in taxes and goes to the state. Thirteen percent goes to the organization running the collective for all services, and there are many. The remaining cash is divided among members of the collective.

We calculated that this meant every man got about 8,100 rubles a year in cash, besides shelter, services and food, which means that, on the whole, he is pretty well off. Of course, he takes the risk of a bad year that all farmers take. On the state farm, this risk is borne by the state.

This farm was the only place in Tashkent where we were able to visit any homes. It was possible to see newly constructed houses and an older house that had been freshly stuccoed on the outside but left unchanged on the inside.

All these houses have electricity, and you'll often see a one-burner electric stove on top of an old range. The water is carried, but not from too far away. Toilet and bathing facilities are old-fashioned— usually a privy and a bathhouse used by a collective group.

One nice feature is a house for recreation with a garden in which there are big wooden benches where men come to rest, if they feel like it, during lunch hours.

In the middle of the area there is a pond with greenish, stagnant-looking water which they told me was used for bathing. There also are showers inside the house.

This is a diversified farming operation, but cotton is the paying crop. They have pigs, sheep, cows, horses, orchards, vegetables and a variety of crops. There is no pasturage for cows, however, so food is grown for them.

Every inch of land seems to be in use. Where small fruit trees are planted, there are crops all around them. Even when the trees are big enough to bear fruit, there's still something growing under them.

There is a maternity hospital and a healthy baby clinic, but for serious illnesses the farm people go to hospitals in town or the doctor visits their homes. There is a nursery, kindergarten and school. Nursing mothers can leave their work and go to the nursery at stated hours when feedings are given (the same applies to factory workers).

In the farm manager's office there are pictures showing the increase in production on his farm. The output is going up steadily, but at the same time land has been added which, of course, increases production on his farm.

Just before leaving we were, as usual, plied with fruit, bread, tea and shashlik. Our hotel had packed for us an enormous number of sandwiches and fruit, but we should have learned by then that there is never any need for taking food with us if we are stopping anywhere.

From the collective farm we drove to one of the biggest textile factories in that part of the country. It makes chiefly women's cotton dress goods and white cotton for household use. It was one of the biggest factories I have ever seen, and it seemed to have an efficient system for controlling the purification of air.

I am not familiar enough with the latest factory machinery at home to know how the Soviet machinery compares with ours, but I didn't think there seemed to be any more need for women to operate these machines than I have seen in American factories.

They say the incidence of tuberculosis is low. They also have a nursery and school, but the school is only for their own workers. Everyone must attend four hours daily for the first four months, then take courses after work as they desire. There is a public bathhouse and a really large medical establishment. The head doctor told us it takes care of 40,000 patients and has 6,700 doctors.

We saw the part of the hospital that deals primarily with accidents, both to workers and their children. We had hoped to go in the afternoon with a visiting nurse to see some of the workers' families, but that proved impossible.

In the afternoon we called on the head of a Moslem group in Tashkent who told us that the majority of people in that area were Moslems and have 20-odd large mosques and a hundred small ones.

As usual, we were taken to a room where tables were laden with fruit. And after we had asked the necessary questions and had eaten what seemed to be a polite amount of the delicious fruit, I rose to go but was told dinner had been prepared for us and the Moslem custom required us to partake of the food.

I was told that the host always expects his guests to eat well to show appreciation of his hospitality and that there is an Arab saying that if you ate well, you lived long.

I responded that in my country, when you reach my age, you are warned against overeating and are told you are digging your grave with your teeth every day of your life. So I promised to taste these generous dishes but couldn't promise to "eat well."

The Moslems there have a school for preachers and a fine library where we saw some interesting books written by hand many years ago, with translations into Persian and other languages written in the margin.

Then we visited a hall where gatherings are held when visitors come and finally the office of the head of the church, who presented each of us with a characteristic embroidered Uzbek cap and gave me two pieces of silk made nearby. He told me he hoped to come to the United States, where I hope to have the opportunity to return his hospitality.

. . . .

The tone changes as Mrs. Roosevelt's reporting on her Russian visit proceeds uncensored. Though she spent a great deal of her time as a social critic in the United States, expressing all sorts of dissatisfactions with the way things were done in her own country, what Eleanor Roosevelt found in the Soviet Union in some respects appalled her—particularly the ways in which the government manipulated the people's thoughts and held sway over their time and energy by controlling every aspect of their work. Given a great deal more space than usual in her "My Day" columns for this Russian reporting, Mrs. Roosevelt was able to develop her thoughts and to present much more detail than in her regular columns (usually limited to 500–750 words). The difference shows: These are among the best pieces of reporting, of social-cultural-political analysis, she ever produced.

NEW YORK, OCTOBER 2—What is the Soviet Union really like? It is a mass of contradictions and it takes study and thought to understand it.

There is one symbol—the dove of peace—that you meet practically everywhere in Russia. I saw it painted on the side of a truck as I was riding through the streets; I looked down on it from the tower of Moscow University outlined in stone below me. A circus I attended ended with the release of a number of doves of peace. Everywhere this seems to be the symbol.

You might think that it was an effort to keep the people reminded of their need for peace. Heaven knows, they don't need a reminder! They suffered enough in the war, and a traveler in Russia is soon aware of it.

But that is not why it is done. It is done to remind the people that they must sacrifice and work for peace because their great enemy, the United States, is trying to bring about a war.

The dove of peace is really intended to teach the people of the Soviet Union that, while they love peace and want no war, the U.S. government is planning an aggressive war and the Soviet government is only trying to protect the people of the Soviet Union from such aggression.

If you forget this, you will be lulled into a security that is dangerous

. . . .

for all of us. But you are going to need much more understanding, much more willingness to learn before you can hope to avoid this war that these people are being indoctrinated into believing that we in the United States might start.

Guns and atomic weapons are not going to win this war or prevent it. Much, much more has to be done, and to explain why I say this, I am going to tell you as much as I was able to find out about what the Soviet Union is today.

I will begin by giving you my interview with Nikita S. Khrushchev, chief of the Soviet Communist Party. You may not agree with my conclusions, but I want to give you the basis for my thinking. So in these articles I will take you to see one thing after another that I saw. Then I will try to evaluate the price that is paid by the people of the Soviet Union for these things, and explain what they mean not only to the Soviet people but to the people of Asia, Africa and South America as well.

On this understanding alone, I believe, can we form a policy which may save us from the war that the people of the Soviet Union dread as much as we do.

I have never felt as cut off from the world as I did in the weeks I spent in the Soviet Union.

It is practically impossible for the people of the United States to believe that isolation such as exists in the Soviet Union can really exist anywhere in the world today.

The only newspapers that can be bought in Russia are the Communist Soviet papers, the Communist German papers, the Communist French papers, and the English Daily Worker. In the Soviet newspapers today you will get six pages of plans for the celebration of the 40th anniversary of the Revolution, you will get two and a half columns, at the most, of world news and the only news about the U.S. that I saw was that we have refused to allow our Negro children to go to school with our white children in Arkansas and Tennessee.

When I pointed out to anyone that this particular difficulty involves only a small segment of the United States—seven or eight states, at the most, out of 48—and that this is not a fair presentation of news from the United States, I was usually met with the remark that the individual with whom I was speaking knew nothing about politics. That is the refuge of all intelligent people in the Soviet Union who want a quiet life.

In trying to understand the Russian thinking, there is one thing we must know. The Russians had a great scientist called Pavlov. His theory—now believed—was that through conditioned reflexes you can mold a human being into any pattern you desire. This has been worked out so that it begins with a child at the age of two months.

I am not sure that these theories are not as important for us to understand as the fact that Lenin is the nearest thing to a saint that the Russian people have to worship. The Revolution of 1917 unified the country. The people were fighting against wrongs, and Lenin symbolizes to them the beginning of a better world.

The war brought to the Russians terrible hardships which are still with them in memory and, to some extent, in actual fact. Khrushchev himself spoke to me of the loss of his son and 12,000,000 men in the war and the destruction of cities, towns and villages. In the last five years, however, enormous physical gains have been made in the daily lives of the Russian people.

The proof of how they feel about Lenin is the long lines that for more than 20 years have wended their way to Lenin's tomb in the Kremlin every day it has been open. People, coming from all over Russia, form the lines that crawl for a mile and a half. I did not realize the length of one such line till I followed it to its beginning and found that it wound back and forth three times in the garden along the Kremlin wall before it began to climb the last half mile of the hill up to the entrance of the tomb. To what do we give such devotion?

I am home and, oh, so glad to be home. But for the sake of our country and our people, I hope that in these articles I can make you see the reasons why our misunderstandings are so great, and point out some of the things we must do if war and extermination are not to be the answer for both the people of the United States and the people of the Soviet Union—which really means the world as well, for we can no longer isolate the results of war.

. . . .

The sheer boldness of Mrs. Roosevelt's decision to request an interview with Nikita Khrushchev is noteworthy. Other reporters had tried and failed even to gain admission to the country, much less the inner sanctum of power at the Kremlin. But her stature in the international world of politics itself, stemming from her years at the United Nations as United States delegate, had put Mrs. Roosevelt in a nearly unique position. She had the full credentials of a diplomatic expert without any official government connection, as though she were a self-appointed ambassador-at-large. And her "My Day" was still syndicated widely enough so that any foreign leader, including Khrushchev, who wanted to say something to the American people knew that Eleanor Roosevelt's column was an excellent way to do so.

NEW YORK, OCTOBER 3—I can best begin this series of articles on the Soviet Union by letting Nikita S. Khrushchev, leader of the Communist Party of the USSR, speak for himself. I was asked to submit

. . . .

my questions, but Mr. Khrushchev did not have them before him when I appeared. And he answered my questions as though he was speaking completely spontaneously.

This first article will cover only in part some of the recorded answers, and while I have his answers in Russian, I can give you only the translation as it came from my interpreter, Mrs. Anna Lavrova, who told me she had translated for my husband at Yalta.

I opened by asking her to tell Mr. Khrushchev that I appreciated his taking the time to see me when he was on vacation and I added that I had enjoyed and had been much interested by my trip in his country. Mr. Khrushchev answered, "Politicians never cast aside political obligations."

Here are my questions and his replies:

ROOSEVELT: I came to the USSR for the newspapers I write for and to use what information I could gather for lectures which I will be giving in the coming year, but I have the hope that being here I can gain greater understanding and clear up some of the questions we get at home from some of our people who do not understand certain things they hear about the USSR.

KHRUSHCHEV: I appreciate your coming here and I want to speak of President Franklin Roosevelt. We respect him and remember his activities because he was the first to establish diplomatic relations between the USA and the USSR. President Roosevelt understood perfectly well the necessity of such relations between our two countries.

He was a great man, a capable man who understood the interests of his own country and the interests of the Soviet Union. We had a common cause against Hitler and we appreciate very much that Franklin Roosevelt understood this task, which was a common task of our two countries. I am very happy to greet you in our land and to have a talk here.

ROOSEVELT: Mr. Khrushchev, may I ask the questions which I have submitted? Then if you have any questions to ask me, I will be happy to try to answer them, and may we have some further informal talk, not for direct quotation?

KHRUSHCHEV: Yes, Mrs. Roosevelt, you are welcome.

ROOSEVELT: At home people would say, "How does the Soviet Union expect us to disarm without inspection when she forced us to rearm after World War II? We reduced our army from 12,000,000 to 1,000,000 men." That would be one of the first questions asked, sir.

KHRUSHCHEV: I believe, Mrs. Roosevelt, we have different points of view on this armament complaint. We do not agree with your conception. We consider that demobilization took place in the U.S. and in the USSR.

You mention that you had 12,000,000 army men but in our country men and women were all mobilized. In our country perished roughly the number of people which you mention made up the army in your country, almost the same number of people. Mrs. Roosevelt, I do not want to offend you, but if you compare the losses of your country and the losses of ours, your losses just equal roughly our losses in one big campaign, one big attack by the Germans.

As you know, Mrs. Roosevelt, what terrible ruins we got and destruction because we lost our mining, our metallurgy. We lost our cities. That is why our country was so eager to establish peace and to establish firm peace. No country wished it so eagerly as our country.

When you consider demobilization, just some circles in your country wanted it. Others thought and believed that the Soviet country would perish as a socialist state, so they just hoped that it will perish, that it will die.

ROOSEVELT: I can't quite understand that. You mean, Mr. Khrushchev, that you think we thought, or rather that some circles believed, that all socialist countries would die.

KHRUSHCHEV: That is exactly. But these hopes failed and you see now that our socialist state was established out of the ruins, has established its economy and has become even more powerful.

ROOSEVELT: I understand, Mr. Khrushchev, but the Soviets kept a much greater proportion of men under arms than we did at that time.

[Dr. David Gurewitsch, who made the trip to Russia with me, was making the recording of the conversation and, at the same time, listening to make sure the translations were correct, since he knew Russian and was allowed to take photographs. So he broke in here to say, "Not just the proportion but the absolute figures were far greater—6,000,000 men under arms in the Soviet."]

KHRUSHCHEV: Dr. Gurewitsch, you may perfectly know the number of your army men, but don't feel so sure of the number of our army men. You don't know it. [Turning to Mrs. Roosevelt] I do not reject that our army was bigger than yours. We approached this question in a quiet way, in a calm way. Then it can be looked at reasonably and easily understood.

Take a map and look at the geographical location or situation of our country. It is a colossal territory. Mrs. Roosevelt, if you take Germany or France, just small countries which keep their army either to defend either their East or their West, that is easy.

They may have a small army, but if we keep our army in the East, it is difficult to reach the West, you see, to use this Western army in the East, because our territory is so vast. Or the army which is in the North cannot be used in the South.

So, to be sure of our security in our state, we have to keep a big army, which is not so easy for us. When people speak about borders, they speak about 3,000 kilometers, which is the distance between the continents. But when we move our army from East to West, it means 3,000 kilometers.

ROOSEVELT: I understand all this, of course, but you have nothing to fear from the North. I understand that at Yalta Germany's defeat was accepted and you did not want Germany built up as a military power and you wanted a group of neutral countries between you and Germany. I understood at that time that these countries were to be free countries but to be closely tied to the Soviet Union, since the USSR was actually thinking of its protection.

Today, certainly, Great Britain, France and Germany are not a military menace. I don't say they might not become so, but they are not today. They are purely on a defensive basis, so I think it is possible to discuss very calmly how a country like the Soviet Union can be secure, which I understand perfectly the need of and the desire for, and still it should be possible not to have in the Soviet Union an army that can be an offensive army, because that frightens the rest of the world.

KHRUSHCHEV: What can I tell you in answer, Mrs. Roosevelt? When we increase our arms, it means that we are afraid of each other. Russian troops, before the Revolution, never approached Great Britain and never entered America. Even in old times they never came to the United States of America, but the troops of the USA approached our Far East, Japanese troops were in our Far East in Vladivostock, French troops in our city of Odessa, and that is why we must have an army. Your troops approach our territory, not we yours.

We never went to Mexico or Canada, but your troops went there, so that is why we have to have an army in case of danger. Before the time when troops will be drawn out of Europe and military bases will be liquidated, of course, the disarmament will not succeed.

ROOSEVELT: The actual type of armament today that is important has changed. It is not what it used to be in the old days. We are reducing our army, but what matters today is atomic weapons, and that is why I imagine the emphasis will have to be on how we can come to an agreement.

What follows is a portion of a subsequent column; Mrs. Roosevelt and Khrushchev carry on a dialogue about arms inspections and reductions the likes of which their negotiators might have had at the round table in Geneva in more formal circumstances. One gets a sense that Mrs. Roosevelt had lost patience with the slow, deliberate process of international arms reduction negotiations and had decided to see what she could do by taking the subject into her own hands and right to the lion's den. The amount of time and space given to the subject of nuclear war and the prospects for nuclear disarmament also reflect a continuing, overriding concern of the late 1950s throughout most of the American populace, which had not yet learned to accept "the bomb" as an inevitable fact of political life.

CINCINNATI, OCTOBER 5—KHRUSHCHEV: We are for international inspection, but there first has to be confidence and then inspection. Mr. Dulles wants inspection without confidence.

ROOSEVELT: I think the confidence and the inspection have to come together. We have to start and gradually increase our plans.

KHRUSHCHEV: Quite right. Only gradually it can be done.

ROOSEVELT: Would you agree to limited inspection if we could make a beginning?

KHRUSHCHEV: But I quite agree. That is what we proposed. We proposed inspection in ports, on highways, on roads, at airports, and it is to be an internation inspection. But in answer to our proposal, Mr. Dulles makes a statement which sounds as though he was making propaganda for the atom bomb, trying to make it palatable. He talks of a clean bomb as if there were such a thing as a clean bomb. War is dirty thing.

But you refused our suggestion. You insist on this flying business and looking at our factories. You know those rockets made the situation more frightful. Now we can destroy countries in a few minutes. How many bombs does it take to destroy West Germany? How many for France? How many for England? Just a few. We have now H-bombs and rockets. We do not even have to send any bombers.

ROOSEVELT: And soon small countries will have atomic bombs.

KHRUSHCHEV: Why not? Research goes on. They learn about it. Let's get together so there shall be no war. We are ready to sign such an agreement now.

ROOSEVELT: Your people certainly want peace, and I can assure you that our people want peace, too.

KHRUSHCHEV: Do you think we, the government, want war?

ROOSEVELT: Not the people, but governments, make war. And then they persuade the people that it is in a good cause, the cause of their own defense. Those arguments can be made by both your government and by ours.

KHRUSHCHEV: That's right. Can we say we had a friendly conversation?

ROOSEVELT: You can say we had a friendly conversation, but we differ.

KHRUSHCHEV: Now, we didn't shoot at each other.

. . . .

Eleanor Roosevelt saw many Russian leaders in addition to Nikita Khrushchev. There was a long list of challenging appointments with ministers and subministers of everything from agriculture to health. She wanted to learn as much as she possibly could about how the Soviet system worked, or (as it turned out) in many cases did not work. And, as always on her foreign trips, she made time available for the arts and for other entertainments, for these experiences too were revealing about whatever place she might be visiting.

A letter Mrs. Roosevelt wrote to Trude and Joseph Lash in New York during her Moscow visit shows that there were moments of laughter and comic relief in the midst of this serious visit to the USSR. "Then we went to Zagorsk, really lovely 15th Cent. Church & a most amusing midday meal at the Greek Orthodox Divinity School! They are stout these gentlemen & eat & drink well. We were plied with champagne & I was glad of my agreement to drink only water. Maureen [Maureen Corr, Mrs. Roosevelt's secretary] found her line—taking one glass— looked upon with incredulity and not accepted!" And later in the same letter: "We have been to a circus, a ballet, & a huge & beautiful amusement park in the evenings!" That she was so widely well received by the Soviets led to the remark "The welcome in spots almost embarrassing. . . ."

These final two selections from Mrs. Roosevelt's columns about life in the Soviet Union are models of astute observation and thoughtful political-cultural analysis. Her largely female readership in the United States would have been especially curious to hear about everyday life for typical Soviet women.

NEW YORK, OCTOBER 9—A large group of Russian women invited me to spend some time with them soon after my arrival in Moscow. They told me they were members of the Committee of Soviet Women, which covers the whole USSR.

The assistant chairman of the committee placed me on her right. She was a professor. On my other side sat Tatyana Zueva, Minister of Culture of RSFSR, deputy to the Supreme Soviet.

All were distinguished women. Two of them wore pins with a gold star hanging from them, distinguishing them as heroes of the Soviet Union or of Socialist Labor.

These were women receiving fairly good salaries and yet none of them probably lived in an apartment which you and I would consider adequate for family needs. Building is going on everywhere in Russia at a tremendous pace, but the needs to rebuild are even greater and most people live in inadequate quarters.

The architecture of the new apartments is drab and dull. Beauty and quality are sacrificed for speed, so that buildings finished only five years ago might have been built 30 or 40 years ago.

The entrance to nearly all apartments resembles that of one of our modern slum-clearance type of buildings—made so that one can hose down the stairs. And if there is an elevator, it is the kind you find in France: small and open like a cage.

While the influence of France is felt in the type of houses and the looks of the streets, the concierge is missing. Instead, most housing units have someone in charge of social welfare who tries to adjust quarrels and difficulties and who has an eye to cleanliness and general behavior of the tenants.

The women told me that since all of them work, the days when people had to queue up for hours to buy their supplies were trying for them.

Now, however, they can telephone and have the supplies delivered. This means they have to shop at a government store where all food prices are fixed by the government.

If they want to buy something from the little open markets in their area, where people who live on the land are permitted to sell any goods they do not need, then they must go themselves and compete with other shoppers. The advantage is that there is sometimes a little more variety.

There is a room in the big stores where children can be left while mothers shop, and while we were in Moscow a big shop, primarily for children, opened. The crowd that went through this new shop on Sundays was simply tremendous.

I asked this group of women whether they would outline for me how a woman in the Soviet Union manages her day. I told them that I thought some of us in the United States wondered how it was possible for a woman with children to work at a full-time job.

They smiled at me indulgently and said the government provided them with many things needed to make this possible. They get up early and feed the family, the older children leave for school and, if there are young ones, they are taken to a kindergarten. Or if a mother works in a factory and has a baby, she takes her baby to the day nursery in the factory.

If there is illness in the family, she is not required to report to work. The doctor gives her a certificate and she can stay home. Wherever they are, the children are fed by the government, the union or the factory organization and the mother picks them up and brings them home at the end of her day's work.

The crowding in apartments means there is always more than one family sharing one unit. So there is usually an older member of the family who at 60 has retired and is glad to watch the children if they must be at home.

There are many restaurants and families go out to dinner on Sunday or sometimes for an evening meal. Sunday is still the day of rest, even in a country where religion is not officially recognized.

These women seemed to think their lives are very easy to manage. My Intourist guide, Anna Lavrova, whose husband is a professor, mentioned to me that on evenings when she is at home and busy sewing, he reads aloud to her in French, a language that he loves.

There is a hunger among men and women alike for education in the Soviet Union, and in the subway, on trains, everywhere, young and old read as though their lives depended on mastering what is on the pages of the book they read.

St. Louis, October 18—As I look back on all my experiences in the weeks spent in the Soviet Union, I want to say first that I understand well the love of the Russian people for their own country.

It is a vast country, with many climates, many resources, many possibilities yet undeveloped in soil, in coal and oil and metals of all kinds. Above everything else, it has vast resources in human beings.

Like all people who have lived close to the soil, there is a devotion for the particular area in which they live. I can see this even in people who left Russia years ago. A taxi driver in New York asked me the other day about his old country and said wistfully: "The village I came from near Minsk was wiped out in the war but I would love to go back and just see that country again. I love it still."

This love of country accounts partly for the Russians' willingness to work and sacrifice when they are told it is necessary for the preservation of their native land. A totalitarian regime which regulates all news makes it impossible for anyone in Russia to understand that there are different interpretations of events from those they have been given.

The fact that none but a Communist newspaper can be bought within the Soviet Union, even though there may be libraries with some magazines giving a fair opinion of the world scene, still means that the mass of people have very little concept of events or thinking in the world outside of their own.

The continuing political struggle at the top for power modifies only minor situations. The terror of secret police may be lessened, certain arbitrary rules may change somewhat. But all of the Soviet Union's leaders have believed in the Socialist doctrine, so the promotion of this idea goes on by different methods, perhaps, but the basic idea does not change. And I doubt if it will change.

This basic Socialistic idea may be modified as time goes on, but that will largely depend, I think, on what the free world is able to prove. The free world will have to believe as firmly that the wave of the future is democracy, freedom and justice and show how good this can be for human beings.

There is no real hope of modifying the beliefs of those dedicated to a Socialist and Communist idea, which still holds that Communism is the final great hope for the happiness of human beings, unless we can prove by deeds that our accomplishments are greater.

In the life of the ordinary man and woman in Russia, all that is good has happened to them since the Revolution. I have told you a little of the advances in education and in medicine. We must recognize that there is an increase in urban living, but where the government is the employer, every man and woman in the Soviet Union has a job.

If a woman has many children, she may stay at home. Otherwise, the basis of all planning is to make it possible for men and women to work and, in spite of their working, to take good care of their children.

There is no comparison between life in the Soviet Union and in the United States, for instance, because the whole objective is based on a different concept. This may modify as the need for a big labor force lessens, but at present it must be the policy of any government in the Soviet Union.

We must remember that the vast number of Soviet people have been peasants, have lived in huts in overcrowded conditions with no sanitation and other comforts, without medical care, without education and that religion was largely used to make these poor conditions of life accepted—a panacea to keep people quiet and make them think of a future life rather than of the miserable present.

So it is natural that the present government stresses for the mass of people the possibilities of education, the giving of medical care, the security of a job and an old-age pension, even though it asks for sacrifices and offers comparatively slow progress in the more modern comforts of living.

These things can give hope to the Russian people, and the signs in the factories which say "Be grateful" have in back of them some real improvements which we must recognize.

In addition, leaders of this regime not only believe in education but they have a real enthusiasm for research and a respect for the scientific mind and the processes which bring advances in the present-day world and which they feel bring them greater security in the struggle with the capitalist world.

It seems to me that this situation calls for understanding on our part, respect for these achievements, but a firmer belief in the possibilities of our own system.

. . . .

After weeks of reporting about serious matters such as Soviet-American relations, Mrs. Roosevelt turned her attention to a squabble in American government involving a fur coat that had been given to First Lady Mamie Eisenhower. Yet even from the ridiculous Eleanor Roosevelt found a way to bring out the underlying substantive issue, in this case the ethics of giving gifts to government officials. More than that, she clearly wanted to express some friendly sympathy for the First Lady because she realized how vulnerable the president's wife is to public scrutiny, a scrutiny that was sometimes mercilessly unfair.

ANN ARBOR, MICH., NOVEMBER 9—Congress, it seems to me, is becoming rather confused about the gifts-in-government question in Washington.

The Constitution bars public officials from accepting gifts from a foreign government, and this has been construed in various ways by the State Department. But as far as I know there is nothing which deprives a person who is not actually in employ of the government from accepting from a foreigner something to show appreciation of kindness or good service.

There is also nothing except good taste, as far as I know, to dictate what the wife of a President shall or shall not do. It is this point that is not touched upon either in the Constitution or in any law I know of. And it is this which I would like to write about because I think Mrs. Eisenhower has been made uncomfortable by criticism resulting from her acceptance of a fur coat from the Fur Trappers of Maine and the Beaver Fur Trappers Association.

The beaver trappers of Maine presented Mrs. Eisenhower with some skins. This was done in the obvious hope that she would have these skins made up and wear them and that a domestic industry thereby would get some sorely needed attention. Not many people know that the trapping of beavers is one of the industries of the State of Maine.

Mrs. Eisenhower herself paid for the making of her coat and it is nobody's business what she paid for having it made up. She was doing an American industry a kindness.

The effort was made, I think, to make her feel that this was wrong in some way, and yet no strings were attached to this gift. She was not asked to award a contract or to change somebody's road or to see that

. . . .

oil was imported here or there. She was simply given a gift which those who gave it hoped would give her pleasure, knowing that if it did and she wore the skins, it would bring them some attention.

Nobody was going to be forced to buy a beaver coat, but they would know where they could buy one. I believe it would have been more unkind and she would have been open to severer criticism if she had refused the gift rather than accepting it.

There is little enough pleasure attached to being the wife of a President, a position that involves a great many responsibilities. Why the press apparently should draw critical attention to a perfectly innocent act of kindness I cannot understand.

Mrs. Eisenhower has conducted herself with dignity and grace in the White House. She has fulfilled the duties expected of her, and this type of criticism seems to me petty and small and not worthy of the American press or the American people.

. . . .

The ongoing civil rights struggle in the United States did not blind Eleanor Roosevelt to the fact that in other countries similar if not worse conditions of prejudice and of domination of one race by another called out for attention. She was among the early prophets of eventual radical change in the politics of apartheid in South Africa. Mrs. Roosevelt supported a call in 1957 for a universal Declaration of Conscience concerning opposition to apartheid.

NEW YORK, DECEMBER 2—People all over the world have been asked to sign a Declaration of Conscience to observe a day of protest against South Africa's apartheid policy. An international committee, composed of more than 150 world leaders from more than 43 nations, has designated Human Rights Day, December 10, as this worldwide day of protest. Particularly in India and in Africa, as well as in many other countries of the world, there will be demonstrations protesting the policy which is felt to be harmful to human relations the world over. Therefore it cannot be the domestic concern of one nation only, but of all nations.

More than 20 American communities have already said they would hold similar meetings. The Very Rev. James A. Pike is the U.S. national chairman and Rev. Martin Luther King, Jr. is the vice president of the committee in this country. The list of those who have signed the Declaration of Conscience is composed of the names of men all over the world who are known to have stood for equal rights for all human beings. It is true that there are peoples who are not as advanced as others, but as a rule this is due to lack of opportunity and can be corrected in one or two generations by education and environment.

. . . .

When I was asked to sign this Declaration of Conscience, I at first hesitated. I felt that a country which needed to look at its own situation and acknowledge the basic rights of all its own citizens and work for the necessary changes which would bring every citizen in the United States the opportunity for complete development of his powers might better perhaps first sign a Declaration of Conscience covering his own country. I signed, however, because the situation here, bad as it is, is not quite the same as the situation in South Africa. The Negroes of our South have good leaders and though their education has been insufficient and their opportunities for advancement certainly not equal, still they have begun their upward climb. They are able to do much for themselves, and on the whole in this country there is a vast majority of people who are ready and willing to help them achieve equality of opportunity in every area of our complicated civilization.

Bitter as the feeling is at present in the South and in spite of the fact that communications between the races in many Southern states seem to have deteriorated, the Supreme Court decision and the feeling of the majority of the people of the nation will eventually, I am sure, bring about a solution to the present difficult situation. Someone suggested to me the other day that it might be started in the South by dividing boys' schools and girls' schools and putting all boys without discrimination into one school and all girls without discrimination into another, which would remove one of the chief objections of the Southerners. Whether this would help or not, I don't know. But I am confident that the pressure of the majority feeling in this nation will be so overwhelming for equal rights for all our citizens that sooner or later this problem must have a solution which satisfactorily safeguards these rights.

....

Home at last for Christmas at Hyde Park, the pleasures and travails of managing an aging country house (her beloved Val-Kill) absorbed Mrs. Roosevelt's attention. It had been an astonishingly full year for Eleanor Roosevelt, full to the brim with work and remarkable meetings with remarkable people. It was time, for a few days, to focus on family and fun.

HYDE PARK, DECEMBER 30—There is an old saying, often quoted by my husband's father, which said "No very stiff frost will come until the springs are filled."

I think our springs in the country must be nearly filled by now. We have had rain and rain and rain. The brook always overflows into my cellar at Hyde Park when it rises above a certain level, and it already has done so.

....

There are certain places in the roofs of the playhouse and my own cottage which we have tried to mend but which, under certain conditions, leak and cause a near-flood in the back kitchen and in one of my living rooms. But during the last heavy rain only the back kitchen suffered.

This, however, is not a happy situation when cooking for a large number of persons, as my people at Hyde Park have been doing the last few days.

My grandchildren are so delighted to go horseback riding every day during the holidays, so the lack of snow or ice does not upset them at all. But the rain does! So, while we are not praying for snow, we are praying for clear weather!

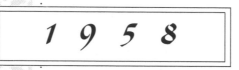

1 9 5 8

Not again until the mid-1980s, when President Ronald Reagan was at the height of his popularity, was a person in the eighth decade of life chosen as the most admired American in a Gallup poll. In 1958 that honor went to Eleanor Roosevelt, who would turn seventy-four in October. Reagan's popularity reflected his solid hold at that time on the White House; he had an official mandate. Mrs. Roosevelt's social role was entirely different. Though she had certainly enjoyed many years at her late husband's side when his party held sway, by 1958 she had been forced by changing circumstances to redefine her role as that of gadfly, speaking more often than not for an advanced progressive minority, making all the more remarkable her choice in the Gallup poll as America's most admired woman.

In 1958 the cold war continued to heat up. All year the news was marked by reports of military advances and scientific progress carried out in the name of international competition, generally with the Soviets. Protracted discussions of disarmament went nowhere. In January the Air Force organized a system of unremitting surveillance aloft, keeping strategic bombers always at the ready should the Russians attack. By May the United States and Canada had formed NORAD (North American Air Defense Command), which included radar stations all across the Canadian tundra. These steps were meant to keep Communists out. Communists already on the loose in America were apparently diminishing in number, or at least in enthusiasm: *The Daily Worker* cut back to once-a-week publication due to declining revenues.

Secretary of State John Foster Dulles, constantly dueling with the Soviets, recognized that outer space could easily become the next battlefield. In January he proposed an international agreement to guarantee the peaceful use of the heavens. At the same time, the U.S. space program began catching up with the Russians'. On January 31

Explorer 1, America's first satellite, was launched by the Army from Cape Canaveral in Florida. In March the Navy launched Vanguard 1. By July the incipient rivalry among the military services in the space program was resolved with the creation of NASA (National Aeronautics and Space Administration). Eleanor Roosevelt's chilly opinion about the space program was unwavering. She recognized the scientific achievements but argued that humanitarian needs on earth should be addressed first, a viewpoint not widely shared at the time.

American foreign policy met with stiff, even hostile resistance in two places in the spring and early summer. Vice President Richard Nixon, on a good-will tour of Latin American countries, was assaulted by a mob in Venezuela; American-sponsored libraries in Lebanon were attacked after U.S. Marines had landed in that country to help quell an insurrection. During this year Mrs. Roosevelt devoted many "My Day" columns to analyzing America's difficult role in world politics. She believed America had a major role to play as the richest, most powerful country in the world, but her most favored tactics had little to do with the Eisenhower administration's preferred tools and strategies, which usually relied on sales of arms to foreign governments. During the dog days of August, the U.S. Navy sent its premier atomic submarine way up north, but not to cool off. The *Nautilus* made the first under-ice crossing of the North Pole, a technical and military triumph.

Heat of an entirely different kind was generated in August when the Russian novelist Vladimir Nabokov's titillating *Lolita* was published in English in the United States. It barely survived several censorship challenges.

The domestic world of education also generated a good deal of friction in 1958. On the positive side, the Democratic Congress and the Republican White House, after much debate, succeeded in adopting the National Defense Education Act to make loans available to students for higher education. The theory was that America needed better students to fight the good fight against Communist influence at home and abroad. Mrs. Roosevelt approved of the program but thought there was no need to link the aid-to-education bill directly to international conflict. Meanwhile, in the South the integration struggle continued. In September, Little Rock, Arkansas, sought more time to effect integration, but the Supreme Court denied the request. By the end of the month, Governor Orville Faubus had closed four public schools in defiance of the Court's orders.

The end of the year saw Nelson Rockefeller, an already prominent American Mrs. Roosevelt admired, take a major step in developing a political career when he won the governorship of New York. The Democratic Party in New York was in poor shape, as Mrs. Roosevelt candidly documented in her "My Day" columns, and while she worked hard to help rebuild it, she generally gave the Republican Rockefeller her support once he was elected.

In 1958 James Agee—who with photographer Walker Evans had produced in 1941 one of the most moving books about the Depression and about poverty in general, *Let Us Now Praise Famous Men*—was awarded the Pulitzer Prize for fiction for his *A Death in the Family.*

....

Long before she joined the ranks of senior citizens herself Eleanor Roosevelt had developed a genuine concern for the financial fate of people who, as a result of age or disability, could no longer earn an adequate income. She had participated firsthand in the debates within the White House about the establishment of the Social Security Administration. While it was a major New Deal victory for FDR and the liberals in Congress to have social security finally implemented, few among its early proponents took into account what inflation would eventually do to the payments the government was beginning to guarantee.

By the late 1950s Mrs. Roosevelt among others had recognized that without periodic adjustments in the levels of veterans', widows', and retirees' government benefits, living on a fixed income could become difficult indeed. The idea Mrs. Roosevelt introduces here—of linking social security payments to inflation—was later to gain broad acceptance as "indexing," meaning that as the Consumer Price Index (the government's main inflation barometer) rose, so too would social security benefits.

NEW YORK, JANUARY 10—I have a letter from a woman who tells the sad story that I hear more and more often these days.

She is a widow whose husband, a war veteran, died 27 years ago and left her to raise five children. She wrote to draw my attention to the fact that even though widows of veterans get a pension, it is not enough for them to live on. Her pension is $54.18 a month.

This woman lives in southern Texas, but even there her pension is not sufficient to live on. She has worked hard all her life. Her husband was a bodyguard for President Theodore Roosevelt on many of his speaking tours.

She is unable to make ends meet because she no longer can work. Her children, she says, are married and have their own families to raise and she does not think it right to burden them with her support.

I feel that it is not too much to ask that each child give her a small amount, yet I have great sympathy for her feeling that after a life of hard work she should be entitled to a pension covering the necessities of life so she need not depend on her children.

I feel a reassessment of Social Security benefits in the pension field

....

should be made. The cost of living has gone up. Of late, prices always seem to be going up and never coming down. Perhaps there should be a sliding scale for pensions to meet the changes in living costs.

I think, too, that pensioners are a group which probably should be given some of our surplus foods, for no one in this country should be on a diet below the standards of healthy living.

Most of these people are old, and perhaps Congress will not think their votes amount to much. But this group is certainly getting larger in this country and, therefore, even from a political standpoint, this situation should receive consideration from both Republicans and Democrats.

....

The Roosevelt family had long since grown used to living in the public spotlight. Judging from the number of them who entered politics or some other form of public service, it seems as though family members had a natural gift for coping with the lack of privacy and the sometimes harsh criticism of the press or of political adversaries. Eleanor Roosevelt was among the toughest of the lot. She could be angered, offended, or amused at what was said of her or of her children, but she was never afraid of such scrutiny.

Still, the experience of seeing herself and her family portrayed by actors in a play was something new even for Mrs. Roosevelt, although she had had an opportunity to read the script by Dore Schary before seeing the play. The self-effacement of her comment on how her own character was portrayed was typical. Although Eleanor Roosevelt was intellectually adamant about many of her ideas, apparently believing with utmost confidence in her own viewpoints, she was touchingly unassuming about other aspects of her personality.

Louis Howe, another character in the play, was perhaps the closest and most durable political adviser to both Franklin and Eleanor Roosevelt, whose support reached back to the 1920s—when FDR made an unsuccessful bid for the White House as James Cox's vice presidential running mate. Howe was a somewhat coarse and rambunctious fellow with an unappealing face, and it had taken Mrs. Roosevelt quite some time to accept him as a Roosevelt insider. Eventually she came to admire and trust him completely.

SARASOTA, FLA. FEBRUARY 4—I saw the opening-night performance last week in New York of the play "Sunrise at Campobello," which depicts nearly three years in the life of my husband.

I found to be quite true what my son, Elliott, had told me about the play. It is remarkably good and well acted, but I was happy that the actors recognized it as a play and did not try to make it too real.

....

As a result, just as Elliott had said, I was able to see it as drama and not think of it as depicting each individual as he or she really was.

Dore Schary, the author, did a remarkable job of gaining an insight into the characters as they were at the time—in 1921. Louis Howe, for instance, who is a delightful and amusing person, could easily have said any of the things that were put into his mouth and I enjoyed the portrayal of him thoroughly, although he could never have looked like the gentleman cast in his role.

I thought Miss Mary Fickett did an excellent job of being a very sweet character, which she is in the play. I am afraid I was never really like Mr. Schary's picture of myself, so I could even look upon the portrayal of myself in a fictional light!

Ralph Bellamy, as my husband, did a remarkable job of showing, in his study at the Institute for Crippled and Disabled, the way people with polio feel and the patience, hard work and determination that goes into doing each new thing. He suggested my husband very successfully.

Dramatically and emotionally, the play carried a real impact. Because it is about a victory over polio and leaves out all political questions, it may have a wider appeal and much more sympathetic audience than if stress had been laid on later political achievements. To people who have had and have overcome polio, it will have a very personal appeal, and it will dramatize for many the character-building that inevitably accompanies a lengthy illness of this kind in which patience and determination play such a great part in final achievements.

In real life, of course, there was one point which came later in my husband's life, as it frequently does in the lives of other polio victims. This was the point in which he made his decision as to whether he would devote himself to his efforts toward recovery or accept his disabilities in order to play a more active role in the life he was leading.

Sometimes, as in my husband's case, such a decision will be to go on with a political career. Sometimes it will be a decision to pick up again a home or business or professional life and work with the disabilities rather than devoting more time to complete recovery.

That is a subject, perhaps, for another play. In the meantime, I want to congratulate Mr. Schary and the producer, the Theatre Guild, and every member of the cast for a remarkably good performance and an extremely interesting play.

. . . .

In her "My Day" columns Mrs. Roosevelt did not go into the question of an afterlife. For her, religion had much more to do with clarifying one's own values and achieving inner peace so as to be better able to accomplish socially useful things in this life. She also saw religion and prayer as means toward a broader end: a worldwide communion of all peoples. In this year's "My Day" column on the World Day of Prayer, Mrs. Roosevelt not only quotes some eloquent lines from the year's chosen prayers, but also notes the crossculturally unifying power of shared spiritual experience.

MIAMI BEACH, FEBRUARY 6—In the South you are apt to see along the highways many reminders of a religious nature. I have always wondered whether the South was really more interested in religion or the weather. Because the South, especially in the warm areas, is a refuge for people who are growing older, those who sponsor these signs think of them as particularly appropriate to the population of this part of the country.

In any case, my visit here coincides with a reminder which has come from the United Church Women. They tell me that on Friday, February 21, the 72nd observance of the World Day of Prayer will take place. This is the first Friday in Lent and Christians all over the world will unite in prayer for a better world and in thanksgiving for our Christian heritage.

Each year a new group in a new part of the world provides the service, and this year it has come from a group of women in Australia. They have chosen two prayers used by the aborigine Christians. The first is:

"Most High Father God, may Your love go into all parts of the earth, and may the people of all nations learn to know your great truths and goodness through Jesus Christ, and so be able to teach their children that only through Him can the peoples of the world have true happiness and lasting peace."

The second one is:

"You know, O God, that a very small leaf on the ground can mean that big roots are underneath, so we pray that even a little light from You touching the heart will mean that men and women will know of a very great love coming from You for them. We pray that this light and love will grow everywhere until everyone will have heard the story of Your way."

These are the prayers for the peoples of the whole world which come from the Australian bush where more than 60,000 aborigines live.

The theme of this World Day of Prayer is "The Bread of Life," and this is the day when throughout the world many peoples will repeat the prophecy of Isaiah: "He shall judge between nations, He shall decide from many peoples; and they shall beat their swords into ploughshares, and their spears into pruning hooks; nation shall not lift sword against nation, neither shall they learn war any more."

Perhaps the time has come when this prophecy shall come to mean something real to the peoples of the earth, who are now capable of self-destruction and therefore need inspiration and intelligence to keep them from committing suicide. Regardless of their religion, people throughout the world are thinking along the same lines.

....

Even if Mrs. Roosevelt's own husband had not been a polio victim, she would probably have viewed Dr. Jonas Salk's scientific effort to find a polio vaccine as one of this century's great humanitarian projects. Born in 1914, the American physician and microbiologist had taught at the universities of Michigan and Pittsburgh (he developed the vaccine at the latter). Polio had remained one of the most frightening of diseases well into the 1950s, and it often struck children who were otherwise in fine health. As the success of the vaccine became an accepted fact, Dr. Salk's fame justifiably skyrocketed. He was unable to attend the awards dinner described in this "My Day" column, but Eleanor Roosevelt, long a supporter of the fight against polio, was a perfect pinch-hitter.

CHICAGO, FEBRUARY 22—The AFL–CIO has given its annual memorial award for humanitarian service during the past year to Dr. Jonas E. Salk, who developed the anti-polio vaccine.

It was presented at a luncheon Wednesday noon at which Dr. Salk was unable to be present because, as he explained in a letter to President George Meany, he felt that he should not allow himself to be lured away from his laboratory. There, he felt, he must work hard and consistently, since research is a hard taskmaster that requires long and constant service.

I felt greatly honored to receive this award, given annually in memory of Philip Murray and William Green, for Dr. Salk and to express his thanks and appreciation for the recognition given by labor to his work.

Being a modest man, Dr. Salk insisted that he accept the award for all those whose work led to the final discovery it was his good fortune to make.

It is obvious that he was correct in giving credit to the army of people who are always responsible for any new scientific discovery, but many people are not as thoughtful in recognizing those whose work led to the final step.

Dr. Salk is one of those scientists who hopes that science can really make a contribution to society and he works as a citizen as well as a scientist to try to bring out the peacetime contributions of science rather than to have us all think primarily of the destructive uses to which science can be put today.

....

*This column reflects the nationwide debate that ensued from the So-
viets' success in launching the first satellite, Sputnik, in 1957. If anything confirmed for the liberal intelligentsia in America that postwar
society had become regrettably anti-intellectual, it was the combination
of McCarthyism's red-baiting on the one hand and the inattention to
serious education as a national priority on the other. Eleanor Roosevelt
sided with those who believed America had been caught off guard. It
was time, she argued, for America to get serious about teaching, about
children, about scientific progress. Unless it were to do so, and soon,
Mrs. Roosevelt worried that democracy would lose its pre-eminence as
the world's most respected political form.*

AUSTIN, TEXAS, MARCH 3—I wish that the New York Herald Tribune
editorial last Friday, entitled "Did Sputnik Wake Us Up?," could be
reprinted in every paper in the United States. It called attention to
several recent opinion surveys in this country on science, education
and history, and commented on the appalling implications of the results obtained. What these surveys reveal is not that we need to copy
the Russian system of education and set up more scholarships for scientists, but that we need to change our attitude in this country toward
learning and knowledge, its value, and the respect due to those who
take the trouble to learn.

This fundamental attitude, for example, is at the bottom of some of
the ignorance cited among students of American history in Indiana.
You may be shocked to read that, out of 90 university students quizzed
on American history, only eight could identify the Bill of Rights! The
explanation might be that in the State of Indiana there was for a time,
with the help and influence of one of their Senators, so much fear of
Communism and so little knowledge about it that few people would
have dared to talk of the Bill of Rights for fear of being called Communistic!

That only four students knew what a "right to work" law is does not
astonish me so much because the name is a misleading one. These
bills have nothing to do with the right to work; they are antiunion bills.
They are designed to force concessions upon the unions to a point
where they cannot maintain a higher standard of wages for their workers, which is the only way they succeed in obtaining a higher standard
for all workers, whether union or nonunion. Also, since the population
of the country constantly increases, it might be excusable if there was
no great accuracy in remembering the exact estimate. But that no one
could name the author of a good history of our country is shocking,
for it reveals how little reading our young people now do.

Above everything else, however, the most disturbing revelation is
the low opinion people in general have about the teaching profession.

There is no question but that in our country we must raise the standards of preparation for teaching, increase the salaries, and recognize teachers in our communities as influential and respected people. Otherwise we will continue to have increasing trouble with juvenile delinquents and uneducated young people. We should remember Thomas Jefferson's admonition that democracy, which we have discovered through the years to be one of the most difficult forms of government, cannot function except with an educated electorate.

The first step is to increase teachers' salaries. The next is to give them better opportunities for education. Finally, every one of us must make it a point, in the locality in which we live, to know the teachers and to give them our support and help. They deserve a place of respect in the community, and they cannot expect to function successfully with their young people unless they are given this recognition.

....

Eleanor Roosevelt had locked horns publicly with the formidable power broker Robert Moses as early as October 1945. Officially, Moses was New York City Parks Commissioner and chairman of the Council of Parks for the state of New York. But between 1934 and 1960, by working his way onto many of the most important state government commissions responsible for the development of both urban and rural areas, he positioned himself so as to influence and even control the decision-making on dozens of public works projects.

Moses often stood for development of exactly the kind Eleanor Roosevelt thought senseless. She believed that too many of Moses' plans were based on a change-for-the-sake-of-change philosophy. As a lover of New York City life, Mrs. Roosevelt was always among those who stood firmly in defense of the architectural integrity of the city's best old neighborhoods. Historically rich and architecturally lovely Washington Square was surely one of these. She sided with the American social philosopher and educator Lewis Mumford, a specialist on the culture of cities, in opposing a Moses-sponsored scheme to split Washington Square Park (the only substantial open, green space in Greenwich Village) in two by extending Fifth Avenue through its middle. Eleanor Roosevelt and friends won the battle.

NEW YORK, MARCH 22—I think I have said before how I feel about the proposition to make a broad roadway through Washington Square in New York City, but I would like to repeat that I consider it would be far better to close the square to traffic and make the people drive around it, as they do around Gramercy Park, than to accept the reasons given by Robert Moses, Commissioner of the Department of Parks, to ruin the atmosphere of the square. Mr. Moses has said that the

....

reason for this roadway is to "give the commercial benefit of the name Fifth Avenue to the group of property owners who are rehabilitating the property south of Washington Square." This is largely done, of course, at public expense.

Any name which is given to the street running south below the square can be picturesque and just as charming as changing a roadway and the character of the square.

I would have liked to see the square kept with at least the north side retaining its old houses, which had dignity and charm. But if now we put a highway through and around the archway or even remove that historic landmark, there will be no definite end to Fifth Avenue. The trees will go, the traffic will be greater. There will be no peace and quiet for those who enjoy the square at present. Fifth Avenue will become an avenue for heavy traffic, like any other avenue in that area, and I cannot see the need.

I join with Lewis Mumford and the Joint Emergency Committee in their desire to keep the square itself an historic place. Too little emphasis is put in this city on points of historic interest, and I cannot bear to see this last little bit wiped out without at least entering a protest.

....

One easily enough gets the impression that Eleanor Roosevelt had a secret source of energy, though perhaps there was no secret after all. The depth of her dedication to the American Association for the United Nations and to other humanitarian activities was itself a source of continuously renewing energy—and for an extra store of courage, even in the face of a blizzard that would have kept more ordinary mortals home and safe inside. Her friend and physician, David Gurewitsch, commented on her prodigious energy: "Medicine can take no credit for her vitality. She owes it to her constitution and to her ability to relax. In addition, she possesses a self-discipline and a sense of duty with which she can drive herself beyond the endurance of most people."

NEW YORK, MARCH 26—I think I must go back a little and tell you of a journey I took last Thursday.

Our executive committee meeting at the American Association for the United Nations lasted until 5:00 P.M. By that time, you may remember, the storm was getting pretty bad.

I had asked my own car to come down from Hyde Park to pick up Professor Arthur N. Holcombe and myself and take us to a conference on disarmament at Arden House, in Harriman, N.Y. In midafternoon my driver telephoned to say he had skidded on the parkway and would not be able to get the car repaired until the next morning.

....

As always when I have said I would go, I felt an obligation to try to arrive at my destination. So, Professor Holcombe being an adventurous soul, I telephoned Roosevelt Zander, from whom I frequently get cars when I need them in New York City. He agreed to drive us to Harriman himself and said that if we left at five o'clock we should make it by seven-thirty, in spite of the weather.

Since that meant we would be there in plenty of time for the evening session, I even toyed with the idea of stopping somewhere along the way for something to eat! As we progressed, however, the storm grew worse.

The Thruway ceased to look like a thruway. We began to pass trucks off the road, and soon the cars going in either direction were none too frequent. At seven-thirty we actually were at the exit where we should have left the Thruway, but the snow had completely obliterated the sign and we went gaily on toward Albany.

We found ourselves in the wilderness, with the storm howling about us, no signs that were readable, and a sense that we were never going to arrive anywhere—plus the disquieting possibility that our gas was going to give out shortly.

Zander had other engagements, and I felt sorry for him. I also felt a little sorry for myself, because I had been idiot enough to wear a spring suit and a raincoat when I started out that morning, and by 9:00 P.M., I assure you, I would have liked a fur coat!

Finally we came off at an exit and found a toll gate. Zander went over to ask where we were, and the attendant came out of his booth, looked into the car and said, "Mrs. Roosevelt, I'm so glad to see you! We've met before, in Tokyo and in Bonn, Germany! You can get gas just beyond the next left turn, then take the first left beyond the gas station, back onto the Thruway, and I'll call a state trooper to guide you back to your proper exit."

We nearly missed the left turn because the snow had covered any signs of it, but we saw a distant light, got our gas, and were back at the toll gate just as the trooper showed up. He led us back almost to the right exit, where a truck had skidded and blocked the road. Zander's big car couldn't get by, but the trooper's little one could, so Dr. Holcombe and I left poor Zander to find another route back to New York, and the trooper took us the rest of the way. We reached Arden House at 10:00 P.M. and enjoyed a very welcome belated dinner.

I feel very grateful for all the kindness that was shown us on the trip, and particularly for Zander's cheerfulness and his good driving, which kept us on the road when we might so easily have skidded into a ditch or impassable snow at any moment. I know many other people had far more serious adventures during the storm, but I was glad when ours were over! And I was glad we'd made the effort, for out of 47 people expected at the conference, almost 30 did manage to get there!

. . . .

Eleanor Roosevelt's record as a mother was a mixed bag of successes and failures. Over the years Mrs. Roosevelt received scores of letters from other women who raised questions about child rearing, about the perennial gap between the values of one generation and those of the next one to follow. Mrs. Roosevelt liked to write about her own upbringing and her own experience as a mother. She hoped to be helpful. Columns such as this one, picked up midway through, are also quite suggestive about how Eleanor Roosevelt's own personality took shape.

HYDE PARK, MARCH 27—The one other thing [children] learn is that real love accepts people with their weaknesses as well as their strengths. You like to respect and admire someone whom you love, but actually you often love even more the people who require understanding and who make mistakes and have to grow with their mistakes.

Sometimes I think that the younger generation has seemed to make more mistakes than the older ones for the simple reason that they have not been given such black-and-white values.

I can remember my mother-in-law saying "Why don't you tell the children that that is wrong?" And I weakly responded "Because I am not quite sure that in certain circumstances it is wrong."

There were no shades of values for us, and we were disciplined in those days to make the best of whatever life turned out to be. Our younger generation, however, has often had a vision of perfection and tried for it and failed because perfection rarely exists and it is only through real effort that one grows to approximate a realization of one's dreams.

. . . .

On what was supposed to be a fence-mending goodwill tour to several South American countries Vice President Nixon found himself the target of insults and vegetables thrown by anti-American mobs. In Lebanon, American libraries had been attacked by hostile mobs. Although the United States had fostered and financed the Marshall Plan to help rebuild Europe after World War II, winning many friends, it had also engendered much hostility in certain hot spots. Usually these were in the less developed nations where American foreign aid was often subject to misuse and where the military situation was unstable.

In this column Mrs. Roosevelt works hard to explain what sort of foreign policy might serve everyone's interests better than the policy

. . . .

underwritten in recent years by the Eisenhower administration. She argues that to some extent it is inevitable for the world's richest, most powerful nation to be resented by poorer nations dependent on the wealthy leader for defense, trade, and humanitarian aid. At the same time Mrs. Roosevelt felt that selling arms never really solves any problems. She favored a foreign aid policy based on improvement of the quality of life, not on dollars for firepower.

EN ROUTE TO LAS VEGAS, MAY 16—We are witnessing these days what it means to be the outstanding power in the non-Communist world. It is our libraries that are burned in Lebanon; it is our Vice President who, on his goodwill tour, is attacked by students and mobs.

The reason is simple. It is not because the attackers dislike Richard M. Nixon personally. Nor is it because the Lebanese have any particular dislike for what our libraries have offered them.

It is because, to them, Mr. Nixon and our libraries stand as a symbol of that which opposes what they have been taught to believe is the great revolutionary movement for the "good" of the peoples of the world.

Our people are justly indignant, and since the kind of power we now possess is rather new to us, we may be inclined to say "Well, they don't want us, so why do we bother to do anything for them or with them?"

This attitude, of course, is a sign that we have gained our power quickly and have not recognized the responsibility that goes with it. If this were to be our official policy, we would do just what the Soviets want and hope for. They would remain as the only ones ready and willing to help the revolutionaries.

I pray that our government, and we ourselves, have grown mature enough to look upon these demonstrations partly as recognition of what our world leadership means and must mean, to regret them but not to let them succeed to the point of forcing us to give the Communist element in the world exactly what it wants.

We believe in freedom and are trying to see that all people obtain freedom. We are not going to look at our interests from the financial viewpoint alone. We are not going to allow our recession to do things abroad that will ruin other economies. We, of course, hold paramount our own interests, but we know that our interests are best served when we consider those of the world as a whole.

No country in our position is loved, but we should make ourselves respected and better understood. Our policy of giving military aid to foreign nations instead of actually raising the living standards in those countries has been a mistake.

This policy may be helpful at home, and it may bring greater financial support from Congress than any other type of foreign aid. For our people do not realize that these shipments of arms are not going to be used against the Communists and will be of no real value, whereas any help we may give in raising, even a little, other people's standards of living will win us friends.

If we now cut down on foreign aid because the Soviets have been successful in stirring up trouble in certain South American countries, in the Near East and in North Africa, we will make a great mistake and lose more friends instead of gaining them.

It may well be that this was not a propitious time for Mr. Nixon to go to certain South American countries. Our State Department should have known that. But we can now be glad that he and his wife have returned safe and sound. These special and spectacular tours had better be given up until we have brought about changes in the feelings of these countries.

I keep repeating that the Moscow challenge is not a military one alone. It is an economic, cultural and spiritual challenge, and sooner or later we will have to face this fact.

. . . .

By simple arithmetic anyone could tell by 1958 that the postwar baby boom would sooner or later clog the nation's schools, which in many communities had not been expanded significantly for decades. There was little argument in Congress or in the state legislatures over whether new classrooms were needed. The issues blocking school construction were both philosophical and political. In the late 1950s Americans were still thinking through the policy issue of whether and how federal aid to education should be implemented. Heretofore most public education had been financed on the state and local levels. And when education aid bills came up in Congress, civil rights or segregationist riders were often attached, making passage difficult if not impossible.

Mrs. Roosevelt was once again ahead of her time on the issue of federal aid to education. She was fully convinced that such an expenditure was a far better investment in the nation's future than a parallel expenditure on new weaponry—or even on the space program—would be. Seeing yet another education bill go down to defeat raised her ire.

HYDE PARK, MAY 24—After a tiring trip in the West, I was happy indeed to arrive back in my little New York apartment from Bismarck, N.D. I had planned to write today about the last few days of this trip, but a more important matter has come up that I want to discuss.

This matter is the shelving by the House Education and Labor Committee of the school construction bill that would provide federal money to help the states improve their school situation by adding more class-

. . . .

rooms before the overcrowding becomes more intolerable than it already is.

How Representative Graham A. Braden of North Carolina, committee chairman, can permit this is beyond my understanding!

The parents of this country should protest through every organization at their command, for their children are going to pay the price of schools so overcrowded that teachers cannot give them adequate attention.

It is a fact that under present conditions the curriculum of the schools is deteriorating and that children, of necessity, will be less interested in learning and have less respect for education because the government of their country does not think it worth paying for.

No democracy can succeed, according to Thomas Jefferson, unless it has an educated people. And we cannot educate citizens under the conditions that our government is now forcing on the people of the country.

An article in the June Esquire magazine tells of some of the things that happen when people do not consider learning important, and these things are happening to our young people today.

The author gives an appalling quotation from Dean William C. Warren of the Columbia School of Law on the shortcomings of college graduates who are entering law school.

It looks as though it is not until our young people reach graduate school that they begin to realize that education was not intended to be mere play but that it is hard work and preparation for life, and that to succeed in the world of today our children must learn during their educational years to conquer difficult subjects.

If the federal government does not take its responsibility for helping the states with their educational problems, or if the states refuse to accept this aid for fear they will have some type of interference, then we are going to fall behind.

It is because we are not willing to pay more for our education and to give it more serious thought that I think we are finding our juvenile delinquency problem constantly becoming more serious.

If we do not pay for children in good schools, then we are going to pay for them in prisons and mental hospitals. There is a distinct tie-up, I think, between the increase of juvenile delinquency and the inadequacy of our public schools.

Of course, this is not the only factor entering into our problem, but it is certainly one of the most important. It seems to me a terrible waste of human material which we are condoning at the present time, but I don't know if it is possible to bring home to our parents how serious this waste really is for our nation.

*Eleanor Roosevelt was in the minority who cautioned about the wisdom
of selling arms to any and all foreign nations who might appear to need
them for defense (and be able to pay). She recognized that arms bought
for so-called deterrence almost always end up being used in some form
of aggression. Such was turning out to be the case at least in the Mideast
and in North Africa. Thus the unruliness of countries such as Egypt,
an arms purchaser from Western nations, could not be blamed entirely
on the Egyptians.*

*Nor could the French and Algerian impasses over Algeria's antico-
lonial demand for sovereignty be blamed entirely on the most direct,
obvious participants. Mrs. Roosevelt saw the too-often meddling hand
of the United States even in this tense postcolonial squabble. The ren-
aissance of Charles de Gaulle as French leader neither surprised nor
delighted her. Eleanor Roosevelt recognized his charisma as just that,
and she feared for the French and the Algerians under his hot-tempered
influence.*

NEW YORK, MAY 29—No one today will think of anything except the
situation in France, for it affects the rest of the world. I cannot help
feeling we are reaping the results of having allowed Gamal Abdel Nasser to come into power in Egypt. Our policies, or lack of policies,
during the last few years are now coming home to roost.

Nasser has been able, with the help of the Soviet Union, to stir up
trouble among the Algerians and to give them a feeling of support in
their fight against France so that no negotiations could be reasonably
undertaken with a hope of some positive solutions.

Now there are no solutions. The French premier has resigned and
General Charles de Gaulle will come to power with the full backing
of the French military forces. De Gaulle has said often enough that
he felt that the United States was not an ally but tried to dictate to
France. That means that he will negotiate with us on a tit-for-tat basis
and try to be tough.

Whether this means the end of NATO, or whether it means just
more difficulty in every move, remains to be seen. There will be no
friendship between our governments, for de Gaulle is a gentleman
made of the stuff of dictators. At least, that was the opinion of those
who met him a few years ago. He may have mellowed and we will
watch his moves with great interest.

The whole situation will be used by the Communists, and it
may well be that they will eventually control France. To believe
that this French situation does not foreshadow serious troubles for us

in Europe would be wishful thinking and putting our head in the sand.

. . . .

Mrs. Roosevelt's private correspondence during this period indicates that on some domestic issues, such as race relations, she had begun to realize that Adlai Stevenson was not effectively in touch with the feelings of either white or black liberal Americans. She began to see that, admirable as he was in the role of intellectual leader for the Democrats, he lacked the political magnetism that is the hallmark of election winners. Nonetheless, Eleanor Roosevelt still looked to Stevenson for visionary ideas on more global problems such as disarmament.

NEW YORK, JUNE 11—Adlai Stevenson, in urging the free nations to rally to achieve a functioning, expanding free world trading system, has stated what seems perfectly clear to anyone who has studied the situation of the non-Communist nations of the world.

He made this statement in his week-end address at Michigan State University in which he pressed his proposal for a committee of experts comparable to the group that laid the groundwork for the Marshall Plan in 1947.

Mr. Stevenson also pointed out that as Britain and France are laying down the creditor role, the United States must take up this role if economic conditions are to be improved. That is why we should have a committee of experts in this country similar to the Marshall Plan group.

I believe, too, we should go one step further and call together the heads of industries, who will have to implement any plans made by this committee.

If we are to negotiate on a broader scale for better trade in the world, we will have to take a good look at conditions at home. We cannot let people at home suffer because it is necessary to make different arrangements in other parts of the world in an overall scheme for economic well-being on a broad basis.

This means that when certain things become unprofitable to do at home, instead of meeting the problem by putting up a high tariff wall, we will have to meet the challenge by changing our own economy, retraining our people, bringing in new industries. All of this takes real planning.

We have not even taken the trouble to plan economically with our neighbor, Canada. There is one area in which we could begin to make headway at once.

The proposals made by the Canadian Prime Minister, John G. Diefenbaker, for a four-point program deserved careful study because cooperation with Canada, our closest neighbor, should certainly show

. . . .

that we can develop mutually helpful ways of doing things such as dealing with our food surpluses.

To go back to Mr. Stevenson's proposal, he added a suggestion to help bring about a peaceful world which I think has great merit. He wants "an international medical research and health year as another way, similar to the International Geophysical Year, for the world to cooperate for survival instead of destruction."

He goes back to his old proposal of ending the testing of nuclear weapons and of coming to a reasonable agreement with the Soviet Union on matters of inspection against violation.

And, most important of all, he suggests acceptance by the West of the principle of Soviet equality and power so that we could divert our military rivalries into competition in science, education, and economic development.

Mr. Stevenson developed all of his suggestions reasonably and carefully, but the thing that is important is the appointment of committees to begin carrying out these suggestions.

Will the present Administration dare to accept these ideas from a Democratic leader, or will it feel that it must persist in doing nothing?

....

Mrs. Roosevelt had many friends in the entertainment business, and it was natural for her to come to their defense when the entire industry found itself under attack by the seemingly endless Communist witch hunt conducted by the House Un-American Activities Committee. Senator Joe McCarthy, the most virulent anti-Communist of them all, was now several years dead, but the spirit of his hostility to anything left-wing lived on, particularly in the minds of the Congressmen who served on HUAC and their staffs. In order to avoid being investigated by HUAC, film studios and other entertainment businesses tried their best to keep their rosters of employees clean of Communist sympathizers.

But the committee's definition of left wing and sympathizer kept shifting, becoming ever more irrational and illusory. Before long, someone whose only offense was to have marched in a May Day parade several years earlier could end up being branded a Communist. The consequences could be deadly: artists and business executives alike were blacklisted by the industry leaders and thus prevented from finding any new employment. Careers came to a dead stop. Yet neither a trial nor even a formal investigation might have been held. Only the insinuations of HUAC had set the ball rolling.

HYDE PARK, JUNE 27—[There is] something I have been wanting to say about the recent House Un-American Activities hearing in New

....

York involving such personalities in the entertainment field as directors, actors, musicians, etc.

Because they refused to answer questions concerning past affiliations with the Communist Party and took refuge in the First and Fifth Amendments, several of them lost their jobs.

I wonder whether the public realizes that many people really believe that nobody has a right to ask anyone about his political affiliations, past or present. We are not at war.

In these cases there was no question of any action to overthrow our government, so the question is based on one's right to hold opinions and beliefs contrary to the usually accepted pattern. Down through history this has been the American citizen's right, and it still is his right to claim, under either of these Constitutional guarantees, the refusal to answer.

In addition, the pattern followed in questioning a person who is willing to answer consists of asking him to divulge the names of those who were Communist party members with him. In wartime this may be necessary, but at present in the entertainment field it is nonsense.

I was taught as a child that to be a tattle-tale and thereby get other children into trouble was a despicable thing, that it was better to bear unfair punishment than to tell on a friend.

This was stayed with me all through life, and I can quite understand the pleading of rights under either of these amendments to prevent being asked about those whom one certainly would endanger by naming.

We do things in wartime because then the protection of our country comes first, but in peacetime we first must protect the liberty of the individual in thinking, speaking and changing his mind.

For these people to have lost their jobs because of the House committee's actions seems unfortunate. They were not in occupations that might endanger our safety. They have a right to earn a living and to live in peace, since they have said that they are not now Communists, and whatever were their former beliefs, they have since learned better.

. . . .

Walter Lippmann shared with Dorothy Thompson the top spot on the country's list of most widely read newspaper columnists for many years. Mrs. Roosevelt usually respected Lippmann's views, but she took issue with him concerning the recent troubles in Lebanon where civil unrest had led to an American airlift of arms in May, to safeguard Lebanese independence and U.S. citizens there. Here Mrs. Roosevelt sounds like a mainstream cold warrior, advocating the use of American military force to help stop even the indirect spread of Communist influence. Her position is at odds with her other pronouncements about how to

. . . .

implement an effective foreign policy in the Mideast. But she was not simply a predictable idealist; there was much of the political pragmatist in Eleanor Roosevelt too.

HYDE PARK, JULY 5—Rarely do I disagree with Walter Lippmann, but his recent column entitled "Against Intervention" seemed to me to contain certain fallacies.

No one could be more violently opposed than I am to putting our soldiers into combat in any country of the world. I think it would bring us misunderstanding and bitterness and accomplish no good.

But, since this is the case, then I think we should support any action by the United Nations that would provide for an expanded international police force to guarantee nonaggression across a country's borders and even providing arms when it is evident the Soviet Union or its satellites are doing so.

A negotiated settlement is not always a happy one, but negotiations should always go on. When we said we would help to protect nations from aggression, however, I think we meant we would throw our whole diplomatic weight and strength into action, backed by the UN police force.

The Lebanon situation is not like Suez. There our allies attacked Egypt. Lebanon is asking for help against aggression, and if we interfere unilaterally we would be doing so at the invitation of a government under attack.

In the case of Lebanon, it is not an open attack but infiltration, although on a large scale. Men from Syria and arms from Czechoslovakia, furnished by Syrians and used by Syrians in Lebanon, are flowing across the Lebanese border. UN observers actually are not enough help to prevent this.

If we do not protect Lebanon in this situation, there will develop throughout the Near East the feeling that friendship with the West has no value. We cannot allow this feeling to become prevalent anywhere in the world.

. . . .

In On My Own *Eleanor Roosevelt explained that even at this point in her career she was still receiving nearly a hundred letters a day, from all parts of the world and covering a host of subjects. Three secretaries helped sort the letters, provided routine answers, forwarded them to offices and agencies that might help the writer, or passed on to Mrs. Roosevelt the ten or so per day that might truly require some fresh thinking or a reply from her. Mrs. Roosevelt usually took a pattern of comments in the flow of correspondence as a sign of an emerging problem she would want to address in a "My Day" column.*

. . . .

At other times Mrs. Roosevelt had a one-of-a-kind opinion and used "My Day" to express it. The average citizen probably did not see the installation of "Don't Walk" signs on city streets as an occasion to raise questions of personal discipline, civic duty, common sense, and avoidance of newfangled technical gadgets. But Eleanor Roosevelt did, and in one short paragraph she reveals quite a lot about her sense of right and wrong.

NEW YORK, AUGUST 13—The new regulations for crossing the street in New York City went into effect last Friday. I really think it would be simpler if everybody were just told they had to cross when the light is green and that they must not cross anywhere but at the street corners and never diagonally. Complicating life with the "Don't Walk" signals and telling drivers that they must yield the right of way to traffic just makes it more complicated.

....

The summer of 1958 was to bring a major change in Eleanor Roosevelt's domestic life. Her landlord in New York announced a $150 increase in rent which Mrs. Roosevelt refused to accept (in a letter to her daughter Anna she called it "ridiculous"). By August 12th she had given up the apartment, moving back to the Park Sheraton Hotel to adequate but smaller quarters.

A plan had emerged, however, to secure a permanent home in New York. She and David Gurewitsch decided to buy a house together on the Upper East Side of Manhattan. Welcome as this decision was, it was also fraught with some tension; only a few months earlier David had remarried, and Eleanor Roosevelt was having some trouble adjusting to the notion that her longtime intimate friend—and her personal physician—was no longer a single man.

There had been a solid basis of love between Eleanor and David, rooted in respect and pure enthusiasm, and now at least a decade old. Their correspondence revealed a strong emotional bond, made all the more remarkable, first, by Mrs. Roosevelt's prominence in the world and Dr. Gurewitsch's relative lack of fame; and secondly, by the fifteen-year difference in their ages, she being the elder. Seen from the perspective of this unique friendship, the idea of their buying a house together made perfect sense.

Little by little Mrs. Roosevelt came to appreciate Edna Gurewitsch's presence in David's life as a positive force. Slowly, relations between the two women warmed, though the need Mrs. Roosevelt felt for David's time and attention showed no signs of abating. In the summer of 1958 the three began a search for a house that lasted until the end of that year, when they purchased a brownstone at 55 East 74th Street. The

....

plan was for the Gurewitsch's to have the upstairs and Mrs. Roosevelt eventually to take over the two lower floors. She could not move in, however, until September 1959 and then only to one floor due to existing leases of prior tenants.

As preparations for her second trip to the Soviet Union were being completed Eleanor Roosevelt took time out to restore her energies by doing a little gardening at her beloved Val-Kill cottage in Hyde Park.

HYDE PARK, AUGUST 22—This past Monday and Tuesday were most gorgeous days up here in the country. The first touch of autumn seemed to be in the air, and it was most invigorating, especially when we realized that there are many warm days still ahead for us.

The goldenrod is coming out fully, and it seems that there are more wildflowers this year—and they are lovelier—than I have ever known them to be. My little garden still flourishes, and this week I pulled radishes and picked beans. And I look forward very soon to a full crop of tomatoes and lima beans. I think we have picked the very last of our rhubarb, but this year has been an exceptionally long season.

. . . .

Although the dateline is Brussels (she is on her way again to the USSR), Mrs. Roosevelt was looking back across the Atlantic to the U.S. political scene. In another of her remarkably prescient observations about politicians who would someday stand at or near the head of their parties, Eleanor Roosevelt here singles out Edmund Muskie, who did indeed go on to become senator from Maine (1959–1980). (In 1968 he was Hubert Humphrey's vice presidential running mate and on his own a leading contender for the presidential nomination in 1972.)

BRUSSELS, AUGUST 29—My attention was attracted the other day by a newspaper article about the election campaign in Maine. Interest is heightened by the fact that on September 8 a Democratic candidate for the United States Senate will be chosen, and a likely candidate is Governor Edmund S. Muskie, the first Democrat to be elected to that office. If he is nominated and if he wins, he will be the first Democratic Senator from Maine.

Mr. Muskie, who has been governor for two terms, is a quiet, tall, good-looking man. I wish he was better known throughout the country, for I think he has the qualities of greatness which might even lead him to be considered for the presidency someday.

He speaks extremely well and is easy to understand, never trying to hide anything or cover up for anyone. I have a hunch he may break the Maine tradition and be elected to the Senate. If he is, he will be

. . . .

an asset there and a personality that will not long be ignored. He will bring dignity and courage to his office and his state.

. . . .

As she had with previous world's fairs, Mrs. Roosevelt took her readers on a guided tour of the fair at Brussels in 1958, bringing out her best travel-writing skills. (She also saw the fair as an arena in which the Soviet and Western blocs were continuing to play out their competition by showing off the best of their cultures.) Much about the American displays pleased her, although she had some doubts about the cultural value of the Yankee exhibition of fast food—and about the Europeans' apparent fascination with it.

BRUSSELS, SEPTEMBER 5—To continue our journey around the American Pavilion at the World's Fair here, we next found ourselves at the exhibit of modern paintings. On display is only the work of artists under 45 years of age, and many parts of our country are represented.

I am told that these exhibits have made a deep and exciting impression on artists from different parts of Europe. Even I—no expert in modern art and in need of far more education and application in looking—came away feeling that I could live very happily with a painting called "Rain" by James Boynton and with one by Kyle Morris, which is untitled, and another by Bernard Perlin called "The Farewell." Also, the caricatures by Steinberg are most amusing and typical of types that most of us have enjoyed.

I went through the business machines area, and all of these displays were carefully explained and demonstrated to us. Unless one had such explanations I do not see how one average visitor going through would find this part of our exhibition interesting, except that, like machinery in any of the other pavilions, it shows our capacity for mechanics.

We soon went through the cocktail lounge and cafeteria, where people not only were eating inside but also taking outside to a terrace their lunches which many had brought with them, buying only a drink in the cafeteria. It is all very well arranged and managed, and I think this is a side of American life that is worth showing to our neighbors who spend so much time over their meals and never seem to understand what we mean when we tell them that we don't like to eat so much or take so much time off to eat, particularly at noon.

When we explain to most Europeans that we work better in the afternoon when we take less time and eat less at our midday meal they seem puzzled. Here we have demonstrated what we mean, and it is astonishing to see how many visitors are eating hamburgers, which they have just bought and taken out to eat on the terrace. This well may turn out to be a real interpretation to the foreigner of one facet

. . . .

of our life, which could mean far-reaching changes in their understanding of America's habits and customs.

....

There is a hint of unhappy things to come in the following brief comment about the two Germanys. Soon movement across the border will be stopped altogether and the city of Berlin divided by a wall that will stand as a symbol of Communist defensiveness until 1989. Although Mrs. Roosevelt made no predictions about where German and Soviet politics might be leading, her antennae were out and she was aware these were meaningful tensions that must be watched closely.

BRUSSELS, SEPTEMBER 10—The newspapers over here tell us that lately there has been a tremendous influx of people from East Germany coming into West Germany. I had read before coming over that it was being made more and more difficult for people to leave East Germany, but they still seem to manage to do it.

The most striking departure, of course, in recent weeks was that of Dr. Josef Haemel, former rector of Jena University in East Germany. He was an older man who had built up the university, and it must have been a terrible wrench to leave, even though he has found new freedom.

....

The reports Eleanor Roosevelt filed about her 1958 trip to the USSR did not match her outstanding reportage during her 1957 visit.

One of the two columns written about the Russian trip that follow focuses in a chatty way on some domestic details Mrs. Roosevelt thought would be interesting to American housewives. The other discusses the wisdom of establishing full diplomatic and economic relations with the Communists in China and the USSR. At this point (and for many years to come) American policy was to refuse to do business with or even to recognize the legitimacy of the Chinese Communist government.

Mrs. Roosevelt's 1958 trip to Europe and Russia was partly a professional journey and partly personal. The World Federation of United Nations Associations was meeting in Brussels (at the World's Fair), and she had been asked by the American association to attend. Going on to Moscow was an independent move for Mrs. Roosevelt, made with a small entourage consisting of David and Edna Gurewitsch and the usual one or two Roosevelt secretaries.

NEW YORK, OCTOBER 3—I feel you might like to know how the beds are made up in Russia, so I am going to tell you.

....

In the hotels each bed has a box spring with a thin pad on top. The sheets are of heavy linen, the bottom one of the two being tightly stretched over the pad and tucked in. The top sheet is a bag with a diamond-shaped large opening at the top. A heavy quilt is slipped in, the bottom is then turned up, and the two sides at the top are turned in. Then, after the Chinese fashion, you crawl into your cocoon from the top and tuck it tightly around you.

If it is very cold you put on top as many extra covers as you need. It seems like the best way to make a bed for warmth in the cold Moscow climate, and I am thinking of trying it for the winter months at Hyde Park.

NEW YORK, OCTOBER 6—I am home again and trying to think through what I have really learned from this second three weeks spent in the Soviet Union.

Only a few people in America can tell you even today what communism really is. But fear of communism has taken hold among us. And fear without knowledge is dangerous.

For instance, some of our businessmen began to equate democracy with free enterprise and to state that there could be no freedom without an economic system called free enterprise. This is obvious nonsense because a number of countries which are not Communist countries but which do not happen to have the natural resources for an overall free enterprise system have had to accept some socialism with their free enterprise. Yet, they are democratic countries and opposed to communism.

It is evident, therefore, that one must separate belief in a form of government from one's economic beliefs.

We in the United States can operate very successfully a free enterprise system because of our vast natural resources, and there is no question but what this type of economy develops resourcefulness, initiative and the many traits that make a man successful in building up his own and his country's success. But we may well have to learn to live with other types of governments and other types of economies, and it is well to look at the realities of every situation and not to deal in generalities or in blind prejudices.

Because we dislike the Communist system we chose to believe that for one reason or another we would wake up someday and find that by some miracle the Soviet Union has disappeared. It is time that, as a people, we woke up to the fact that it has not disappeared.

The Russian people are well-disciplined, amenable to direction, healthy, and determined to build a place in the sun for themselves and their country. They accept sacrifice, they do without many things that we consider essential to decent living. They do this out of fear of war and under compulsion, but there is acquiescence in the compulsion.

We must constantly remind ourselves that we are judging people who 40 years ago under the czars had no freedom, practically speaking. They had no education and very little opportunity for health services. Today they have education, free excellent preventive medicine, medical care which is adequate and also free, and a standard of living for the mass of the people which is far above what they had under the czars.

This does not mean, of course, that some people are not living below their old standards, because the mass is being considered here—the people, 200,000,000 of them—who make up the work force and the building force of this country. The government shapes the lives of the people from the time they are babies. The government believes it needs highly educated people, and the government believes in scientific research. It does not have to ask the people about it, but the people are given the benefit of what science in every line can discover, and they soon learn its value.

The United States as a nation, I think, should face the realities of the present world situation.

In eight years the Chinese, percentagewise, from all I can learn, have come along faster than the Soviets in the same amount of time. They still need the Soviets, but the time may come when they will have as much, or more, power than the country which has helped them to develop. We know little or nothing of what goes on in China, but perhaps it is time for us to realize that this is dangerous ignorance.

Look back on the historical picture and try to decide whether the time has not come to make some kind of arrangements with both the Communist Chinese and the Soviet Union. By refusing to trade we are forcing them to build up their own ability to produce the very things they might buy from us. By coming to no agreements we and they have a growing apprehension of war.

By closing our eyes to the existence of Communist nations we are neither helping the more liberal forces within these countries nor are we hurting the growth of their power. All we are doing is wasting time in making a settlement which must sometime come if we are not to destroy the whole world through an atomic war. And every day the settlement by war or by peaceful agreement becomes more costly to us.

If we face the fact that we are dealing with our equals, that they have a right to be recognized as equals, that both of us have a right to ask for the kind of safeguards which we feel will bring us some sense of security, accepting the fact that none of us starts with any sense of confidence in each other, then we may find solutions.

Once we face these realities and necessities we can negotiate, but it will require the best brains that we can muster and our best and toughest negotiators. The sooner we stop talking about war as though it were a possibility, the sooner will we face the realities of this situation before us and begin to find solutions to the problems of today.

. . . .

On her visit to the World's Fair in Brussels Mrs. Roosevelt had greatly enjoyed Harry Belafonte's extravagant stage show at the American pavilion. She wrote a long and colorful "My Day" column about this marvelously multilingual, handsome, charming, and black entertainer who so successfully represented all that was good about the melting-pot culture of the United States. His show made her proud, but the experience of racial discrimination his family had back home in New York in their search for housing made her ashamed. It gave Mrs. Roosevelt the occasion to make again a point she brought up frequently during the years of the civil rights struggle: that Northern cities by no means could claim to have a clean record on civil rights issues. To earn the privilege of criticizing the more conservative South, Northerners would first have to put their own house in moral and legal order.

NEW LONDON, CONN., OCTOBER 20—I am sure that every New Yorker was shocked the other day to read that Harry Belafonte and his charming wife and baby were finding it practically impossible to get an apartment in New York City except in what might be considered segregated areas or in a hotel. I have long been saying that in the North we have only one step to take to meet the Supreme Court order of nonsegregation in schools, and that is nonsegregation in housing. In New York State we have the laws necessary to achieve nonsegregated housing if we saw that they were diligently respected.

There was a time when prohibitions against various racial groups were more prevalent than today. For instance, Jewish groups were much more concentrated in specific areas than they are now; and the same kind of thing was true of the Italians, the Irish or the Germans. Gradually these barriers have broken down, until it now remains for us to see that the barriers against our Puerto Rican and colored population also disappear.

There are beginnings to encourage us. The Committee on Civil Rights in Manhattan, for example, has issued a pamphlet on housing co-ops which may be the answer for a number of people. Some private builders who are planning and constructing co-op apartments are particularly interested in seeing that there is no discrimination in any project where they have invested their money. These cooperatives, of course, vary in price and location; some are in the suburbs, others can

. . . .

be found in the city. Many of them, however, are not in areas conveniently located for individuals of special interests. Therefore it is important that we press for the general freeing from restrictions of all New York City property.

Real estate people often frighten themselves and their clients by saying that property taken over by a Negro family forces the whole area quickly to become a Negro area and that property values go down. This, of course, depends upon the white people in the area. If they move out from places because of prejudice or fear, the character of the neighborhood inevitably will change and the value of the property may decrease. But if they learn to live with their neighbors without discrimination of any kind, they will soon find that their neighborhoods become simply mixed neighborhoods—neither all-white, nor all-Negro, nor all-Jewish, nor all-Italian. We are a mixture of races in New York City, and every neighborhood should in normal course become a mixed neighborhood.

I can think of nothing I would enjoy more than having Mr. and Mrs. Belafonte as my neighbors. I hope they will find a home shortly where they and their enchanting little boy can grow up without feeling the evils of the segregation pattern. Discrimination does something intangible and harmful to the souls of both white and colored people.

. . . .

By the time Theodore Roosevelt succeeded to the presidency in 1901, after President McKinley was shot, his niece Eleanor was a young woman of twenty-five. Her admiration for him was already fixed, and the hindsight of many years had only underscored what she believed back then: he was a giant among men. She particularly admired the vigorous combination of physical and intellectual activity that characterized his personal style. Many of the themes of FDR's administration and the years Eleanor Roosevelt spent working for the United Nations could be seen in rough outline in the Theodore Roosevelt presidency. Among these themes were a serious concern for the natural environment, an activist role for the United States in international affairs (trying to keep world peace while exercising ever-increasing influence for American economic interests), a distaste for monopolistic business practice, a love for the reading and writing of history.

The young Teddy Roosevelt is most often recalled as the leader of the Rough Riders, a volunteer cavalry regiment that served in Cuba in 1898 during the Spanish–American war. But he also won the world's most coveted accolade as a peacemaker, the Nobel Prize (in 1906), for his role in ending the Russo-Japanese war. There is more than fondness in Eleanor Roosevelt's recollections of him; there is the deepest respect.

. . . .

NEW YORK, OCTOBER 25—We are celebrating this month the 100th anniversary of Theodore Roosevelt's birth. No one in public life ever had any meaning to me before I became old enough to be conscious of this uncle of mine as a public character.

I grew up in my grandmother's house, where politics was almost never mentioned, and it was only when I began to read the newspapers myself that I became conscious of the first cartoons of Theodore Roosevelt as New York City police commissioner with very prominent front teeth!

Uncle Teddy was always kind to my brother and me because we were the children of his only brother who had died. We stayed with him at times in Oyster Bay and later, when he became President, even once or twice in Washington. He was always a fascinating, colorful personality, but I am afraid when I was young I was occasionally more worried by his energy and the physical activities he expected of us all than I was impressed by his mental achievements.

Now I realize how varied were his intellectual interests, how widely read he was and how much he developed the various sides of his nature so that life could be enjoyed in many different ways.

He had a tremendous influence over the young men who were starting out in life when he was already active in politics. He preached the responsibility of each and every citizen of our country for the government of our country. He did not expect that all of us would go into politics as a career, but I think few young people came in contact with him without being given the feeling that they must do something for the community in which they lived.

He was a wonderful father, as those who have read his letters to his children will realize. He was a historian, he was a sportsman, a politician and a statesman.

It is hard for most of us to realize that as a boy he suffered cruelly from asthma, and it was only his indomitable will that built the strong physique which could withstand the many physical tests he imposed upon himself throughout life. His friends were often put to these physical tests as well. And I am afraid that having built his own strength by force of will he looked upon anyone who could not match him as somehow lacking in some traits of character which he considered essential to being a really valuable human being.

He was a loving and loyal friend and his courage was not only physical courage but had a certain moral and spiritual quality. You might not agree with his point of view, but you knew that he expressed his own convictions and that he himself would live up to the same standards he set for others.

He had a feeling for social justice which was ahead of his time and, because of this, he earned from some people a familiar criticism that

I have heard many times since—namely, those whose interests he interfered with said he was a "traitor to his class." He was really only a pioneer, pointing the way that this country had to follow if it were going to be true to the ideals on which it was founded.

As time goes by, great characters stand out more clearly from the pages of history, and I think it is safe to say that people are going to read the books that now exist and that will in the future be written about Theodore Roosevelt with greater and greater interest. They will feel that he was one of the men who influenced the thinking of our country and moved us forward along the lines of social justice and humanitarian interests, which are today the areas that furnish us with the only alternative to communism.

....

Boris Pasternak's Doctor Zhivago, *an epic treatment of the tragic upheavals of twentieth-century Russia, was completed by 1955. The same social and political tensions it so effectively evoked (class conflict, intellectual and spiritual repression) were very much alive in post-Stalinist Russia under the often brutish leadership of Nikita Khrushchev. The book was banned in the Soviet Union and, after being smuggled out, was first published in Italy in 1957. Worldwide acclaim soon followed. Pasternak was compelled by official Soviet pressure to refuse the Nobel Prize in 1958.*

Mrs. Roosevelt writes about a particularly awkward period for Pasternak when it appeared he was being unofficially exiled from his own country. She, like most other progressive intellectuals, saw the Pasternak case as proof positive of the intellectual aridity of Soviet thinking. Eventually Pasternak did return to his beloved Russia to spend his last years (he died in 1960) at an artists' colony near Moscow.

HYDE PARK, NOVEMBER 3—It was sad to read Boris Pasternak's plea to Premier Khrushchev to be allowed to remain in Russia. The announcement that the Soviet winner of the 1958 Nobel Prize for Literature would be allowed to leave Russia seemed to indicate that the government felt he was not a good citizen and would be glad to get rid of him. But Pasternak's letter should convince anyone of his love for his country.

Everyone tells me that his novel "Doctor Zhivago" is beautifully written, and it obviously must have great merit to have won the Nobel Prize. Ordinarily a country is very proud when one of its citizens wins this prize. But official wrath has apparently been aroused because of the critical passages in "Doctor Zhivago." Although I have not read the book, I have read excerpts from it which are, I imagine, the ones considered critical. Some of the descriptions seem to me beautiful and

....

very poetic. The critical passage I read was that voiced by certain characters who criticize both the last days under the czars and certain things under the Revolution.

It may well be that an idealist who embraced the Revolution, looking for the millennium, would find many things to criticize, for human beings rarely attain the millennium. But to punish a man for writing an outstanding novel in which his characters state a variety of viewpoints seems both unreasonable and unwise. A strong state can take criticism, particularly criticism which is voiced by someone who truly loves his country. To keep alive a fear of punishment for voicing one's honest opinion seems to be possible only in a very backward country with a very backward people. I hope the Soviet Union will rise above its past and that Mr. Khrushchev will show, by his treatment of the plea now voiced by a man who has brought honor to his country, that there is real advancement in the freedom for all intellectuals.

....

Eleanor Roosevelt was among a tiny minority who, in these still early years of the development of full-scale television programming and the advent of significantly increased amounts of leisure time in the average American's weekly schedule, said "Stop; let's think this over." Mrs. Roosevelt takes the point even further to warn her readers about the negative impact of passivity and the positive benefits of a life—like hers—filled with a lively variety of labors and creative pastimes.

NEW YORK, NOVEMBER 5—If the use of leisure time is confined to looking at TV for a few extra hours every day, we will deteriorate as a people.

Actually, preparation for the use of leisure time should begin with our schoolchildren. The appreciation of many things in which we are not proficient ourselves but which we have learned to enjoy is one of the important things to cultivate in modern education. The arts in every field—music, drama, sculpture, painting—we can learn to appreciate and enjoy. We need not be artists, but we should be able to appreciate the work of artists. Crafts of every kind, the value of things made by hand, by skilled people who love to work with wood or clay or stone will develop taste in our people.

These are all things that can give us joy and many of us will find that we are capable of acquiring a certain amount of skill we never dreamed we had, which will give an outlet to a creative urge. But these things must be taught, and in the age now developing about us they are important things. For if man is to be liberated to enjoy more leisure, he must also be prepared to enjoy this leisure fully and creatively.

For people to have more time to read, to take part in their civic

....

obligations, to know more about how their government functions and who their officials are might mean in a democracy a great improvement in the democratic processes. Let's begin, then, to think how we can prepare old and young for these new opportunities. Let's not wait until they come upon us suddenly and we have a crisis that we will be ill prepared to meet.

....

Eleanor Roosevelt's personality embraced a wonderful combination of the liberal experimentalist, always open to a potentially good new idea, and the habitual traditionalist who liked to do some things the same way, year after year. Eleanor's approach to celebrating Christmas was grounded in her traditionalism, both its religious and secular sides. In this year's Christmas "My Day" column she explains her best-loved activities at this holiday.

While Mrs. Roosevelt certainly had the option, given her age and professional stature, of making the Christmas week into a respite from writing, even from thinking about worldly matters such as politics and the economy, that is not what she chose to do with her time. After a brief break for Christmas itself, she returned to a more typical theme for a year-end column. In it she throws a few darts at one of her least favorite labor leaders, Jimmy Hoffa, who at this time was trying to organize the New York City police and firemen into a union. Mrs. Roosevelt had many times before expressed her sympathy for public employees' right to organize while at the same time standing firm in her opinion that they ought not to be permitted to strike because of their obligations to the public.

Thus, even if someone other than Hoffa had been leading this effort, Eleanor Roosevelt would have been skeptical. Hoffa had become president of the Teamsters in 1957 and his union was expelled from the AFL–CIO that year because of rampant corruption. His tempestuous career continued through two convictions for jury tampering and fraud (1964), release from prison by President Nixon (1971), and his disappearance and apparent murder (1975).

Hyde Park, December 25—Christmas is here again, and I hope that at this season we will stress the religious side of the celebration. Of foremost importance for the world to remember is that the story of the Christ child is the one that really gives meaning to this day for every Christian everywhere.

I always go to midnight service in our church in Hyde Park because I like to begin the celebration hearing the familiar religious carols and being reminded of the heart of this season, which is "Peace on earth, goodwill to men."

....

During the day we return, of course, to the enjoyment of all the other traditions which we have absorbed in this country—Santa Claus and his reindeer and the Christmas decorations which every year become more evident in every village and in every city.

I love the Christmas lights and sometime during the Christmas season I always try to drive after dark one night down Park Avenue in New York City where the trees make a long stream of light and many windows are decorated. Then I proceed over to Fifth Avenue and down to Washington Square and up the whole length of Fifth Avenue where so many shops have outstanding decorations.

I love to look at the big tree in Rockefeller Plaza, which is always a joy. This little excursion is one of my annual Christmas pleasures.

NEW YORK, DECEMBER 31—One of the big news stories during the recent newspaper strike here was the announcement of the projected drive by the Teamsters Union to organize New York City's 24,000 policemen.

The article I read said that this threat has been made by Henry Feinstein, president of City Employees Union Local 237 of the Brotherhood of Teamsters, acting on behalf of James R. Hoffa, international president of the Teamsters. Mr. Hoffa is at present the temporary head of a nationwide campaign to bring all policemen, firemen and other state and county municipal workers into his union.

This, of course, is going to bring us up against a long-discussed question. Is it possible to allow employees in occupations that are necessary to the safety of the public at large in a city to be under the direction of any other organization, which would be outside the jurisdiction of the city government or the state government or the federal government?

I think most of us agree that these employees should have ways of presenting their complaints or grievances to their employer—whether it be city, state or federal government. And there should not only be special requirements for such employment, but there also should be special consideration, for in taking this kind of employment these people do give up for the public good a certain amount of independence. And one of the things that most people have felt had to be given up is the right to belong to a union, which of course is a part of the labor organization as a whole.

Mr. Hoffa is undoubtedly a very intelligent man, but I see signs in the moves he is making that point in the direction of trying to get control of employees in vital services of a city, such as New York City or any other city throughout the country.

If you think this through you must recognize the threat that the head of one union might arrive at. He could conceivably become a more important dictator than the overall leaders of the AFL–CIO labor organizations as a whole could possibly aspire to be.

Government administrations can be wrong and, when the voters decide that they are, those holding office soon find out on election days.

But unions cannot be above government. Dictator is perhaps a harsh word to use in connection with Mr. Hoffa, but he should give it consideration when he deals with the real necessity to protect the people of a big city. When one tries to organize the police and fire departments of a big city one can come dangerously near to usurping the powers of government.

These are random thoughts that have been going through my mind since reading about the projected Teamster action, and I think the situation should be given serious thought by the leaders in the labor organization, for they are responsible for the leaders of the individual locals.

For instance, Mr. Feinstein has said that he would establish picket lines outside all police depots and supply stations with the intent of cutting off the delivery of supplies for heating buildings, gasoline for police cars and other commodities. He also boasted, according to what was reported, that because the police commissioner had ruled that policemen could not join the unions they were "going to give the commissioner a taste of the economic force and pressure of the Teamsters Union."

This brings up another age-old question, which has been discussed many times: "What about control of the Army? That is the way dictators come into control."

It seems to me that Mr. Hoffa is getting a little bit arrogant and somewhat dangerous!

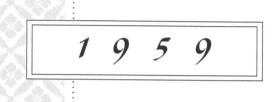

_1 9 5 9_

President Eisenhower did not have an easy task in front of him as the 86th Congress convened in January 1959. His Republican administration was poised to do partisan battle on almost all the issues with a Congress heavily weighted in the opposition party's direction. The Democratic-to-Republican ratios were almost two-to-one. And, for the first time since 1925, the Senate rejected a presidential nominee for a cabinet post (Lewis Straus, to be Secretary of Commerce), handing Eisenhower a bit of humiliation.

Among the first steps the government took in the new year was to recognize Fidel Castro's regime as the legitimate power in Cuba. Eleanor Roosevelt and most Cuba-watchers felt that the dictatorship Castro's forces had overthrown had been the greater of two evils.

The civil rights campaign received a boost in February when public schools in two Virginia towns desegregated without incident—showing that it could be done graciously. That same month brought disaster to St. Louis when one of the worst tornadoes on record struck the city, leaving an estimated $12,000,000 worth of damage in its wake.

Another step in the process designed to ring the Soviet Union with non-Communist Western allies took shape in the spring when the United States signed defense agreements with Iran, Pakistan, and Turkey. Eisenhower proudly signed a bill in March admitting Hawaii as the forty-ninth state. But his administration lost a key player when Secretary of State John Foster Dulles resigned in April due to ill health and died five weeks later at the age of seventy-one. Eleanor Roosevelt was not a fan of Dulles' ideas, but she paid him gracious tribute as a loyal public servant.

Canadian neighbors to the north joined in celebration with the United States when the St. Lawrence Seaway opened for the first time, creating a usable commercial shipping passage all the way from Duluth to the Gaspé peninsula and the Atlantic. In another act of international cooperation, some five thousand Japanese nationals who had been U.S. citizens prior to World War II but had renounced their citizenship during the war had their American status restored, reflecting the fact that both Japan and the United States had by now put the war behind them.

The next U.S. nuclear-powered submarine to be launched, the *George Washington*, could itself launch a Polaris missile, and this technological step forward in artillery changed the balance of power in cold-war disarmament talks. Something else potentially incendiary also hit American shores at midyear: D. H. Lawrence's famous novel, *Lady Chatterley's Lover*, the erotic scenes in which proved too hot for the Post Office to handle. It was banned from the mails, and whether Eleanor Roosevelt read it for entertainment or out of curiosity was not disclosed in her "My Day" column.

The summer of 1959 brought some portents of trouble to come for the United States in Southeast Asia. At Bienhoe, South Vietnam, two American soldiers were killed by Communist guerrillas on July 9. In Laos the political situation continued to destabilize, and by the end of August the State Department had begun sending significantly increased military aid to that struggling country. Mrs. Roosevelt found herself, like most Americans, divided about the wisdom of these moves. She clearly wanted to thwart the spread of communism but kept searching for ways to do it without tanks and guns.

The so-called Republican recession was in full swing by summertime, with unemployment riding high at 1,400,000 people out of work. The administration had trouble finding effective means to bring the numbers down. A major strike at U.S. Steel complicated economic matters considerably throughout the country because the ripple effect of the strike touched twenty-eight other steel producers and 95 percent of the steel industry. In early October the president invoked the Taft–Hartley act to break the strike (forcing a resumption of work and arbitration of the dispute). Mrs. Roosevelt had been opposed to the Taft-Hartley legislation for years, but she too believed the current steel strike was doing the country unjustifiable harm. The economic slowdown in the country was substantial enough by fall for the federal government to introduce a food stamp program to help particularly depressed areas.

Two celebrities captured the attention of most Americans in the latter part of the year, and "My Day" had much to say about each of them. Nikita Khrushchev, premier of the Soviet Union, visited the United States for six days, including a stop at President Roosevelt's grave at Hyde Park, where Eleanor received him. And Charles Van Doren, a highly trained intellectual and academic who impressed the country with his brilliant recall of facts, figures, and concepts on the TV quiz show *The Sixty-Four-Thousand Dollar Question*, was caught in a conspiracy with the producers: He confessed to having been coached by the television network about the questions he would be asked in the "isolation booth" on the show. For a nation trying hard to retain its optimism and self-respect while beset increasingly with challenges to its economic, legal, political, and moral authority, the incident was not what America needed.

. . . .

Eleanor Roosevelt felt she had to do a careful dance around very few issues so as not to offend or alienate certain readers or political allies, but birth control was one. Even so, this column is not the only one she wrote about the rapidly expanding world population; the subject came up at least once a year in "My Day." Mrs. Roosevelt's reading on the subject (and on related issues like the world food supply, which she also treated in "My Day") was extensive enough for her to see that if left unchecked, population growth would run away with itself, creating a tragedy of enormous dimensions, particularly among the poor. Yet she did not move to the point in her thinking where she could advocate explicitly that family planning was at least every good citizen's moral responsibility and, perhaps, every good government's best policy.

NEW YORK, JANUARY 2—There is an organization in Washington, D.C., that will celebrate next month its thirtieth year of work, and yet I think very few people are conscious of the importance of what this particular organization has been doing. It is called the Population Reference Bureau and it publishes the "Population Bulletin," which is used by many newspapers, magazines and colleges as reference material on this all-important question of population.

This organization is trying to tell the public that a crisis really threatens us. It is finally getting recognition and support from some small foundation grants, but it needs much more understanding on the part of the public to really get across to the people the message of the world situation on population today.

The Bureau of the Census recently released population projections that indicate that there could be 100,000,000 more people in this country by 1980. This is approximately half again as many people as there are now in the United States—and this increase would come about in the short period of 22 years.

In 1929, when the Population Reference Bureau was founded, the world population was increasing by about 56,000 each day. By 1945 world population was increasing by about 70,000 each day, and today, every single day, the rate of increase is up to 137,000.

. . . .

More and more organizations are beginning to see the danger signals. Where is the food coming from? True, we are making new discoveries, and new sources of food will become known in the next few years.

But perhaps the most important thing in the world is a wise and sane approach to the constantly increasing birthrate.

If we read back to the early days of American history, we will be impressed by the fact that out of families that consisted sometimes of 10 to 15 children, only perhaps three or four lived to old age and many more never lived beyond their early twenties. Many women died in childbirth. You can find in many New England cemeteries the names of three wives, each of whom bore their husbands a certain number of children. And frequently the death of the mother and the baby was recorded together on the tombstone.

Science has helped us wipe out these tragedies, but we are still expected to meet the problem that our greater knowledge has created. Fewer people die in other parts of the world through famine and epidemics. And if we are fortunate enough to wipe out war and even eventually to teach people to drive their automobiles more safely, we will gradually eliminate two major causes of death.

It is a challenge to our intelligence to meet this situation on a worldwide basis and find a sane method which will not outrage the religious or physical needs of human beings.

....

A contest of wills was one Eleanor Roosevelt would win more often than not. As a debater, a writer, and a parent, she was not inclined to back down easily once she had formulated a strong opinion. John F. Kennedy, U.S. Senator from Massachusetts, and his advisers must have known that they would meet stiff resistance when they decided to challenge Mrs. Roosevelt's claims (made in speeches and an earlier "My Day" column) that the senator had spent far too much money on campaigning and certainly too much of his own father's money for the campaign really to have been kosher. No one knew at the time that this bit of political laundry-washing in public actually would turn out to have involved a former First Lady and a president-to-be. In 1959, the argument was more a matter of a senior member of the Democratic Party, Mrs. Roosevelt, chastising a junior member, Senator Kennedy, with the latter wincing because he could not get satisfaction.

FORT BRAGG, N.C., JANUARY 6—A few days ago I received a letter from Senator John Kennedy telling me that I had been completely misinformed as to the fact that his father had any paid representatives

....

working for him in any state of the Union, or that Mr. Kennedy senior has spent any money around the country on Senator Kennedy's behalf.

My statement to the Senator had been that it was commonly accepted as a fact that these things had been done. And that while it was obligatory on anyone to build up an organization if they wished nomination or election, in any case an extravagant use of money to achieve these results was not looked upon with favor.

This brought forth from the Senator the statements paraphrased above and he writes:

"I am certain no evidence to the contrary has ever been presented to you. I am aware, as you must be, that there are a good many people who fabricate rumors and engage in slander about any person in public life. But I have made it a point never to accept or repeat such statements unless I have some concrete evidence of their truth.

"Since my letter to you, I assume you have requested your informants to furnish you with more than their gossip and speculation. If they have been unable to produce concrete evidence to support their charges or proof of the existence of at least one 'paid representative' in one state of the Union, I am confident you will, after your investigation, correct the record in a fair and gracious manner. . . ."

Since my information came largely from remarks made by people in many places, I think I should give my readers Senator Kennedy's own statement. That is the fairest way I know of dealing with a situation of this kind.

. . . .

Eleanor Roosevelt was accustomed to being the one who gave to other people, but she had a great capacity for enjoying favors done for her. The next column is a journalistic equivalent of a Norman Rockwell painting about the positive qualities of the American melting pot and about the tradition of exchanging kindness among strangers. In a world filled with the tensions of the cold war and the civil rights struggle and other intractable problems, the incident described here really did warm Mrs. Roosevelt's heart. And it happened smack in the middle of the toughest city of them all: New York.

NEW YORK, JANUARY 26—A few days ago I was scheduled to leave New York by plane at nine o'clock in the morning. The weather was bad, however, and when the time came for me to leave the Park Sheraton Hotel, where I live, the rain was coming down in sheets. No taxis were available at either entrance of the hotel, and after ten minutes of waiting I began to grow worried, for I had to reach Idlewild and I was afraid I would miss my plane.

Suddenly a man came up beside me and in a gentle voice said:

. . . .

"Mrs. Roosevelt, my wife and I live in Woodmere and my car is in the parking lot. We would be very happy to drive you to Idlewild if you would allow us."

I looked at him in great surprise, for we had never met before. I hesitated to put him to so much trouble; but my situation was growing desperate, and so I gratefully said: "If I don't get a taxi before you get your car, I would be most happy to go with you."

He arrived with his car a few minutes later. His wife got in with her bags and I got in with mine, and we started off.

After a few minutes, my host turned toward me. "Don't worry about my driving," he said. "I am an old truck driver."

I smiled, because I was not in the least worried about his driving. I was just wondering if I would make the plane on time.

Then, as we waded through traffic, he said: "Where could it happen but in America? Here am I, an ex-truck driver. I have a nice home now, and a nice wife." He glanced at her. "You can see she is very nice."

I agreed as I looked at the pretty little woman sitting behind us.

"I have two nice children—one in Boston University and one in high school, and both doing well," he continued. "Last night we went to see 'Sunrise at Campobello,' we stayed in the same hotel you live in, Mrs. Roosevelt, and now I am driving you to the airport and talking to you. Where else could it happen but in America?"

I surmise it could happen in some other places in the world. But as I think over the difficulties of getting in touch with government officials, or even with retired individuals like myself, I realize that perhaps this is a country in which contracts are easier. It is good to feel that they are—and to know that, in a way, we still have the feeling which must have existed in the early pioneer days of being a part of a big family. There are many variations, of course, but still the people of the United States are a big family.

This little incident, and the kindness which prompted the offer to take me to the plane, gave me a feeling of warmth and pleasure which I can hardly describe; but many other people must experience the same kind of willingness to help in an emergency. The fact that we had not been previously acquainted was no insuperable barrier because we were part of the American family.

....

In the northeast corner of Arizona and the northwest corner of New Mexico are situated several of the most vibrant and historically important Native American tribal lands. Some of the Indian groups here, such as the Hopi who are referred to in the next "My Day" column, have been here, living on the mesas, for over a millennium. Others,

....

such as the Navajo, are more recent arrivals, but even their culture far outstrips the Anglo (meaning, generally, Caucasian or European-based) by several hundred years.

The Taos Indians to whom Mrs. Roosevelt refers were the architects of one of the most remarkable structures in the world, their pueblo, a three- to four-story kind of apartment complex, now almost ten centuries old, built in the adobe style of mud bricks, sticks, and straw.

Mrs. Roosevelt articulated a simple principle in her columns about the troubles Native Americans face: Most can be traced directly to the history of oppression of the Indians by the white man, and therefore it was high time for sensitive reparations, financial and otherwise, to be made.

HYDE PARK, JANUARY 31—You must be beginning to think that all the Indians in the United States are having a difficult time—and I think you will be right! Ever since I first publicized an appeal from an Indian I have received many more. Today I have two more communications.

The first of these is from the Taos Indians of Taos, New Mexico, begging that the Bureau of Public Roads be urged to change the route for a road that is being planned to go through the Taos Indians' "sacred lands." They oppose this road because they feel "it would destroy the unique beauty of this historic area."

The other was sent me by someone who in the year 1955 read a statement by an Indian chief named Dan Katchongva. The writer had clipped this statement from the Arizona Daily Sun of Flagstaff and saved it. It is a very moving plea and one that I think deserves republication today. So, I will give it to you in full, for the people of the United States must awaken to their obligations, through their government, to the American Indians. Chief Dan Katchongva wrote:

"This land is ours and has been from the beginning. We came here first. We hold this land under instructions from our Great Spirit. All of the matters concerning land and the animals were worked out long before the White Man came to us.

"The White Man has come upon us long after we, the Hopi, and other Indians in this area have worked out for ourselves how to live. Our land was well established where each tribe would live. The Hopi people, after many generations of migration, came to this area because it was pointed out to us by higher powers. The White Man came and after becoming strong because of our help started to take all the land, homes, and owner property away from us. We have suffered untold hardships as a result. We are still suffering.

"Every time we work up to a point where we feel that we have everything we need, then a new policy or program comes from Washington, and immediately we are forced to go on that plan without our consent, prior knowledge, or consultation.

"The White Man seems to have forgotten his religion, his obligations to the Indians and his promises, but continues to try to force us to his ways.

"Sometimes we are put in his jail, his prisons, and have come to this time now without sheep, horses to work our farms, our very own land. These lands have been taken from us by the Navajo with the help of the United States government.

"Today we find ourselves confined to a small area. Today I am without houses because Indian Bureau officials have confiscated them because I wanted to take care of them in the way the Hopi did for generations before the White Man came.

"Many of our people are sheepless because they refused to follow Indian Bureau policies. As a leader of my people, I have never been consulted about any of this, nor have I given my consent to these policies.

"I have always objected to anyone coming upon our land to take our natural resources. We have long known that the wealthiest part of this great land is here beneath us. But we know, too, that these resources must not be used for purposes of war nor to destroy other people. These things are to be used only for peaceful purposes and then only after the land matter of the Hopi has been settled.

"Our way of life is good and well planned out for us by the Great Spirit and we have been warned never to depart nor deviate from it. Our land is not selfish. If we take care of it by the way we live and by prayer, by performing our ceremonies and by adhering to the instructions of our forefathers, then we may enter the everlasting life and not destroy ourselves."

. . . .

Much as Eleanor Roosevelt respected good doctors, she was no fan of the American Medical Association, nor was she convinced that psychiatry and psychotherapy had much to offer over the more clear-cut advantages of a good home life and parents who knew how to balance love with discipline. There were several points in Mrs. Roosevelt's life at which it might have been reasonable for her to seek psychotherapy (when she lost an infant child, when she found the struggle for family control with her mother-in-law too intense, when she realized the truth about her husband's extramarital relations). But she saw them all through, with the help of her religious faith, the love of her family and friends, and an iron will.

This column takes off from a television panel discussion show hosted by Dr. Karl Menninger, co-founder with his brother William of the

. . . .

Menninger Clinic in Kansas, where they developed various techniques for treating mental illness.

NEW YORK, FEBRUARY 16—Instead of asking me for a speech, Dr. Menninger said the plan was that he and I would exchange points of view on a variety of subjects. He and his colleagues were the scientists—and they are presented with the problem that exists, namely, mental illness from babyhood through to old age; and they were trying to find the answers and the best answers to every problem put before them. As we talked, I realized that I was of course interested in this problem of treatment, but that fundamentally I was more interested in the problem of prevention. Why was it we had to have mental illness? If we could discover it in children and learned the proper treatment, why couldn't we also study the reasons which brought it about and try to prevent the causes?

I had to confess that at first I had been impatient with the ease with which many people turned to psychiatry to solve personal problems which I felt were problems that self-discipline required one to settle for oneself. But I had come to realize that psychiatry could be of infinite help to people. It could bring about better results and perhaps prevent long struggles which an individual otherwise might have to go through in order to gain self-mastery without any understanding help. But I still believed that it was important for the individual to struggle for himself and to feel the sense of achievement in his own self-reliance and self-control. If this is not one of the results of psychiatric treatment, I am always nervous about the final outcome.

....

Sophie Tucker seemed an all-American institution to most of her vast audience during her extraordinarily long career as a nightclub singer, but in fact she had Russian origins. Tucker, known in the hearts of her adoring fans as "the last of the red-hot mamas," had been on stage through the burlesque and vaudeville eras (like Mrs. Roosevelt, she was born in 1884), had known the rowdy English music-hall circuit, and then had become America's most famous nightclub singer of torch songs, those poignant ballads that could break your heart even if you were happily in love. Eleanor Roosevelt was not much of a nightclub patron, but she knew a shining star when she saw one—as she did in Pasadena (she was in Los Angeles for AAUN work) the night she and Sophie Tucker met.

NEW YORK, MARCH 9—I began to worry about getting to Pasadena in time for dinner and the evening meeting, remembering that the freeway between Los Angeles and Pasadena between five and six o'clock can be very crowded and very slow. Fortunately for me, Mrs. Hershey Martin, with whom I stayed, had arranged that they would call for me after dinner at her house and take me over for the evening speech, after which I would go to a reception. This worked out very well, and when it was all over Mrs. Martin and I joined her husband for a very short time at Sophie Tucker's opening at the Ambassador Hotel.

I had never met this remarkable entertainer who, at 71, as she told us, is still going on with her regular entertainment programs and making a success of it. Miss Tucker told us that she had given away $3,000,000 for charitable purposes during her career and she thanked all those who had helped her to do this. She came to meet me at the end of her performance, saying it was high time we should meet since she had known my boys for a very long time. She is full of life, and I could not help thinking what an extraordinarily vivid personality she has.

. . . .

The voices of two of America's most eloquent and persuasive journalists—Eleanor Roosevelt and Martha Gellhorn—combine in the next column to produce a stunning statement about the insanity of nuclear war and a plea for progress among all nations in learning to resolve disputes without resorting to global violence. As a newspaperwoman, Martha Gellhorn met Mrs. Roosevelt in the White House in 1934; their friendship bloomed and continued until Eleanor Roosevelt's death in 1962. They had the deepest respect for one another (as the Introduction to Volume I, Eleanor Roosevelt's "My Day," 1936–1945, written by Gellhorn, attests). Gellhorn was a distinguished war correspondent in Europe from the Spanish Civil War throughout World War II and afterward.

TEHERAN, IRAN, MARCH 16—A powerful and timely book, "The Face of War," by Martha Gellhorn, has recently been published by Simon and Schuster, and I would like to urge that this book be read carefully by the leaders in every nation of the world, certainly in the Soviet Union as well as in the United States.

Martha Gellhorn, as an experienced journalist, writes extremely well—almost too well to make the reading of this book bearable. In fact, at times I had to put it down and close my eyes and try to think of other things. It is the account of her war experiences during eight years in 12 countries. She tells not only of the men at war but of the countless human beings—men, women and children, and especially children—who lived through these wars and bore the brunt of the horror which was man-made.

One of her statements I think none of us today should ever forget.

. . . .

"From the earliest wars of men to our last heart-breaking worldwide effort," she writes, "all we could do was kill ourselves. Now we are able to kill the future."

On the last page of this book, which so graphically describes the face of war, she writes: "If we will not learn, is there any hope for us? The answer is that we cannot help hoping; we do not control it. We are given a supply which only runs out in death, perhaps because each one of us knows love, the source of hope. . . . But this is our final chance to learn. The second World War was an evil that men could stop; the unknown nuclear war will have no end. No peace treaty will stop the interminable, invisible poison dust. The war of the universe will be carried on by the wind. War is a crime against the living and always has been; no one can begin to imagine the size and the shape of the crime of nuclear war. . . . Where will the survivors be, outside the limits of civilization, not worth immediately killing—and what can they hope for, what can they create again to the honor of mankind, knowing that the earth and the air and the water are incurably tainted, and that they have nothing to hand on to their children and their children's children except disease, a withering end to the last of the race? . . . To preserve freedom? What freedom? For whom?"

These are very pertinent questions. This book forces you to think them through. There was a time when you could believe that to be willing to die for your country and to fight for it might have ennobling effects upon the character of man. With nuclear weapons that day is past, for you preserve nothing for the future or for anyone but a slow and certain death.

Is there no wisdom among us today which will force us to use and to develop the machinery set up after World War II in the United Nations so that the peoples of the world—all of whom will suffer if nuclear warfare breaks out on the face of the earth—can use their collective genius to prevent the destruction of the future?

. . . .

On March 12, Mrs. Roosevelt, her granddaughter Nina now seventeen, daughter of son John Roosevelt and his wife, Anne, and the usual entourage of secretaries had left New York for a pleasure and business trip to Iran and Israel. They would be away a month, keeping to a hectic schedule of social and unofficial diplomatic meetings and passing through Paris and London en route home. But even in remote parts of Iran and Israel Mrs. Roosevelt found the time and the means to write her "My Day" columns and to transmit them back to New York.

This column bears a foreign dateline and concerns a slice of life in an African country, but it derives from a not-so-unusual interview Eleanor Roosevelt had in the States before departing. From her White

. . . .

House years until her death, Mrs. Roosevelt was perceived by countless people around the world as the right one to go to for help—no matter whether the problem was personal, institutional, or governmental. Mrs. Roosevelt kept an appointment schedule that would have worn down a woman half her age, and she made a point of remaining accessible to strangers who, more often than not, deserved some assistance. As Martha Gellhorn said of Eleanor, "she was not a brilliant conversationalist but she was a genius at listening," which was Mrs. Roosevelt's way of becoming able to make a useful response.

SHIRAZ, IRAN, MARCH 17—Just before I left on this trip I had a most interesting visitor back in New York—a young African from Kenya who is a medical doctor.

This young man, Munjai Njoroge, was born in Kenya in 1926. After obtaining his early education in Kenya, he earned his Bachelor of Science degree in Hygiene at the University of South Africa in Pretoria in the Union of South Africa.

Somehow he became the pen pal of a New York schoolboy and was encouraged to believe that if he came to America he would be able to get the more advanced education that he wanted. He had to survive various financial crises, but finally reached New York by way of London with three cents in his pocket. He borrowed his fare to California and enrolled at Stanford University, from which in due time he received his BS and MD degrees.

He then held an internship at Kings County Hospital, New York, and later received an appointment at Presbyterian Hospital, also in New York.

Now he is planning to return to Africa as Kenya's first American-trained physician. He hopes to establish there the first modern hospital for Africans, administered by Africans, in a rural area, and he is being helped in this enterprise by the Medical International Cooperation Division of the International Rescue Committee.

I feel sure that this group is cooperating in its work with the World Health Organization and that the maximum good can come out of this enterprise.

Kenya is a British Crown Colony and Protectorate which is working toward its independence. It is about one and a half times the size of California. It has a population of a little over six million people, who are mainly engaged in agriculture.

What hospitals now exist in Kenya are in towns, so in the rural areas only a few government and missionary clinics serve the people. Most of the doctors are Europeans or Asians. They have done remarkable work, but few speak the language or understand the background of the people they serve. There is now only one other African private doctor in Kenya, so Dr. Njoroge on his return will be the second African doctor and the first trained in the United States.

This is an exciting project, and help will be needed to see it materialize. But I am sure there will be interest on a broad scale in this young man who had the determination and courage to travel more than halfway around the world for his education.

This is a great opportunity for the American people to show their interest in helping an area of the world where the Soviets are very ready to give "technical assistance" in order to prove that they understand the needs better than we do.

. . . .

Among the reasons for Mrs. Roosevelt's visit to Iran was the fact that her daughter Anna and Anna's husband, Dr. James Halsted, had been working for two years at an Iranian hospital, helping to educate native doctors, nurses, and patients in advanced medical procedures.

Mrs. Roosevelt's group was well looked after by the American ambassador, and the presence in Iran at this time of Henry Morgethau, Jr., a longtime Roosevelt family friend and adviser, also put Mrs. Roosevelt at ease in what were sometimes rather primitive conditions. The next two columns, filed from Tel-Aviv and London, focus on her experiences in Iran and Israel and are typical of her traveler's reports from the field, almost a set of rough notes meant to be digested at a later time.

Ramadan is the month-long Islamic holiday commemorating the first revelation of the Koran to Mohammed.

TEL-AVIV, ISRAEL, MARCH 25—It is the season of Ramadan in Iran, where we were last week, and it is the practice of all Mohammedans to fast from sunrise to sunset. So they eat two large meals, at sunset and before sunrise! Right in the middle of the season are the two weeks observed by Iranians as we observe our Christmas, with gifts for the children and great family gatherings!

Soon after our arrival in Teheran I went to the Nemazee Hospital, a fine building that is well equipped and staffed but unable to take all the patients they hope to have when they are better financed. There also is a nursing school, and there's a clinic for the care of eyes, both of which they hope to enlarge. This could become a fine medical center and, with close cooperation with the university, it could develop into a fine teaching hospital.

Trachoma and tuberculosis are the biggest medical problems. There is need for all the young American-trained Iranians to work in different parts of the country, but it seems as though much still is centered in Teheran itself and too little spread out into the country.

. . . .

We visited two of my daughter's friends, one in a big house with a lovely garden and the other in a small house. Everywhere there are flowers, and water is much used for decoration, as in Pakistan and India. Almost every garden has an eight-inch-deep reflecting pool. I visited the university hospital, where I was told there is an enormous waiting list of chronic cases, and some of these people come and lie at the door and on the steps hoping to get in. We also saw the Red Cross maternity hospital and a prenatal clinic in town that also lacks funds to meet its needs. One section of this hospital is for foundlings brought in by the police—abandoned babies who are cared for here and at a year old given out for adoption.

Many well-to-do people wear Western clothes, but many women wear a kind of large enveloping cloth which covers them from head to foot and which is drawn around the lower parts of their faces. Partly this is protection against dust which through much of the year flows everywhere. It is amusing to see the latest type of high-heeled shoes beneath this coverall, if the lady is a lady of fashion.

LONDON, APRIL 6—In Eilat we lunched with the major and afterward took a trip in a glass-bottomed boat to look at the coral and the beautiful colored fish of the Red Sea. Four years ago they had one boat; today they have ten. That is perhaps a good way to gauge the growth of Eilat.

The fish are many and varied, but I was particularly fascinated by a kind of sapphire-blue variety which, darting through the water, looked more beautiful than any of the others. We were told we did not have time to go out to the best coral beds, but what we did see was interesting and we were grateful for the time allowed us for this little trip.

We took the plane at 3:30 and flew directly from Eilat to Beersheba. There is no real landing strip there; the planes just land in the field. But everyone was waiting to greet us and take us at once to the opening of the Youth Center at 4:30. This is a Youth Aliyah Day Center.

With the new influx of immigrants to Israel, these day centers have proved very valuable for the older children from 14 to 17. They have to learn Hebrew as quickly as possible; and at the same time, if they come from countries where they have a regular education, they must not be allowed to fall back in their studies. It might be difficult to fit them into the regular school system, so the day centers provide both educational and vocational work. They also provide a place where many children of the community come to play together. The director is usually chosen because of his capacity for giving special guidance to this age group, and by the time they go into the army they will be prepared to get the maximum out of their training and vocational experience. The boys remain two and a half years, the girls two years.

Although a cold wind blew up as we sat on the platform in Beersheba during the dedication of this center, no one seemed to notice it—least of all the youngsters who played and sang for us. A group of girls danced for us in bare feet on the board platform, and I felt they certainly would gather many splinters in their feet. But not a girl seemed to experience the slightest discomfort, and I thought again what hardy youngsters these were.

We were fairly frozen by the time the speeches ended. I felt very much honored in having the Youth Center dedicated in my name, but I must confess I was glad when we were able to get back in the car and drive around the town. It has grown completely different from my recollection of four years ago. Then there were 20,000 people in it; now there are 42,000.

On my very first visit, seven years ago, I saw a young man and his wife who had just arrived and settled in a little two-room house. Three years later I saw them again. They were better settled, they were happy because he was a good carpenter and had plenty of work, but she had no children and felt there was a shadow in the house. This time I asked the major if I might go and see them again, and to my joy I found that they have two children, a boy and a girl. Their garden is growing, and her husband, in his spare time, is adding two and a half rooms to the house. These are substantially built, and the wife told me with pride they would have a bathroom. Her icebox already stood in the kitchen, though the roof is not yet on.

After our drive around, we returned to Hias House. This was built as a hostel for visiting engineers and technicians of every kind who constantly come on business because the two factories which were here four years ago have now grown to six. A great deal of research is being carried on, for UNESCO has established a desert research project which seeks to find what kind of things grow best here and how the area can be reclaimed in the best possible way.

. . . .

Even for Eleanor Roosevelt the slightly lunatic experience of buying a camel, inspired by granddaughter Nina, was something new. Nina hoped to ship the animal back to America, a plan that never worked out. This column carries on the Israeli travelogue and shows that, tourist though Mrs. Roosevelt was, she was also considered equal to a visiting head of state. Her appointments list included European royalty and key government leaders from Israel. The Ben-Gurions were among Eleanor's favorite friends in Israel. Other Israeli leaders over the years had occasionally given Eleanor Roosevelt pause by seeming belligerent with their Arab neighbors, but in her estimation David Ben-Gurion was the kind of diplomat who could help Israel grow while contributing to

. . . .

*peace in the Mideast. Foreign Minister Golda Meir would herself be-
come prime minister in 1969.*

LONDON, APRIL 8—When we were in Jerusalem we went down into
the tombs from which have been excavated the 71 members of the
Great Sanhedrin, which dates back to antiquity. After looking at these
excavations, we decided that the nicest thing about them was that the
land around was being turned into a playground for children and that
trees were planted there and that the view out over the valley was
really beautiful.

All the desire that people had for permanent graves buried deep in
the rock so that they would not deteriorate fast seems to me so foolish.

I would rather be out in the open, with the sky above me where my
early remains can disappear rapidly. For my spirit, I am sure, will enjoy
the soft rains and the sunshine and the white snow in winter and the
fact that children can play happily in the garden.

From there we proceeded to the zoo, which is a biblical zoo and
includes all the animals that are mentioned in the Bible. Nina at once
went to look for the camel that we had bought and which it now
develops we may not be able to bring home with us. Unfortunately,
there was some kind of celebration in the town and the camel had
been loaned for the day to entertain the children.

If Nina's camel, which she named Duchess, ever does reach the
United States—with the beautiful saddle given to us by Sheik Suleiman
of Beersheba—I am sure it will give much pleasure to many children
in the neighborhood.

After our visit to the zoo I returned to the hotel to keep my appointment with Queen Elisabeth of the Belgians. She is just as full of
life and interest as she was when I saw her last year in Brussels. She
had already visited one of the children's villages and, just as happened
to her in Russia, she fell in love with the children and wanted to
embrace them all.

Late that same afternoon we went along with several other people
to tea with Prime Minister and Mrs. David Ben-Gurion. Mrs. Ben-
Gurion is wonderful in her care of her husband, and what a remarkable
man he is! His eyes snap as though he were a young man when he is
talking about something he is vitally interested in, and he gives you a
feeling of resourcefulness, courage and flexibility in his thinking,
which is quite extraordinary.

At dinner that night with Mrs. Golda Meir, the Foreign Minister,
I had the pleasure of meeting several members of the government,
among them the Minister of Education. They all seemed to possess
strong personalities, with good qualities of leadership, and this perhaps

is the distinguishing feature that accounts for their success in meeting problems that must at times seem insoluble.

. . . .

Over the twenty-six years that Eleanor Roosevelt wrote "My Day," her readers became accustomed to one thing: their correspondent was an opinionated lady. They also got used to the sometimes jerky style of the column; the art of the graceful transition was not very much hers. But the following column, on two entirely unrelated subjects—the DAR and a Tennessee Williams play—is nonetheless pithy and entertaining.

What annoyed Eleanor Roosevelt about the Daughters of the American Revolution was that membership in the group was based not on merit but on bloodline: only those who have ancestors whose participation in the American Revolution of 1776 can be documented are taken in. She felt that the DAR membership was more often smug than sensible, and over the years she had engaged in verbal tussles with them— each side assuming that the other had lost the argument. No matter how much good work the DAR may have done to preserve and mark historic places (an effort Mrs. Roosevelt certainly applauded), their ultraconservative politics forever disqualified them from her approval.

When she talks about a play she had seen recently, Mrs. Roosevelt again shows us that contemporary drama in which the agonies and passions of tortured souls are displayed onstage is not the genre she really likes. For her, the drama of starkly defined political ideas—as in Odets' Waiting for Lefty—*was far more moving than the drama of enigmatic feelings—as in Beckett's* Waiting for Godot.

NEW YORK, APRIL 28—The ladies of the Daughters of the American Revolution have just held their annual meetings in Washington. These meetings were of interest to those of us who really believe in the United Nations and think that if these worthy ladies could be enlisted in what we consider the right lines of endeavor they would find themselves doing a much more valuable service than when they are on the other side of the fence.

However, they think differently, and so we are treated each year to absurdities. They waste their time in a very sad manner.

Why should they make statements to the effect that the United Nations should be removed from the United States and that the U.S. should not be a member? The UN is in the U.S., it is a going concern, we are a member, and the UN is going to stay here. The ladies of the DAR might much better make up their minds to the facts and see what they can do to make their organization really useful.

There is an attack going on now, I understand, on UNICEF, one

. . . .

in which the DAR is probably taking a part. And if the DAR really studied UNICEF and did something to help it, they would discover that this UN agency is doing a great deal for the children of the world. How much better this would be than being entirely negative and doing a destructive piece of work.

One night last week I went to see the Tennessee Williams play "Sweet Bird of Youth." It is a powerful play and beautifully acted. And the little quotation on the program gives one an inkling of one idea that is brought out:

"Relentless caper for all those who step
The legend of their youth into the noon."

Who has not known that in varying degrees nearly all human beings have to fight the desires of youth which often do not die with the passing of years? This is one of the tests of the growth of maturity.

And the last plea made so well in the play by Paul Newman for a recognition by each one of us of the beast that lives within us is perhaps a wise admonition. But do we have to go through quite so much sordidness of detail? Granted that much of it is true.

To me the man who came barefooted from the hills and made himself a power and was willing to sacrifice even those he loved most (if he understood love at all) to his own ambitions is perhaps the most horrifying of all the characters because we have seen and recognized it so often. Strength that goes wrong is even more dangerous than weakness that goes wrong.

Sometimes, it seems to me, Tennessee Williams wants to put in words and incidents things that are better left to our own imaginations and better faced when we are alone and must face ourselves.

Perhaps I am wrong and perhaps we need what Tennessee Williams does. The stirring that he gives to each one of us may be a necessity, but I find it more pain than pleasure. I have never met this playwright, but if it is true that one lives with one's characters, life cannot be very pleasant for him.

. . . .

Eleanor Roosevelt could not and did not distance herself from important political events which had no immediate connection to her. Instead, she looked for the general implications for all citizens within whatever circumstances were at hand and out of these she formulated an opinion and recommended action. When she read about an especially egregious example of Southern racism, Mrs. Roosevelt felt that the insult and threat posed by it touched her life too, not just the life of the black man. Subsequent reports showed he had been murdered by a white vigilante gang that was never brought to justice.

. . . .

NEW YORK, APRIL 29—On last Sunday morning in two New York newspapers I read front-page stories about a group of men who took a Negro from a prison in Mississippi, where he was awaiting trial on an accusation of possible rape of a white woman, and beat him and removed him to parts unknown. He had been left unguarded, at least so the story was told, and the mob just walked in and took him out of his cell.

Up to the time I write this no one has been found who could be charged with the responsibility for the kind of cruelty for which we and our three allies at the end of World War II tried the makers of policy in Nazi Germany.

We have not reached the point as yet, thank God, when mass murders of people in gas chambers are going on, but when a mob does not wait for the action of the law, then you are no longer a law-abiding nation.

This occurrence in Mississippi was not something that could be shrugged off by the rest of the country by saying "Well, this is unfortunate. But it did not happen in our community." Nor can it be explained that it happened in a particular area where people are so conditioned by their past that their emotions have led them to forget their obligation to be law-abiding citizens.

This was something about which we all have some responsibility. If we in other parts of the country do not express our feelings of shock at such conduct, then we are as guilty as the men who actually were in the kidnapping group.

It was only a few people who decided that they wished to eliminate a certain group of people in Germany, but it grew to such dimensions that six million Jews died in the prison camps. When you begin to allow yourself to override the law you do not know where you will end. When you begin to allow yourself a kind of self-righteous prejudice against another race or another religion, you do not know what the end may be, and in the end you may suffer as did those who sowed the seeds of World War II by their policies.

This can be seen in the films of the Nuremberg trials. Here were the men who thought they would never suffer as they saw others suffer, and yet they were condemned to hanging. The mobs that lynch today may well be running before future retribution, or their children may be in the years to come.

There is nothing that concerns the people of only one section of our country. This unspeakable behavior in Mississippi concerns all of us. And if we feel strongly enough none of our citizens will dare to stand up against a real moral reaction to what happens to our own citizens who may be of another race and color but who are American citizens and entitled to equal justice before the law.

Eleanor Roosevelt's beloved Val-Kill Cottage was cozy, even humble compared to FDR's austerely grand ancestral home on the Hudson River at Hyde Park, New York, a mile or so away. The living room in the converted furniture factory was crammed with books, overstuffed chairs in cotton slipcovers, and photographs of family and distinguished friends and visitors. Val-Kill is now a National Historic Site, administered by the Park Service.

ELEANOR ROOSEVELT
HUMANITARIAN AND DIPLOMAT
1884 - 1962

ELEANOR ROOSEVELT
5¢ U.S. POSTAGE

ELEANOR ROOSEVELT
5¢ U.S. POSTAGE

HYDE PARK, N.Y.
OCT 11 1984
12538

Eleanor Roosevelt
USA 20

FIRST DAY OF ISSUE

"FIRST LADY OF THE WORLD"

An envelope and a 5¢ stamp bearing her portrait (left) was produced by the Post Office Department not long after Mrs. Roosevelt died in 1962. A first-day-of-issue cover (right) also includes the 20¢ stamp issued in October 1984 to celebrate her hundredth birthday. The postmark was, of course, Hyde Park, Eleanor Roosevelt's legal and emotional home. (*U.S. Postal Service*)

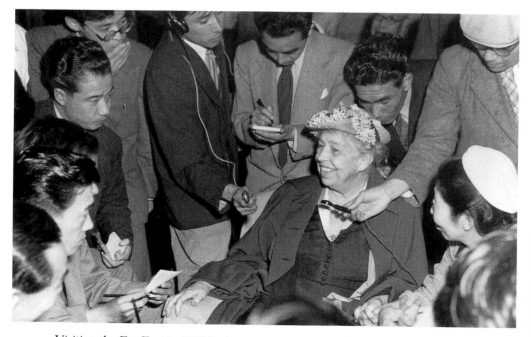

Visiting the Far East in 1953 both as a representative of the World Association for the UN and as a private citizen, Mrs. Roosevelt was swamped with requests for press interviews. Here she fields questions from Japanese reporters. Though her schedule of public appearances was daunting, she relished the opportunity to promote the UN's cause and to bring messages of good will from America. (*FDR Library*)

Andrei Gromyko had been the Soviet Union's ambassador to the United States in the 1940s and later played a key role at the United Nations, where he and Mrs. Roosevelt often found themselves at odds ideologically. When Mrs. Roosevelt left her post at the UN in January 1953 in the clean sweep of Republican patronge following Eisenhower's election, the tributes to her were many. None meant more than the respect she was accorded by Gromyko, one of her ablest foes. (*AP/Wide World Photos*)

The year 1953 took Mrs. Roosevelt to Eastern Europe. She and her friend Dr. David Gurewitsch (at left) relax aboard the new Yugoslavian president's yacht on the Adriatic. Marshall Tito, who ruled Yugoslavia from 1953 until 1980, seemed to many Western liberals, including Eleanor Roosevelt, a strange but welcome creature, a liberal Communist. (*FDR Library*)

B. C. Gardner, chancellor of McGill University, Montreal, applauds as Mrs. Roosevelt accepts an honorary doctorate of laws in November 1953. Such honors were particularly gratifying to her—she eventually had dozens of them—because she had never attended college. (*FDR Library*)

Especially after World War II, when the harsh truth of the Holocaust became known and the establishment of Israel as a state was underway, Eleanor Roosevelt was an indefatigable worker for the Jewish cause. Chosen woman of the year more than once by Jewish groups, she was always ready to join in fundraising efforts for the budding new country in an ancient land that she had visited and found fascinating, even inspiring. This photograph was taken in Akron, Ohio, in early 1954. (*FDR Library*)

For decades after FDR died in 1945, heads of state visiting America made pilgrimages to his grave at Hyde Park. Such visits usually involved Mrs. Roosevelt, who delighted in showing her guests the grounds and the presidential library, filled with memorabilia from the war years and before. On Memorial Day 1954 the guest was Emperor Haile Selassie of Ethiopia. To her right is Herman Kahn, Library director. (*FDR Library*)

The boys from nearby Wiltwyck School came every summer to Val-Kill for a picnic, and Mrs. Roosevelt often rolled up her sleeves to assist (as here, in 1954) in dishing out what even she—the mother of six—considered huge amounts of food. The socially disadvantaged Wiltwyck children were mostly from New York City. Eleanor Roosevelt believed that a country atmosphere and good discipline would help any child develop along the right track. (*Olga Norbin; loaned to the FDR Library by Stella Hershan*)

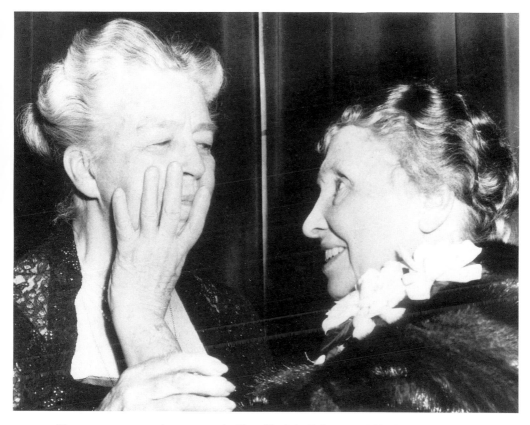

Two great communicators met in New York in February 1955 when the American Foundation for Overseas Blind gave a testimonial dinner for Helen Keller at which Eleanor Roosevelt was a guest. Miss Keller admired Mrs. Roosevelt's dedication to social causes and to promoting respect for the handicapped. Eleanor Roosevelt applauded Keller's exuberant and courageous determination to live a full life despite her handicap. (*UPI/Bettmann*)

Ten years after the end of World War II Europe was still plagued by serious problems with refugees and displaced persons. Among the most heartrending situations were those of the orphans of war and its aftermath. In 1955, at Cambous, near Montpelier in southern France, Mrs. Roosevelt had a tête-a-tête with a Moroccan Jewish refugee orphan. Eleanor Roosevelt had a magic touch with children everywhere. (*Omicron Photos*)

(*Left*): Mrs. Roosevelt frequently disagreed with Connecticut Representative Clare Boothe Luce when she served in Congress from 1943 to 1947, but her career was one the former First Lady admired. In Rome in the spring of 1955, the two women shared thoughts about the international scene. Mrs. Luce was then American ambassador to Italy; Eleanor Roosevelt represented the American Association for the UN. (*FDR Library*)

(*Below*): Day in and day out, decades of continuous work for Mrs. Roosevelt meant that her relationship with her secretaries (here Maureen Corr) went far beyond mere loyalty. Eleanor Roosevelt kept up a voluminous correspondence, produced several books, delivered countless speeches, and hammered out her "My Day" column (and others for monthly magazines) with the consistent energy of a well-oiled machine. This is her office in her New York apartment (211 East 62nd St.) in 1956. (*Cowles Communications, Inc.*)

Eleanor Roosevelt was married to the man who served longer than any other in the White House and supported the man who failed in three consecutive attempts to become president. Many in the country's liberal wing looked to Governor Adlai Stevenson of Illinois as their conscience and intellectual standard-bearer. Mrs. Roosevelt sometimes urged greater warmth upon him but always found his ideas persuasive. Here she rallies with the governor at the Democratic National Convention in Chicago in 1956, where he won the party's nomination for the second time. (*FDR Library*)

The labor movement had few more staunch supporters than Eleanor Roosevelt. Although she could be critical of labor leaders whose vanity made them grab at unjustified power and unionized public service workers who wanted to strike, she used her "My Day" column repeatedly to explain rank-and-file viewpoints to a not-always-sympathetic public. She was a guest at the 1956 Amalgamated Clothing Workers convention in New York. (*Samuel Reiss*)

Mrs. Roosevelt had doubts about the commercial and entertainment uses to which the young medium of television was being put in the late 1950s but participated happily in a UNICEF Halloween Party at the United Nations in 1957 with the children's TV celebrity "Captain Kangaroo." Eleanor Roosevelt had became something of a television celebrity herself as moderator of round-table discussions of social and political issues. (*FDR Library*)

Eleanor Roosevelt's reporting from behind the Iron Curtain in 1957, particularly her interviews with Premier Nikita Khrushchev (whom she visited at Yalta in September), broke new ground for American journalism. The United Feature Syndicate editors extended her "My Day" columns to accommodate the serious and detailed text she filed from deepest Russia. The interviews revealed a Khrushchev at once more human and more rigidly ideological than had been seen or heard before. (*UPI/Bettmann*)

In Jerusalem in March 1958 Mrs. Roosevelt was shown the famous Dead Sea Scrolls by Hebrew University president Professor Mazur. Israel's roots in antiquity fascinated Eleanor Roosevelt, and she discussed in her "My Day" column the complex, volatile mixture of Judeo-Christian, Arab-Islamic, and other cultures in the Middle East. (*David Harris*)

In June 1960 part of Dore Schary's *Sunrise at Campobello* was filmed in the Roosevelt family residence at Hyde Park. Between takes Mrs. Roosevelt chatted with the film's stars, Greer Garson (who played the young Eleanor Roosevelt) and Ralph Bellamy (who played FDR). Mrs. Roosevelt counted playwright Dore Schary among her friends and did provide some insight and information to encourage his work, but she and her children found it strange to see their lives transformed into those of literary and historical characters. (*FDR Library*)

It took Eleanor Roosevelt several months to warm to Senator John Kennedy, particularly after the failure of the draft-Stevenson movement she had helped to spearhead at the national convention. Kennedy was candid about his gratitude for Mrs. Roosevelt's support, and she saw in him the promise of greatness. (*USIA/FDR Library*)

The threat posed to the world by the atomic bomb was much on people's minds in 1960 as the United States and the Soviet Union made the arms race ever more intense. Joining Mrs. Roosevelt at a peace rally in New York were two distinguished politicians who had worked throughout their careers for the cause of peace. Norman Thomas, on Mrs. Roosevelt's right, ran for president many times under the Socialist Party banner; Alf Landon, former governor of Kansas, ran against FDR on the unsuccessful Republican ticket in 1936. (*FDR Library*)

Seventy-two-year-old Eleanor Roosevelt carries her own suitcase to a plane at New York's LaGuardia field in 1960. Fiercely independent and determined, Mrs. Roosevelt traveled thousands of miles every year until the last few months of her life. (*Lawrence Jordan, Jr.*)

At Eleanor Roosevelt's funeral in Hyde Park in October 1962 three American presidents joined other friends and family to bid her farewell. From left: Jacqueline Kennedy; President John F. Kennedy; Vice President Lyndon Johnson; former president Harry Truman; Bess Truman; former president Dwight Eisenhower; Margaret Truman. (*AP/Wide World Photos*)

Eleanor and Franklin Roosevelt are buried beneath a plain white marble marker in a simple rose garden at Hyde Park. (*FDR Library*)

I am sick at heart and ashamed that I belong to a race that can commit the same kind of cruelty that made us shudder when it came to the fore in Nazi Germany. We shudder when we hear of it today in Communist Russia and in Communist China.

What has happened to us that we do not see in this kind of action the seeds that will bring destruction upon us all in the future?

. . . .

Another way of pushing forward the campaign for civil rights was to applaud those works of art that showed how compassion and courage could triumph over discrimination. The black actor Sidney Poitier already had a distinguished list of credits in stage drama and film by the time Mrs. Roosevelt first saw him.

HYDE PARK, MAY 2—The other evening I went to see Sidney Poitier in "A Raisin in the Sun." Lorraine Hansberry wrote a delightful play which, incidentally, I had read in manuscript, but Sidney Poitier brings it to life and he is well supported by all the other actors.

This play has been praised by all the critics, so they do not need my praise to add to its popularity. But I would like to thank both the author and Mr. Poitier for an evening that had real meaning, and I hope meaning that will sink into the conscience of America.

. . . .

Mrs. Roosevelt had seen the face of poverty and hunger many a time. She had also crisscrossed the breadbasket heartland of America, repeatedly witnessing the growth of the country's vast agricultural business and its capacity to create surpluses of food. Added to these firsthand experiences was careful study of data about the world's hunger and population problems—as part of her job at the United Nations and, later, simply as a concerned citizen. Thus, when Eleanor Roosevelt wrote about famine-relief projects, she knew whereof she spoke, and she did so with deep conviction.

In this case she takes up the issue of why the United States does not seem able to help a neighbor, Haiti. She can see the record of complicated political factors, but for her the issue is hungry people in one country and overfed people, overstuffed grain elevators, in another—and how to help out. She introduces the novel idea of using food itself as part of an international loan. And she praises a man who became one of her favorites in the Senate because of his consistent humanitarian principles, Hubert Humphrey of Minnesota.

FLINT, MICH., MAY 5—It seems to me that we have been left in ignorance of the situation in Haiti which, because of our past history

. . . .

of concern about that land, should be of concern to everyone of us.

In the Congressional Record there is a speech by Senator Hubert Humphrey of Minnesota in which he brings out the fact that because of a long drought there has been famine in Haiti which affects 45,000 men, women and children. This condition has existed for over a year and even if the rains were to come now the people would have no seed left with which to plant crops, and no animals left to sell in order to get money to buy seeds. Both a French priest and a Baptist minister report starvation conditions among the people and pitiable conditions among the children.

In his speech Senator Humphrey pointed out the curious fact that we, who are so near to Haiti, not only are slow to act when we hear of such a situation in which our surplus food could be used, but there is no machinery set up by which we can do this. At the same time he points to the fact that in the District of Columbia there are 7,000 children in the grade schools who have an inadequate diet and there is no school lunch program.

The President was upheld the other day by the Senate in his veto of a rural electrification bill and he repeatedly upholds his Secretary of Agriculture, who has allowed a condition to arise where we have no plan either for helping hungry children at home or for helping people who have starved for over a year in a neighboring island. All of this when we ourselves have more food unused than we know what to do with. This looks as though Democrats as well as Republicans must accept responsibility for this deplorable situation.

There was a time when our citizens believed that a good harvest was the gift of God. We needed it and we were thankful for it. Otherwise, we would have no Thanksgiving Day. I think with a little serious planning we could help people all around the world to improve their own food supplies and to profit by our ability to grow food and our luck in having good harvests.

Then we could really thank God again for His rain and His sunshine. We could really be confident again of the value of our land and we would have earned the gratitude of the people in Haiti.

True, we probably recognize in Washington that the government of Haiti under a past President, Col. Paul E. Magloire, got itself into a very bad economic situation by the now-familiar method of having a dictator who exploited the people and made a fortune for himself and ruined the economy of his country. But the people who starve have no realization that this is probably one of the reasons why their government today is unable to help them. They are conscious of only one thing—that they need food and it isn't there.

We could make food part of a loan to help the present government to rehabilitate its economic situation, but I think we have a right to ask for some type of supervision of the economic use of whatever loan we make.

The pattern of dictatorship repeats itself too often and even if they now have a government that has every intention of helping the people and honestly administering the government departments, still they may need some expert financial advice. This could be given on a technical-assistance basis through the United Nations if not through us, but we must not let people so near to us continue to starve.

....

One frequent theme in "My Day" was the idea that when it rains, it rains on everyone. The Roosevelts were not excluded from the simple pleasures or the occasional annoyances of daily life, certainly not in their beloved New York City of which Eleanor Roosevelt, in particular, was proud.

NEW YORK, JUNE 10—This is a busy city! One would hardly believe that with its vast number of hotels there would ever come a time when getting a room in a New York hotel would be difficult. Yet, one of my sons had to ask me for a couch in my apartment to sleep on Monday night.

However, I see in the paper that 10,000 Rotarians from 72 nations opened their 50th annual convention on Sunday night in Madison Square Garden. This will go on for six days, and they expect to have 16,000 in attendance. In addition, the Dental Association is meeting here and the mayors of the country are meeting, also.

Altogether, New York City must be looked upon with favor by the various groups as a place to hold their meetings.

....

Fourteen years after FDR's death the international praise of his life and career continued. In 1959 Mrs. Roosevelt took note of a plan to honor FDR by giving his favorite summer home the status of nearly sacred land.

NEW YORK, JUNE 18—I was gratified to see in one of our newspapers recently that the Governor of Maine and the Prime Minister of New Brunswick, Canada, have suggested that Campobello Island, or at least some part of it, shall be made an international shrine.

I imagine this would include the purchase and preservation of the land and the house which once belonged to my husband. He was very fond of the waters lying all about this island and he cruised far afield.

....

Until his illness I think he enjoyed his holidays on the island itself as much as any other relaxation in his busy life.

It was there, of course, that he contracted polio, but the seeds of the illness he had brought with him and it only developed after his arrival. After his illness he was unable to do some of the things he had most enjoyed, and so he returned only twice for brief periods to the island. But he always remembered it with affection, and if this suggestion should go through I am sure that it would have pleased him.

....

Much traveling for the AAUN filled this part of the year for Eleanor Roosevelt. While out West she once again visited her son Elliott at his ranch and accepted an invitation to serve as the central speaker at a civic forum in a Colorado town. Mrs. Roosevelt was popular all across the country as a lecturer and derived much of her income from speaking engagements. She had become a master at the essentially impromptu speech, following only a couple of rules she had picked up along the way from some of the great political orators she had heard over the years. She would write down the first and last sentences or paragraphs of her speeches, to be sure the speeches would have a frame and some order, but otherwise she trusted to memory and imagination to carry her through. David Gurewitsch gave her another bit of advice: keep lots of garlic in the diet because it enhances memory, and Eleanor adopted this practice. She also did her homework and brought to events such as this one a real sense of joy about seeing the process of democratic dialogue in action. It restored her faith at a point when the quality of political discourse in the country had been brought ever lower under the lingering influence of McCarthyism.

MILWAUKEE, JUNE 25—On Sunday the weather proved fairly good and Elliott took me over to Grand Junction where the Daily Sentinel, which has published my column ever since the earliest days, was sponsoring an afternoon meeting at which I was to speak and an evening dinner at which I spoke again.

Grand Junction considers itself the center of activity for the Western slope of Colorado, and Mr. Preston Walker, who is the publisher of the Daily Sentinel, has followed in the footsteps of his father who was the publisher before him. They have been in the newspaper business and in politics and interested in every new development in the state of Colorado as far back as anyone of the family can remember. They are strong believers in the United Nations and so my three-o'clock speech was on the UN.

The dinner in the evening was for leading citizens from neighboring towns, and when you speak of neighboring towns in Colorado it covers

....

an extended territory. One neighbor drove 260 miles to attend the dinner.

Those in attendance at this affair were primarily interested in the improvement of their own communities and much of their time is spent in working on local situations. Mr. Walker, however, wanted me, if possible, to show them how our home situation touched the world situation and how closely what we do at home affects the world situation and our leadership of the non-Communist world.

That was easy enough to do and after I finished we had a period of questions. I think I have seldom had more interesting questions, which showed considerable thought on the part of these people regarding world problems.

....

Mrs. Roosevelt practiced her belief that a couple of hours sleep after a long nighttime flight was all that was required for a person to bounce out of bed and face the new day feeling fresh. The astonishing productivity of her life may be explained as much by her metabolism as by her sense of duty and love of hard work.

MILFORD, CONN., JUNE 29—Miss Corr and I caught a 6:30 plane to Chicago, where we spent a comfortable night at the Blackstone Hotel. On Wednesday morning we were on our way to the airport again at a quarter before 11, she returning to New York while I went on to Milwaukee to speak in the evening for the Wisconsin Home Economics Association. A four-o'clock press conference preceded the dinner and speech at the auditorium, after which I took the 11:20 plane back to New York.

I like night flying. If you can sleep—and I usually can—the trip is over quickly; and even if you do get in at 4:10 in the morning, you can still have a couple of hours in your own bed and wake up feeling fresh and ready to start a new day.

....

On many occasions incidents of racial discrimination provoked Eleanor Roosevelt's moral outrage and inspired some of her best newspaper writing. In this instance one of the most prominent black families in the world became the object of a racial insult that made Mrs. Roosevelt ashamed of her own country. Dr. Ralph Bunche was the first black to be a division head in the Department of State; he entered the UN in 1946 (the same time as Mrs. Roosevelt) as a director of the Trusteeship Division; and he was awarded the Nobel Prize for Peace in 1950 for his work as principal secretary of the UN Palestine Commission. But the

....

prominence of the Bunche family was neither here nor there to Mrs. Roosevelt; the issue was fairness.

HYDE PARK, JULY 13—I don't know how other people feel about the story last week on the refusal of a swank tennis club in Forest Hills, L.I., to permit Dr. Ralph Bunche's son—who has been taking tennis lessons at the club from the pro—to become a member and play there. I can only say I felt mortified that in the North we still have a club, the West Side Tennis Club, which is not ashamed to say that it bars Jews and Negroes from membership.

The members of this club may think themselves better than people of other races, and they may think that in their club and in their homes they can be justified today in refusing admittance to people on a basis of race, color or religion. But I would like to point out to them that bombs do not discriminate in this manner. When these people have helped the rest of us to lose the uncommitted areas of the world where two-thirds of the world's population exist, which are largely of non-Aryan race and of many religions and many colors, then perhaps they will realize what they have done to give us a Communist world—if not to destroy our civilization completely.

I hope that no colored champion and no Jewish champion will play tennis at this club again.

Of course, this kind of discrimination will not hurt the Bunches. They have too many open doors to feel a slight of this kind. But how can we in the North ask of the South the sacrifices that we are now asking if we countenance this kind of snobbish discrimination?

If you can't play tennis with Negroes, how come you are willing to let them be drafted into your army and die for you? I am ashamed for my white people. I am one of them, and their stupidity and cruelty make me cringe.

. . . .

Among the many points Mrs. Roosevelt admired in Adlai Stevenson's vision of America's future role in international affairs was the idea that, with a large investment of energy and dollars, the United States could become the world leader in exporting ideas about peace and the materials necessary to preserve it. Such materials would not be bombs but butter, not arms for warfare but hands to help—in medicine, farming, and education. She chose this vision as an important beacon to follow, and thus when she learned of similar proposals from other quarters, she gave them solid endorsements. Note here the clever use of her own uncle, President Theodore Roosevelt, as a symbol of a previous generation's outmoded world view.

. . . .

HYDE PARK, AUGUST 4—Another idea, which has considerable appeal to me, has recently been put forth and, if carried out, I'm sure it will succeed in creating a new picture of America in many parts of the world.

The primary idea is to emphasize our leadership in the cause of peace, and the suggestion for going about it is both novel and practical.

This would entail taking six of our ships that are now in "mothballs" and putting them in condition to sail. These would include a hospital ship and a small carrier, and their mission would be to tour the world to cope with disasters and meet any special needs in the underdeveloped areas of the world. Planes from the carrier would be available to fly far inland if necessary.

Such a fleet would be called "The New Great White Fleet." President Theodore Roosevelt, in 1907, sent the original great white fleet around the world to demonstrate our military strength. But this new fleet would travel only on missions of mercy and peace.

....

A little over a month away from turning seventy-five, Eleanor Roosevelt has the energy and enthusiasm to make two professional appearances in two different New England cities, driving on conventional highways between them (no interstate superhighways had yet been built), in the middle of summer without the comfort of air conditioning—all in the space of eight hours. Her motivation in this case was just the same as it was in her work for the UN: to promote international dialogue and to let foreign visitors see that America did not want war.

KITTERY, ME., AUGUST 6—On Tuesday Miss Corr and I left Hyde Park at nine o'clock in the morning and drove up to New Haven, Conn., where a summer seminar for foreign students at Yale is in progress. After spending an hour with them, we drove on to Cambridge, Mass., where at 4:30 Mr. Henry Kissinger introduced me to the Harvard summer seminar for foreign students.

It was a long day but one that I enjoyed very much, as I am deeply interested in these students who come to our country to take back to their countries a better knowledge of us and our way of life.

....

The withdrawal of European colonial powers and the peaceful transition to democratic home rule in former colonies was one of the developments in Africa that Mrs. Roosevelt praised most strongly. Those Africans who played leading roles in their countries' liberation struggles became her heroes too. President Nkrumah of Ghana won great respect worldwide for his leadership. An invitation to join the British Queen's Privy Coun-

cil meant, at least symbolically, that he became one of the Crown's advisers. (Not many years later, Nkrumah's statesmanship turned increasingly autocratic. He was ousted from power in 1966.)

NEW YORK, AUGUST 17—We should not pass over without mention the Queen's action in making Kwame Nkrumah a member of her Privy Council. We must say a word of appreciation for the long and patient lifetime work which was what the Prime Minister of Ghana really celebrated when he went from Accra to Balmoral Castle. Here was a man, the hereditary chief of the Nzima tribe, who had lived in a mud village of the Gold Coast, had been in a British jail, but now was the Prime Minister of the new country of Ghana. It was a really great occasion, not only for him but for the colored peoples of Africa, and we congratulate both the Prime Minister and the Queen.

....

Mrs. Roosevelt rarely expressed any sense of impatience with the pressures of being a public person and rarely indicated that her self-imposed grueling schedule had become wearying. But here she does. However, she knew that the demands put on her time by countless interest groups, by autograph seekers, and by those just with a story to tell that somehow confirmed their connection to her life at one point was all evidence of the influence and impact she had achieved.

TULSA, OKLA., OCTOBER 9—Here I am speaking to a Jewish Community Council on Israel and so my audience is more or less restricted to this group, but they tell me that the Negro Chamber of Commerce wanted so much to have me come and meet with them, if only for 10 minutes, that the synagogue has opened its doors to this group also.

One of the great difficulties on these trips is that so many groups would like you to spend just five minutes or 10 minutes or "just look in" on them. They don't seem to realize that this would give one no time for rest or to prepare for the lecture one has come to give.

There seems always to be the inevitable press conference, and today there was one TV program and two other groups that wanted interviews as well as the two newspaper representatives and a group of journalism students from the high school. I got through rather quickly, however, as most of the radio and TV questions were identical.

Sitting in the waiting room in Kansas City, and, in fact, I find this true now wherever I stay for more than a few minutes, the desire for autographs was quickly manifested. It used to be that people would only ask apologetically for their children or grandchildren but now they ask for themselves without shame.

I was reminded of the movie star with whom I once commiserated when I saw him surrounded by autograph seekers. He said: "Yes, it is a nuisance, but there is only one thing I would mind more and that is if they didn't want it."

Being 75 years old and having spent most of my life in the public eye and having met a great many people, I suppose I must expect that some would want to come up and remind me of when we last met. Sometimes it is a real thrill, too, as it was when a young man wrote me a note from across an aisle, saying, "I served with your son in the raider battalion in World War II. He was a grand commander and so was Carlson." That gave me a thrill and I passed it on to Jimmy with great joy and pride.

. . . .

Mrs. Roosevelt's great faith in the UN is evident in this column, in which she expresses her belief that even a political dilemma as old and thorny as the Chinese–Tibetan one could be resolved through UN-sponsored negotiations. Ethnically and spiritually distinct from the Chinese, Tibetans nonetheless had known some degree of Chinese control ever since the eighteenth century and a long period of Mongol control before that. In 1911 Tibet had reasserted its independence—which it maintained until 1950, when the Chinese again invaded. Earlier in 1959 an anti-Chinese uprising was crushed, and in its aftermath the Dalai Lama, Tibetan Buddhism's spiritual leader, fled the country.

Mrs. Roosevelt was open to the idea of writing on behalf of the Dalai Lama not only because she recognized him as a man of peace but also because the Tibetan cause was another facet of the West's own struggle to resist the further spread of communism.

NEW YORK, OCTOBER 16—I was visited on Tuesday afternoon by one of the Dalai Lama's brothers. He and a second brother have come to the United States to speak before the United Nations on the situation that faces Tibet.

I asked him whether it was true that the people in that mountainous country had been kept at a very low standard of living and that, therefore, the Communist Chinese, who emulate the Soviet Communists, felt justified in moving in to establish what they felt were reforms. He told me that the Dalai Lama had already planned to move on four different fronts to bring some changes into the old agricultural system of the country and to improve the standard of living for the people. And he added that these changes had been opposed by the Communists in the country and that an increasing number of Chinese Communist troops had come in until the people who loved the Dalai Lama had felt that he was in danger personally.

One of the most serious results, of course, of forcing the Dalai Lama

. . . .

to leave Tibet is the fact that a very large number of his people left with him, and they are all now in India. This has added a new problem to the refugee situation. India is finding it extremely difficult to provide the proper kind of food for these thousands of people who must be fed and housed.

I am glad that the situation is being brought before the United Nations and I hope that the nations of the world will give help to these refugees and bring the weight of world opinion to bear on the entire situation. Only thus can peace come to Tibet and the traditional ruler returned in peace and be allowed to try to work out the problems of modernization and contact with the outer world, which now becomes necessary in spite of the remoteness of the people in that country.

It points up to us that there is no area of the world that is remote any more and that all of us are going to feel whatever happens, no matter how far away it is.

....

Though long before any voters would cast official ballots, the time for preliminary decisions about presidential candidates for the 1960 elections had arrived. Mrs. Roosevelt by herself could not, and would not have wanted to, make or break anyone's presidential aspirations. But everyone in the Democratic Party who was considering a race for the White House knew that not having Eleanor Roosevelt on his side would be like going on the tennis court without a racket. From her viewpoint, however, her endorsements of Stevenson in both of the two preceding campaigns had given her a bitter taste of defeat she had not known since early in her husband's career, when he ran as vice presidential candidate on James Cox's losing ticket in 1920.

She assumed it wouldn't be Stevenson again running for president on the Democratic ticket, but who would it be? There was plenty of talent from which to choose. In this column Mrs. Roosevelt alludes to "Texas' favorite son"—and could mean either the aging Sam Rayburn, Speaker of the House, or the ambitious Senator Lyndon Johnson.

NEW YORK, OCTOBER 23—I have been seeing a number of people in the past few days, all of whom are thinking primarily about politics at home and are committed to their chosen nominee in the Democratic campaign. They all argue equally seriously for their particular candidate!

In Texas, of course, one cannot escape becoming aware of that state's favorite son. And former President Truman hinted rather broadly down there that while Missouri will have a favorite son in Senator Stuart Symington, if the Senator cannot be put across, then Texas might be the recipient of Missouri's influence and vote.

....

Not having any votes that I can count on or any desire to find myself really involved in a preconvention struggle, I listen to everybody's arguments. And I would really enjoy my position more if it were not for a little nagging feeling that perhaps, at some point along the way, I, like everyone else, have an obligation to decide which of the candidates has the qualities necessary to meet the problems of the present day. I shall resist this little nagging thought as long as I possibly can.

. . . .

Although Mrs. Roosevelt uses the pronoun we *in this column about the unsophisticated level of taste that characterized American television viewing habits in the late 1950s, one cannot help suspecting that she did not include herself in the indictment at all. For one thing, Eleanor was not a television watcher. Other than the occasional news program, her schedule had no time in it for TV. She got her news from a large selection of local, national, and international newspapers and newsmagazines, and she found her entertainment in live music and theater or in books.*

NEW YORK, OCTOBER 30—There was what might be called an amusing item in the newspapers the other day, giving the ratings of various television shows shown for the half-hour period last Sunday afternoon from 5:30 to 6:30.

Here is the way the ratings came out: "Lone Ranger," a repeat film, 10.8, Leonard Bernstein, 7.9; Chet Huntley, 4.0. These ratings perhaps justify what some of those people who plan programs on TV are constantly saying—that the public does not even want good music more than it wants a little excitement which it can view without any effort in the way of thought.

It appears we are back at the same old stand. We are given in our newspapers and on TV and radio exactly what we, the public, insist on having, and this very frequently is mediocre information and mediocre entertainment.

. . . .

Mrs. Roosevelt, as head of the family, had laid down the law in the early years after FDR's death when a rash of squabbles among her strong-willed children had brought everyone in the clan into conflict. There were fights over how to use the family land at Hyde Park. There were disagreements over who among them could or should write about the late President's political legacy, his place in history. There was a tussle over son Elliott's approach to editing the childhood letters of his father. Eleanor's response was to rein them all in by extracting a promise that in public, and in print, Roosevelt family troubles would not be aired.

. . . .

She discusses in the next column her son James' book, Affectionately F.D.R, *and gives it as fair-minded a review as a mother could. What does not emerge here is that behind the scenes in the family there had been a good deal of nail-biting about potential lawsuits stemming from the candidness of some portraits in James' book. Joseph Lash indicates that by the time it was published, however, calm had somehow been restored among the Roosevelt "boys."*

New York, November 19—I have never mentioned in this column the book written by my oldest son, James, about his father, called "Affectionately F.D.R." No father could have asked for a more understanding and sympathetic tribute from a son, and it is certainly written with deep affection.

I have a slight reservation about some things that are said in the book about other people, but not about my husband. The reason is that I think they reflect the observations and feelings of a very young man, perhaps at the time not quite capable of understanding certain things and who, therefore, was impatient.

For instance, he criticizes the housekeeper who was with us during all the years that we were in the White House and in doing so, of course, in an indirect manner he criticizes me. For he does not seem to realize that whatever Mrs. Nesbitt did she did under my direction.

And as a young man he just was not aware of the many things that made the housekeeper's job in the White House a difficult one. There was more to it for Mrs. Nesbitt than merely to try to provide the President of the United States and his guests with the best possible food. There were doctors in the White House to whom she had to listen. There were budgets to be considered. And there were times when we tried out things for the sake of some policy that was being urged upon the people.

For example, I remember well feeding everyone for a time on the same menus that had been worked out for people on relief in the days of the Depression by the home economics experts in the Department of Agriculture. These menus were designed to keep one healthy, but certainly not to give one pleasure. And I remember well the day when the author of this book, my son James, said to me pathetically at lunch: "If I paid five cents extra, Mother, could I have a glass of milk?"

And there was the time Amelia Earhart, who was staying with us on a brief visit, said she was hungry and could get nothing to eat in the late evening. This was because she did not know how to go about it! And my son, John, found the icebox locked at night and was outraged!

I am quite sure no one complained of the food during a short period when we were trying out some of the very good recipes one particular lady left with us. She had been visiting the White House to do research on some of Martha Washington's and other First Ladies' favorite recipes. But at other times it is quite likely that the meals were not always to the liking of many of our friends or members of the family.

I think I know good food if I stop to think about it, but too often I do not stop to think about it, so I know I'm no great help to a housekeeper.

In one or two other cases, too, I think the book reflects youthful opinions. But, on the whole, in its main objective I think it achieves a remarkable warmth, and both my son and Mr. Sidney Shalett, who worked with him, must be pleased with the results they achieved in "Affectionately F.D.R."

Although Mrs. Roosevelt does not use the phrase oral history *in this "My Day" column, what she describes here is just that. She had a marvelous knack for telling family tales in such a way that not only the details of one famous family emerged in full relief, but also the social, political, and even technological background of the time emerged clearly as well. Eleanor Roosevelt combined the talents of a fine raconteuse and those of an amateur museum curator. She takes us on an insider's guided tour of the Roosevelt mansion at Hyde Park.*

HYDE PARK, NOVEMBER 23—We drove up to Hyde Park late Friday afternoon, and at dinner our guests were Mr. and Mrs. Robert Atkinson and two gentlemen concerned with getting the statements of people on historical monuments which perhaps will be of interest in the future. We discussed going around the Hyde Park house next day and recording what I usually tell visitors whom I take about personally.

At nine on Saturday morning I started on the recording trip, covering as much as possible from the first to the third floors. Shortly they are going to open some nature trails here, and the little ice house and stable will also be open to visitors. I therefore added a short recording on my husband's love of trees and his constant interest in planting them, as well as some comments about the stable.

I find that showing young people the ice house is a very interesting way of making them aware of the changes that have come about in our way of life. Such a thing as an ice house, of course, does not exist today, but up to the time of my mother-in-law's death we had no electric refrigerator in the house. My mother-in-law and my husband always worried that in a mild winter the ice would not be thick enough to cut and store. I told Mr. Atkinson that I thought we ought to simulate ice, with straw laid between the cakes, so that young people might get an idea of how ice was kept in a period which, after all, is not so long past. It was always brought to the big house daily and put in from the outside around the so-called cold rooms, which had doors also into the kitchen. One cold room was for meats and vegetables, the other for milk, cream, butter and eggs.

I also show the young people my mother-in-law's store closet, where she kept supplies of preserved fruits and vegetables, jams, jellies and pickles for winter use. But she was not quite as old-fashioned a housekeeper as my grandmother Hall. When I was a little girl, she would take me into her storeroom at Tivoli every morning. There I would hold one bowl while she measured all the flour that would be needed that day, and then, in another bowl, all the sugar that would be required. This was brought in barrels which stood side by side in the storeroom. Tea and coffee were also measured out, but that custom had passed by the time I became familiar with my mother-in-law's housekeeping. Even now I sometimes feel a little guilty when I do so little housekeeping.

Dr. J. Cotter, the park service archaeologist, made me tell them about my husband's horse, Bobby, which he and his mother had given his father about a year before his father's death and which continued to be my husband's horse for many years.

Up in the playroom on the third floor they had looked through some books in the children's bookcase and found one in which Franklin Jr. had pasted an ex libris which said: "Half hours with the worst famous writers." The other day my granddaughter looked through these books and said she was sorry that her mother had not had the foresight to take some of them for my great-grandchildren's edification.

After the recordings were over, I greeted some 20 girls from as many countries who had come up from Vassar to see the house and library. Two correspondents and a photographer from Latin America had also come for an interview, so I did not manage to get away until well after 11 o'clock.

....

Senator John Kennedy of Massachusetts had not yet won over Eleanor Roosevelt to his camp. She recognized his growing influence and aspirations, but among the emerging presidential candidates in the Democratic Party, Kennedy received less attention from Eleanor than anyone. Nonetheless, she took more of an interest when she began to see that the senator could handle even the toughest of personal and political questions with aplomb. The process of Mrs. Roosevelt's warming to Kennedy was slow, but it had begun.

NEW YORK, DECEMBER 1—The American Roman Catholic bishops made a statement on birth control a short time ago which seems to

....

me the only possible position they could take. I cannot quite understand why the newspapers are making so much of it, and bedeviling
Senator John F. Kennedy for a statement.

This is a religious question and has always been understood. In reply
to a question on the birth-control issue and its relation to foreign aid,
Senator Kennedy gave a wise answer, I think.

It would be unwise for any national administration to grant aid to
another nation for this particular purpose. If the other nation finds it
essential to its well-being to undertake birth control, that is its own
concern, as Senator Kennedy has said. If any organization or individuals in any country feel it is important to help a second country keep
down the birth rate, that is the decision of that organization and of
those individuals.

The government of a country which has as many people, for instance, as we in the United States have of varying religions and beliefs,
should not, as a government, take official action in a subject which
enters into the religious and domestic affairs of another nation. It will
offend some of its own citizens and it might easily offend some section
of the people in the other nation.

No government, however, should have the right to prevent individual citizens or organizations from giving help if they were asked to do
so by the government or individuals or organizations of another nation.
This practically is the stand which Senator Kennedy stated, and I think
it was a sensible and correct stand for him to take, as it would be for
any other candidate of whatever religion.

. . . .

*As a diplomat Mrs. Roosevelt had learned that a badly worded agree-
ment could turn out to be worse than no agreement at all. But her sense
of the underlying instability of peace in the world made her look upon
most international steps toward workable, if imperfect, accords and
treaties as progress worth praising. Declaring certain unpopulated areas,
like Antarctica, off limits to nuclear tests struck Mrs. Roosevelt as the
only sane approach to take. And although she guessed wrong on a resolution of tensions between Great Britain and Argentina over the Falkland Islands, her "My Day" columns show why she had hopes that a
Falkland crisis might be averted. She saw Britain's eventual withdrawal
from those very distant islands as one more appropriate step the former
colonial power might take in the name of peace.*

NEW YORK, DECEMBER 4—It is encouraging to read the newspapers
and find accords chronicled.

For instance, a 12-nation pact makes the Antarctic a science reserve

. . . .

through a treaty just signed in Washington, D.C. The treaty bars military activity and outlaws atomic tests in this area.

The nations signing are: Argentina, Australia, Great Britain, Chile, France, New Zealand, Norway—all of whom have some claim on territory in the Antarctic but who have agreed to freeze these claims. In addition, the treaty was signed by Belgium, Japan, South Africa, the Soviet Union and the United States. Of course, this treaty cannot come into being until each nation has ratified it according to its constitutional procedures.

This treaty will ease some tensions. For instance, there has long been a great deal of feeling between Argentina and Great Britain over the Falkland Islands, and it may be that they will now come to realize that they are not really anxious to control this area as they thought they were.

An agreement also has been signed between the Soviet Union and Great Britain on the expansion of cultural exchanges, and this might mean the end of Soviet jamming of the British Broadcasting Corporation programs.

....

It wasn't just the fiery style of John L. Lewis' leadership of the United Mine Workers that, over the years, had alienated Eleanor Roosevelt. It was a whole set of specific moves he had made that seemed to her to run counter to good taste, good sense, and good Democratic politics. For one thing, Lewis, who at first was a New Deal supporter, became FDR's staunchest labor critic, withdrawing his support altogether to back Wendell Willkie in the 1940 presidential election. During the war he led the UMW in several coal strikes, earning the wrath of public and presidential opinion. In 1948 Lewis had drawn a heavy fine for the union for failing to obey a court order to end a protracted strike. All of this was too much for Mrs. Roosevelt to forgive until she could see Lewis' retirement coming and believed that at last he would relinquish his crown.

Frances Perkins was FDR's Secretary of Labor from 1933 to 1945.

NEW YORK, DECEMBER 18—I have not always had the warmest feelings toward Mr. John L. Lewis but when one reads that, at 80, he is about to resign, having led the miners for 40 years, one goes back over the past and realizes that as their leader he did a magnificent job.

When Mr. Lewis started out, no one knew what conditions were for mine workers, protective legislation was rare in many states, and it was not till he really began functioning that the situation for miners began to improve.

I have thought of him at times as a demagogue, but I often recall

....

Frances Perkins' admonition to me when she was Secretary of Labor. She invited me once to meet some of the labor leaders, and I made a critical remark about Mr. Lewis. With more knowledge and deeper insight, she said: "He is a very good labor leader. He just happens to be the type who would always say 'Mama knows best.' In his case it would be 'Papa knows best.'"

Perhaps for those he led it was essential to have this type of labor leader, so we must be grateful for his accomplishments, congratulate him warmly, and hope for him happy and contented years of retirement.

....

What Mrs. Roosevelt loved most about Christmas (aside from a little shopping on Fifth Avenue and seeing the lights on Park Avenue or at Rockefeller Center in New York) was so traditionally American that any Christian reader of "My Day" could easily identify with her. The sense in which Eleanor's "My Day" column was much like a letter from a friend is evident here again as she closes out the year in a quiet and hopeful way.

HYDE PARK, DECEMBER 28—Christmas is over and I hope that many of us went either to midnight service or to the service on Christmas Day to remember the spiritual origin of our holiday. The custom of the giving of presents and the Christmas tree, of course, has come to us from many different lands, and many of us have observances that take us back to the lands of our forefathers.

I used to like best the early morning ritual of Christmas stockings in my husband's room with the smallest children sitting on his bed; but now I think it is the Christmas dinner, with the bringing together of those who are near enough and hearing from those who are far away. When possible we telephone before we sit down to dinner, which makes this midday meal the most meaningful time of getting together.

I always love the midnight service on Christmas Eve, with its music and lights followed by the drive home through the quiet countryside after we have celebrated an event which brought about the greatest influence for good among vast numbers of people in the world. Our warmest and best instincts spring from the teaching of the Man who was born in that manger on Christmas Day so long ago, and the spirit that He brought to the world is the spirit we count on today to bring us peace on earth, good will among men.

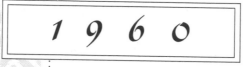

1 9 6 0

To no one's surprise but to many Democrats' delight, 1960 began with an announcement by John F. Kennedy that he would indeed run for President. Kennedy entered a crowded field of primary election campaigners, and he began his formal pursuit of a term in the White House without the endorsement of Eleanor Roosevelt. By summer's end he had secured the latter; by election day in November—though only by a hair's-breadth—he had secured the former. The year 1960 had the feeling about it of a new era trying to be born, and Mrs. Roosevelt used many of her "My Day" columns to comment on the changes.

It was not as though the Republicans had made a shambles of things. On the contrary, in his January 1960 State of the Union address President Eisenhower had the pleasure of reporting a $200,000,000 budget surplus and a forecast of record-breaking prosperity. Vice President Richard Nixon tossed his hat into the ring as a presidential candidate two days later and rode the Republican wave of success almost to victory, at least in the popular vote, in November. Eisenhower planned a trip to Japan in January after the two countries had signed a mutual defense treaty, completely reversing their deadly adversarial relationship in World War II, but anti-American sentiment ran too high in Tokyo for the President's visit to be safe, and he stayed home.

In the civil rights struggle, early February brought two important events. In Greensboro, North Carolina, four black people staged what came to be known as a "sit-in" at a whites-only lunch counter: the first of many such confrontations. As a tactical form of nonviolent civil disobedience, this was an approach Mrs. Roosevelt would support. The Senate ratified the Twenty-third Amendment to the Constitution, which banned poll taxes in federal elections. These taxes had been used to exclude poor people from the ranks of registered voters, especially in the South.

In the primary election campaigns, some of JFK's opponents and some people in the press insinuated that the Senator was unfit to be President, not for lack of talent but because of his religion. As a Roman Catholic, these critics claimed, Kennedy necessarily would be a pawn of the Vatican. The Senator replied "I don't think my religion is anyone's business," but the issue dogged him throughout the campaign. Eleanor Roosevelt saw the religion issue as bogus but also dangerous. She feared for the country should a qualified candidate be defeated because of a religious prejudice. Kennedy's early victories in the Pennsylvania and Massachusetts primaries, however, created great momentum for his candidacy.

A series of embarrassments in 1960 for the United States in relations with the Soviets weakened the country's position in world affairs. In May a U-2 spy plane was shot down over Soviet territory, and Eisenhower had to admit that the U.S. had had reconnaissance planes flying over the USSR for years. At a major-power summit conference in Paris in mid-May Khrushchev demanded an apology from the U.S. but did not get what he wanted. The Russians promptly withdrew from the meeting. In late June a ten-nation disarmament conference also disbanded after failing to reach any agreements. Fidel Castro, the Cuban revolutionary leader, now president of the Republic, proved increasingly cantankerous as well. Eisenhower struck back by cutting Cuban sugar imports by 95 percent, a move that may have hurt Cuba but displeased American housewives. Rightly or wrongly, these Republican foreign policy setbacks strengthened the Democrats' chances of recapturing the White House.

The national conventions in July served up these two party tickets: Kennedy and Lyndon Johnson (Senator from Texas since 1948) for the Democrats; Nixon and Henry Cabot Lodge, Jr. (former Senator from Massachusetts, defeated by Kennedy in 1952; representative to the UN, 1953–60). Much of the rest of the year Americans were absorbed by campaign news. Television played a bigger-than-ever role in this campaign, introducing for the first time the live presidential debate. There were four debates, and although the political commentators gave different scores to Kennedy and Nixon concerning their answers to questions, almost everyone had to agree that Nixon suffered badly from the stiff image he projected under the glaring lights. Kennedy seemed to inspire more confidence with his evidently greater finesse.

When the election finally came, Mrs. Roosevelt felt satisfied that she had thrown her support to Kennedy, though never as heartily as she had for Stevenson. Like a true Democrat, she was glad to see another liberal headed for the White House. Before the year's end the selections President-elect Kennedy announced for cabinet and other posts won her approval as well, with the possible exception of the appointment of Robert Kennedy, the new president's younger brother, as attorney general. Thus the year ended on a hopeful note with a rising tide of fresh energy in Washington and throughout the land.

....

Over the years Mrs. Roosevelt stuck assiduously to the principle that workers in the public sector cannot be granted the same kinds of rights to strike or otherwise stop work as can workers in other businesses and industries. Whenever a strike came about or was threatened, for example, by firemen or nurses in public hospitals, Mrs. Roosevelt urged all the parties involved to keep everyone at work—for the public's good— while the labor dispute was resolved through arbitration. Many in the labor movement, which otherwise had Eleanor Roosevelt's support, felt she had betrayed them when she would make such pronouncements.

"My Day" columns were also quite often used to point out that certain admirable accomplishments had been made by women (especially when these came in fields of endeavor traditionally restricted to men). The labor-management mediator in this strike was a heroine in Mrs. Roosevelt's view.

BOSTON, JANUARY 4—New York City has just gone through one of its periodic transit crises, with a threatened strike averted by an agreement reached only at the last minute in the cold gray dawn of New Year's Day.

As in previous threats of a transit strike, there was the usual cliff-hanging drama staged by the opposing parties at the bargaining table. The Transit Authority could offer only so much, President Michael J. Quill of the Transport Workers Union held out for more, the Mayor intervened with stop-gap measures whereby the city would up the ante, and a compromise was finally reached that will provide an uneasy peace for another two years. Meanwhile, millions of New Yorkers were filled with anxiety, business concerns were uncertain whether employees could get to work on Monday, and vital services for the city's population were in danger of drastic disruption.

In a situation of this kind, of course, one comes up against the question of the public welfare versus private interests. There are strikes that can be conducted without really hurting the welfare of the general public. Unfortunately, the transport workers on buses and subways are engaged in an occupation which does vitally affect the daily life of the general public. I have long felt that all such occupations will have to have a code different from that ordinarily used, where it is simply a matter of collective bargaining between an industry and its

....

employees and not a situation where the everyday life of the citizen is involved.

If no new automobiles are produced over a period of time, for instance, some people may regret it but their daily life can still go on. But to cut off the means of transportation by which people reach their daily employment, to cut off the flow of milk or food into a big city, to cut off power from a big city—all these things adversely affect the daily lives of masses of people not involved in the controversy. The workers employed in such industries should, on the one hand, have special protection and special consideration. But they should also have special obligations, because the welfare of the people as a whole dominates the welfare of any special group.

It was of interest, I think, to see that a woman, Mrs. Anna M. Rosenberg, headed the Mayor's mediation panel in this situation. Mrs. Rosenberg has earned for herself the respect of both labor and management. Busy as she is with her private business, she is always available to do a public job in the interests of the general welfare. We, as women, should be proud of her accomplishments and New York City generally should be proud of her as one of its distinguished citizens.

....

The year 1960 kept up the pace of Mrs. Roosevelt's travels for the AAUN and for other speaking engagements. Many of the datelines for "My Day" columns this year will come from out-of-the-way cities and towns across America. Mrs. Roosevelt, now seventy-five, traveled frequently and fast: sometimes a twenty-four-hour trip out of New York would have her appearing in three states and four cities, flying home on the red-eye express, and going back to work the next day before noon.

A column filed from Needles, California, combines two familiar elements in Eleanor Roosevelt's writing. One is her direct use, by quotation, of a sample of the voluminous correspondence she received; the second is her plain-spoken denunciation of racial discrimination. She had a skillful way of indicating what behavior is right and what is wrong, from an ethical viewpoint, without ever pointing the finger of blame specifically at anyone.

NEEDLES, CALIF., JANUARY 11—I have received a letter touching on a problem that we, as Americans, should think about. It reads:

"I hope I am not taking up your time and wasting it. I am an American Negro 33 years of age, born and raised in Los Angeles. I have a problem and I consider it a serious problem. In 1953 I completed a course for a licensed beautician at the Los Angeles Trade Technical Junior College. I passed the state board examination and received my California license.

....

"I applied for work in various beauty salons and department stores and also outside. I have always been turned down flat because of my race. So in late 1953 I moved to San Francisco, where I went through the thing all over again. Department stores would advertise in the newspapers for a hairdresser. I would call up, give them my name, and they would say come right over. When I got there, they looked at me as though they had seen a ghost.

"Finally, I got a job. I stayed there for two years until I decided to make my home in New York. I have lived in New York since 1955. I applied for my hairdresser's license, which I now have. I live in Greenwich Village. I have applied for jobs at one of the city's large department stores, and also at a large hotel. I have applied in Greenwich Village in shops along Eighth Street. They won't have me. They have told other people: 'What would our customers think of a Negro man working on their hair?'

"I am at a loss. I have some special customers and I do their hair at their homes; but to make ends meet I have to work as a janitor. Why should this be? I have trained as a beautician. I was in the war, overseas. I was in the Navy from 1944 to May 1946. I don't think in terms of race, but I am growing bitter to think that I am not hired because of race. How can I improve my skill unless I can practice?

"If you have any suggestions, or can help me in any way, I would be grateful. All I want is a job to begin in my profession. I am willing to work up if that is required."

I have left out a few things, such as the suggestion that this young man work in Harlem. That requires a special kind of training, however, and he does not want to specialize in it. I have asked a number of people if they would have any feelings about having their hair washed or done by a colored man. I have found that very often women prefer to have their hair done by men rather than women. This has always seemed to me ridiculous, because women are quite as good as men in this profession. Sometimes men take more trouble to improve themselves by study, and a great many foreigners have had more intensive training abroad than some of our women. But if you are willing to have your hair done by a man and you have no objection to his being of foreign nationality, then I cannot see why one should object to a colored person; and a number of the people I have asked feel as I do.

Perhaps there is really more timidity on the part of those who own the beauty parlors: they often have a fairly hard time running them anyway, and don't want to add to their troubles. This is quite understandable; yet it seems to me unfair that an American citizen trained in a certain kind of work cannot find employment in his profession because of the color of his skin.

I hope a great many people will think this over, because this is distinct discrimination in employment.

. . . .

Eleanor Roosevelt had no qualms about juxtaposing distinctly unrelated topics in a single short column. In the following piece we read an excerpt from a "My Day" column that also discussed hearing aids, the stigma attached to wearing one, and the new technology available to help the hearing impaired, among whom Eleanor Roosevelt was one. Having finished with that topic, Mrs. Roosevelt moved on to heaping praise, once again, on Adlai Stevenson for his foresight in international affairs. Fair or unfair, the dig at Vice President Nixon is a good example of political sarcasm, proving that, elderly and refined lady though she was, Mrs. Roosevelt had a sharp tongue and wasn't afraid to use it in print.

SYRACUSE, N.Y., FEBRUARY 1—On Thursday night I went to the Roosevelt Day Dinner given by the New York Americans for Democratic Action. As usual I had many guests from foreign countries at my table and enjoyed them very much. Mr. Dore Schary was a remarkable master of ceremonies. He and Mrs. Marshall Field should be proud of the way in which they planned the dinner and carried it out. In spite of a number of short speeches and two major ones, we left the hall at 11:00 P.M.

I had the pleasure of presenting the ADA citation to Adlai Stevenson, praising him for his foresight in his campaign four years ago when he asked that we negotiate to ban nuclear tests.

The Republican standard bearer in the coming presidential campaign called it "treasonable nonsense" at that time, but it has become part of his own party's program. He will probably be praising the work that his party has begun to do and, with his usual facility, he will forget that he ever opposed it or that Adlai Stevenson advocated it in the campaign four years ago and was given a citation because of his foresight. Mr. Nixon never has anything but hindsight.

. . . .

On the new issue of radioactive waste disposal, Eleanor Roosevelt was one of the earliest lay writers to address the problem. She had no easy solutions to offer but recognized a need for public involvement in the decision-making about how to cope with this new dilemma.

NEW YORK, FEBRUARY 4—Now I must report on something that has just been brought to my attention. My correspondent writes:

. . . .

"At least three bills are now before the House of Representatives which would take control of atomic waste sea dumping from the hands of the AEC and place it where we believe it rightly belongs—in the hands of the United States Public Health Service."

These bills are HR 8187, 8423, and 7014.

My correspondent is temporary chairman of the Lower Cape Committee on Radioactive Waste Disposal, and he lives in Wellfleet, Mass. He says there are several other citizen groups in the East that are urging active Congressional intervention in the problem of radioactive waste disposal in our coastal waters. These other groups have been active in New Jersey, North Carolina, Texas, Connecticut, Florida, and elsewhere.

The dump site off the tip of Cape Cod, which is my correspondent's concern, is barely 12 miles off the Boston shore and in the heart of the Atlantic sea lanes leading into Boston harbor. According to the newspaper story sent to me, there are included among the dumped radioactive material isotopes yielded by the development of the first atomic bomb—the bomb that exploded over Hiroshima.

Hauled out to sea in a metal drum, they were dropped over the side of a vessel in 250 feet of water in 1946. And, until a few months ago, over a period of nearly 12 years, ships returned to the dumping site regularly with more waste cargoes, whose potential hazard can only be guessed at.

It is now discovered that in 1954 the National Committee on Radiation Protection specifically recommended that radioactive waste disposal be carried out in depths of at least 1,000 fathoms, or 6,000 feet. The Lower Cape Committee says:

"If atomic dumping with its grave implications to life and human well-being can be initiated and carried out without the knowledge and consent of citizens of areas which can receive contamination, we believe this is a matter for the U.S. courts."

This situation is one, I think, that very few of the people of the United States have been conscious of, and it is time that we got a little more information.

. . . .

Not alone in declaring her strong conviction that the Baltic states deserved to be free of Soviet domination, Eleanor Roosevelt was nonetheless among the most forthright in saying so. The grip maintained on satellite nations by the Kremlin was fierce at this point in the cold war. But Mrs. Roosevelt's many years as a UN delegate had schooled her in dealing with recalcitrant representatives of the Soviet state head-on, without mincing words.

. . . .

LOS ANGELES, FEBRUARY 10—A great many people in this country are still sympathetic toward the Baltic states—Lithuania, Latvia, and Esthonia—which years ago were deprived of their freedom and incorporated into the Soviet Union.

The Soviets would have us believe that the majority of the people in these countries accepted the loss of their freedom with gratitude, but there are in our country many people who remember that these states were forcibly incorporated into the Soviet Union. They remember vividly that there was no vote taken under any foreign auspices or in any way that could have given the people a chance to vote freely.

When this was done, in 1940, I can recall that my husband and I both felt that it was a very sad thing. But by the time the Yalta meeting was held Russia felt so strongly that these states were part of her mainland that it was not possible even to consider them in the same way as the Iron Curtain countries along the western border were discussed.

The natives of these Baltic states who are in the United States have an undying hope that the day will come when their native lands are again free.

Of course, it would be difficult to persuade the Soviet Union that it would be in a stronger and safer position if it were to grant freedom to these countries. It would be hard to convince the Russians that these countries would then owe them such a debt of gratitude that there would be a friendly tie that probably never could be broken.

In this world, however, most of us are motivated by fear—governments more, perhaps, even than individuals—and, therefore, such action by the government of the Soviet Union seems a very remote possibility. But the hope still lives in the hearts of those who are in America and who can remember with such deep affection and devotion the countries of their birth.

Perhaps someday there will be such security in the world that any area that wishes freedom will be allowed its freedom. If we can achieve such a state, the movement of people everywhere will be without any interference, since humanity will really have learned the meaning of brotherhood.

....

On the road with Eleanor Roosevelt, the intrepid seventy-five-year-old itinerant lecturer: anything could happen, and often did, but the lady remained unflappable. The following story about a travel nightmare made a good column, and we sense a small degree of pride that Mrs. Roosevelt felt in her own spunkiness. Her concern continued to be less for her own safety or convenience and more for her obligation to keep her appointments. Misery, of course, loves company, but Eleanor Roos-

evelt was not one to complain. She had no time to complain. She had to get to her next appointment!

As if this February disaster were not enough, one night in March 1960, Mrs. Roosevelt found herself sleeping on a bench in the Louisville, Kentucky airport, grounded by a snowstorm. Instead of taking a hotel room, she lingered in the airport and caught the next available flight back to New York, a flight that landed at 5:30 A.M. . . . , just in time for her to go home, freshen up and proceed with another working day.

WASHINGTON, FEBRUARY 17—Well, after a rather hectic week-end, I got back to Hyde Park Monday morning to fill an early engagement there—though I must admit I was 40 minutes late.

I feel very guilty today that I did not keep my secretary more carefully informed on Sunday as to my movements, since apparently the newspapers and the radio frightened everyone to death by making them think I was lost. And all the time I was very easy to locate, since I was sitting in a very comfortable, warm Greyhound bus waiting for a line of trucks nearly 12 miles long to move.

I had left New York on a TWA flight for Pittsburgh, Pa., at 8:15 Sunday morning. We had to leave from the hangar on account of the weather. Then we had a little rough weather in the air, so that breakfast was delayed until around 9 or 9:30 o'clock. But none of us had any idea that there was any question about landing in Pittsburgh until the captain told us we were "holding" over the city until the runway was cleared.

Finally, we were told we had to land in Columbus, Ohio, because the Pittsburgh airport said that no sooner were the runways cleared than the snow was blown right back on them again.

I was slightly disturbed because my luncheon date in Pittsburgh was at noon and I had no idea if there was any way to get from Columbus to Pittsburgh even in time to speak after lunch.

In the Columbus terminal I had a call from Pittsburgh that informed me that the lunch had been called off. I then asked it it would not be better to take a plane right back to New York, since the roads were bad and I might not get to Pittsburgh in time for dinner.

The airline was sending a bus to take the passengers from the delayed trips, so when I told the Pittsburgh people this they urged me to come on the bus, since they felt sure the roads would be clear and there would be no difficulty. Feeling an obligation to meet my dinner engagement at least, I started off a little after one o'clock.

The bus was practically filled, and I really admired the spirit of those passengers. Everyone had had his plans upset, but there was laughter and joking with the bus driver and a kind of good-humored friendliness that I rarely feel in any other country in the world.

We went on quite rapidly for about two hours and a half and then our troubles began. In West Virginia the road is only a two-lane highway. It was not very well cleared, and as far as policing goes I saw no state police until they came to look for me sometime around 9:30 or 10 o'clock in the evening.

What happened was that the trucks, not having chains, got stuck on the grades and traffic piled up behind them in both directions until there was a line 10 to 12 miles long outside the little town of Washington, which is across the West Virginia border in Pennsylvania.

I have the Governor of Pennsylvania, Mr. David Lawrence, to thank for the fact that the state police finally came to inquire if I would not be willing to walk a mile to where we could get on an alternate road and perhaps get around the jam. The young bus driver held me firmly by the arm and insisted on walking all the way with me. His friendliness and cheerfulness all the way I shall always remember.

We had had no dinner, though some of us had been able to get off and get some sandwiches and coffee at a little wayside stand. One young man got a bun with some ham and brought it to me. And Mr. William Cohen, who had joined me in New York City as he was going to the same meetings, was as solicitous as he could be. People are always kind and look after me with care.

I felt sorry to leave my fellow passengers behind to go with the state police, but I thought of the 11 o'clock train that I must catch if I were going to make my Monday morning appointment in Hyde Park, so with many apologies I started off. Once in the police car, we took a back road and made quick time, but it was evident that I would not make my 11 o'clock train. I did, however, make an 11:36.

So, I filled my Monday morning engagement and enjoyed the rest of the day in Hyde Park. On Tuesday I spoke before the Hyde Park Rotary Club at noon, and then to Hartsdale to speak for the American Association for the United Nations at 8:15 P.M.

....

One of the battles lost in the 1936–1939 Spanish Civil War was that fought by the Republican loyalists to convince the world that they were not heavily infiltrated by Communists. This was as much a moral as a public relations battle, and years later it was still being discussed. In her "My Day" columns of those years, Mrs. Roosevelt had made it clear that her sympathies lay with the Spanish Republicans. Almost a quarter of a century later she was still sticking to her guns by echoing the Spaniards' own plea for refugee assistance.

Among the Spanish loyalists Mrs. Roosevelt so much admired was the greatest cellist of the century, Pablo Casals (1876–1973). Casals would not visit the U.S. because of his continuing political opposition to the Spanish dictator, Francisco Franco, whom the United States had chosen to recognize (in a hotly debated foreign policy move) because of a presumed need to maintain military bases in Spain.

WASHINGTON, D.C., MARCH 7—I have an appeal from a small group of people who six years ago formed an organization called Spanish Refugee Aid, Inc. Their object is to help 120,000 Spanish Republican refugees who today, 20 years after the Civil War in Spain, are still living in Southern France. Pablo Casals, the cellist, and Lazaro Cardenas, former President of Mexico, have lent their names to this small working committee.

We in the United States are deprived of hearing Pablo Casals perform because we recognized the Franco government, against which Casals and the Spanish Republicans had fought so valiantly. Some people still persist in believing that the Republicans in Spain were Communist-controlled because the Communists came to their aid— for which the Republicans were quite naturally grateful. But the refugees who have lived all these years in France are not Communists. They are Spanish patriots who wanted their country to be free. Now the committee in this country wants not only to go on with the aid in clothing and food which they have been able to distribute, but also to build for the old people a home near Montauban, a small old provincial town in South Central France. They need help very badly. I hope that some people will remember that this was a war for liberation, and will be sympathetic to these patriots.

....

At the end of a long discussion of whether capital punishment is a valid way to achieve justice or to deter future crimes (Mrs. Roosevelt consistently argued "no" on both points) is an illustration of Eleanor Roosevelt's fearlessness about whether crime and criminals might ever touch her life. Having lived in the public spotlight for decades, she was well aware that from time to time some disturbed or angry person could try to do some harm to her husband or to her. The attacks on President Truman and on members of Congress in the 1940s and 50s by disgruntled Puerto Rican nationalists, which Mrs. Roosevelt spoke about in "My Day," had not frightened her. Not even direct threats to her own life seemed to give her pause about carrying on with her work. This excerpt begins toward the end of Mrs. Roosevelt's column.

SARASOTA, FLA., MARCH 14—Our knowledge of human beings is limited. We cannot know all about any other human being. For the protection of society, if a human being seems dangerous we have a right to limit his contacts and thus protect others from the danger. But I

....

doubt if we have a right to take away a gift which we alone cannot give. For that reason I believe the movement against capital punishment is growing stronger in our country. It is a good thing to have people think about the problem at this time. I hope many people will give it serious reflection and come to the conclusion that I have—that human beings have no right to take each other's lives.

On Friday morning my secretary, Miss Corr, and I left New York by air and had a fairly good trip to Tampa, though we ran into a tropical storm just before landing which made us almost an hour late. Trouble with the plane's flaps twice forced us to return to Tampa after taking off, and I finally decided to drive to Sarasota because I was to speak there in the evening and it was getting late. It took so long to arrange for a car that I did not reach the Sarasota airport until 6:30 P.M. A few brave souls who had waited for our arrival escorted me immediately to the dinner where I was to speak, while Miss Corr took our belongings and went to my uncle Mr. David Gray's home.

While we were at the dinner a telephone threat was received against me and one of the gentlemen present. Apparently the sheriffs of two counties were alerted, but we proceeded calmly with dinner and I was unaware of any of the excitement until the morning paper brought me the news. I can't say that such things disturb me much, but I am sorry that my uncle, who lives here and loves Sarasota and the South, has to be dragged in on any kind of disagreeable performance

....

In another example showing Eleanor Roosevelt as a muckraking journalist, in the tradition of Lincoln Steffens, Ida Tarbell and Upton Sinclair, a "My Day" column turns to a subject Eleanor had written and spoken publicly about many times in her career. To Mrs. Roosevelt the notion that a country as rich as the United States could not (or, more to the point, she had frequently said, would not) provide adequate housing for all of its citizens, even the poorest, was simply scandalous. The years-long effort in her committee at the UN to write a Universal Declaration of Human Rights had included debate with delegates from all kinds of cultures around the world on such basic points as every individual's right to adequate shelter and food. And they had all agreed: such rights were inalienable. Mrs. Roosevelt was convinced that America must rebuild its cities and must start by eliminating the ghettos. Often during the Depression she had seen highly disturbing living conditions when, it was said, fully "one third of a nation" was ill-housed, -clothed, and -fed. To find conditions even worse in 1960, when middle-class per capita income had reached a new peak, was simply not acceptable to Eleanor Roosevelt.

....

NEW YORK, MARCH 21—I have just received some rather startling and even shocking material on a crisis which faces the cities of our nation as a result of the deteriorating slum conditions that exist almost everywhere. I think all of us should become more aware of this crisis than we seem to be at present.

New York City alone, for example, has 7,000 acres of slums, with some of the worst areas in Harlem. If the density of the population of Harlem were applied throughout the city, all the people of the United States would be housed in Manhattan!

Various factors have contributed to the worsening of slum conditions in our cities. Those who can afford to get away from the big cities, for example, move to the suburbs, and in recent years the greatest migration throughout our country has been of this kind. The result is that the city dwellers who are left behind are more and more going to be predominantly in the low-income group. And of this group, the larger proportion are nonwhite.

Washington, D.C., is already more than 50 percent nonwhite. In six years the Los Angeles nonwhite population increased 45 percent, while the white population increased only 12 percent. New York's nonwhite population is up 41 percent as against a 6-percent increase in its white population.

Hence the slum problem is becoming one of the really serious problems of the U.S., and it had better be faced by all city dwellers. What it means is that we have to modernize all of our cities, and the best place to start is with the slums. Today we have 22 million slum dwellers in our cities as against 20 million farmers. Our federal expenditure per farm family is $3,000 per year as against $84 spent on the slum family. Again, studies just completed in the public schools of Atlanta show that students from the slums perform 30 percent below their natural capacity, compared with those from average homes. In other words, squalor seems to slow down their natural abilities and talents, and it is hard to teach children who are hungry, cold and poorly clad.

America has more than five million people in slums with gross incomes of less than $2,000 a year. Since most of this is used for food, clothing and medicine, they cannot afford to pay the rent which private capital would require to provide adequate shelter. The only answer yet found is to build public housing for the low-income groups. But to this one constantly hears the reply: "There is no money in housing the poorest people well; there is money in housing them ill." Slum landlords therefore continue to take a 30 percent return on slum housing. As a result, taxes will go up in cities because the poorer people remaining need more public services.

It is time we faced this whole problem squarely. We will get poorer and poorer citizens unless we change the housing in which they spend their childhood, and this can only be done by clearing out the slums of our big cities. The health of the future city dwellers and the health of our whole country depends on providing young people with an environment in which they can grow instead of deteriorating.

....

In the appreciation of the arts, when one's sense of taste has been solidly consistent for years, it can be particularly hard to embrace the new; Eleanor Roosevelt did her best. She had no taste for the comic grotesque, but that is what she saw in Duerrenmatt's modernist play, The Visit. *The Swiss playwright's dark sense of irony was far removed from Mrs. Roosevelt's bright optimism about the human soul. Similarly, in music, the piano concerto she refers to by the Hungarian composer Béla Bartók (1881–1945) can be challenging even to someone schooled in traditional Western symphonic music.*

NEW YORK, MARCH 22—Last week I went to see the Lunts at the New York City Center in a revival of "The Visit" by Friederich Duerrenmatt. From my point of view it is not a very pleasant play, but it was beautifully acted and certainly it gave one more to think about than does the average theater performance.

I also had the pleasure on Saturday night of going to the New York Philharmonic and hearing Fritz Reiner conduct a most interesting program. Rudolph Serkin was the soloist, and Concerto No. 1 by Bartók was played. The whole program was new to me and I was not at all sure I understood the music. Nevertheless, I realized later that the music left me with a sense of grandeur and that the evening was a very satisfying one.

....

Eleanor Roosevelt was an articulate voice in the beginning of the debate about apartheid, thirty years early. The crackdown in South Africa she refers to in this column concerned repressive measures taken against South African blacks as their few remaining civil rights were stripped away and as their most influential political party, the African National Congress, stumbled into a trap. It was eventually banned, with Nelson Mandela, its leader, imprisoned. But these events were not so far from home as one might think, according to Mrs. Roosevelt, who saw a direct link to the civil rights struggle in America. She had moved by this time from the position of being an observer to one who here recommends and endorses specific actions ordinary citizens can take to keep the heat on Southern segregationists.

HYDE PARK, MARCH 26—We have all been very much upset by the situation in South Africa. But equally upsetting has been the news

....

from Alabama, where nine college students were expelled from school for their sit-down strike. A visitor came to tell me that when a sympathy strike was attempted on behalf of these students, the police set up gun posts around the college campus, tapped the telephone lines to the church where meetings were being held, and altogether created an atmosphere so much like South Africa that it is not comfortable for an American citizen to think about.

Fortunately, students in colleges in the North have realized that the students in the South will need help, so within hours $1,000 was expedited from campuses in the North to the beleaguered students in Alabama. I think we should organize to support these students in any way it is possible to do so.

As I have said before, I do not think boycotting lunch counters that are segregated in the North has much value except in letting off our own steam. But I do think that refusing to buy South African goods— such as lobster tails, diamonds, caracul coats, etc., none of which we buy every day—and at the same time refusing to buy anything at all from chain stores that have segregation of any kind in our South will have a very salutary effect.

It is curious that the United States and South Africa have much the same problem. However, the degree, thank heavens, is different. But we must move forward here at home or we cannot protest with sincerity what goes on abroad.

....

Man's inhumanity to man was a phenomenon Eleanor Roosevelt could neither understand nor tolerate. When she saw a case of inhumanity being passed off as a rational, civilized, and necessary form of behavior, she spoke out to condemn it. The subject here is chemical and germ warfare. Mrs. Roosevelt's own memories of the horrors of World War I, in which there were few controls on the use of such weapons, are no doubt behind her thinking here.

NEW YORK, APRIL 5—I was very much surprised the other day to be sent a clipping from a March 25 newspaper saying that "the Army asked Congress today to approve an increase in its budget next year for stepped-up development work on the chemical and biological weapons of war."

In World War II it was my understanding that by mutual consent germ warfare was ruled out, but now we see by this clipping that Major General Robert J. Wood, deputy chief of the Army's research and development program, says that the Army feels it necessary to develop germ and gas warfare systems "which can complement the nuclear deterrent."

....

This seems to me unthinkable. We are becoming less and less civilized every day and also totally impractical. Spending large sums of money on a horrible type of warfare when already we have the certainty that bombs will bring complete destruction seems hardly necessary.

Must we create more and more ways of destroying human beings? Is it really necessary to "complement the nuclear deterrent," which can already give us complete annihilation and cannot deter anything?

. . . .

Enormous patience for her friends and family but little for herself: such was the case with Eleanor Roosevelt who from some viewpoints was a driven woman (though fortunately driven by her dedication to good causes). She approaches the annoyance of an injured foot like a soccer player hurt in the middle of a game. She keeps running, right through the pain. Help comes from her friend David Gurewitsch, who was also her physician. The doctor and his wife Edna had joined Mrs. Roosevelt not long before in buying a house on New York's Upper East Side, with two apartments, one for Eleanor on two floors at the bottom, and the other for the Gurewitsches on top.

NEW YORK, APRIL 6—My life has been changed for me for the next few days because I very stupidly stood between two cars on a street on Sunday afternoon and only watched the oncoming cars from the left. I heard a car start up, but I did not realize it was the car on my right.

The next thing I knew something bumped into me and I lost my balance and fell down. I was up again in a minute and retrieved my umbrella and my handbag and went on to the appointment I was about to keep.

But I found that my right foot was decidedly painful and I could not put my weight on it, so I hobbled along and hoped it would improve. I made my little speech for cancer research at the benefit where I was going, and then, fortunately, my friends, Mr. and Mrs. Joseph Lash, took me home.

At home I found a group of little girls who had come in for an interview. After a few minutes I left them with their chaperones to have some cocoa and cookies and excused myself and went upstairs to ask Dr. David Gurewitsch to look at my foot and do something to it so I could keep my dinner appointment.

At this point I was not walking with great ease. He did what he could and I managed to dress and get to the dinner, which was given by the coat and suit industry for the benefit of Brandeis University. I made my speech sitting on a high pillow in a chair!

On Monday morning Dr. Gurewitsch took me up to the Medical

. . . .

Center for an X-ray. Nothing is broken, fortunately; I have only some torn ligaments. I now have two hand canes and a beautifully taped leg and am confined to my apartment for a few days—something that has not happened to me for a long while.

I had to ask my youngest son John to fill my place at a meeting in Providence on Monday, and I was certainly grateful to him that he was able to go. I am also grateful to the many people who have called and asked about me. But I am annoyed with myself for being so foolish as to let myself get knocked down, for I should be old enough to watch what is around me on every side.

....

The idea of national health insurance had come up in the 1930s from the American Socialist Party, and New Deal thinkers gave it serious consideration, finding that the financial woes of the time made it impossible to add it to what was then still a new program: Social Security, introduced in 1935. But after World War II President Truman made national health insurance one of his primary political goals. Even in the waning weeks of his lame duck administration, he was still trying to find enough votes in Congress to get a national health insurance bill passed. Eleanor Roosevelt consistently supported the campaign for health insurance for all Americans, but especially for those who were unable to pay for medical services themselves—and that often meant the elderly. She had no particular plan to put forward but instead argued the broader point about the public's entitlement to such help. Truman was gone; Eisenhower was soon to go; Mrs. Roosevelt was still around, still pressing the same point. (It would be five more years before Medicaid and Medicare were approved, with leadership from a Democratic White House and Congress.)

NEW YORK, APRIL 9—At the hearings this week on changes that would benefit the aged in our Social Security system, a real argument developed that was aired on the front pages of our newspapers. James B. Carey, president of the International Union of Electrical Workers, backing a Democratic bill to add health insurance features to the Social Security system, had it out with Senator Everett M. Dirksen, who quite naturally came to the defense of the Administration. The union leader insisted that the Administration had surrendered to "the American Medical Association and the insurance companies."

Now, anyone who has any volume of mail must know by this time that one of the real grievances of the older people in this country, who number about 16 million, is that Social Security does not give any health insurance. Sooner or later all of them need medical care, hos-

....

pitalization, expensive medicines and special provision made because of certain kinds of physical handicaps.

And I was very much surprised the other day when the President said he did not think that insurance was at present necessary. When he was asked questions at his press conference he suggested that a rise of one-half of one percent in the tax might be a way to meet the needs. I see, however, that Arthur S. Flemming, Secretary of Health, Education and Welfare, says that the Administration "with a real sense of urgency" is trying to devise an acceptable system under which this insurance would be available.

This seems, then, to be largely a financial question, and it ought not to be difficult to find out how something as necessary as this could be done.

There is no question in my mind that Social Security benefits are inadequate and cannot be considered to be meeting all the needs of an older person. If all the Administration does is to make a long-drawn-out study, then it is going to be accused of woefully neglecting the real interests of the older people. And these needs are urgent because the help must be given now and not after the people are dead.

． ． ． ． ． ． ． ． ． ．

The leadership in the White House that helped bring about the medical insurance legislation discussed above came from President John Kennedy, his vice president, Lyndon Johnson, and from President Johnson's subsequent vice president, Hubert Humphrey. All three had been dedicated supporters of the concept for years. Similarly, each had actively supported the many proposed civil rights bills struggling toward adoption in the Senate, only to fall at the feet of filibustering, segregationist senators. When the Senate finally passed a civil rights bill, Mrs. Roosevelt knew it was time to applaud. Once again, she links the U.S. crusade for civil rights to the situation in South Africa.

NEW YORK, APRIL 11—It is a good thing that the Senate has finally passed the civil rights bill after an eight-week fight, with 42 Democrats and 29 Republicans in favor. This is only the second civil rights legislation to pass the Senate since the Reconstruction Era. The first civil rights act of 1957 was also a voting rights measure. Already those who want a really fair bill giving the Negroes their full rights are denouncing this bill, and I am quite sure that it will continue to be denounced. But I hope that it is at least a step in the right direction.

All of us in the Democratic Party, I think, owe Senator Johnson a vote of thanks. He has risked repercussions among his Southern colleagues and among his own constituents. He has made it possible for the Democrats to claim equal, if not more, responsibility for the pas-

． ． ． ． ． ． ． ． ． ． ． ． ． ． ． ． ． ．

sage of the bill, which of course should never have had to be passed—
for the right to vote should be something which every citizen of this
country enjoys without any question. Since it was necessary to pass
the bill, however, we are fortunate to have had a parliamentary leader
with the skill of Senator Johnson.

My one fear is of intimidation, which I feel sure will be tried to
prevent Negro citizens in the South from registering and voting. I hope
the Attorney General can find ways of protecting the registration and
of preventing retaliation when the Negro citizens of the South exercise
their constitutional right.

It is notable that the House of Commons in London unanimously
approved the resolution deploring South Africa's racial policies and
urging the British government to voice a strong feeling of disapproval
at the forthcoming Commonwealth conference. It is difficult to imagine the kind of atmosphere that will exist at this conference—with
Ghana, India and Great Britain itself, as well as other Commonwealth
countries, protesting the policy of one of their members.

Things seem to go from bad to worse in South Africa, and nothing
seems to move the people there but fear. When you have to arrest
hundreds of Africans and formally ban two African political groups,
you are not living in a safe community or one that has reached a point
of understanding where reasonable living conditions can be arranged
between the races. It is a very sad situation and one where the fundamental rights of human beings are so clearly involved that world
public opinion is turning completely against South Africa.

. . . .

*Just over 100 years before Adlai Stevenson proposed that the presidential
campaign process would be improved by instituting one or more "great
debates" on television between the candidates, Abraham Lincoln and
Stephen Douglas had established a model for such encounters, a custom
"more honored in the breach than in the observance" in American political life. Stevenson lamented the absence of direct contact between
the key candidates and lamented the absence of extended dialogue between candidates and interviewers from the press and other segments
of society. His own two campaigns had been hurt by the fact that he
shone best when actually discussing issues at some length—not when
forced into trading quips with the press or when having to defend himself
indirectly against unfounded criticism from his opponent, but never
face to face.*

*Mrs. Roosevelt deeply respected Stevenson's insights and gave his
proposal for what became a key element in the 1960 presidential campaign her warm support.*

. . . .

NEW YORK, MAY 19—The suggestion made the other day by Adlai Stevenson would, I think, go a long way toward bringing real knowledge to the people about Presidential candidates and their policies.

Mr. Stevenson's suggestion to have a "great debate" on television would be a real step forward in having a rational campaign conducted.

I do not think anything is as good as actually seeing the candidates in person, but if they had this free time on the air and were obliged to engage in a debate with opposition candidates on issues during this time, I think the people would grow accustomed to listening and watching that hour on TV. They would get a far clearer concept of what was at stake and of which was the candidate best equipped by character and knowledge as well as experience to meet the issues of the future.

With the summit conference in Paris ending before it even had a real chance to get started—and in an atmosphere that undoubtedly means that Mr. Khrushchev will now devote himself to thinking of all the ways in which he can embarrass and irritate the West—we are going to need to know what plans the two major parties here have to meet one of the most serious situations that this country has ever been up against.

. . . .

It was no secret that Eleanor Roosevelt was not a warm supporter of John F. Kennedy in his quest for the presidency; she still had her mind and heart set on Adlai Stevenson as the ideal candidate, despite his losing record on the level of presidential elections. The Senator and Mrs. Roosevelt had not been foolish enough to trade many barbs in public (actually, she had given the Senator a harder time than he would have dared to give her); but they had disagreed on certain issues, and Eleanor Roosevelt felt that Kennedy had made his way nearly to the top of the Democratic Party a bit too much on the easy ride provided by bundles of money from his wealthy father. Mrs. Roosevelt saw in the Kennedy clan a great deal of talent but also what appeared to her as an unappealing smugness.

In this context it was hardly a surprise that negative comments made by Eleanor Roosevelt about John Kennedy would be exaggerated by those Democrats who were frustrated with her or, worse, would be twisted out of shape by Republicans who were happy to find any wedges they could to drive between one important Democrat and another. The Republicans knew it was going to be a close contest for the White House and that a party divided against itself would be unlikely to win. So we see Eleanor Roosevelt trying at once to clear the air about her opinion of Kennedy but at the same time trying to avoid mending any fences. She does not give the Senator even a single word of positive recognition.

. . . .

PITTSFIELD, MASS., JUNE 8—I have just received a clipping in the mail which repeats something I have been told a number of times and which I would like to refute. It quotes me as having said as regards Senator John F. Kennedy "that he may write about courage but he has little of it himself." And it goes on to say that I have said if the Presidential race were between Nixon and Kennedy I would not vote at all.

Both of these quotations are entirely incorrect.

I never said either.

I am not coming out for any candidate until the national convention. This is the stand I have taken from the very beginning and it would take some very compelling reasons to make me change this. And if I did so I would certainly explain my reason for the change clearly.

It is quite true that there are times when one may not like the candidates presented by either party, but one has an obligation to choose and to vote on the record of the party, for democracy does not function when the people do not take responsibility.

....

Three days later the political sands had shifted. Realizing that she had been acting a bit too idealistically (in thinking that somehow, without bold action from his supporters, Stevenson would be nominated anyway), Mrs. Roosevelt rolled up her sleeves and prepared for a good old-fashioned Democratic Party convention tug of war over the biggest prize of all—the presidential nomination. Always on the lookout for workable compromises among competing but friendly colleagues in her party, she endorsed the idea of a Stevenson–Kennedy ticket. Hindsight would show her that this combination never really had a chance. It overestimated Stevenson's desire to run again (he remained an "unannounced candidate," at best willing to accept a draft by the convention), and it underestimated Kennedy's determination to sit in the Oval Office. The vice presidency would never have satisfied JFK.

The evidence of Stevenson's continuing popularity was substantial, and Mrs. Roosevelt duly reported it in her "My Day" column. Her office became an unofficial "Draft Stevenson" headquarters. The flow of mail and telegrams and calls fed her optimism about his candidacy . . . if only they could get his name placed in nomination.

One key element in Mrs. Roosevelt's strategy for Stevenson was to persuade JFK to drop out of the presidential race himself and then to endorse Stevenson, opening the way for the Stevenson draft at the quickly approaching convention. She pleaded with Kennedy through her "My Day" column and through various behind-the-scenes channels. The Kennedy machine would hear none of it, although JFK had a solid respect for Stevenson's intelligence and record of public service. Mrs. Roosevelt recognized that only a groundswell of public opinion in Stev-

....

enson's favor could get him into the running at this late date, and so she offered her readers a lesson in grass-roots political organizing to help them see that the miracle Stevenson needed could indeed be brought about by a few weeks of intense hard work.

HYDE PARK, JUNE 11—Because I decided on Thursday of this week to change my mind since I felt the world situation was so serious we needed to give the people of this country the opportunity to vote for the best possible man and the best possible ticket that the Democrats could put in the field, I came out for Stevenson and Kennedy, signed a petition addressed to the delegates of our Democratic National Convention, and made a statement explaining my action.

Ordinarily, I would think it did not make much difference what I did, but my political mail is of very great interest at the present time. The people seem to want a man of maturity with proved administrative ability and experience in dealing with the heads of government in all parts of the world, and this man is quite obviously Adlai E. Stevenson.

Two things made me feel that a simple citizen such as I am had an obligation to speak out. One was a statement on the part of Prof. Arthur M. Schlesinger, Jr. of Harvard and Prof. Henry S. Commager and Joseph L. Rauh, Jr. They said that as Stevenson was not a candidate they were coming out for Kennedy. At the same time Chairman Paul M. Butler told a California group for Stevenson that, since Stevenson was not a candidate, they were not entitled to any headquarters space in the area where other Democratic candidates would be accommodated during the Democratic National Convention.

This led me to decide that it would be wise to ask Mr. Stevenson to clarify his position on being a candidate, and I hope in my next column, or perhaps before that in a statement, to be able to give you his answer. I feel sure there is a growing groundswell among a great number of people in this country indicating trust and confidence in Mr. Stevenson in our present critical world situation. I think we should recognize this, for it will mean greater unity and strength for him as a President.

I have not mentioned the other Democratic candidates because it seems to me that Senator John Kennedy is the one who undoubtedly stands out as having the greatest chance for the nomination. I realize, of course, that Senator Lyndon Johnson has a number of votes he can control and that in the convention there can always be maneuvering if there is not a quick decision. But the likelihood of a quick decision and the fact that Senator Johnson is so much needed as the leader of the Senate and that Senator Stuart Symington is, on the whole, looked upon as a very useful and strong Senator but has not developed great national strength have given me the feeling that our strongest ticket would be Stevenson and Kennedy.

I realize that I am being presumptuous in expressing my opinion when there are so many people with greater political knowledge and experience than I can possibly hope to attain, but sometimes the voice of the average person needs to be heard. And this is a time when I think it is well for the average person who has strong feelings to speak out.

NEW YORK, JUNE 16—I am getting telegrams from different areas of the country which say something like this: "Our grateful thanks for your endorsement of Adlai E. Stevenson. He is not an active candidate himself, but he remains the candidate of millions of Americans." The wires come mostly from heads of committees, but individuals have sent messages, too.

All I can say is that it looks to me as though Governor Stevenson is simply not a candidate from his point of view, since he does not seek the nomination, but that he is the Democratic candidate for President for millions of Americans. In this sense, he is our candidate for the convention of 1960.

HYDE PARK, JUNE 30—The State of California is certainly being active on behalf of Adlai Stevenson. One reason probably is because California is Vice President Nixon's home state. It seems to me that more people in California than in some of our other states seem anxious for a change to a Democratic administration in Washington.

Governor Edmund G. Brown of California has indicated that he leans toward Senator John F. Kennedy, though he is still uncommitted, and I imagine the activity on the part of groups for Mr. Stevenson makes the Governor think twice about coming out definitely for one candidate over any other one.

It is obvious to me that more and more people are joining the bandwagon for Stevenson, but I am told that at the convention the bandwagon probably will roll for Kennedy and that it will be very difficult for any of the "hoi polloi" who have joined the Stevenson forces even to get into the convention and make a noise about their choice. Perhaps it is well, then, to make all the noise they can now!

I have before me an amusing draft notice sent by one of the California committees to Mr. Stevenson. In it he is notified to appear at the convention to show cause "why he should not be drafted as commander-in-chief of the U.S. armed forces for four years of service."

I seem to receive in the mail every day a new idea about what could be done to emphasize the feeling of the people that lies back of this draft movement.

One of these suggestions strikes me as particularly good. It is that all over the country groups working for Stevenson plan a dinner on the 10th of July. The hours, of course, would vary so that they would coincide with the dinner that is being held in Los Angeles that night for the delegates and various other important people in the Democratic party and at which Mr. Stevenson will be one of the speakers.

Then, the suggestion goes on, at each dinner throughout the country a message should be drafted urging the delegates to nominate Adlai E. Stevenson for President, and that these messages should be delivered to the chairman of the dinner in Los Angeles with the request that they be read to the assembled delegates.

I would only add for myself that I would like to see the messages contain a plea to Mr. Kennedy that he throw his support to Mr. Stevenson and run as the Vice Presidential candidate so that the ticket would be as strong a one as the Democrats could put in the field.

. . . .

In the final week before the Democratic convention in Los Angeles, a certain degree of political realism was finding its way back into Eleanor Roosevelt's otherwise enthusiastic thinking about the prospects of a third Stevenson presidential candidacy. One of the more sobering facts the Stevenson camp had to face was that the tidal wave of last-minute endorsements they hoped for (from prominent Democrats like Eleanor Roosevelt) was still at best only a wavelet. By now a Kennedy endorsement for Stevenson was seen as clearly out of the question. There were hopes that former President Truman would switch his allegiance away from Senator Stuart Symington in order to bolster Adlai Stevenson's chances, but what Truman said was a great disappointment. Having taken off the boxing gloves when she entered this year's campaign, Mrs. Roosevelt pulled no punches here in suggesting that Truman probably could never have appreciated Stevenson anyway, for the former president was a deal-making pragmatist while the former governor of Illinois was an idealistic intellectual.

Kennedy responded to Truman's speech with a press conference in which he gave a bravura performance of his diplomatic skills, his gentlemanly behavior, his conviction and resolve about seeking the presidency. Mrs. Roosevelt could see by now the writing on the wall: Somehow, like it or not, Kennedy was the man either to beat or to run with. Either way, it was time to pay him some respect.

NEW YORK, JULY 5—I listened to former President Truman's statement Saturday, as I imagine many people did, and while I very much regret his resignation as a delegate to the Democratic convention, I was relieved to hear that he will perhaps be in Los Angeles next week. I

. . . .

imagine he has been persuaded to be somewhere where he can be consulted.

I fully share his desire for a free convention, with delegates really listening to all sides of every question and sizing up every candidate and making up their minds without any coercion, but who knows better than Mr. Truman that such a convention never existed and probably never will? Human nature is human nature, and no human being is ever completely free of the feeling that he must consider where he may be harmed and where he may be rewarded for the actions which he takes.

If, state by state, we will go to work to clean out bad bosses, we shall greatly improve the caliber of the individuals who run the machinery of both parties. If rules and regulations are passed which make it possible for the rank-and-file party members to have a voice in various decisions, right up to the choosing of their representatives in conventions, than we shall have done something that may give us more participation by the people and cleaner politics.

Mr. Truman said many kind things about Senator John Kennedy, and he said that he was in no way removing his backing from Senator Stuart Symington, but when he went on to enlarge at length upon the virtues of Senator Lyndon Johnson it was evident that he has a well-formulated idea of where the delegates' voting strength should go. He would like to see it transferred from both Senator Kennedy and Senator Symington to Senator Johnson. I doubt that his feeling will be unanimously echoed in Los Angeles.

Interestingly, it now appears that Senator Kennedy and Senator Symington had better court Senator Hubert Humphrey's backing. It seems rather ironical that a man who had to withdraw from the race because he was defeated still holds the trump cards.

The most conspicuous point in Mr. Truman's statement, of course, was his naming so many possibilities as candidates, some of whom have hardly been mentioned before, while completely omitting the name of Adlai E. Stevenson. I remember well when President Truman forced Mr. Stevenson to run in 1952. I remember that, having done so, he was surprised to find that he had not nominated someone who would cleave to him, but someone who had a mind of his own. But of course no one has failed to understand Mr. Truman's reasons for not caring about Mr. Stevenson. They are two totally different people.

Mr. Stevenson will remain a great figure in the country, whether he is nominated or not. Without any office, he is still the only one of all the candidates who forces the knowledge upon you that he has entered a room even before he speaks.

NEW YORK, JULY 7—Most people who heard the broadcast of Senator John Kennedy's reply to former President Truman must have been impressed both by what he said and the way he said it. He was most courteous to Mr. Truman.

Certainly no one could have misunderstood his statement, however, that he had given long thought to becoming President and, having decided to try for this place of power and responsibility, hoped to win and would not withdraw.

Senator Kennedy made a good plea for youth, and he showed from past history the part young men had played in the shaping of world events. And he noted, too, there would be young men in many of the new nations who would be cast in difficult roles in the years ahead. The Senator did not seem to be on the defensive but appeared to be a perfectly assured and confident person.

I still feel that a Stevenson–Kennedy ticket would not only be the best for the country but for our political party, too.

But as an example of what the Kennedy speech did to several people around me, one man remarked at the end of it: "Well, I hope the Democratic party wins. I am for Adlai Stevenson, but if it turns out to be Kennedy, there are many people, I think, who will support the ticket with a sense of greater assurance because they heard this press conference."

. . . .

To the barricades, but graciously. Her sense of humor intact and careful not to alienate anyone in the Kennedy camp, Eleanor Roosevelt did what she could to push the Stevenson noncandidacy one more time, now in Los Angeles, the night before the convention was to begin. She tells a humorous story about herself and reports in ample detail about the jockeying for position that always goes on behind closed doors at a national convention. Although Mrs. Roosevelt appears to have sensed that she wasn't going to get exactly what she wanted out of this one, it is just as clear that in the tumultuous world of party politics she felt right at home.

Los Angeles, July 12—I arrived in this city in the middle of the evening Sunday after a most pleasant and quick trip by jet from New York.

I discovered on arriving at the airport that, despite the fact I had told my grandson I had a car to meet me and I would appear at National Committee Chairman Paul Butler's dinner as soon as I had done one or two little errands, I was still met by a determined group of people who wished to have me whisked away in an official car escorted by motorcycles and a charming girl guide. This was something I learned long ago I could do without with great pleasure. So, the kind people who wanted to do everything for me found me a most reluctant guest.

. . . .

I insisted on getting my own bags, and on finding the car which I knew had been sent for me and which was a modest little economy car, I discovered that the very delightful young driver was named John Kennedy. He told us his name with a sheepish grin, and added that he came from Illinois and was for Stevenson.

The kind hosts who met me had arranged a welcoming group bearing Stevenson banners at some distance from where our plane landed. So, after getting our bags, we walked down and greeted them. They had met Adlai Stevenson at the airport the day before; in fact, it was, I was told, the largest demonstration that had ever been seen at the airport.

How much value there is in demonstrations and people's signatures we will find out in the next day or two. I am afraid that the delegates who come here with the votes that will nominate the candidates are not very much affected by the banners and the signatures and the telegrams that pour in.

I reached the dinner in honor of Paul Butler to find the speaking about to begin. I was urged to come and sit on the dais and asked also to speak, but since all the candidates, including Mr. Stevenson, who is still a candidate waiting for a draft, were on the list of speakers, I felt that someone from the outside would be out of place. I was glad of the chance, however, to listen to each man state to this audience of several thousand what he thought was important.

Of course, I know I am prejudiced, but it seemed to me that the man who made the most sense, who analyzed the situation before us most clearly and told us what should and could be done about it, was this undeclared candidate, Mr. Stevenson.

From the main dinner we went into another room where Dore Schary was presiding over a second dinner, and there I spoke for a few minutes before the candidates were asked again to speak. This time I left immediately after speaking, since my watch said it was 2:30 A.M., though according to California time it was still only 11:30 P.M.

Monday morning dawned with beautiful weather, which the Californians tell me they are putting on for the convention, and apparently as much activity as can be put into a day was planned.

The newspapers, of course, are announcing that the Kennedy band-wagon is rolling according to schedule, and the news of Governor Pat Brown's announcing for Kennedy, though he said he had not released the California delegation from their first-ballot vote for him, was met with great rejoicing by the Kennedy forces. Many of the delegates, however, are Stevenson delegates, and such a division is also true of some of the other states, though they are being heralded as sure to turn to Senator Kennedy.

So, if Senator Kennedy wins on the first two or three ballots, we will all be able to go home on Thursday and we will know in November how the people feel.

I am truly sorry that Mr. Truman is not going to be here, for somehow he belongs at a Democratic convention.

....

The die is cast. Kennedy has won the nomination, and it is necessary now for the party to close ranks and to begin healing wounds suffered in the primaries and preconvention jostling for position. Certain realities must be faced, too, about the contest the Democrats are about to enter with the Republican standardbearer, Richard Nixon.

NEW YORK, JULY 18—As I listened to Governor Stevenson and Senator John F. Kennedy on TV Friday night, I thought Mr. Stevenson did a splendid job of introducing the Presidential nominee, and that Senator Kennedy's speech was remarkably forceful and forthright. I particularly liked the way in which he told the people that he was going to have to ask a great deal of us. Anyone who reads the papers these days must be aware of this fact.

WESTBROOK, CONN., JULY 20—While I am happy that so much spontaneous affection and appreciation was shown for Mr. Stevenson's qualities of statesmanship, I cannot help feeling rather relieved that he will not have to head the campaign against Vice President Richard Nixon. This will not be a pleasant campaign, and in many ways I feel that Senator Kennedy is better fitted to organize and plan it.

....

Eleanor Roosevelt, along with a handful of congressional activists showing a serious concern for the environment and the global supply of vital natural resources, was among the first to recommend urgent study of the nation's fossil fuel supply.

NEW YORK, AUGUST 1—A correspondent has drawn my attention to the fact that Concurrent Resolution 73, which calls for the creation of a joint committee to study the need for a national fuels policy, is still awaiting action in Congress. According to my correspondent there is no opposition to this resolution by the small oil companies, but the international group of oil companies is fighting it. Why should they object to such a study?

Vice president William R. Connole of the Federal Power Commission made a statement some time ago that stressed the incredible rate at which our "energy" resources are being used up. He said, "All the fossil fuel consumed in the history of the world prior to the year 1900 would last only five years at today's rate of consumption." Surely there can be no question about the necessity of studying our sources of fuels and carefully watching their rate of depletion.

The coal industry in this country has been a sick industry for a long time. In the last year or so, the deplorable conditions of the people in the mining areas of West Virginia have attracted much well-deserved sympathy. The most shocking part of it is, however, that these conditions are far from new. In the depression years of the early '30s the mining industry suffered terribly in West Virginia, Kentucky, Pennsylvania and southern Illinois. People lived in conditions that should not be permitted, under our American standards.

But we have not yet been moved to make a really fundamental study of the difficulties which must be met, and which I think could be met by a national fuels policy. Certainly this August session of Congress should take up Concurrent Resolution 73 and start a study which cannot be ignored and which will be acted upon.

. . . .

Now the irresistible force meets the immovable object. The Kennedy campaign found a way, perhaps something of a pretext, for its candidate to make an appearance in Hyde Park on a day when Eleanor Roosevelt would be at home at Val-Kill. A luncheon was arranged at which she and JFK could have what they really wanted, a time to talk privately and alone. The air had to be cleared between them, and they both recognized their party's need to rally behind the selected candidate. Kennedy may have had little to yield to Mrs. Roosevelt on specific policies, but he was far too astute a politician to think that running all the way without her endorsement would be smart. He did not come to Hyde Park begging, but he did come asking.

What JFK got was a challenging but supportive encounter with the grande dame of American politics. Her sense of how the presidency actually works is evident in this column. There is but one president, and yet his decision-making must be informed by contributions from many minds that do not think in his same style. Thus Mrs. Roosevelt was still promoting the idea of involvement in the Kennedy campaign, and perhaps the administration, of her own favorite candidate, Adlai Stevenson.

When the luncheon was over, Mrs. Roosevelt and Jack Kennedy emerged beaming. An alliance of sorts had been forged. The candidate is said to have remarked about this meeting with his sometime critic: "I am smitten by this woman; absolutely smitten."

New York, August 17—In my conversation with Senator John Kennedy at Hyde Park Sunday, I was anxious, needless to say, to find out

. . . .

if he and Adlai Stevenson had planned to work closely on foreign affairs during the campaign.

I knew there would be no question of Representative Chester Bowles working closely with the Senator, because it was for this purpose that he withdrew as a candidate for re-election to Congress. And I felt sure that it would be easy for Senator Kennedy and Representative Bowles to work together.

Senator Kennedy has a quick mind, but I would say that he might tend to arrive at judgments almost too quickly. Therefore, it seemed important to me that he should have a good relationship during the campaign with Mr. Stevenson, thereby demonstrating that their philosophies are sufficiently similar so that they could work well together in the future, even though Mr. Stevenson has a more judicial and reflective type of mind.

I was pleased to learn that the Senator already had made plans much along these lines. It gave me a feeling of reassurance.

Our Democratic candidate is a likable man with charm, and I think that already, since the convention, the difficulties and responsibilities that the future may hold for him as President have opened up new vistas for him and brought about a greater maturity.

I think Senator Kennedy is anxious to learn. I think he is hospitable to new ideas. He is hard-headed. He calculates the political effect of every move. I left my conversation with him with the feeling that here is a man who wants to leave a record of not only having helped his countrymen, but having helped humanity as a whole.

I had withheld my decision on joining Herbert Lehman as honorary chairman of the Democratic Citizens Committee of New York until I had a chance to see and talk with our Democratic candidate. After Senator Kennedy's visit, I telephoned my acceptance to serve with Mr. Lehman, and I told Senator Kennedy that I would discuss what help in the campaign I could give, for I have come to the conclusion that the people will have in John F. Kennedy, if he is elected, a good President.

As the weeks go by I hope I will have an opportunity to see our candidate more and to know him better, but I have enough confidence in him now to feel that I can work wholeheartedly for his election.

Senator Kennedy was met by a very large crowd Sunday morning when he landed at Dutchess County Airport on his way to Hyde Park. I had sent my car and two friends, Dr. and Mrs. David Gurewitsch, to meet him.

Dr. Gurewitsch got out of the car to go forward and welcome the Senator. Mrs. Gurewitsch stayed in the car and, while waiting there, asked several people in the crowd if they were Democrats or curiosity-seekers. To her surprise, she found that most of them professed to be

Democrats. Both she and Dr. Gurewitsch reported to me later that the applause upon Senator Kennedy's arrival was astonishing.

Perhaps it was a case of public tastes changing somewhat as the years went by. There may have been other factors too. The popularity of "My Day," although not of its author, if the opinion polls could be trusted, was waning slightly. Mrs. Roosevelt's publisher, United Feature Syndicate, was receptive to the idea that "My Day" should become a three-times-per-week column instead of six. And, like it or not, Mrs. Roosevelt was slowing down, if ever so slightly. She had been on the six-columns-per-week schedule for all of twenty-four years with hardly any interruptions. The syndicate sent out a notice on its wire to subscribing newspapers, indicating that following Mrs. Roosevelt's European trip this fall (her last long voyage), the new format would be introduced. Among the changes was the matter of length: Eleanor Roosevelt would write longer pieces now, though fewer of them. From here on, many of the better columns are actually well-developed essays. The syndicate dropped the official name "My Day" because the column was no longer daily and much less a diary of Mrs. Roosevelt's activities. But for all intents and purposes, these changes were cosmetic. The spirit and purpose of Mrs. Roosevelt's newspaper writing carried on the same, and the "My Day" title was so fixed in everyone's mind that it stayed in common use to the end.

. . . .

Some in the Nixon camp truly believed that Kennedy, as a Catholic, would be forced by the Pope to call Rome before making any important decisions. There were some in both parties whose ethnic and religious prejudices were such that the idea of an Irish Catholic as president made them dizzy with distaste. In either case it came down to the same question: Would America finally elect a Catholic president, breaking the apparently rigid pattern of entrusting the nation's highest office only to those with Protestant backgrounds?

The issue had surfaced concretely in 1928 when the four-time governor of New York, Alfred E. Smith, a Catholic, ran for president and lost to Herbert Hoover. There were other issues in that year's campaign, to be sure, but one that cut down Smith's chances of victory was the question of his trustworthiness in international affairs as a Catholic who might be compelled by the Vatican to act somehow against the nation's better interest. The attacks made on Smith's character were unscrupulous but effective. The Roosevelts, Eleanor and Franklin, thought they were scandalous. The Kennedy candidacy gave the country a fine chance, Mrs. Roosevelt thought, to break an old and harmful habit by putting someone other than a Protestant in the White House. Although she was no fan of the Catholic church's social policies, she was com-

. . . .

pletely unsympathetic to anyone who would use religion as a test of suitability for government service.

Dr. Norman Vincent Peale, a prominent Protestant clergyman, was widely influential, primarily because of his longtime best-selling inspirational book, The Power of Positive Thinking.

NEW YORK, SEPTEMBER 21—At the start of our national election campaign it seemed that every newspaper I read complained about the dullness of the campaigning, that neither candidate seemed to be able to lift it out of the doldrums. The people were not being reached, they said, with anything that really mattered to them.

Since the religious issue was injected, however, by a few clergymen—some of whom probably thought they were helping the Republicans—more interest seems to have been aroused. And I was interested to read that Dr. Norman Vincent Peale some days ago disassociated himself from the National Conference of Citizens for Religious Freedom, a group that charged a Roman Catholic President would be under "extreme pressure from the hierarchy of his church" to align the foreign policy of the United States with that of the Vatican.

Religious freedom cannot just be Protestant freedom. It must be freedom for all religions. It is a long time since I sat in my office and read the scurrilous literature that came into the Democratic headquarters in Alfred E. Smith's campaign. Nothing quite so bad is reaching me now. But some of the letters sound hysterical and purely emotional.

The question seems to me fairly simple. The Constitution gives us all religious freedom and we are not to be questioned as to our religious beliefs.

Some people maintain that the Catholic Church is not above working to get certain public privileges for its private institutions. This can be done, however, only by the passage of certain laws.

To tell a man he cannot run for any office in this country because he belongs to a certain religion or is a member of another race—even though he is required to fulfill all the obligations of citizenship, including fighting and dying for his country—is completely illogical and unconstitutional.

I have fought to prevent the Catholic Church from being granted certain school privileges which I think interfere with our accepted beliefs on the separation of church and state, but I will fight equally hard for the right of any American citizen to serve his country in any capacity.

....

Mrs. Roosevelt's columns about political unrest among the Soviet satellite nations turned out to be farsighted and accurate readings of how people in those countries felt for years about their forced subjugation to Soviet rule. Here, on the occasion of a visit to the United Nations by Soviet Premier Nikita Khrushchev, Eleanor Roosevelt throws down a simple but profound challenge to the Communist leader.

NEW YORK, SEPTEMBER 26—Some of the things Khrushchev says, if one does not stop to think about the realities of the situation, might prove alluring to certain states—as when he inveighs against colonialism. Yet if one surveys the world scene closely, it is clear that colonialism is practically dead. In a very few places there has been some resistance on the part of colonial powers, but the great majority of the nations in Africa which are now becoming free have been granted this freedom by the colonial powers.

If Mr. Khrushchev really believes in the self-determination of people, he should allow a free election under United Nations supervision in Estonia, Latvia, Lithuania, Albania, Hungary, Bulgaria, Czechoslovakia, East Germany and Poland—all Russian satellites. No other great nation boasts so many subject peoples. It may well be, as Mr. Khrushchev would undoubtedly claim, that they are anxious to be a part of the Soviet Union, and would in any case continue as Communist states. The latter may be true, but I am not quite so convinced that all of them would want to remain subject to the Soviet Union. In any case, Mr. Khrushchev can prove this at any moment by asking the UN to supervise an election in each of these countries, where a secret ballot will be used.

....

Eleanor Roosevelt was not above using satire to score a few political points. Vice President Nixon's performances in the second and third televised presidential debates were good grist for her mill. Without having to impugn his ideas, she could put the spotlight on him as the weaker candidate anyway. Her words are a little less than kind, but then the Republican bigwigs took their shots at Kennedy, too. Although Mrs. Roosevelt yearned for a political climate in which the intelligent discussion of ideas is the main method of sorting out who ought to carry an election, she knew as well that personality and charisma—even a candidate's sense of humor—are elements that cannot be ignored. Seeing the candidates on television heightened her feeling for just how important surface impressions could be.

NEW YORK, OCTOBER 12—I have waited to talk about the second "great debate" between our respective candidates for the Presidency because I wanted to hear as much as possible of the reactions of other people.

....

The most general opinion I get is that the make-up man and the lighting helped Mr. Nixon very much.

I am not quite sure that this satisfies me completely, for I had to look at Mr. Nixon twice before I recognized him. Furthermore, it would seem to me that the objective in these debates was to get to know the two candidates as they are, not as some make-up man wishes to make them appear. This question, however, does not seem to arise with Mr. Kennedy, as I understand he decided that it was more important that people get to know him as he is.

Lighting, of course, can affect both candidates greatly, but that depends entirely on the technician at the time—and when all is said and done this is not a beauty contest. These two men are trying to tell us what future they believe the nation faces and as nearly as possible along general lines what their ideas are as to next steps.

On this score, this was a better debate than the first meeting. Both sides were sharper. Mr. Nixon was more finished, but it seemed to me in the details of dates and figures Mr. Kennedy was perhaps more the master of information. This perhaps is only natural because as a Senator he would have sat in on many of the debates, whereas the Vice President is not expected to be present at every session and frequently has to be away, so he could not follow details as closely.

This second debate, it seems to me, did not give either side a clear-cut advantage over the other. Several people have told me that they wish the candidates could contest strictly in the form of a real debate— just two men answering each other, minus the interjections on the part of the reporters. In that way we could get a clearer concept of what was in each man's mind. We would get more real information.

Los Angeles, October 17—I wonder whether the rest of the people in the nation watching the third debate between the two Presidential candidates could have been as amused as I was at the little interchange concerning President Truman's "bad language." How virtuous can we really be in the U.S.? How many children do you really think have never heard anyone in their environment say "go to hell" or "damn?" Somehow I think the morals of our children will survive Mr. Truman's speech, and I cannot join Mr. Nixon in his virtue because he reminds me too much of a little story we used to laugh about in our family for many years.

My mother-in-law, like Mr. Nixon, felt that no gentleman ever used bad language. When by chance my husband said "damn" in front of the children, she would draw herself up and say: "Franklin never used to use bad language. He has learned it from his little boy Johnny, whom you, Eleanor, allow to spend so many hours in the stable!"

Somehow these occasional expressions by the man of the house never have seemed to me to have had a very bad effect on any of the children in any of the families I have known. Of course, there are paragons of virtue. I can remember once being on a trip in West Virginia during the Depression to look into some mining conditions. We had traveled all day and were very tired. Two ladies and one very gentle man, a Quaker by religion who could not allow himself any violent letting off of steam, were in the party. When we suddenly blew a tire at 2:00 A.M. on a mountainside about 10 miles from the hotel where we were to spend what remained of the night, I am afraid the two ladies said many things which were not ladylike. All the gentleman said was, "Too bad, too bad," as he walked up and down the road while we waited to get the tire replaced. We had two hours of sleep that night because we had to start at six the next morning, but nothing ever stirred Mr. Clarence Pickett to bad language.

I wonder, however, if this is really a criterion by which we choose the best man to be President of the United States. History perhaps will record that Mr. Truman was a great President, and a little sense of humor might help in understanding his occasional lapses in language.

From his remarks elsewhere in the debate, it would seem that to Mr. Nixon the principle of holding on to the small islands off the coast of China is more important than what is happening, and what may happen, to the people on these islands. This discovery may shock a good many people, but it did not surprise me.

The Vice President did a very good advertising job for his future speeches on this TV debate. On two occasions he said that he was going to make in the coming week a major speech on the subject on which he was questioned. Then, apparently on the theory that no one would dare interrupt him, he proceeded to talk quite a lengthy time in order that no one would notice that he had said nothing!

Mr. Kennedy may plan to make major speeches on some of these subjects, but he didn't mention it—he answered the questions as they were put. He did have to correct certain statements made by the Vice President, but that is to be expected. On the whole, I felt that he told us more than did his adversary.

. . . .

One of the better topics for a book Eleanor Roosevelt could have written with great authority was the role of the First Lady in American politics. She had more experience in and near the center of power in the White House than any other woman in the country's entire history. She was one of the most active First Ladies, both by inclination and because her husband's handicap from polio created a need for her to travel and observe many places when he could not go. Yet she was also one of the most family-minded First Ladies and kept very private about serious

. . . .

*family matters. Despite Mrs. Roosevelt's awareness of her importance
as an ally of the president, she did not presume to be an official member
of his government. Nor did she think any First Lady ought to be.*

*But Mrs. Roosevelt by 1960 sensed a change in the role of the First
Lady, a change coming about not only because the Republicans, she
observed, had drafted their president's and vice president's wives into
political service, but also because television created so many new opportunities for the candidate's exposure as a family man. There never
was a stronger campaigner for equal rights for women than Eleanor
Roosevelt, but here we see her recommending that the presidency and
the country would be better served if the First Lady were to keep to her
traditionally secondary role.*

NEW YORK, OCTOBER 21—As we watch the Presidential campaign un-
roll, I wonder how many have noticed one rather interesting change
in the modern type of campaign. This was brought to my attention
the other day when a young newspaper reporter said to me: "Do you
really think that the decision as to a man's fitness for the office of
President should depend, in part at least, on what kind of a President's
wife his wife will be?"

I looked at her in surprise for a moment, because it had not dawned
on me what changes had come about since Mr. Eisenhower's first
campaign.

Apparently we have started on a new trend. I can't remember in my
husband's campaign, nor in Mr. Truman's, that such a question could
be asked. Some of the children or I would accompany my husband
on the various campaign trips, and if we were around at railroad stops
he would introduce us to the crowd in a rather casual manner. He
often said "My little boy, Jimmy," when Jimmy was as tall as he was!

My husband insisted always that a man stood on his own record.
He did not bring his family in to be responsible in getting him votes
or in taking the blame for his decisions. I think he sometimes found
it amusing to let me do things just so as to find out what the reaction
of the public would be. But nothing we did was ever calculated and
thought out as part of the campaign in the way we feel that Mr. Nixon
plans every appearance with his wife.

There must be times when the whole situation becomes practically
unbearable, I would think, for the woman of the family. And I hope
that we will return to the old and rather pleasanter way of looking
upon White House families as people who have a right to their own
lives.

The wives, of course, have certain official obligations, but they are
certainly not responsible for their husband's policies. And they do not

have to feel that sense of obligation at every point to uphold the ideas of the man of the family.

With so many people around a President who say "yes" to everything he says, it is fun sometimes for the family around him to say "no" just for the sake of devilment—but that should be a private family relaxation.

. . . .

Now, practically on the eve of the election, Mrs. Roosevelt offers her readers some observations about the candidates' characters, reading backward from the kinds of reactions the two men seem to elicit in the crowds who turn out to see them as they crisscross the country, scrambling for votes. Eleanor Roosevelt is growing ever more positive in her endorsement of Senator Kennedy—given where she started only a half-year or so ago, a fairly remarkable turnabout. Remarkable not only because it indicates her flexibility at seventy-six, but also because it demonstrates Kennedy's force of character, his capacity to rouse the nation out of what Mrs. Roosevelt argued had been an eight-year-long, almost nightmarish slumber of Republican mediocrity.

St. Louis, November 2—I do not know what will happen on November 8 any more than anybody else knows, but as I go around the country and hear about crowds that have greeted Senator John F. Kennedy and the smaller crowds that have greeted Vice President Richard Nixon, one interesting observation is forcing itself upon me. The crowds that greet Mr. Kennedy want to shake him by the hand, or sometimes they just want to touch him, or sometimes they just want to look at him. This, I think, means a sense of identification between the people and the candidate.

Mr. Nixon has tried to be outgoing and his pretty wife says she loves campaigning because she loves people. But from all that I hear the feeling of the crowd is very different, and I know of only one thing that makes this difference. It is this: when the people finally decide that someone is their man—that he understands them and cares about them—though they may not agree with everything he says or does, they are still close to him and they trust him and they believe in him.

If I am right in this analysis perhaps we are going to have someone who can draw from the people of the United States the greatness that underlies all their everyday concerns. We need it badly at the present time. No one man can meet the problems that are going to face the next President. He must have around him people who are conscious of their greatness, and if we are watching this sense of identification with their candidate and their trust in him we will see a great people

. . . .

rise to the challenge presented in the very difficult days that face us at home and abroad.

This will mean for the United States the greatest opportunity to serve the world that any nation has had and I hope we accept it and rise to the best that is in us as a nation.

....

The arrival of a newborn in the president-elect's household, the little boy the nation would soon be calling John-John as he romped around his father's oval office, was too delicious a topic for Eleanor Roosevelt to ignore.

PORT HURON, MICH., NOVEMBER 28—National and international news sink into the background when a baby is born, especially a baby to a President-elect of the United States. This particular baby has upset his mother's and father's plans considerably, but the parents seem quite happy to change their plans in view of the circumstances!

Mrs. Kennedy very wisely had prepared her daughter for the fun of having a baby brother by letting her play with her little cousin. Still, with all the preparation in the world there is apt to be a little jealousy when a second baby comes home. One counts on the motherly instincts of a little girl as shown to her doll, but it does not always work out that way when it comes to a real live baby in the house taking much of the attention and care which has previously been showered on baby number one.

I can well remember an occasion when my one and only daughter, who was the oldest child of the family, dumped a whole box of powder on her baby brother's face. They were 20 months apart, and motherly instincts did not show so strongly at that early age. Perhaps when Caroline Kennedy gets her own baby brother home a little care will have to be taken to make her feel really happy about this addition.

Everyone will be sending warm congratulations to the Senator and his wife and wishing this new small boy happy days in the White House.

....

A frequent theatergoer and avid reader, Mrs. Roosevelt experienced many a play and book over the years that displeased her. Usually, if she bothered to make a negative comment at all (she was disinclined to do so), it would be brief and dismissive. The stage version of Advise and Consent *upset her so deeply that she gave an entire, lengthy column to it. The fact that the play had won the Pulitzer Prize in no way swayed Mrs. Roosevelt toward thinking that she too must applaud it. The fact that the acting was excellent made no difference. What moved her most deeply, and toward real anger and depression (almost to a call for cen-*

....

sorship), was the bleakness of the picture the play paints of America's political process. Eleanor Roosevelt feared for a country that could take the message of Advise and Consent *literally as the only truth to be told about the morality of its men in politics.*

NEW YORK, DECEMBER 16—Sometimes a small thing that seems unimportant may touch off more important things, and so today I am going to write about a play I saw on Wednesday evening of this week. The play is "Advise and Consent," written by Loring Mandel and based on the Pulitzer Prize-winning novel by Allen Drury. . . . As I sat through the performance I felt a sense of complete depression and disgust.

The play is beautifully acted and holds one's interest from beginning to end. But in this drama for ourselves and for all the world to see we are depicting all the worst things that can be found in political situations that are brought about by the weakness of human nature, the way in which scheming people can play upon human nature, and the man who is willing to lie because he thinks the ultimate good will be a justification.

We saw all these things depicted with extraordinary skill. Even the man cast as the President of the United States made arguments and excuses that must have caused uneasiness among those in the audience who noticed the evident effort to have the stage character resemble President Eisenhower.

It was a shock to see the office of the President included in the general downgrading of human beings who go into politics with legitimate ambitions but who are still weak, small, vindictive, determined to gain their own ends whether good or bad, and ruthless where anyone except themselves is concerned.

I have watched this game of politics for many, many years, in fact since I was a girl, and I know how ruthless and how utterly discouraging it can be. I think I know how to remember one's friends and how to fight against one's enemies. But I have seen this done without stealing, without double-crossing, without threats. And I have seen good men who were invulnerable. I have seen men triumph over all the pettiness and meanness and incredible temptations that faced them, and I still believe that on the whole the majority of human beings are decent and good and strong and straight.

I cannot bear to see depicted on the stage nothing but the worst side of our public life.

If this were wartime I think one would cry treason at this play. And since we are really engaged in a war, it is time we woke up to it. Perhaps it is good for us to see ourselves at our worst, but it is certainly not good to see only our worst. We must also be inspired by the best that is in us.

As the play proceeded I grew angrier and more depressed. I came out of the theater with the feeling that if there is someone who could write a true picture for the American theatre of the real values in our life and in our government, this should be done and done quickly in order to counteract the harm that this play will do us at home and abroad.

Young people seeing this play will be discouraged from entering into politics. Why should they look up to any of the characters who walk across the stage during the three hours it takes to act out the drama? I think perhaps the fact that the play is so well done is something to be deplored.

. . . .

The period between the election and inauguration of a new president is always one bright with anticipation and fraught with tough choices. Who would agree to serve in which high-level posts? And whom to appoint—to serve the country's and the party's best interests while offending the fewest people? Kennedy made many moves of which Mrs. Roosevelt was fully supportive. There were hopes within the Roosevelt family that Franklin Roosevelt, Jr., might get the nod from Secretary of Defense-designate Robert McNamara for the position of Secretary of the Navy. FDR, Jr., however, was passed over but not appropriately informed, and there were some hurt feelings.

Mrs. Roosevelt herself could not help wondering whether she would be called upon again to represent the United States at the United Nations. The question became even more concrete when, after not being appointed Secretary of State, Adlai Stevenson was chosen by Kennedy as ambassador to the UN. Stevenson and Kennedy discussed the possibility of a role for Mrs. Roosevelt there, and it was agreed that she would be invited to sit in as an observer. But her time for such activity had passed, and the best advice of friends, family, and doctor was to forego the opportunity. Mrs. Roosevelt also declined Kennedy's invitation to sit in the presidential box at the inauguration, declining apparently with a bit of pique that Stevenson had not been chosen secretary of state. She sat in the front rows below the podium that brisk day in January, wrapped in a mink coat and an army blanket, and, according to Joseph Lash, was brightly encouraged by the stirring speech President Kennedy delivered.

In this year's-end column, her willingness to forgive the president-elect his apparent nepotism in appointing his brother Robert to a cabinet post is indicative of her eagerness to see the new president off to a good start.

. . . .

HYDE PARK, DECEMBER 27—I think the storm of protest which has been aroused by the appointment of Robert Kennedy to the Attorney-Generalship is beginning to seem foolish. Granted that he is young, granted that he has no long experience as a lawyer behind him, he nevertheless has integrity. His ability seems to be unquestioned and it is just possible that he understands certain phases of his brother's programs better, and has a more comprehensive knowledge of them, than anyone else that the President-elect has been able to find.

In this case, I doubt whether the President-elect is choosing his brother. I think he is choosing a man whom he believes will get some of the things done which he wants to accomplish.

With an Attorney General who will use his powers to the limit, a good deal can be accomplished along the lines that I am sure the future President wants. Much can be done for civil rights, something can be done to control racketeers.

It may well be that after careful thought and search the President-elect has decided that the qualities needed to carry through this job are found in his brother. This judgment may be good or bad, but it seems to me that we might wait with a little more calm to find out whether President-elect Kennedy's objectives are better obtained through the way he has chosen, or whether he should have observed the unwritten tradition that having members of your family in positions of government where they carry real responsibility is dangerous.

1 9 6 1

Dwight David Eisenhower did not have an easy time of it during his last month in office. As president he had to wrestle with the possibility of cutting off diplomatic relations with Cuba, which had become increasingly restive under Fidel Castro's revolutionary Communist leadership. Eisenhower gave the country something serious to think about in his final State of the Union address when he warned that the United States, indeed the Western capitalist world, stood a good chance of being taken over from within by the technocrats who run what he called "the military-industrial complex." He urged that political control over the fate of the nation be revitalized lest big corporations, especially those with vested interests in seeing the arms race grow ever more intense and costly, end up dominating the society. Eleanor Roosevelt respected this speech and its main theme.

The eyes of the world, including Eleanor Roosevelt's, were on Washington for the inauguration of the new president, John Kennedy, on January 20th. By and large Mrs. Roosevelt was impressed with his performance. She joined the Congress in granting the new leader a honeymoon during which it was hard for him to do anything wrong. Among his early innovations was the first live televised presidential press conference, and Mrs. Roosevelt recognized that no one who had come along in quite a while in American politics was better equipped to shine in such circumstances than JFK. She thought he represented the country and her party well indeed.

There were hopeful and stressful measures to be taken in foreign affairs during the Kennedy honeymoon. In March the new President called upon all nations in the Western Hemisphere to join in an Alliance for Progress, a grand economic development program. At about the same time Kennedy's administration had to take a stand about the increasing presence of Communist Chinese troops in Laos: The expansion of communism did not fit with the promises Kennedy had made in his inaugural address that the United States would go anywhere and do anything necessary to help preserve freedom.

A brighter measure aimed at the same goal was the President's establishment, by executive order later ratified by the Congress, of the Peace Corps. Eleanor Roosevelt was delighted. Late in the year the Agency for International Development was created, another wing of government designed to do what private philanthropy and investment had long done for third world and other distressed areas. Again, Mrs. Roosevelt was pleased: The two new agencies harmonized well with her own lifelong activities and social values.

Soon—in April—one of America's most embarrassing foreign policy disasters on record hit the newspaper headlines. The White House had given its full sanction and cooperation, through the CIA, for a Cuban invasion intended to oust Castro or at least to make secure the U.S. Naval Base at Guantanamo Bay. Most of the participants were Cuban political exiles who wanted to recapture their homeland. The invasion was a military botch within forty-eight hours, and Kennedy had to take the brunt of the blame. He weathered the storm of criticism with surprising aplomb. Mrs. Roosevelt treated the subject discreetly in her column by emphasizing how well the President had done at cleaning up the public relations mess caused by the failed invasion.

The country once again found things to crow about soon enough, but Eleanor Roosevelt was not among those who enthusiastically applauded the news that astronaut Alan Shepard had made the first suborbital flight (300 miles up) by an American. The Soviets had sent a man into orbit about a month earlier, to the chagrin of the American space program. Nor did she applaud Kennedy's bold announcement that the United States would set for itself the goal of landing a man on the moon by the end of the decade. In Mrs. Roosevelt's view there were still far too many unsolved human problems on earth to justify such huge expenditures as the space program would entail.

By midsummer the worldwide concern about the potential spread of Communism was intense enough to push the White House into proposing the biggest military budget on record, including a significant buildup of reserve troop strength. The President wanted to make a clear show of force vis-à-vis the Soviets. A rock-solid symbol of the capitalist-communist standoff was foisted upon the Germans and the world when, in August, the Soviets erected the infamous Berlin Wall to shut off East Berliners from the temptations of the so-called decadent life in democratic, capitalist West Berlin. The free world was appalled.

By 1961 Mrs. Roosevelt had begun to slow down somewhat, yet compared to most people her schedule of trips to AAUN meetings, lecture dates, family visits, and so on still looks like that of an unusually active much-younger person. At seventy-seven she could claim proudly to have visited within the year at least thirty cities and towns in the United States and Canada requiring overnight travel from New York. She did take some vacation this year, but the flow of newspaper columns continued to be steady and impressive.

. . . .

No one in America understood better than Eleanor Roosevelt that the presidency is not a one-man show: it is a team effort, resting on the shoulders of a great many appointees. If the president and his closest advisers do not choose appropriate leaders for each department, no amount of well-honed ideology will suffice as a substitute to give the country a clear direction and successful programs. Mrs. Roosevelt watched the Kennedy appointments process with a critical eye and came away pleased. She saw the outlines of a domestic and foreign policy shaping up in ways she could support, a fact that was a welcome relief to her after eight years of Republicanism. Among those people mentioned in this column is one of Kennedy's most popular choices: John Kenneth Galbraith, the Harvard economist and author whose 1958 book The Affluent Society *had been a best-seller.*

NEW YORK, FEBRUARY 1—It was natural that the Republicans in the Congress should sit in somewhat "cool disapproval," as described in one of our newspapers, during President Kennedy's first State of the Union message. For there were grave differences between the outgoing Republican Administration's point of view on the overall state of the Union at home and abroad and the picture painted by the new President.

For eight years now the people of the United States have been treated like children. They have been told that all is well, and because a majority were still comfortable and we were apparently not actually at war the pleasing picture painted for us was easily acceptable. In the past few months the burden of unemployment has been steadily mounting, however, and signs here and there have pointed to the fact that difficulties were coming to a head both at home and abroad, and the time has come when the American people must be rudely jolted into an acceptance of the fact that we are in trouble.

Much of our ability to meet our problems depends on the people of this country being actually willing to face them. It has been proved over and over again that we are resourceful, vigorous, capable people, and can usually meet any challenge that we really understand. We have been lulled only temporarily, I hope, into indifference and apathy over the past few years. Now the question is whether this has really

. . . .

seriously affected our character as a people or whether we will face the challenge now put before us with zest.

I do not think it will be difficult for our people to understand the challenges at home. We have able economists who can explain the needs not only to our industrial leaders but to our people as a whole.

In the field of foreign affairs, however, the President has perhaps a more difficult challenge. There has been for a longer period certain trends of thought in the State Department that will have to be reversed. President Kennedy has named a wonderful team, but under that team much change must come about in the thinking of many of those who carry out foreign policy both at home and abroad. Certainly, anyone who listened to the State of the Union message or who has read it with care must be impressed by the President's comprehensive grasp of the many problems that face the nation.

There are still many things, of course, that have not yet been thought through in all their implications. I have a feeling that the fundamentals of our defense policy have still not been completely covered. The Peace Corps, it seems to me, should be more closely linked to the defense of the nation than has so far been done so far as one can tell. And our diplomatic approaches to representatives of other nations must be warmer and more flexible, or some of the fundamental things that the Administration wishes to accomplish will be stymied by the wrong people handling policies which they either disagree with or do not understand.

That there is the will in this Administration and the ability to meet the problems before us seems apparent from everything that has so far been said and done. On the whole, every appointment gives one greater confidence in the ability to appraise where definite qualities in the people can be useful.

For instance, the appointment of Dr. Kenneth Galbraith as Ambassador to India is, I think, a most fortunate one. Here is a man with keen understanding, with training in all the areas where India most needs help, a sensitive human being who will, I feel sure, understand the leaders of the Indian nation. Appointments such as this give one hope that the challenges in foreign affairs are going to be met.

Neither the domestic nor the foreign aims set by the President can be accomplished overnight, but that there is a will which has not existed before—a will to face the realities before us at home and abroad and to get the cooperation of the people of the U.S. by telling them the truth—augurs well for the future solutions which the President hopes for.

. . . .

Bold initiative always seemed to Eleanor Roosevelt one of the hallmarks of truly presidential leadership. Her standard, of course, was her own

. . . .

husband's tenure in the White House, especially his remarkable first term, when he seemed to be lifting the country out of its economic doldrums step by steady step, with one new program after another. The problem of how the United States could distribute its food surplus more effectively so as to help the poor at home and abroad was an issue that had troubled Mrs. Roosevelt for years. Kennedy's announcement of a food stamp program struck her as eminently sensible. One of Kennedy's key administrators in this area was a quiet, unassuming man, with a background as a clergyman, hailing from the prairies of South Dakota: George McGovern. At thirty-eight McGovern was typical of the young liberal intelligentsia who came to Washington to join the Kennedy team. McGovern combined compassion with administrative and political know-how to get the job done. He would go on to serve as U.S. Senator from 1963 to 1981 during which time he made a famous bid for the presidency itself as an anti-Vietnam war candidate of the Democratic Party in 1972, losing to Nixon.

NEW YORK, FEBRUARY 3—President Kennedy's second press conference was again, I think, a great success. He is being honest in his answers, which is really the one safeguard in a situation where you can be heard by the entire country and where nothing you say will be forgotten.

I am particularly glad, also, to see that a plan for using food stamps in certain areas is going to be worked out and used here at home to bring about a better distribution of our surplus food. Both Agriculture Secretary Orville L. Freeman and Mr. George McGovern, the Administration's director of the food for peace program, must be getting knowledge all the way down the line—from their civil service subordinates who are the ones acquainted with the past and the present most intimately. They no doubt have knowledge that was available in the recent past but which they had not been called on to give.

Food stamps, under the plan now suggested, would be issued through local authorities to needy families who can use them to get designated foods at regular markets, and already the list of foods to be available has been increased. This will be in addition to the expansion of the regular distribution of food to the needy which the President ordered the day after he took office.

All this and much more shows that action is coming in the wake of words and I think the country is beginning to feel the lift of knowing that something is being done to meet our problems. Everything may not work out perfectly, but one does have the feeling that there will be no letup in effort until solutions are found.

From Waltham, outside Boston, where Mrs. Roosevelt was attending a Brandeis University trustees meeting, she filed a column that included comments about a man destined to become a martyr to one of her own most serious causes, civil rights. Though the outlines of Dr. Martin Luther King, Jr.'s thinking about race problems in America were already clear at this time, he was still on the way up to the heights he achieved as an organizer, an orator, almost as a saint in the civil rights movement. Mrs. Roosevelt recognized his talent.

WALTHAM, MASS., FEBRUARY 6—In the past few days I have twice had the opportunity of hearing Dr. Martin Luther King speak—once at the annual Roosevelt dinner of the Americans for Democratic Action, on Thursday night, and again on Friday afternoon in New York at a meeting at Mrs. Dorothy Norman's home.

Dr. King is a very moving speaker. He is simple and direct, and the spiritual quality which has made him the leader of nonviolence in this country touches every speech he makes. He speaks, of course, for that Southern organization which is gradually gaining support all over the United States—the Congress of Racial Equality, known as CORE. Its new national director, James Farmer, impresses me as a very intelligent and capable man.

....

The ideas behind "My Day" columns were frequently sparked by Eleanor Roosevelt's voracious reading of newspapers. All her life in New York she read on a daily basis several of the city's livelier papers. (At most points there were at least three serious newspapers from which to choose.) Whenever she traveled, Eleanor read the local newspapers too, for in the editorials and in the papers' particular slants on the news she could find out what public (or at least news media) opinion outside New York really was. And whenever she could get them, Eleanor perused foreign newspapers as well. Among her favorites are two mentioned in this column. Looking at L'Express from Paris was one of her ways of keeping her skill in French active. Not to have a usable second language was, in Eleanor Roosevelt's estimation, unacceptable and simply lazy.

NEW YORK, FEBRUARY 22—In reading the Manchester Guardian of Great Britain the other day I came across an interesting article by John Cole, who reports that the Labor Party is now demanding that South Africa's membership in the Commonwealth be suspended until it agrees to change its racial policies.

Also over the week-end I read in the French newspaper L'Express

....

an interesting article about the one man who seems to be the possible successful negotiator between various factions in Algeria and also between Algerians and the French government. He is Ferhat Abbas, and his aim always has been to find solutions without violence.

. . . .

As Eleanor Roosevelt aged, her lifelong distaste for military conflict as a way to resolve international disagreements hardened into a philosophical position. The frequency with which her calls for disarmament appear in "My Day" columns rose as the years went by. The threat of worldwide extinction by atomic or hydrogen bomb accounts for much of this shift in attitude. But even more than that it was Mrs. Roosevelt's cumulative sense of loss, when she thought of all the young men and women in so many countries—friendly and enemy—who had been killed or maimed in the wars she had known. (She had been fourteen years old when the Spanish–American war broke out in 1898; thirty when World War I came in 1914; fifty-five when World War II began in 1939; and sixty-six at the outset of the Korean War in 1950.)

NEW YORK, FEBRUARY 27—Along with a group of young people, I was invited the other evening to a screening of the film "The Bridge," which has won several awards in Europe. It is the story of a group of young German recruits late in World War II, when Hitler became desperate and began calling up boys only 16 years old. The film depicts their exploits in a heroic light, and one can understand that it would give the German youth a sense of love of country and pride in the idealism and courage of its young soldiers. But the story's exaggerations make the film hardly believable, and apart from propaganda purposes I can see little real value in it.

One of the boys looked at me for a moment and then asked the inevitable question: "If you know that war has been like what we have just watched, and you are still talking about the possibility of any kind of war, we find it hard to understand. It seems to me that war would be unthinkable to those who knew that the results were such as those we have just seen."

This is a difficult statement to answer, for it involves our distrust of each other in different parts of the world, as well as the difficulties in general of developing understanding. In the last analysis, it does force you to think whether the older generations—which have seen as many as three wars—have really put enough emphasis on the need for enhancing the value of human life, and on the need for a clearer understanding both of the harm that has come through past wars and the futility of now contemplating suicide in so many areas of the world.

The first step, I think, toward a greater understanding of the world's

. . . .

problems is to broaden all of our thinking. These are problems which no longer affect only one nation but the world as a whole. Certainly, we are the one nation that ought to be able to think in comprehensive world terms. We have no need to seek more territory, nor have we any reason to be jealous of any other nation in the world. We are powerful, resourceful and inventive.

We are now, for example, talking of a "peace force," but are we not thinking on too small a scale? Why is the Peace Corps not part of a whole new defense plan which touches the lives of every American citizen, making it essential that in youth each of us learns to give some service to our country at home or abroad? After we go on to our own work in the world, we Americans should still hold to that sense of obligation to serve. We should live up to our own beliefs, giving others in many lands the opportunity of choosing between the products we produce, both cultural and material, and that which is produced by others who hold different views. Above everything, we must insist that we learn to live together in the future and that the primary aim of a nation is no longer to learn to die for one's country. It is more difficult, but far more necessary, to learn to live for one's country.

. . . .

By now Mrs. Roosevelt's opposition to the idea of giving federal aid to private schools (in particular to Catholic parochial schools) was well known. What is interesting in this column is the argument she makes against the whole idea of private education in the first place. Eleanor Roosevelt herself was a product of elite private schools in America and Europe. Her husband, children, and scores of relatives and close friends and their children had all attended the finest prep schools in America. Yet here we find her arguing that the country and most individuals would be better off if everybody went to public school. This is a burst of thinking characterized by a strong populist and leveling impulse not seen often elsewhere in Mrs. Roosevelt's writing.

WALTHAM, MASS., MARCH 6—High officials of the Roman Catholic Church in the United States have announced that they will press for an amendment of the Kennedy Administration's education bill to add provisions for long-term federal loans to private schools. According to newspaper stories, the officials, who include cardinals, archbishops and bishops, took the position that unless some such provisions were included they would fight passage of the measure. Interestingly enough, top churchmen of no other denomination have come out with such demands for federal aid to private and religious schools.

I believe that in this matter we must go back to Jefferson's original concept. A democracy must provide for public education since it is a

. . . .

form of government that could not function without education. But from our nation's earliest days the specifications were that our public schools were to be open to all children in the U.S. on an equal basis. Our great concern at the present time should be to make sure that all of our citizens profit from this original concept, and, further, that we do not continue the type of segregation which has made it impossible for some of our people to be the educated citizens that Jefferson felt were a necessity in a democracy.

Throughout our history, those who have wanted to send their children to church schools or to private schools have done so at their own expense. In point of fact, however, the great majority of our children in the U.S. have been educated in the public schools.

I personally think that the public schools would probably be better if all of us felt an obligation to send our children there, except under certain specific conditions. I can see the value of private schools, for example, as laboratories where experiments in education can be more easily tried than in the public-school system. Ever here, however, I begin to think as the years go by that these gains are counteracted by the lack of more universal interest on the part of parents who send their children to private schools because they feel that greater opportunities in the education field may be found there along the lines they wish.

It is true that the large number of Roman Catholic children attending religious schools in this country does put a burden on their church. It is therefore perhaps not strange for the church to feel that when they remove a large number of children from the public schools they should be compensated for so doing. Yet from the beginning in the United States there has been a very strong feeling on the separation of church and state. Indeed, when efforts of the present kind are made to blur this separation, it hurts the real freedom of religion which should exist in our country. I believe such freedom can not exist to a full extent if religion is put into channels against which there is an almost automatic feeling of disapproval among large numbers of people in this country.

. . . .

What to think about Fidel Castro? Liberals in Congress and elsewhere in American politics were caught in a bind when, in 1959, the revolutionary guerrilla leader surprised the world by overthrowing the right-wing Batista regime that had successfully courted American favors for years. Castro emerged as a charismatic orator and brilliant propogandist. His Marxist-Leninist program was totalitarian and benefited the working class by redistributing wealth formerly held by the middle class.

Those in America who recognized how repressive the Batista regime

. . . .

had been and who favored a better deal for Cuban workers had to be pleased. At the same time, Castro's cozy relationship with the Kremlin made everyone nervous. At this point we see Mrs. Roosevelt acknowledging the validity of Castro's revolution and of the claims that the Batista regime had been backed by American capitalists with vested interests in the Cuban economy. What the White House and CIA were planning for Cuba in about two weeks was still unknown to Mrs. Roosevelt, as it was to the rest of the country.

HYDE PARK, APRIL 12—In all probability the Cuban situation will come up for discussion before long in the United Nations. In the meantime we hear, day by day, one rumor after another of people being trained to invade Cuba as guerrillas. Yet we know, and they must know, that unless they get cooperation from Cubans themselves on the island there will be little chance of overthrowing Castro's regime.

The objectives of the revolutionary government, as Castro stated them in the beginning, certainly met with complete approval from the people of Cuba. The Cuban people had been exploited by business groups from many countries, including the United States. Money had been made there and a corrupt government had profited, but the people themselves saw no benefits coming to them from whatever was taken out of their country. Certainly, the United States could not quarrel with the objectives of the revolution as they were stated and we could certainly not expect the Cuban people not to uphold this revolution.

This, however, is no longer a Cuban affair only. One difficulty has arisen perhaps partly because of the shortsightedness of the U.S. government. Now it is the growing influence of the Soviet Union that frightens not only the U.S. but the whole Western Hemisphere. All the assurances that come from Dr. Castro that he is not a tool of the Communists sound somewhat empty. They leave one unconvinced when one has watched Soviet infiltration and growing Soviet control in other areas of the world.

I am glad to see that President Kennedy has ruled out the use of American troops in any invasion of Cuba. But let us hope that the Cuban people themselves will begin to question how much control is being handed over to the Soviet Union. Dr. Castro might find it to his own benefit to talk this whole question over with President Kennedy, who would perhaps be able to throw some light on the willingness of the Soviets to step in and take over control while they insist that they are in no way tying strings to any of their aid.

. . . .

When the Russians put Sputnik (the first satellite) into orbit on October 4, 1957, the event sent shockwaves through the United States' scientific,

. . . .

*academic and political communities: How could the U.S. have allowed
its arch rival in the Cold War to pull off such a technological coup? To
a large degree, America was still playing catch-up four years later when
the Soviets again had a space breakthrough. Russian cosmonaut Yuri
Gagarin became the first man to fly in earth orbit, riding a space capsule
called Vostok 1. It was an impressive technical triumph and a courageous voyage, but it left Mrs. Roosevelt cold. Not only did she feel that
space-program dollars (or rubles) would be better spent on solving earthly
problems, but she was convinced that cooperation through the UN made
far more sense than engaging in an international competition of space
exploration.*

NEW YORK, APRIL 14—It is certainly almost breathtaking to think that
a man flew into space and was gone 108 minutes circling the earth
and during the trip talked to the ground by radio.

I don't know, of course, what this means to scientists. It means little
of interest to me except that the world is becoming smaller and smaller.
In time, I suppose, we will find some real reason for wanting to communicate with the other planets—if there are human beings living on
them. It will be exciting to find if their ways of life are better and more
interesting than ours and it will certainly add new dimensions to our
whole existence.

The fact that we in the United States should not be prepared to send
a man into space as yet seems to me quite unimportant. This is the
kind of thing in any case which should be under the sponsorship of
the United Nations and information which is of value should be shared
by all nations.

I am sure that there are matters of climate and perhaps many things
which I do not know about which should be of value to the world as
a whole, and this should certainly not be controlled by one nation
alone.

That is why it seems to me important that agreements should be
reached in the United Nations and that all information should be centered there for the use of the world as a whole.

We certainly congratulate the Soviet Union and can quite understand that the students at Moscow University held a celebration.

The Soviets, naturally, have great pride in being first to achieve
scientific advances which some of us look upon as more or less in-
comprehensible developments but which we feel sure will eventually
have more meaning to all of us.

. . . .

*It has always been difficult for middle-of-the-road political thinkers in
America to fathom why anyone would ever freely choose to support a*

275

Communist regime. Because such an attitude cannot be comprehended, so the argument goes, it must not really be true. And if it is not true, one can then assume with confidence that workers and peasants living under a Communist regime would rather have a democracy—and, by extension, would welcome to their country swarming bands of liberators should any be available in the outside world.

It is to Eleanor Roosevelt's credit as a foreign policy analyst that she did not swallow this too-easy line of thinking—as the CIA and White House did when they decided to back an invasion of Cuba by frustrated Cuban exiles based in Florida. Also to her credit and, as she says, to President Kennedy's after the fiasco, is the fact that once the abortive invasion was over, she was quick to recommend that America admit its mistakes and make reparations.

NEW YORK, APRIL 24—From the newspaper accounts it would seem that our Central Intelligence Agency was not very well-informed as to the internal situation in Cuba. One account suggested that on the one hand we had underestimated Castro's hold on the people of Cuba, and, on the other, that those who might have wanted to revolt would be unable to do so, since the government had become a police state.

I wonder if we are not falling back on this second idea and ignoring the fact that there may be large groups of people in Cuba who find themselves in better condition today than they were under Batista. It is difficult, of course, to find out. Yet, from what one reads, the exiles seem to be drawn largely from the intellectual and business groups of Cuba, whereas conditions among the poorer people may be such that Castro has been able to improve the hopes they hold for a better life. In that case, the greater number of people would not be inclined to join with the rebels. Since a successful invasion in this instance depended upon an uprising among the masses in Cuba, it should have been evident to our people that this undertaking was premature.

Lies are evidently easy to fabricate in the present atmosphere of Cuba. Dr. Raul Roa of Cuba charged that a Sherman tank was involved in the landing on Giron Beach, but it now turns out that the tank actually was one of Russian make. Again, an American Social Security number, given as proof that it was an American pilot who was shot down in Cuba this week, turns out to be a number belonging to a Connecticut cabinetmaker who has never flown a plane and says he has no interest in Cuban politics!

On the whole, it seems to me that even though the President's statement was correct that no American would take part in a Cuban landing, still we were involved in a way. This is perhaps not conductive to giving other nations the feeling that we are actually going to consult with the other Latin American states on all matters concerning our neighbors in this hemisphere, and that we will not act on our own.

Certainly, the votes in the United Nations have not been encouraging. We lost out on the resolution to have the inter-American organizations use their good offices to negotiate the difficulties between Cuba and ourselves. Even more serious, our Latin American friends at first refused to go along with the resolution for financial support to the U.N. in the Congo situation, and agreed only after an all-night session.

....

President Kennedy spent much time and effort in the early months of his new administration trying to instill in his fellow citizens a new sense of the drama of their moment in history. He issued numerous calls for sacrifice in the name of justice and peace. Yet his own administration would produce the greatest-ever peacetime military budget, and he would advocate an expensive and exotic space program as a national priority that could not help but overshadow more humble goals such as eliminating hunger or illiteracy. Mrs. Roosevelt was moved by the new president's fervor. His values seemed essentially right to her. Nonetheless, as the next two columns show, her own values were more than slightly different.

HYDE PARK, MAY 1—In his Chicago speech on Friday night, President Kennedy declared that the goal of his Administration and his programs is to build an America which will fulfill its own promise of greatness. He added that in doing so the nation would "prove to a turbulent world that human welfare in the context of human freedom is the foundation of the future of the race. We would like to show here a civilization where every citizen is free to pursue those goals which his talents and his capacity permit, unhindered by artificial barriers of ignorance or prejudice."

This means, as I see it, that the President believes we must set our own house in order. Since we are engaged in a worldwide struggle with another ideology, we must realize that guns never really change ideas. We must have new ideas to fight those in which we do not believe, and the place to demonstrate what we believe and what we can do for people is here at home.

....

The American space program—a Kennedy-administration top priority—was running almost neck-and-neck with the Soviets'. The first United States manned suborbital flight occurred on May 5, as astronaut Alan Shepard rode a Mercury program space capsule and splashed down

....

to safety in the Atlantic Ocean. Universally and instantly recognized as an American hero, Shepard won Eleanor Roosevelt's applause as well, although she had her reservations about the short-term value of exploring even nearby "outer space."

HYDE PARK, MAY 8—Commander Alan Shepard's flight into space was exciting news. For us this is the beginning of more and more experiments until the day comes when we will know whether there is human life on the stars and what it is like, if so.

I must say, however, that this seems to me some time off. I am still more concerned with what happens to us here on earth and what we make of our life here than I am about these remarkable experiments. I know they have great value, and undoubtedly important discoveries arising from these experiments will help us here on earth. But I hope we are particularly careful not to send our man into orbit as the Russians did until we are sure that the return has been safeguarded as far as is humanly possible. The differences between our system and that of the Russians is a regard for human life, and I do not want to see us lose any of this regard.

We must congratulate astronaut Shepard—and, incidentally, his wife—for the courage and endurance in the training period leading up to this triumph. Let us hope that all those who carry forward these extraordinary achievements will come home as successfully to receive a grateful nation's acclaim.

....

This column demonstrates Eleanor Roosevelt's liveliness of mind at age seventy-six, when by most people's standards a view of the world based on long-established habits would seem not only likely but also forgivable. Not so for Mrs. Roosevelt. In her meeting with the new Secretary of HEW, Abraham Ribicoff, she showed an admirable capacity to let go of old models for social assistance and for considering creative new alternatives. Her concept of a junior Peace Corps for the domestic scene contributed to the development by the Kennedy administration of what later became VISTA—staffed not by high schoolers but nonetheless bringing home to the United States the same attitudes and skills the Peace Corps itself was just then beginning to spread throughout the third world.

NEW YORK, MAY 17—When I was in Washington last week Mr. Abraham Ribicoff, Secretary for Health, Education and Welfare, was kind enough to see me, and I was impressed, as I always am, by the infinite patience that a public official has to have. There are always so many people who want to see the head of a department—just to talk about

....

the one small thing they are interested in—and I often wonder if the real work that the man himself wants to do does not have to be done after the regular working hours are over.

The world has changed and our situation has changed. Organizations that were needed 20 years ago might not be needed at all today or might be much more efficient today if certain changes could be made. Mr. Ribicoff said he needed time and discussion and advice from a number of people before he could make up his mind what were the basic changes it would be wise to make.

He spoke of the fact that my husband had inaugurated a certain number of things that had proved successful in meeting certain situations at the time. And I was glad of the opportunity to tell him that I hoped there would be no feeling that tradition demanded duplication of the past.

For instance, there is talk, which I hope will materialize in action, of creating for our high-school youngsters a "domestic corps," somewhat similar to the Peace Corps. This seems to me a very good idea, but I sincerely hope no one will blindly insist on following the setup of the original Civilian Conservation Corps camps that were established during my husband's term of office.

The CCC camps were very necessary for that day and had to be organized in the way they were, but if we now organize camps with the same objectives of doing soil conservation, forestry work and rehabilitation in depressed areas, there will certainly be better ways of organizing than we could arrange for in the days of the Depression and certainly a better program on the educational side can be devised.

. . . .

One phase of an ordinary mortal's life conspicuously missing from Eleanor Roosevelt's was retirement. As though her regular schedule of newspaper writing, book writing, lecturing, working for the AAUN, and keeping innumerable social and philanthropic dates were not enough, she periodically still let herself take on other responsibilities. In the next two columns we find her engaged in some ad hoc, extracurricular international diplomacy.

Following the Bay of Pigs fiasco in Cuba, there were many prisoners of war the U.S. wanted to retrieve but was hamstrung to do so effectively because of its weakened diplomatic position in dealing with a triumphant, defiant Fidel Castro. Mrs. Roosevelt was persuaded that she could help. The respect she had commanded as a negotiator at the UN underlay the idea of asking her to join a citizens' committee that would try to work out a plan to buy back the prisoners by shipping to Cuba a much-needed supply of farm tractors. The idea was to get the outline

. . . .

of a deal worked out, then to turn the matter over to the White House and Congress for implementation.

But what rarely happened in Eleanor Roosevelt's long diplomatic experience did happen here. The whole project backfired, with Mrs. Roosevelt and her two fellow committee members coming in for quite a blast of criticism from Congress where it was felt that they had overstepped their bounds.

Serving on the committee with Mrs. Roosevelt were Dr. Milton Eisenhower, the former President's brother and himself a prominent educator, and labor leader Walter Reuther, president, AFL–CIO.

BOSTON, MAY 26—Early last Monday morning I took a plane to Washington to sit in on the first meeting of the Peace Corps. My day was slightly complicated by the fact that Premier Fidel Castro has sent over 10 of the prisoners he held from the recent invasion, with the proviso that if they got a firm agreement for us to send 500 tractors to Cuba they could stay over four days after Tuesday noon to make any detailed arrangements for the liberation of some 1,200 men captured during the invasion. If they got no firm commitment, they were to return Tuesday at noon, and they had given their word of honor to do so. I met with Dr. Milton Eisenhower, the head of Johns Hopkins University, and Mr. Walter Reuther to discuss the next steps in the Cuban situation.

It was decided that as the Cuban prisoners were being flown to Washington by the immigration authorities and would arrive at 1:30 that we should have a meeting with them at that time and not see the press until we had heard from the prisoners exactly what Premier Castro's offer was and we had decided what our answer would be. We felt quite sure that we must ask for a list of the 1,214 (or whatever number above that it might be) prisoners and that some provision of verification should be made as they returned to the United States and to whatever countries they wished to go. For the rest we would wait.

At 1:30 Mr. Reuther, Dr. Eisenhower and I met with these 10 men. One or two of them were very young. Most of them were in command of some unit. They were all intelligent and fine-looking men. They told us exactly what had happened. Immediately after a Premier Castro speech early last week they asked to meet with him and they gave their word that if allowed to come over to the United States they would return. They were elected by their fellow prisoners.

They gave us in detail Castro's offer and he added that he wished it understood that he was not making an exchange of men for machines but was asking for indemnity for the damage done by the invasion. The world will make its own decision on this particular point, and it seems to me unimportant, since the machines must be delivered or we cannot save men's lives.

We made a firm commitment, but we asked to send a committee of experts back with the men when they go because it seemed to us that the type of tractors asked for by Castro were not suitable for the uses he said he wanted them for. We will try to get experts in agriculture and machinery to return with the group.

We immediately asked Mr. Joseph M. Dodge, who for a time in President Eisenhower's Administration was Director of the Budget and is now living in Detroit, to be treasurer of our group. And we are making an appeal to the country as a whole to raise $15 million. As the tractors are delivered the men will be returned on the same ships. We have asked that the procedure for verifying the list of prisoners which we have asked for shall be worked out along with the manner of the exchange.

I hope all of you who care about human lives, for whom I think we have some responsibility, will send your contributions to Tractors for Freedom, Freedom Box, Detroit, Mich.

HYDE PARK, MAY 29—In the Congress it may not be very popular to be trying to free those who landed on the beach and were captured in Cuba. But the people of this country seem not only to want freedom for their soldiers but to be anxious to help the farmers of Cuba. It is good to know that there is kindly feeling for the Cuban people all over the United States.

I must say I have been completely surprised by the reaction in Congress. None of the three members of our committee ignored the Logan Act, which forbids individuals to negotiate with foreign governments, and there was consultation with our government before any announcement was made of a reply to President Castro. That a humanitarian gesture by our people in response to an offer by the leader of a small nation like Cuba could be considered as an act of weakness on the part of our people or of our government, however, is beyond my understanding. The United States has too much strength and too much dignity, it seems to me, ever to consider an action which will save lives and help the people of a small and neighboring country as an act of weakness. Rather it seems to me to be the action of a strong nation and its people to help the people of a weaker nation.

There is no comparison with such a situation as occurred during the Hitler regime in Germany. Then an exchange was offered of human lives for trucks, but the war was on and this was war materiel. No answer at that time could of course be made. The only similarity that can be noted in the two offers is that some types of minds seem to link together human lives and machinery. President Castro has been careful to state, however, that he considered the tractors are to benefit the farmers, to help them grow more food and raise their standard of living; hence, he considers the machines as an "indemnification" for any harm done during the invasion. Since the harm done was comparatively slight, indemnification may be somewhat exaggerated. But this was the way the offer was made, and the people of the United States do not seem to quibble about what they pay if they can free human lives. President Castro stated that if the prisoners did not return from the U.S. with a firm agreement, they would serve from 30–35 years of hard labor.

The reaction of South American countries seems to be in sympathy with the people of the U.S. There have been student demonstrations and collections are apparently being taken up to add to this fund. Mr. Reuther, Dr. Milton Eisenhower and I were not the only ones who wanted to do something in answer to President Castro's offer. There were already started a number of different groups who want to collect money for this purpose. I think most of the people will send what they collect to Tractors for Freedom, P. O. Box Freedom, Detroit, Michigan.

I am indeed saddened by the attitude of some of the members of the Senate and the House. Had it been only an attack on the part of Republican members, I might have felt that it savored of partisan politics. But that is not true, so I realize it is a genuine difference of opinion. I regret it particularly where I have high esteem for those who are in opposition.

I do not believe that there is any weakness or kow-towing to President Castro in taking up his offer, nor do I think it hurts the dignity of the U.S. in any way. Neither do I think that the law of the land is flouted by the manner in which this is being done. I not only believe in obeying the law but I hope that respect for the law is going to grow in our own country, since we are the nation who would like to see a world governed by law rather than by force.

I fully realize, however, that even where the law is concerned it is man-made and people must live according to their consciences. With the deepest respect for those who differ, therefore, I still am glad that the three of us serving on this committee felt our consciences dictated some kind of action in view of the responsibility we carried. I hope very much that the great warmth of response from the people of the United States will in the end be of great service to our country.

. . . .

A frequent theme in Mrs. Roosevelt's thinking about the possibility of substantial disarmament was the economic question of what would happen to the workers and natural resources being devoted to military

. . . .

activity if the country were ever to lean in the opposite direction, toward peace. Over the years she considered this question from many angles, sometimes writing about the need for re-education of workers in the military, sometimes suggesting concrete ways that certain military-oriented companies could turn their energies to peacetime production. She found in a speech delivered by her favorite political leader of mid-century, Adlai Stevenson, a fine discussion of the topic on broad terms and wanted to pass along his best thoughts to her readers. Eleanor Roosevelt heartily agreed with Adlai Stevenson: to make the hoped-for conversion in the economy, government and industry must together invest in planning ahead.

HYDE PARK, JULY 12—One of the arguments constantly brought up as regards the sincerity of the United States in desiring disarmament is the point that our economy could not stand giving up the continuation of full military production. And very important to the overall picture on disarmament was the statement made in Geneva by Mr. Adlai Stevenson, who heads our delegation.

In a speech before the Economic and Social Council he said that an accord to limit arms would provide the opportunity to turn "our resources from production of instruments of death to the production of the manifold things we need for a better life for our own citizens and for the citizens of other nations."

In his speech he recognized the fact that a changeover period that comes abruptly nearly always causes a time of disruption, but if it is planned for it can be accomplished very quickly and the difficulties can be minimized.

I was interested to read that Mr. Stevenson said such plans are really being considered in Washington. I hope they will be carried out to the point where business, particularly the big business of mass production for war, will know exactly step by step what they will be able to do and what world needs they will begin to fill. There are needs all over the world crying out for consideration, and I don't believe we have reached the point of pinpointing what our great industries could do if they turned their energies from military production to production to meet certain basic needs throughout the world.

Mr. Stevenson also said that Washington hoped the day would come when preparation for a changeover would not be merely an "academic exercise," and then he added that from our point of view there was "no higher priority than genuine disarmament and the building of greater confidence and trust among the great powers, who have life and death for the human race in their hands."

Mr. Stevenson's speech must have been of great interest to many of the representatives of the 18 countries present who represent different areas of the world. It must have given hope that even though we are telling our Soviet adversaries that we will take stock of our military situation and prevent any deterioration that will tempt them to such acts in the Berlin crisis as might lead to war, nevertheless our aim and objective is—and will always be—peaceful accommodation and development for the good of the human race as a whole.

....

Mrs. Roosevelt had written earlier about the value of bilingual education; here she advocates a kind of bilingual citizenship test. Her discussion in this case and in previous columns about foreign-language skills emphasizes the positive side of the issue. She saw no reason to put anyone down simply because he or she could not speak or write English. The other side of this debate, in education and in the courts (concerning citizenship tests), was that without a common language, the culture might tend toward fragmentation; that without an ability to use the common language, a student or a citizen would be shut out of normal political discourse and disqualified for many jobs. It is a bit surprising that Mrs. Roosevelt did not take up these aspects of a highly complex question.

NEW YORK, JULY 14—There is a very interesting civil case coming up soon in the New York State courts. It involves the question of the right to vote on the part of a Puerto Rican citizen who was educated in American history and government under the American flag in Puerto Rico, but in the Spanish language—not the English language. Here on the mainland he must take a literacy test in the English language before he would be granted the privilege to exercise his right to vote.

It will be interesting to see the outcome of this case, for it will affect a large number of people who came here as grown-ups and who are American citizens, trained under the American flag and having all the essentials required to pass a literacy test which includes a knowledge of our history—except that they speak only the Spanish language.

Somehow it seems to me this is an important test. I can only believe that when we have citizens whose native tongue may be anything but our accepted English and whose tradition should allow them all the rights of citizenship, including the use of their own language for qualification as voters, that they should be allowed to exercise that right.

....

Should anyone have any doubts that in 1961 Eleanor Roosevelt was still a sprightly woman with a sense of humor, full of enthusiasm for her favorite political candidates, this excerpt from the column of August

....

30, *should put those doubts to rest. Mrs. Roosevelt had supported Robert F. Wagner, Jr. in the New York City mayor's office throughout his tenure, which began in 1954. But it wasn't just this Robert Wagner's work she admired. The mayor's late father had been a longtime U.S. senator from New York and an ardent supporter of FDR's New Deal, particularly with effective labor legislation.*

The column for September 1 once more indicates the pleasure Eleanor Roosevelt took in traversing the city (here she is on the Upper East Side) and hobnobbing with other lively Democrats such as Adlai Stevenson who, as so often in the past, charmed her with a witty remark.

NEW YORK, AUGUST 30—I have been attending meetings this week— some indoors and some on street corners—on behalf of Mayor Robert F. Wagner in his campaign for re-election.

When one is making these short speeches, climbing up a ladder onto a sound truck and trying to speak above other noises of passing traffic, I often wonder how much sense one really makes.

HYDE PARK, SEPTEMBER 1—The other evening in my touring around the city in New York's mayoralty campaign I suddenly found myself a guest with Adlai Stevenson at one stop. This was a rally to raise money for the reform club in the Yorkville section of the city. It happened that Mr. Stevenson, like myself, had a warm interest in young Harry Sedwick, who is running for one of the local district leader offices, and I surmise that our Ambassador to the UN was also brought into this local situation by some younger member of his family!

This happens to us all, but with his usual wit Adlai Stevenson told us how in every political situation he had been admonished not to get into local politics and now his inclination was to rise and say, "Gentlemen, I wish to say a few words to you on disarmament."

However, when it came his turn he explained his particular interest in the young candidate and his genuine interest in good government, and it was as usual a pleasure to listen to him. I think perhaps it gave him an amusing interlude from the more serious business of the special session of the UN.

Mrs. Roosevelt would have defended to the death the principles that speech should be free, that anyone lobbying for a cause should have access to advertising space in the news media. At the same time it annoyed her greatly when she saw industrial lobbies organizing vast war chests of funds to pay for disinformation campaigns directed at an unsuspecting public. One such, in her opinion, was the lobbying effort by the pharmaceutical industry, designed to keep consumers believing that only brand-name medicines could help them heal or find relief.

The idea that generic drugs, priced much lower, might serve just as well had been around for a long time but had not found a champion in Congress until Senator Estes Kefauver of Tennessee (Stevenson's running mate in 1956) took charge of the issue. Mrs. Roosevelt, of course, was perceived by many throughout the land, especially the elderly and the dispossessed, as a one-woman lobby for their causes. The fight to make low-cost generic medicines available was a natural one for Eleanor Roosevelt to join.

NEW YORK, SEPTEMBER 8—Senator Kefauver and Representative Emanuel Celler of New York have sponsored a drug industry antitrust bill (S 1552) that will go a very long way toward correcting many of the abuses and deficiencies of current practice. This bill would have the effect of increasing competition and diminishing the temptation to fix prices. It would put teeth into the regulation and control of drug manufacture by the Food and Drug Administration. It would make better known to physicians those drugs which are potentially dangerous and, most important, it would stimulate prescriptions by generic name through the provision of long-overdue central control over the naming of drugs.

Prescribing drugs by generic name was first advocated by the Citizens' Committee for Children of New York in its own intensive study of the impact of modern prescription drugs on the family budget, made some three years ago prior to the Kefauver investigations.

The director of one large hospital indicated in his testimony before the committee that prescription by generic name would result in savings annually of tens of millions of dollars and would reduce drug costs in his own hospital by some 40 percent.

The raising and policing of standards and the encouragement of prescribing by generic name would, in itself, be sufficient reason for enthusiastic support of the Kefauver–Celler bill. But the strong, well-financed drug industry lobby continues to becloud the issue for the newspaper reading public.

. . . .

Mrs. Roosevelt spent most of her days wrestling with questions and issues on a big scale, but she had a disciplined ability for paying attention to details as well. She recognized that in human relations the details of our behavior with one another eventually add up to either a positive impression or a negative one. Although she was quick to forgive others when minor slip-ups caused her displeasure, Eleanor Roosevelt set an unusually high standard for herself. It didn't matter whether she was dealing with a congressman or a cab driver.

CHICAGO, OCTOBER 4—I hope I will be forgiven if I inject a little story in this column which is a confession of guilt. I am writing it because I hope that the wrong I inadvertently did may be rectified if my victim should happen to read this column. I realize it is purely of interest in New York City, but perhaps the rest of my readers will be amused and forgive my turning to something so personal.

About two days ago I left a taxi to go into a shop. I thought the driver could back into a place by the curb and wait for me, and I thought he understood I was coming right out and that this was what I expected him to do. There was 60 cents due on the meter when I got out.

I was only a short time giving my order in the store and I came out to find no taxi. I wandered up and down the block, stood at the corners and looked and finally a gentleman getting out of a taxi, thinking I was looking for one, offered me his. In desperation I took it, explaining to my driver that I was still looking, as we drove slowly away, for my original taxi.

I cheated that driver out of 60 cents, plus a tip, and I feel guilty. So, I would be grateful if, on the chance that particular driver sees this item of confession, he would send me a note telling me where I could reimburse him.

I use taxis so much in New York City that most of the drivers know where I live, but it might be difficult for someone who does not know to find out and come to collect his money. So, I make this confession in the hope, which I realize is very slight, that my unintentional dishonesty can be rectified.

. . . .

Historian Arnold Toynbee is credited with the provocative remark "Those who refuse to study the past are condemned to repeat it," and Eleanor Roosevelt could not have agreed more heartily. She had seen in America and elsewhere (here the case in point is Germany) a kind of willful amnesia in which the terrors and mistakes of the past (slavery, genocide) were wiped out from memory. With those painful memories gone, she feared, similar errors of judgment could easily begin all over again.

From the time of World War I onwards Germany stood in Mrs. Roosevelt's mind in a special category: an aggressor nation the morality of whose leading people could not fully be trusted. Nazism confirmed her worst suspicions about the dark side of the German culture and collective conscience. She had heard all the standard explanations for the

. . . .

rise of National Socialism and then Nazism and the holocaust under Hitler's regime, and even when these explanations made some political sense, they never added up, in Eleanor Roosevelt's opinion, to an acceptable ethical excuse.

In an unusually serious tone in the next column, Mrs. Roosevelt once again takes Germany to task. The occasion was her reaction to a film that stunned the public. The war crimes trials that were the subject of the film were conducted at Nuremburg, Germany in 1945 and 1946.

NEW YORK, NOVEMBER 1—The other night I had the good fortune to see a preview of a film which will not be shown publicly throughout the United States until December and then it will be released simultaneously in several other countries. It is called "Judgment at Nuremberg"—a Stanley Kramer production that stars Spencer Tracy, Marlene Dietrich and any number of other very fine actors and actresses who have given outstanding performances.

It must have taken courage to produce this film at this time—a time when most of us have forgotten what went on in Germany before and during World War II, let alone having any recollection of World War I.

As the film unrolled I could not help remembering an incident when, after World War II, I met a woman in devastated Germany with whom I had warm and affectionate ties. We had roomed together many years ago in a school in England for nearly two years. I asked her how she could have supported Hitler, with her strong Christian feeling of the obligation to live according to Christ's teachings. Had she known what her people were doing to the Jews?

This was her answer: "You people are as responsible as we Germans are. We were humiliated after World War I. Hitler seemed to give us back some of our dignity. When we began to have an inkling of what was really happening, he had complete control. And so we never looked over the hill and we never knew what was going on in Germany."

In this film we see portrayed one of the last trials at Nuremberg and the attitude and performance of the postwar German people. There were no Nazis. They had all hated Hitler. Couldn't the Americans understand that they were good, fine people who would never have countenanced such cruelties had they known about them?

The effort of the charming woman to win over our chief judge is an interesting study. She was so plausible, so sweet, but it made me think of things which we in America should remember today. The old judge was not won over or fooled because he was steeped in American traditions of justice. Many of those around him had lost their ability to think clearly and live up to their own standards. The ease, the charm of the young German woman; the agreeable, friendly men—how could they have really done what they did?

But in speaking to the repentant German judge the old American of Maine said: "You went wrong when you allowed your first man, whom you knew to be innocent, to go to death."

After watching the trial and listening to the eloquent pleas on both sides and having heard the old judge's final summing up, in which only one of his colleagues concurred but which condemned the four German judges to imprisonment for life, there comes the final statement on the screen: "Not one single man condemned in these trials, and not one of these men sentenced, is still serving his sentence in Germany today."

It was hard for me to believe a short time ago when I was told that 80 percent of the men serving in government positions today in Germany were once in Nazi government positions. It is always explained that of course they could look nowhere else for competent people, so how could the present government do anything else?

We have forgotten our fear of Hitler. That fear is over and done with. We now fear only the Communists, and certainly Mr. Khrushchev is doing his best to intimidate the world. But I hope and pray he is not succeeding, for we must keep some balance in the situation of today. We must not forget the past.

The German people were responsible for what happened in Germany. They did not react quickly enough because they felt, as my friend felt, that Hitler was giving them back their dignity. But you must not for any reason abandon the clear look at the realities of a situation.

. . . .

A life as rich as Eleanor Roosevelt's could not help but be filled with colorful memories. Although she had long since discontinued the summertime family treks to Campobello Island in New Brunswick, Canada, she did carry with her fond memories of the years the Roosevelts spent time there away from the pressures of Albany, New York, and Washington. Eleanor Roosevelt had never become a sailor herself, but she admired anyone who had: one such salty fellow was her late husband Franklin, about whose boat she reminisces here.

NEW YORK, NOVEMBER 8—The past few days have been the most beautiful autumn days and I had the good luck to be driving through Connecticut and part of Massachusetts.

I spoke in Mystic, Connecticut, at a meeting sponsored by the Marine Historical Association. The seaport museum there has been con-

. . . .

siderably developed since I saw it a few years ago and has as many as 4,000 visitors on a summer's day.

Much of the history of the sea and seafaring people in that area of New England can be traced in this museum. And not the least interesting item to me personally is the small sailing boat called the "Vireo," which my husband brought up on the deck of a destroyer to Campobello Island years ago. He had given his own larger schooner to the government during the war, and he wanted a smaller boat in which the children could learn to sail.

Campobello is a good coast on which to learn to be a sailor. The tides are unusually high. They usually run from 20 to 25 feet, and in narrow passageways there may be a succession of small whirlpools. A really knowledgeable navigator, if the winds are out, can often get home by working the eddies along the coast.

This takes long experience but my husband had that, and while he was a careful seaman at times he could be rather adventurous! Seeing the little "Vireo," I am sure, could recall many happy and interesting memories to the boys in our family.

. . . .

In most Americans' minds New York City is the quintessential shopper's paradise, with more variety and quantity than anywhere else in the country. But it was for Eleanor Roosevelt also home base, where the demands of work and social life left her precious little time for such frivolities as shopping—even for Christmas presents (a top priority) for her ever-expanding brood of grandchildren and great-grandchildren.

San Francisco was a different story. Her trips to the West Coast usually had a relaxed and playful air.

DENVER, COLO., NOVEMBER 29—San Francisco is one of my favorite American cities, and though I love the view from the hotels at the top of the hill, I prefer staying down in the city itself, partly because I nearly always want to shop. Suey Chong in Chinatown always tempts me with lovely pieces of silk, and Gump's is the most marvelous place to wander around in and get ideas for Christmas gifts for friends who have everything in the world.

I shopped in both places when I was there because Mrs. Langdon Post, who is working for the Bonds for Israel organization, made every possible arrangement for my comfort. Transportation, therefore, was anything but a problem.

I also saw two of my nieces, having breakfast with them and their children, and Agar Jaicks, my nephew-in-law, drove me around Tuesday morning, so I lost no time and had a chance to visit and still make

. . . .

my 11:00 A.M. plane to Los Angeles. These glimpses of young members of my family in different places are always a joy to me.

. . . .

For decades, Mrs. Roosevelt was a loyal and active supporter of the Wiltwyck School for boys. She cared enough about the school to be willing to use her "My Day" column unabashedly to advertise its fund raising programs. The event described in this column—a professional boxing match—in any other context would have met with Eleanor Roosevelt's decided indifference or even scorn (she disliked violent sports). But here, she joined the proud alumni of the school in their appreciation of boxing champion Floyd Patterson.

WALTHAM, MASS., DECEMBER 4—Tonight (Monday) at 9:00 P.M in New York City there will be a dinner and a closed-circuit TV of the Floyd Patterson–McNeeley world heavyweight championship fight. Floyd Patterson is a graduate of Wiltwyck School and he has continued to be an inspiration to all the boys who are pupils there. These boys come by assignment of the city's courts, and many of them are from Harlem. They need inspiration, and to have one of their own make good is a tremendous one.

Floyd Patterson made the suggestion of this closed-circuit TV and dinner, and tickets may be obtained at the Four Seasons for $65 each, of which $50 is tax-deductible as a contribution to Wiltwyck School. At this school many New York City boys are striving to learn how they can succeed in life despite the handicaps which life in New York has imposed on them. If you care for this spectator sport, tonight's event offers you an opportunity for an interesting evening.

. . . .

The finale to Mrs. Roosevelt's West Coast trip this year was a lecture in Los Angeles at which she encountered picketers and hecklers. But she had seen and heard it all before and was more than ready to deal with the unruly crowd face to face and in print. And over the years she had learned that taking rude and ill-informed or dishonest opponents seriously was a short route toward giving their ideas more credence and attention than they deserved. Her preferred tactic was the old literary one of satire and rhetorical dismissal. Eleanor Roosevelt the writer could deliver a feisty knockout punch.

Mrs. Roosevelt's hecklers, she guessed, were linked to the John Birch Society, an ultraconservative right-wing group opposed to just about everything Eleanor or Franklin Roosevelt ever stood for. Among the things she backed which the Birchers attacked was the ACLU (American Civil Liberties Union), founded in 1920 by social worker-author and

. . . .

Nobel Prize-winning suffragist Jane Addams; by Norman Thomas, the leader of the American Socialist Party; and by Roger Baldwin, who became ACLU's director. Against the liberal tradition represented by citizens of this caliber, Eleanor Roosevelt thought, there wasn't much her hecklers could say that merited any serious concern.

NEW YORK, DECEMBER 15—I was amused to find myself, at a lecture Wednesday night, picketed by a new group—one, I suppose, which is an offshoot of the Birchites.

There were only a few in the group, standing outside and handing out lists of what they said was a part of all the subversive, Communist and Communist-front organizations I have ever belonged to.

Their leaflets were headed by these words:

"Even more than either hell or a woman scorned, there is no fury quite like that of a liberal about whom someone is publishing past performance data."

I can assure the gentleman responsible for the information being handed out, Roger Abel, that I am not in the least annoyed—only vastly amused.

Some of the organizations mentioned I have been connected with for very good reasons at the time. Others I have never even heard of, but that may be because the time is so long past that I have forgotten about them. That they were mentioned on this list as being either Communist, subversive or Communist-front organizations does not make them any one of these things.

I doubt that listing the American Association for the United Nations as subversive makes it so. I think this would be news indeed to a great many on the board of directors. Some of them may even be so excited as to want to take legal action against Mr. Abel, though I hope not, for I feel such accusations are always better met by ridicule and allowing time for the real truth to come out.

I noticed also that this group made the mistake of so many others—of listing the American Civil Liberties Union as a Communist-front organization. This long-established and respectable group is repeatedly being confused with the American Civil Liberties Congress, which I believe has been questioned as a possible Communist-front organization.

I am enormously interested in knowing that I have been associated with the National Lawyers Guild. I am not a lawyer, so I wonder just how I served in that organization.

I could pick organization after organization on the list and question the exactness of the information, but the greatest wonder of all is how any group can spare the time or money for such piffling work. What good do they do? This is the question the public sooner or later will decide.

. . . .

To the ideologically hidebound conservative in American politics, at this point in the cold war the idea of giving any sort of aid to noncapitalist nations or to third world countries whose governments were sympathetic to the Kremlin was anathema. Mrs. Roosevelt reasoned differently. Her subject here is one she tackled many times in her "My Day" columns because it moved her deeply. What to do with American food surpluses, spawned by improvements in agriculture and by government subsidies to farmers? She could not accept the idea that—with a substantial portion of the American underclass still going to bed hungry at night and with millions literally starving in other parts of the underdeveloped world—it could make any political or moral sense for the United States to horde its food supply. Ideology, she believed, was a cruel master for an empty stomach.

NEW YORK, DECEMBER 18—I believe American food surpluses should go to hungry people; and since women and children are rarely responsible for the political thinking in many Asian and African countries, I question whether food should be withheld for political reasons. Yet if I were in an elected position, I should doubtless feel strongly the responsibility of listening to everyone in the country—even to such unimportant people as our American Nazi leader Mr. Rockwell, who admitted at one time that his party consists of only eleven people. Though I disagree with him violently, I understand why elected officials must pay attention even to such unimportant minorities.

When all is said, however, I think the best American policy—especially where such things as food are concerned—would be to think out ways of using our surpluses to the maximum to help feed our own people, and then to sell or to give to the areas of the world where people are hungry, without regard to their political beliefs. I feel somehow that agricultural surpluses are gifts from the Lord and it is not up to us to decide what shall be the political ideology of hungry people.

. . . .

Buried in a late paragraph of this nearly year-end column is a statement reflecting one of Eleanor Roosevelt's most important observations about the state of political thinking in America at the time: ". . . it is the willingness to abdicate the responsibilities of citizenship which gives us our feeling of inadequacy and frustration." In fact, this plain-spoken column neatly summarizes most of Mrs. Roosevelt's key insights about the psychological and political meaning of the nuclear terror unleashed

. . . .

upon the world over Hiroshima in 1945 in the name of peace. And it reasserts her unwavering belief that only through the rule of international law and the practice of continuous negotiation, sponsored by the UN, could the world keep itself safely back from the brink of another war.

NEW YORK, DECEMBER 20—What can one woman do to prevent war? This is the question that comes my way in any number of letters these days.

In times past, the question usually asked by women was "How can we best help to defend our nation?" I cannot remember a time when the question on so many people's lips was "How can we prevent war?"

There is a widespread understanding among the people of this nation, and probably among the people of the world, that there is no safety except through the prevention of war. For many years war has been looked upon as almost inevitable in the solution of any question that has arisen between nations, and the nation that was strong enough to do so went about building up its defenses and its power to attack. It felt that it could count on these two things for safety.

There was a point then in increasing a nation's birth rate: Providing more soldiers. There was a point in creating new weapons: At their worst, they could not destroy the world as a whole.

Now, all a citizen can do is watch his government use its scientists to invent more powerful ways of achieving world destruction more and more quickly.

As I travel around this country I cannot help thinking what a pity it would be to destroy so much beauty, and I am sure this thought crosses the mind of many a Russian traveling through his country—in fact, the mind of anyone traveling anywhere in the world. Peoples of the world who have not yet achieved a place in the sun must feel this even more deeply than those of us who have had years of development and acquired resultant comforts and pleasures.

A consciousness of the fact that war means practically total destruction is the reason, I think, for the rising tide to prevent what seems such a senseless procedure.

I understand that it is perhaps difficult for some people, whose lives have been lived with a sense of the need for military development, to envisage the possibility of being no longer needed. But the average citizen is beginning to think more and more of the need to develop machinery to settle difficulties in the world without destruction or the use of atomic bombs.

Of course, if any war is permitted to break out, it is self-evident that the losing side would use atomic bombs if they were available. So the only thing to do is to put this atomic power into the hands of the United Nations and have it used only for peaceful purposes.

Here is where the individual comes in. To the women and the men who are asking themselves "What can I do as an individual?" my answer is this: Take a more active interest in your government, have a say in who is nominated for political office, work for these candidates and keep in close touch with them if they are elected.

If our objective is to do away with the causes of war, build up the United Nations and give the UN more control over the weapons of total destruction, we should urge that world law be developed so that people's grievances can be heard promptly and judiciously settled.

We should begin in our own environment and in our own community as far as possible to build a peace-loving attitude and learn to discipline ourselves to accept, in the small things of our lives, mediation and arbitration.

As individuals, there is little that any of us can do to prevent an accidental use of bombs in the hands of those who already have them. We can register, however, with our government a firm protest against granting the knowledge and the use of these weapons to those who do not now have them.

We may hope that in the years to come, when the proper machinery is set up, such lethal weapons can be destroyed wherever they are and the knowledge that developed them can be used for more constructive purposes.

In the meantime, no citizen of a democracy need feel completely helpless if he becomes an active factor in the citizenship of his community. For it is the willingness to abdicate responsibilities of citizenship which gives us our feeling of inadequacy and frustration.

As long as we are not actually destroyed, we can work to gain greater understanding of other peoples and to try to present to the peoples of the world the values of our own beliefs. We can do this by demonstrating our conviction that human life is worth preserving and that we are willing to help others to enjoy benefits of our civilization just as we have enjoyed it.

1 9 6 2

Accomplishments in the civil rights campaign during the last year of Eleanor Roosevelt's life represented the realization of justice after a long period of patient, persistent effort. The year began with a rapprochement between the Democratic White House and the leadership in the black community that the Eisenhower administration had not been able to achieve. In January, Roy Wilkins, President of the National Association for the Advancement of Colored People, praised JFK for his active role in civil rights. Kennedy's administration responded with a stepped-up effort.

But civil rights for black Americans was not the only grand moral cause to which the White House wanted to recommit America. Speaking in Berlin in February, Robert Kennedy, the new attorney general, denounced the recently erected Berlin Wall as an offense to all freedom-loving peoples. This clear posture won the president's brother some favor in Mrs. Roosevelt's eyes, for she too saw the wall as a symbol of tyranny. In late March the Supreme Court decided a case called *Baker* v. *Carr.* The decision empowered federal courts to force reapportionment of seats in state legislatures where patterns of discrimination brought about by gerrymandering had been proved to exist. This gave new and effective leverage to the federal government to create a more equitable voting situation for blacks and other minorities who had been shut out of the political process.

In another civil rights case decided near the end of its term, in June, the nation's highest court addressed not the race issue but the religion-in-the-schools issue by ruling that compulsory prayer in the public schools was unconstitutional. Mrs. Roosevelt thought the decision was a good one, but she argued that the history of religion should be taught to students of all ages. When the next school year began, a significant step toward racial integration of higher education was taken when a black student named James Meredith—whom Eleanor Roosevelt admired—was admitted to the University of Mississippi against severe opposition. Only two weeks after Mrs. Roosevelt died in November the President issued an executive order that realized a dream the former First Lady had held dear for many years. Kennedy's order said that federal government agencies must eliminate discrimination based on race or religion insofar as it occurs in federally funded housing.

Mrs. Roosevelt's lifelong tendency to comment critically or supportively on matters of domestic and foreign affairs showed no signs of abating in her last year. She applauded President Kennedy for the muscle he exercised in condemning a steel-industry price hike and forcing a price rollback. As sympathetic as she was to labor, Eleanor Roosevelt could not see why the inflation in steel prices was justified. She also lent her support to Kennedy's approach to dealing with Southeast Asia. In Laos, in particular, the threat of a Communist takeover was putting the containment theory to a hard test. The U.S. sent naval and ground forces in May to aid the anti-Communist Laotians, and Kennedy called it a "diplomatic solution." Neither Mrs. Roosevelt nor many other Americans could yet envision the nightmare of an American war over the same issue in Vietnam that was soon to begin.

Most Americans thought the year 1962 remarkable because of NASA's string of successful orbital flights for the country's first team of solo astronauts. There were astronaut space trips in February, May, and October. Eleanor Roosevelt remained singularly unimpressed; she had simply not developed an interest in seeing the world from on high. Seeing it up close and firsthand in a human way remained Eleanor's priority. In her final year, at seventy-seven, she took numerous trips again across the country for AAUN and other work, and she made one more sweeping visit to England, France, and Israel, each now as familiar to her as home. There were, however, fewer and fewer visits to Hyde Park, and finally New York became for her what it had been at the beginning—a magnet, her center of gravity.

By the time autumn had begun Mrs. Roosevelt's health was deteriorating rapidly. Her last column was published on September 27. In the November elections the Democrats retained their solid control of both houses of Congress; Richard Nixon lost the race for governor in California and another Kennedy joined the exclusive club of senators (Ted Kennedy, Massachusetts). But the year's major event—the U.S.– Soviet standoff in late October over the reported presence of missile sites in Cuba, a standoff in which Kennedy demanded and won a conciliatory response from Castro and Khrushchev—was something Eleanor was too ill to comment upon publicly. We can only suppose that she shared the world's terror for a few days as a head-on collision between the two great nuclear superpowers seemed inevitable, and then shared the world's great relief after Kennedy and Khrushchev, for different reasons, decided not to risk war and mutual annihilation.

. . . .

Mrs. Roosevelt had not known such energy in Washington since the first hundred days of her husband's first term as president: the Kennedy administration had the country hopping. There were new programs, new study groups, new initiatives of all kinds. Despite whatever lingering testiness there might have been between the Roosevelt clan and the administration, Mrs. Roosevelt wanted to be part of the action, and the White House clearly wanted her on its team. The 1962 columns begin with a typical Eleanor Roosevelt whirlwind of meetings, social engagements, and domestic and foreign travel.

PARIS, FEBRUARY 16—Before coming over here my last two days in the United States were spent largely in Washington, D.C., and I want to tell about them before writing about my current month-long trip.

On last Monday morning in the White House the President opened the first meeting of the Commission on the Status of Women. After very brief preliminaries and upon being introduced by Secretary of Labor Arthur Goldberg, President Kennedy put us all at ease by starting the conference off on a note of levity by remarking that he had appointed the commission in self-defense—self-defense against an able and persistent newspaperwoman, Miss May Craig. No other lady of the press has waged a longer or more persistent battle for the rights of women than has May Craig, and I am sure she is flattered by the President's recognition of her tremendous interest in the field of women's equality.

After the morning session we had lunch in a downstairs restaurant that did not exist in my day there but which must be a tremendous convenience for those working in the White House today. A guide showed us around the White House, telling us about certain things that have been changed under Mrs. Kennedy's direction and which she explained to the American people over two television networks this week.

The basement floor and the first floor for entertaining have certainly been made far more attractive than ever before. Mrs. Kennedy has succeeded in having presented to the White House some really very beautiful pieces of furniture and decorative pictures, which add enormously to the interest of these rooms.

We kept ourselves strictly on schedule all day and opened our afternoon meeting promptly at 2 o'clock at 200 Maryland Avenue, below the Capitol, where the Commission on the Status of Women will have its permanent office.

. . . .

We soon began to discuss the best way to organize to achieve the maximum of work not only on the six points laid down in the President's directive to the commission but in other situations which will certainly arise. The commission will try to make its influence felt concerning women's problems not only in the federal area but in state and local areas and in industry as well as in women's home responsibilities.

The effort, of course, is to find how we can best use the potentialities of women without impairing their first responsibilities, which are to their homes, their husbands and their children. We need to use in the very best way possible all our available manpower—and that includes womanpower—and this commission, I think, can well point out some of the ways in which this can be accomplished.

I was glad to hear brought up the question of part-time work for women and of better training in certain areas because the possibilities available to women could be more widely publicized and education could be directed to meet and prepare for these new openings.

The Vice President and Mrs. Johnson gave a delightful reception at their home in the late afternoon for the members of the commission.

The meetings continued through Tuesday morning and into early afternoon, and I felt that the discussions had brought us to a point where we could get the staff to continue with the organization and start some of our subcommittees to working very shortly.

I was back at my home in New York City by 5:30 P.M. on Tuesday and a few people came in to say goodbye at 6 o'clock and then I packed and dressed and was ready to leave the house a little after 10 o'clock. My secretary, Miss Maureen Corr, and I left by Air France for Paris at midnight and had a most delightful trip—smooth and comfortable. We are now at the Crillon Hotel, where I always feel at home because of the many months I've stayed here when we used to hold meetings of the General Assembly of the United Nations in Paris.

Henry Morgenthau III met us at Orly Airport and told us of the plans made for doing two educational television programs, and a little later we were joined at the hotel by Professor Alfred Gorsser for discussion of our joint responsibilities on the programs. By this time it was 7:00 P.M. Paris time, though only 1:00 P.M. New York time, and after a delightful dinner we felt well adjusted to the change and feel well prepared for busy days ahead.

. . . .

Her month-long trip would take her from New York to Paris, to Tel Aviv and other points in Israel, to Switzerland, across the Continent to London, and back home. It was an ambitious itinerary for an energetic college student, not to mention a member of the senior set. That

. . . .

Eleanor Roosevelt was still as hungry for learning and as eager to encourage learning in others as she ever was becomes quite clear in this column as she reports on visits to academic sites in Israel. Her encounters with Israeli leaders were all based on friendships she had begun on previous trips.

The longer format of Mrs. Roosevelt's column at this point (since the change to a three-days-per-week schedule), permitted her to write rather extensive travelogues. After finishing her visit to Israel, the Alps were the next destination, and the journey brought with it some sweet reminiscences involving two newlyweds named Eleanor and Franklin.

ST. MORITZ, SWITZERLAND, MARCH 5—The day before we left Israel we visited the library of the Hebrew University, which is one of the great libraries of the world. I was astonished to find so many copies of books dealing with my husband, with Theodore Roosevelt and with Abraham Lincoln. I hope that some day Carl Sandburg will visit this library and see that even in this small and faraway country the feeling for Lincoln which he has tried to inspire is being encouraged.

I was very grateful to the director, Curt Wormann, who gave us a considerable amount of his time, and I was happy to meet also the rector of the university, Professor Racah, and to see the lecture room which has been named for me. From the university there is a wonderful view, which is true for so many of the public buildings in Jerusalem. One of the rather sad things we saw in the library were some books from the old university on Mt. Scopus—one book with a bullet buried in it and another that had been badly marred. This must have happened during the fighting, though it is hard to understand how fighting could have gone on practically within the old university itself. Today, by arrangement, the new library is allowed to bring a load of books once a month from the old library.

It was a great pleasure also to call on Prime Minister Ben-Gurion in his office for a short time. He was in fine form—as vigorous and as dynamic as any man could be. I believe that among those in the younger generation who understand him and follow him so staunchly, he is affectionately called the "old man," but I think this is used in the sense that to them he seems quite ageless, belonging as much to their own generation as to any other.

Minister of Education Abba Eban was kind enough to invite us to a very delightful dinner the very last day, which was filled to overflowing with pleasurable experiences. Mr. Eban's dinner took place in the King David Hotel, where we were staying prior to our early-morning departure, and during it I had the pleasure of sitting by the Attorney General, who amusingly recalled the hectic round of public appearances on his only visit thus far to America. Earlier in the day, at lunch at the home of Foreign Minister Golda Meir, I was glad to see our own ambassador, Mr. Barber. He is still new in Israel, but I am sure they are going to like him.

It was an all-day trip on the 28th, the first part by plane to Zurich and then by train to St. Moritz. That train trip is one of the most scenic in the world and we enjoyed every minute of it. I kept being reminded of the trip from Denver, Colorado, up to Aspen. Both are beautiful, but this one for us was more dramatic because of the snow on all the mountains.

I had never seen St. Moritz in winter before. I remember it as a girl of 15 and then again driving from Augsburg up here with a pair of horses in a victoria when my husband and I were in Europe the summer after our wedding. This is considered to be the end of the season, but there is still snow on all the mountains, people are skiing and you still get the full flavor of winter. When the sun is out in the daytime, you are warm despite the crisp and cool air. Only as the sun goes down do you realize that this is really winter and that you are several thousand feet above sea level.

....

Showing only the barest signs of travel fatigue, Mrs. Roosevelt makes a humorous confession about nightlife in gay Paree. Then she takes an insightful long-distance look at the GOP's presidential candidate prospects for 1964, guesses that were almost perfectly accurate. George Romney did become governor of Michigan. Barry Goldwater, senator from Arizona, did fight off a Rockefeller challenge for the Republican presidential nomination in 1964, but he was badly beaten in the election by the incumbent, Lyndon Johnson, who succeeded to the office upon Kennedy's assassination in November 1963.

PARIS, MARCH 12—Back in Paris after an easy trip from Zurich last night, the youngest members of the party went out for more entertainment, but I have discovered that entertainment means less to me than a good night's sleep.

From newspaper reports, a recent Gallup poll would indicate that if Mr. Nixon really means that he is not in the running at the next Republican convention, then the choice lies between Governor Rockefeller and Senator Goldwater, and the margin has narrowed considerably between them. This will make the Republican convention much more interesting than it has been in the last few years because it will indicate whether the party as a whole believes it should be clearly reactionary and ultraconservative or reflect the slightly more liberal views, in certain areas, held by Governor Rockefeller.

Of course, the Republican Party is looking frantically for someone

....

who may still not draw the line too clearly between Republicans and Democrats. A good many people think that should George Romney of Michigan be elected governor of that state he might be one of the contestants at the convention. But this seems hardly credible. Mr. Romney will have had a very short time to show whether or not he is an able governor, and it is not likely that the Republicans would want to put a man of such slight experience into the position of President or make him the nominee. Politics may be partly a question of instinct and imagination, but experience has something to do with it too. It takes time for a newcomer to learn to gauge public opinion, to watch people, to react, often unconsciously, to the waves of feeling in the atmosphere, and to acquire that sense of timing without which few politicians are ever really successful.

Some hold that a President need not be a politician. But the fact is that he is the leader of a political party, and hence it seems to me that if for the first time in many years the Republican Party decides to come out firmly as ultraconservative it will not be likely to choose a middle-of-the-road, untried politician.

To be sure, the choice between Rockefeller and Goldwater is likely to be made difficult by a number of factors heretofore unresolved in a political convention. But the choice between Goldwater and Romney will be a most interesting one. Many of those for Mr. Romney will say he is the best man and therefore does not have to be primarily a politician, but unfortunately the political party, usually to a great extent, governs whoever holds political office.

All of this means that the next few months are going to be very interesting for the rank and file of the Republican Party. The cleavage between ultraconservative and middle-of-the-road liberals is going to be full of controversy, and for once the Democrats—whose ranks this time seem to be undivided—can sit back and calmly watch.

. . . .

From her position as the country's most experienced resident of the White House, Eleanor Roosevelt enjoyed commenting upon how First Families present and past went about fulfilling their public obligations. She was even-handed in her treatment of fellow First Ladies throughout the years, often expressing genuine sympathy for them because she knew how difficult the job could be. It was the same, she realized, whether one was a Democrat or a Republican. But no First Lady drew more outspoken and enthusiastic applause from Mrs. Roosevelt than did Jacqueline Kennedy. As a young mother, as a serious interior decorator with a respect for history at the White House, as an ambassador for the U.S. when traveling abroad, Jackie scored well in every category in

Eleanor Roosevelt's estimation. The column included here is but one of several from this year in which Mrs. Kennedy is admired and praised.

PHILADELPHIA, APRIL 2—I hope that the nation, in welcoming Mrs. Kennedy home, will show her that we are really grateful for her undertaking the strenuous if interesting trip just concluded, because she has certainly enhanced the popularity of America and Americans, and this is not always easy to do.

In London someone asked her if she had really had a chance to sleep enough. With the characteristic resilience of youth, she replied that she had already slept too much! How wonderful it is for us to have a young, intelligent and attractive First Lady with the interest and enthusiasm which she has shown in her trips to India and Pakistan. I am sure the pictures which told of this trip have acquainted many people with these areas and will be valuable in broadening our knowledge of another part of the world.

. . . .

As Mrs. Roosevelt gained perspective on her husband's accomplishments as president she also refined her appreciation of what their uncle, Theodore Roosevelt, had accomplished when he held that office from 1901 to 1909. It appears that her sense of Teddy Roosevelt's progressivism lay at the root of her respect for his political achievements. At the same time, she had some left-over childhood fascination for this vigorous and intellectually lively man. It seemed to her that in several ways the first Roosevelt president was a model the country would do well to think about seriously. The idea of preserving Teddy Roosevelt's homes for the public benefit was a plan Eleanor Roosevelt could easily endorse. Her reflections on the subject brought up family anecdotes that show how far back in American history the Roosevelts had started to make their presence felt.

NEW YORK, APRIL 4—I was much interested to read that the National Park Service will shortly be authorized to take over and administer two shrines in New York State—one, the birthplace of President Theodore Roosevelt on East 20th Street in New York City; and the other, Sagamore Hill on Long Island, which was built in 1884 and served as the summer White House during Theodore Roosevelt's presidency.

Sagamore Hill, which President Roosevelt built and lived in for years, is well known and a good many people are attracted to visit this house, which is so full of reminders of one of our most colorful presidents.

I have always regretted, however, that more people did not know of the two houses on East 20th Street which belonged to Theodore Roos-

. . . .

evelt, Sr., father of President Theodore Roosevelt, and his brother, James Roosevelt. It was in the senior Theodore Roosevelt's home on East 20th Street that this most interesting family lived and where most of the children were brought up. The home itself is very typical of the way of life of a comfortable merchant in the New York City of that day.

Later the two brothers built houses on 57th Street when that location was looked upon as really out in the country. And I remember a distant cousin and friend of the family who lived on Washington Square, Mrs. Weeks, who said, when her son Frederick told her he was going to a housewarming party in those 57th Street houses, that she hoped he was spending the night!

In my young days I always felt that Mrs. Weeks was our tie to the past, because she loved to tell the younger members of the family how in her youth she had danced with General Lafayette at a ball given for him in New York when he came back for a visit long after the Revolutionary War.

....

Although Eleanor Roosevelt had never had the benefit of a formal university education in the liberal arts, she had been recognized worldwide as a preeminent model of the liberally educated person. Her collection of honorary degrees from major and minor universities and colleges around the globe falls just one short of three dozen.

She had thought deeply about what constitutes good education, and she wrote about it often, whether on the level of child-rearing practices or graduate school curricula. Amassing a quantity of knowledge was important, yes; but far more important, Mrs. Roosevelt argued, was learning how to learn and how to find out what one does not yet know. Her position is neatly in line with such other American philosophers of liberal education as John Dewey and Robert Hutchins.

In the second column included here, Mrs. Roosevelt's continuing devotion to the boys at Wiltwyck School once more shines through. In their case, the educational approach had to be, she maintained, one grounded in love and sensitive personal attention. The development of a strong, self-respecting personality was the basis for intellectual growth, according to Mrs. Roosevelt.

SLIPPERY ROCK, PA., APRIL 11—As the volume of knowledge about our world increases, programs of study are becoming more and more complicated, and we must strive harder to give our children the kind of education that would fit them for a life that must be lived in a changing world. Science has moved so rapidly forward that every child must have a basic understanding of certain scientific principles.

....

Perhaps the most important aspect, however, is to provide each child with the knowledge of how to use his mind—how and where to go when he wants to learn new things that he had not had an earlier opportunity to learn or perhaps when he wants to delve more deeply into some special subject.

A disciplined mind is essential for every man and woman today. And a balance must be kept between the science that presses in on us from so many different areas and the natural tendency that many of us have to turn to the humanities and the arts for our real enjoyment and the expression that is essential to good emotional development.

A disciplined mind is essential to analyse problems, and a basic knowledge covering many subjects is essential to finding the lines to follow in searching for solutions.

Every citizen is involved in safeguarding the future of our country, and one of the best safeguards lies in a younger generation able to understand the world in which they live and to give the leadership at home and abroad that is so vitally needed.

SAN DIEGO, APRIL 23—A little incident at one of the picnics which I have held annually for the Wiltwyck boys at Hyde Park will, I think, emphasize how much a personal contact means for these youngsters whose background is often such an unhappy one. As I was greeting the boys on their arrival at Hyde Park, one little white boy stopped in front of me and said:

"Mrs. Roosevelt, do you remember me?"

"Yes," I answered, "I remember all of you. I have seen you at school and many of you were here last year. Of course, I remember you."

The little boy, with determined face, looked me straight in the eye and said: "Mrs. Roosevelt, what's my name?"

I had to explain that there were 100 boys and that I could not remember all of their names because I was an old lady and my memory was not as good as it once was.

He then told me his name. But he was so anxious to be identified by someone that, within five minutes, he stood before me again demanding:

"Mrs. Roosevelt, what's my name?"

To have a friend who knows you by name gives you a sense that you are not alone in the world. This is above all else what every single one of the Wiltwyck boys needs.

. . . .

The following column shows Eleanor Roosevelt moving smoothly through several disparate worlds in the course of one day. Crosscountry travel, household affairs, lobbying for women's rights, discussion of edu-

. . . .

*cational philosophy and management, catching a little sleep, enter-
taining a foreign dignitary, taking in a challenging play. Yes, Mrs.
Roosevelt had help from secretaries, chauffeurs, and friends to keep all
of this running on time, but the sheer expansiveness of her interests,
responsibilities and enthusiasms is a wonder to watch.*

WALTHAM, MASS., APRIL 30—We landed in New York half an hour
late. This meant that I had only a short time in which to get tidied
up, catch up with what was going on in my own home, and then pick
up the Assistant Secretary of Labor, Mrs. Esther Peterson, before
going to the courthouse in Foley Square for a hearing that Congressman Zelenko was holding on equal pay for equal work. Mrs. Gladys
Tillett, our member on the UN Status of Women Commission, was
also present to give her testimony, for this question is one that affects
other countries as well as our own. The dignity of women's equality
when they meet in government, professional and industrial work is
important the world over, not just in the U.S.

I was through by 20 minutes before 11 and on my way to a Brandeis
University committee meeting on education, which is always held before the board meeting later in the afternoon. I came home for a
hurried lunch and to say goodbye to Mr. Clark Eichelberger, who was
leaving for the meeting in Monrovia, Liberia, of the World Federation
of UN Associations. Then I returned to the board meeting and some
very warm discussions which I thought extremely valuable and interesting.

By 4:40 I was home and quite ready to sleep for an hour and a half
before I had the pleasure of having Mrs. Norman bring Mrs. Indira
Gandhi to dine here before going to see a play together. What a charming woman Mrs. Gandhi is! Being vitally interested in her country and
its policies makes her both knowledgeable and extremely interesting.

I was relieved to find that Tennessee Williams' play, "The Night of
the Iguana," beautifully acted as it is, left her—as it did me—a little
baffled in trying to figure out what was the message the author meant
to give his audience. But at least it left us with much to talk about.

....

*Milovan Djilas of Yugoslavia was a man whose fall from grace in the
Communist world was complete: From the position of confidant and
adviser to Marshal Tito and from the position of vice president of the
country he fell to the lowest rank, that of common criminal, all because
the Communist system could not tolerate his dissenting views.*

*Djilas was first dismissed in 1954, jailed in 1956 for supporting the
Hungarian revolution, and had his term extended in 1957 when his
book* The New Class *(a critique of the Communist oligarchy) was pub-*

lished in the West. Freed in 1961, he was soon arrested again in 1962, to be held for four more years. Djilas' 1962 book Conversations with Stalin, *in which Stalin's reign of terror is exposed, may have provoked Tito's rage against his former colleague. Mrs. Roosevelt found his case an appalling indictment of the closed mind of communism.*

NEW YORK, MAY 16—I have been saddened by two news items of the past couple of days.

The first was the word of the return to prison of Milovan Djilas, former Yugoslav Vice President and formerly close friend of Communist dictator Tito.

Djilas is an extraordinarily courageous man, and he evidently is determined to make his own people realize that the worst thing that can happen is to be prevented from thinking and saying what one honestly believes. The Communist court had decided that because the trial would deal with certain Communist beliefs it should be held in private. Djilas protested this action, saying that everything he was now being tried for had already been published and was now public property.

Nevertheless, the trial was held in secret, and Djilas was sentenced to nearly nine years in the same prison where he has already spent a considerable part of his life.

He probably will not be treated too badly, but the mere fact of confinement is in itself a terrible punishment. One may hope that Tito's good sense will make him cut this sentence as soon as the heat and the attention of the moment has worn off.

But that will not wipe out the blot on Yugoslav justice or reduce the resentment against the general Communist idea that people who merely state their honest belief can be thrown into jail. No regime and no beliefs can be on a very firm footing if they cannot stand open criticism and truthful expressions of disagreement. The only way to growth and improvement is through differences of opinion and experimentation. The Soviet theories are no more perfect than are any other kind of theories, and if all criticism and disagreement have been barred there is no chance for any improvement.

The world will be waiting to see what Tito's action will be. If he is counting on the forgetfulness of people, I think he will be surprised to find how often Djilas' name will be mentioned by the peoples of the world in the months to come.

. . . .

Eleanor Roosevelt's reportorial style was heavy on facts and figures. Usually the most literary thing she could manage was a well-told anecdote or a scathing one-liner when she criticized the ideas or behavior

. . . .

of someone she found harmful to society. But here is a rare instance of Mrs. Roosevelt's use of an extended metaphor. The idea expressed is abstract, but no one who has studied her life will miss the readily apparent, though no doubt unintentional, applicability of these thoughts to Mrs. Roosevelt herself.

ATLANTA, JUNE 4—A human life is like a candle. It is lit when a baby is born. It reaches out perhaps at first only in the effect even a very tiny life can have on the immediate family. But with every year of growth the light grows stronger and spreads farther. Sometimes it has to struggle for brightness, but sometimes the inner light is strong and bright from the very beginning and grows with the years.

None of us knows how far it reaches but I am quite sure that even a young life that is not allowed to grow to maturity has left behind it influences for good which will grow and broaden as those who touched this life grow themselves.

The great people of the world spread the major light. They leave behind them accomplishments which touch the lives of thousands, perhaps even millions, of people. But they are strengthened by all the little lights and perhaps could never have accomplished their great ends without the little lights which reached out and inspired them in their own particular circle.

. . . .

That religion is one of the binding ties holding society and family together was a truism for Eleanor Roosevelt. But at the same time she took many positions over the years in opposition to certain political and moral teachings of her own church and of other religious institutions. Respectful as she was of clergy, she accepted none of them as infallible. Nor did she believe that a truly democratic society would long survive if religion were in any way imposed upon or denied the people. Freedom of choice and full tolerance for differences were to her the sine qua non of a society with a healthy attitude about religion.

Thus the furor that broke out when the Supreme Court ruled unconstitutional a New York State Board of Regents prayer meant for use in the state's public schools seemed to Eleanor Roosevelt completely uncalled for. She was all for prayer as an integral part of a child's upbringing, but never for imposing prayer on anyone. Having lived through the agonizing experience of McCarthyism's anti-intellectualism about communism a few years earlier, Mrs. Roosevelt was still sensitive to the dangers of restricted religious liberty posed by right-wing Christian zealots (who denounced the Court's decision).

. . . .

HYDE PARK, JULY 5—The nation's governors, in their annual meeting in Hershey, Pa., had a wordy wrangle regarding a resolution to be submitted to Congress for an amendment to the First Article of the Constitution, which of course deals with freedom of religion and the separation of church and state.

All this, it seems to me, stems from a misunderstanding of what the Supreme Court ruled regarding the New York State Board of Regents-written prayer and the saying of it in the schools of the state under state direction.

The fact is that this is a prayer written and backed by the government of the state and directed to be used in the schools, and which the Supreme Court has declared unconstitutional. The prayer is innocuous, but this procedure would be an injection of state interference in religious education and religious practice.

Under our Constitution no individual can be forced by government to belong to a special religion or to conform to a special religious procedure. But any school, or any group of people, or any individual may say a prayer if he or they so wish if it is not under the order of the government or connected with government direction in any way. This seems to me very clear in the Supreme Court decision and conforms exactly, I think, with the Constitution.

It is my feeling that many of our newspapers put sensational headlines on stories pertaining to this decision, and people have suddenly—without really reading the court ruling themselves—reacted emotionally.

Someone reported to me that he had heard a man on the radio in tears saying that he never thought he would live to see the day when God would be outlawed from our schools. Another told me that a Southern woman wrote to her daughter in New England, saying that she was horrified to find that the Supreme Court was controlled by the Communists and, of course, the Communists were controlled by the Eastern European Jews. Such nonsense, such ignorance is really vicious.

One hears it said, of course, that at present in the South the accusation of communism is rather loosely bandied about and covers whatever you happen not to like. Not to know, however, that the Jewish communities of Eastern Europe are constantly trying to get away from those Soviet-controlled countries because they do not have security or equality of opportunity makes the accusation of their influence in communism and adherence to it a show of complete ignorance of the situation as it really exists. If any people have a reason for disliking communism, it is the Jews.

When unthinking emotions are aroused we usually find that whatever prejudices are held are channeled by the emotions into expressions that have nothing to do with reality but simply are an outlet for the prejudices.

Years ago, in the South, I can remember my husband telling me when he took to Warm Springs the first nurse who had been trained in physiotherapy and had worked for the State of New York that he hardly dared mention the fact that she happened to be a Roman Catholic. He hoped—before anyone discovered this fact—that her kindliness of spirit, her skill and her helpfulness would have won a place among the neighbors where she was going to work.

He was right, but he could not help being amused when an old man came to see him and said: "Miss —— is such a good woman. But I thought when I heard she was a Roman Catholic she ought to have horns and a tail!"

This attitude has worn off somewhat, but in certain areas, such as where the author of the letter I have mentioned comes from, one can still find astounding beliefs about the Roman Catholics and the Jews.

There is a general lack of knowledge, too, about what communism is and how much influence it may have in our country. And the emotional reaction to a Supreme Court decision, such as we are witnessing, seems to me to be the product of an unwillingness to read with care what is actually said and an unwillingness to look at the Constitution and reread the First Amendment.

I thought the President's comment was one of the very best. The Constitution does not specify that we are not to be a religious people; it gives us the right to be religious in our own way, and it places upon us the responsibility for the observance of our religion. When the President said that he hoped this decision would make us think more of religion and our observance individually and at home, he emphasized a fact which I think it would be well for all of us to think about.

Real religion is displayed in the way we live in our day-by-day activities at home, in our own communities, and with our own families and neighbors. The Supreme Court emphasized that we must not curtail our freedom as safeguarded under the First Article of the Constitution.

. . . .

The following column could have been written by a clerk for a superior court justice who needed to collect well-thought-out opinions from steady minds to help him make up his own mind about a complicated decision. It also shows that Eleanor Roosevelt had a fine capacity for putting questions of ethics above issues of political allegiance. She knew that the fabric of American society is woven in part from the strands of the long tradition of Anglo-Saxon common law and Judeo-Christian

. . . .

ethical behavior. Anything that might unravel this fabric could be dangerous to us all, Mrs. Roosevelt contended. Behind the seriousness in her tone here was the recent history of the country's struggle through McCarthyism. As much as Mrs. Roosevelt was opposed to communism, she was equally opposed to seeing the democratic process in America debased while in the pursuit of alleged Communist sympathizers.

HYDE PARK, JULY 6—I have received from an academic group in California a petition concerning the difficulties of a teacher having once been a member of the Communist Party, left it at one point, and tried to get back in several years later when he felt there was a chance, under Khrushchev, the party would be reformed.

While being perfectly frank before the investigating committee about his own activities and views, he refused to inform on other persons because he felt this would be morally wrong. He is charged with violating the Dilworth Act "by refusal to answer questions about other people" and, of course, with having been a member of the Communist Party within the last five years with the knowledge that it advocated the overthrow of the United States government.

The academic committee defending him narrows its defense to two points. First, it feels the case will really be judged on the point of forcing a person to become an informer. Second, it feels there is implicit in the case "the right of an adherent of politically unorthodox ideas, namely a member of the Socialist Workers party, to remain a teacher."

These points, if they go to the Supreme Court for decision, will be important because there are a great many people who feel that our whole standard of ethics is opposed to the child, or man or woman, who informs on someone else. And if the court should base its ruling on this point alone, it would be a highly important constitutional decision.

The fact that the man himself evidently holds extremely unorthodox views, as do some of the men on the committee defending him, does not really detract from the importance of having a decision reached on that point.

Many persons instinctively feel that it is wrong to force someone to inform on someone else, and particularly when we are not at war, it seems we should think carefully before overriding a principle that has been one of our basic ethical teachings as far back as many of us can remember.

. . . .

Eleanor Roosevelt went into a journalist's rage when the Senate was persuaded (she thought hoodwinked) into voting down the Kefauver bill that would have made generic drugs affordably available. Mrs. Roosevelt

. . . .

was well aware that politics is not just the art of compromise but also a hardball game in which elected officials will sometimes do almost anything to collect votes. Self-interest had its limits, in Mrs. Roosevelt's value system, however, and this case, she thought, was one of flagrant disregard for the general public's needs.

The political cartoonist referred to here is Herbert Lawrence Block (born 1909), who was associated throughout most of his career with the Washington Post *and who had twice won the Pulitzer Prize (1942, 1954). Mrs. Roosevelt calls Senator Eastland of Mississippi a Dixiecrat, using a term popular at the time for those Southern Democrats whose positions on such issues as segregation were so conservative that their fellow party members thought they might as well be Republicans.*

NEW YORK, AUGUST 6—I don't know how some of the rest of the country may feel about the matter, but Herblock's cartoon the other day of Senator James O. Eastland and Senator Everett M. Dirksen, that Dixiecrat–Republican combination, reading the news of the horrible infant deformities resulting from the use of untested drugs, made shivers run up and down my spine. In the waste basket behind those two prosperous, comfortable men is the Kefauver drug reform bill, which they helped to defeat in the name of free enterprise, and the caption under the cartoon has the two saying to each other: "Yeah, it's almost enough to make you want to do something."

How much longer are the people of this country going to stand for men in the Senate who act from pocket interest, not from real intelligence and study? What can the world think of a country like ours that does not control its drug industry but succumbs to the lobby of drug manufacturers? These are evil men who combine together to scratch each other's backs. When in the Southern states some of our citizens try to exercise the basic American right of registering and voting, only to have young hoodlums break up their meetings, there is no censure from these gentlemen. Yet somehow the two things—the situation in Georgia and the situation on the control of the sale of drugs—have a connection. If you don't want your fellow citizens to have the right peacefully to protest their wrongs or to try and remedy them, what could be more natural than that you should be among those who consider free enterprise more sacred than human lives? I hope that all over this country there is a mounting knowledge about both situations. Believing as I do that people are basically good and sound, I cannot believe that there will not be a tremendous revulsion against those who hold the materialistic point of view of Senator Eastland and Senator Dirksen.

The beginning of the end for Eleanor Roosevelt came in July. She had not been feeling well, finding herself inexplicably tired more often than not. A blood transfusion was tried, to pick up her energy, and there was some temporary relief. A palsy had developed, and when such elementary things as holding a cup of tea or writing with a pen became unmanageable, she was truly frustrated. Her mind remained as lively as ever, and she pressed on with an only somewhat restricted round of appointments, and of course with her newspaper column. She was still helping with the writing of her last book, Tomorrow Is Now.

Around August 4 Mrs. Roosevelt spent two days in the hospital, recovering from a severely high fever. A column cited below comments on that harrowing experience. At the same time she and the rest of the family were coping, but not too well, with a period of upsetting troubles in son Elliott's life. Elliott had married for the fifth time in 1960, and since then neither his emotional nor his financial life had been stable. He and his new spouse had become somewhat dependent on Mrs. Roosevelt and the family at large; the responsibility weighed heavily on Eleanor.

But there was an event coming that brightened her spirits and helped her recover, if only briefly, from the virus attacking her system. Surrounded by doubters who were sure she could not make the trip, Eleanor Roosevelt headed off to Campobello Island one last time. In anticipation of this final journey, she reminisced about the island playground her family had enjoyed for so many decades.

NEW YORK, AUGUST 10—Next Monday they will be dedicating the Franklin D. Roosevelt Memorial Bridge between Lubec, Maine, and Campobello Island.

The "beloved island" was what Mr. and Mrs. James Roosevelt called Campobello after they first discovered it in the summer of 1883, when they were looking for a good climate for their young son Franklin to spend his second summer. From that time on, part of every summer was spent on the island itself and sailing the waters nearby. James Roosevelt loved to sail and bought a two-masted schooner called the "Half Moon" in which he explored the coast and neighboring waters, and by the time little Franklin was seven he was presented with a small sailboat of his own.

One of the best sailors of the island, Captain Eddie Lank, taught the youngster the mysteries of the Bay of Fundy tides, how to ride the eddies along the shore when the wind gave out, and how to be a really good sailorman. In fact, Franklin Roosevelt was one day to be probably as good a navigator of the coast as could be found, with a very intimate knowledge of all the inlets and rivers and harbors, so that even in a fog he could usually get into port.

The island itself had been granted to Admiral Owen, who had moved out there from Great Britain and built himself a white clapboard house on one of the promontories looking up the two rivers running down on either side of Eastport, Maine. He brought people out with him to settle the island over whom he had the power of life and death. He built a small church, and his daughters did an endless labor of love in cross-stitching the altar carpet and the runners leading up the aisle.

Gradually Admiral Owen and his family faded out of the picture, but the sturdy villagers and fishermen who came with him stayed on. They built their weirs to catch the herring, and in the two little American coast villages of Lubec and Eastport the herring industry thrived. Slowly greater prosperity came and grew.

The people wondered why the line between the United States and Canada had not run outside of Campobello Island. The legend, which may be entirely apocryphal, is that our negotiator, Daniel Webster, was given plenty of liquid hospitality before approving the line which ran between the mainland through the narrows where the tide was particularly swift. This left Campobello on the outside and part of Canada. But it has never seemed to matter a great deal, because the fishermen come from islands on both sides and they trade in Lubec and Eastport.

When my husband was a boy there was fine timber on the island, but forest fires and speculators have taken much of that away. You can still walk on deep mossy paths through dark mysterious woods and come out at a number of points on the other side of the island. If you face the rivers, you can have the most beautiful sunsets laid before you in an unbelievable panorama. If you stay a little distance from Lubec, you can almost think you are looking on Mont Saint-Michel on the coast of France. There are an endless number of islands to visit, an endless number of waterways and constantly changing scenery, but everywhere the rocks come down to the pebbly beaches, with the pine trees clinging precariously as far as they can cling and the water lapping the beaches and the rocks below.

If you cross the island and look out toward the Bay of Fundy and Grand Manan Island in the far distance where the gulls have their nesting place, you find yourself on the most beautiful crescent beach called Herring Cove. Here the fishermen put out their lobster pots. Inside the beach, which is more or less sandy, there used to be a lake called Glen Severn in which it was warm enough to swim. There are also ponds on the island which, when the sun reaches them, warm up and make pleasant swimming pools. But unless you are a hardy native, you had better stay out of the waters of the bay on either side or you will turn blue after a very few seconds.

My husband had two special trips which he enjoyed. One was in a canoe which he had bought from an old Indian chief named Tomah Joseph. It was a birch-bark canoe, and only the skillful could maneuver it successfully. He would circle the island in the canoe, taking a whole day, and eat lunch up by Head Harbor light in a little inlet which gave so many fishing boats protection.

His other special challenge was to say to his young friends: "We will go around the island on foot, but nobody is permitted to leave the rocks and beaches." He knew what his guests rarely did, that there would be at least two places where they would have to swim from one rock to another as the water surged in and then sucked out again. He always made merry if anyone gave up and climbed to the top—or, halfway around the island, decided he had seen all he wished to see of the beaches and rocks and pine trees above.

When we lived there the one telephone, which could hardly be called a good connection, was at the postmistress' office in the village. There was no electric light, and the water supply for use in the house was somewhat sketchy and always restricted. Lamps had a horrible way of smoking, and going to bed by candlelight was no great joy to those who wished to read at night in bed. But you never had hay fever or any of the other allergies which beset people in summer climates. The sun was warm and delightful in the daytime, and at night your pine logs took the chill off the evening air. So it was always the "beloved island" and it remained so even in memory when my husband was no longer able, because of his attack of polio, to go there and live the life which he enjoyed.

Now there will be a bridge from Lubec to the island instead of the little ferry which always took our cars across in the later years. People will cross with ease, and there will be less and less division between the U.S. and Canada. Still, those of us who remember the past will have a nostalgic feeling for the days when you could spend a month or six weeks, virtually cut off from the world and all its troubles, enjoying to the full the "beloved island."

....

Few people make it to age seventy-eight without suffering some kind of illness that sets them back for a while. Eleanor Roosevelt was one who had. And when she had the normal colds and flus, or other shocks to her system (such as giving birth, losing her husband, or getting bumped by an automobile), she was back to work and out in the world again within just a few days. Writing here in the third person, she describes her stay in the hospital in early August, her choice of this voice and viewpoint suggesting something about how foreign the experience of being ill was to her.

But she was indeed ill. As Mrs. Roosevelt approached her death, there was a good deal of squabbling within the family and circle of close friends, including her doctor, David Gurewitsch, about what measures should or should not have been taken to prolong her life. The arguments could only be resolved by an autopsy, which confirmed the prevailing medical explanation of her final decline. Although the immediate cause of death was pinpointed as aplastic anemia (bone-marrow failure), the root of the problem lay in her distant past. In 1919 she had had a tuberculosis lesion, and the TB was unfortunately reactivated by the steroids prescribed to help treat the anemia. Aplastic anemia had no easy cure, but in Mrs. Roosevelt's case the disease was greatly exacerbated over the remaining few months by the spreading of TB throughout her system. Near the end, there was one, or perhaps two, strokes. She was truly incapacitated, a condition that her loving family and friends found very difficult to believe.

This August column ends with the rhetorical question "is it really worth it?" Mrs. Roosevelt's private comments to family and intimate friends at this time revealed clearly enough that she was preparing to let go, for in various ways she began answering her own question, and the answer was no.

CAMPOBELLO ISLAND, N.B., AUGUST 13—This is written by a layman and for the layman. In this case you must imagine the layman as a reluctant patient, told by a firm doctor a few nights ago back in New York that the patient must go at that very hour to the hospital.

The patient in this case had a rather high temperature and wasn't looking very much at anyone, when two strangely gentle but rather large and solid creatures bundled her on a stretcher. Out they went and the patient, feeling like a fiery furnace (because it seemed as though at every minute another cover was placed on the stretcher) was placed in an ambulance.

Once in, all the patient could think of was the black hole of Calcutta. That was what it was like—air that could be cut with a knife. Begging for a little more air, the patient was told she might catch cold on the slow, bumpy ride through the New York streets. The patient thought of all Dante's infernos and decided that if it was possible to live in that heat perhaps Beatrice did not have such a bad time!

Finally a stop, and the stretcher was moved out. Another one came along, and the patient was wheeled into a room where she was told: "Slide over; we will hold the stretcher."

The patient slid, the stretcher disappeared. As it went out, the doctors came in. They went through the usual examinations. They had just finished and decided to go and talk to each other, when a nice young doctor with a tray carrying many articles of torture appeared. He went about his business very methodically, and in the course of the next ten minutes or so the various needles he was supposed to use had been used. "I've finished," he said cheerily. "Good night."

There was nothing the patient wanted more than to be left alone. And that good night sounded hopeful—but she was wrong. A nurse appeared, took blood pressure, pulse and temperature, looked at the patient cheerily and said: "Wouldn't you like some nice orange juice?"

The patient knew that orange juice would taste like everything else at that moment—white cotton batting. But she said, "Oh, yes, thank you. Perhaps a little grapefruit juice mixed with it, as orange juice is rather sweet."

The nurse agreed. But as she went out, a gentleman from the hospital entered and asked: "Sorry to bother you, but what were your mother and father's names?" These were given, when almost apologetically he asked: "And the date of your birth?"

The door had hardly closed when another young lady with a tray full of articles of torture appeared. She went about her business, efficiently and silently. She finished, and the door opened again. This time the nurse just wanted a temperature, a blood pressure, a pulse. A few minutes later and the patient, who had allowed her eyes to close, heard a firm voice say: "Turn on your side," and a nice soft spot of the anatomy received two firm pricks.

Now, thought the patient, there could be nothing more. But she was quite mistaken. It would be so nice for the patient to have a cool alcohol rub—"we will just take your nightgown off." When it was over and the nightgown was back she knew that she was cooler, but this patient had developed a peculiar desire to be left alone and to go to sleep.

Vain was this hope. The doctors came back to say a cheery good night. When they had gone, the nurse said cheerily: "Now wouldn't you like something to drink?" Every time she turned, the patient had been given a glass of water because she found it easier to drink than anything else. But this nurse said: "How about a little cranberry juice?"

The patient vaguely remembered that once she had a particular liking for cranberry juice. But she felt sure it would taste like cotton batting when it arrived, so she said: "Let's try some, but let's add some water too."

The cranberry juice came, and it tasted like cotton wool. The patient added some water and finally swallowed it. Then, after a short interval, the routine temperature, pulse and blood pressure was gone through on the right-hand side. Just as it was finished and the patient thought

"Perhaps I will now be able to sleep," the door opened again and an efficient lady entered and took blood pressure on the left-hand side!

By that time the patient had learned not even to protest. Just let all the Alice in Wonderland people do whatever they wanted to do. Perhaps some day it would cease to be like the Mad Hatter's tea party, and she would be allowed to go to sleep. Midnight—and by dint of making believe she was asleep—she actually got three hours without interruption.

This was a night in a hospital. When the patient suggested to the doctors that it was not exactly restful, they looked at her in mild surprise. "What do we have laboratories for?" they said. "This is why we want you in the hospital."

Eureka, they have you there! You get well, but is it really worth it?

. . . .

The seemingly endless flow of newspaper columns from Eleanor Roosevelt was interrupted briefly in August for the Campobello vacation and in early September, when she was again not feeling well. Then it started once more. We cite here what is almost the last of the columns to illustrate a particular point.

In none of Mrs. Roosevelt's final columns did she even attempt to address the idea that she was soon to retire and soon, possibly, to die. In her final days and weeks the same combative moral concern for justice in the world held her attention as it had for decades. With the exception of the column about her nights in the hospital, Mrs. Roosevelt never succumbed to the temptation of writing about her own suffering. We leave her now, as she sounds out yet another clarion call for government and foreign policy based not on short-term selfish motives, not on fear, but rather on a genuine desire to promote peace in the world through sharing the American bounty with common people everywhere. Her consistent thesis appears here again: We cannot make peace by selling everyone the instruments of war. An old lady now herself, she goes out with a bang, urging her countrymen to press on in the quest for imaginative new ideas.

NEW YORK, SEPTEMBER 14—I often wonder, as I note how nervous we seem to be about Communist build-up in our world, why our country does not use new initiative to think out fresh approaches to the uncommitted people all over the world.

It has always seemed to me that we never present our case to the smaller nations in either a persuasive or interesting way. I think most people will acknowledge, for instance, that we have given far more military aid to these nations than economic aid. It is not very pleasant to palm off this military equipment on people who really are not looking

. . . .

for it. The fiction is that they are being given military aid so that they will be better able to cope with any Communist attack. But all the nations where we do this know quite well that it is pure fiction and nothing else. Practically none of them could withstand a really determined Soviet attack.

In view of this, why don't we offer them something they really want? For one thing, most of them would like food. Many of them, as they watch the development of the bigger nations, want to establish the beginnings of industry. But they know that wider training of their people is essential before they can make industrial advances, and hence a primary need is aid to their educational system.

Frequently I hear people argue in reply: "Well, look what has happened in Ghana. They are completely under Communist influence." Yet I wonder if this is quite true. Some Communist influence has doubtless proved effective. But we must realize how much more Russia has done in other areas of the world to persuade the young of the efficacy of their system. Unlike the Soviets, we have not established a college for these young foreigners. We have not brought them here at our expense and supported them during their years of study, nor have we indoctrinated them at every turn.

We have allowed them to come to this country on the exchange program arranged by our two governments. But I can't say that we take a great deal of trouble about them once they are here. These students, no matter what their official subjects may be, quite naturally want to study our country as a whole, and they want to find out what may be wrong with our way of life, our government and our people in general. It is important that we prevent them from being disillusioned about us.

It might be profitable to us if we would study what is really good in Soviet education and in their way of life. We can't have a premium on all the good things. We know that there are fundamental differences. We are a Christian nation; they do not believe in God. We are anxious that people should learn to think for themselves and not simply accept what somebody else has told them. But there are good things in the Soviet world and we should give them credit for these. Then, on our own initiative, we should develop a program that we believe will be of greater advantage to the newly developing nations of the world.

Similarly, we might profit by the study of other cultures of the world. The nations of Asia have some of the most ancient civilizations and philosophies, yet rarely does it occur to us that we might learn from them—or that they might offer to the newly developed nations ways of thought that would be far superior to anything we could suggest. In the same way, we might learn from the West African tribes described in Allard K. Lowenstein's "Brutal Mandate." These people are Christians and they have said over and over again that they have no use for communism. But we still persist in thinking of them as bush savages who have nothing to contribute to the rest of the developed world.

I have an idea they have a great deal to contribute. I was struck by the fact that some of the young Harvard graduates working in Tanganyika with the bush people came to have great respect for their ceremonies. For instance, before you could ask them to do any work, they had to welcome you with traditional ceremonies; and they had to ask you about all of your family and you had to reciprocate. This is indeed a gracious custom, and I can see why our young graduates came to respect these people and their customs and to hope that we would not wipe them out.

I would like to see more of such new approaches to people all over the world. If we use new initiative, forget about Russia as a rival, and think about what we can offer as a nation, I am sure we would benefit greatly.

. . . .

The difficulty of letting go of a great and colorful life falls not only to the individual living out that life and to her family, but also to all those who worked with her. The editors at the United Feature Syndicate for which Mrs. Roosevelt produced "My Day" and her later columns sent messages out over the wire to their subscribers indicating that Eleanor would soon be resuming her writing. Three times in the autumn of 1962 specific dates were set for the next columns to appear. Each time a devoted and respectful audience was disappointed. The sunset hour had come now for "My Day," and at last there was silence.

Epilogue

In a contest to determine who among all of Eleanor Roosevelt's colleagues and friends admired her most, quite probably Adlai Stevenson would have won. Adlai and Eleanor shared certain habits of mind and character. Both were passionately rational; both were doggedly loyal to one another and to the liberal cause; both had a certain distaste for the hurly-burly of backroom politics, yet both had what so many politicians lack completely: vision. Stevenson and Roosevelt shared a sense that the world community in their time had sunk lower in terms of moral turpitude and had risen higher in terms of aspirations to achieve peace and fairness than ever before. Each struggled to reconcile the extremes of the century they called their own (the Holocaust, for example, on the one hand; the realization of civil rights, on the other). Eleanor Roosevelt and Governor Stevenson vibrated to the same string. In his capacity as UN ambassador, and as her friend, Adlai delivered the eulogy for her in the UN General Assembly. Paraphrasing a Chinese proverb Eleanor herself loved to quote, he said of her: "She would rather light a candle than curse the darkness. Her light has brought warmth to all the world."

Although the three volumes of selections from "My Day" that end here provide a substantial overview of Eleanor Roosevelt's thinking and by themselves represent what most mortals would consider a substantial lifetime achievement, "My Day" was but one of Eleanor's many productive activities. A truly full portrait of Mrs. Roosevelt shows her not only as a writer but as a mother, a presidential adviser, a social reformer, a diplomat, a world traveler, a political activist, a philanthropist, a philosopher, a gardener-knitter-homemaker, and a lifelong student. Like all great heroines, the story of her life enlarges the scope of our own. Here indeed was the fully realized person Emerson, Thoreau, and Whitman had sought after in their transcendentalist calls for true Self-Reliance. Eleanor Roosevelt was, if anything, fully awake and alive.

Her biographer and friend Joseph Lash perhaps summarized best why Mrs. Roosevelt was so singularly impressive. Looking back over all the years of Eleanor's devoted and indefatigable work for so many good causes and on behalf of so many individuals, Lash remarked that "many of her fellow workers of those days have yielded to age, disillusionment, conformity and comfort." Not so with Mrs. Roosevelt, said Lash, for even in her last busy days Eleanor remained as much as ever "the tribune of the dispossessed and the keeper of the country's conscience."

Index